The Complete Idiot's Reference Card

15 Questions to Ask Yourself When You're Choosing a Pet

1. How much money am I willing to spend for a pet?

2. How much money am I willing to spend (or can I spend) for my pet's housing, feeding, veterinary care, and general upkeep?

3. How much time do I have to spend each day playing with, training, feeding, grooming, housekeeping for, and all-around caring for my pet?

4. Do I want a pet that can jog, play football, and/or do home improvement projects with me?

5. Do I want a pet I can cuddle?

6. Do I want a pet that is best seen and not touched?

7. Do I want a pet that is demanding of my attention or one that really won't mind if I'm not home all the time?

8. Do I want a pet who requires a lifetime of training and reminders that I am the boss?

9. Do I want a pet who will get along with kids?

10. Who will care for my pet when I'm not at home?

11. How active am I (now, be honest), and how active do I want my pet to be?

12. Am I allowed to keep pets where I live?

13. What type of food am I willing—and not willing—to feed a pet.

14. Where will my pet sleep?

15. Why do I want this animal?

D0557081

Where to Find Your New Pet

The Breeder: A dedicated, reliable, ethical breeder could be just the ticket for, among others, a new dog, cat, rabbit, mouse, rat, ferret, frog, budgie, hedgehog, tortoise, chinchilla, or even a tarantula.

The Pet Shop: The pet shop isn't the best choice for every pet, but it can be an excellent source for small animals and fish. If frogs and lizards are your passion, look for a shop that deals only in reptiles and amphibians.

The Animal Shelter: At the shelter—a necessary safety net in a world of pet overpopulation and neglected pets (and ill-prepared pet owners)—you will find dogs and cats and perhaps some other types of animals, as well.

The Rescue Group: Today there are rescue groups for purebred dogs and cats, ferrets, rabbits, rats, potbellied pigs, iguanas—heck, for just about every animal in this book.

The Streets: It's not right (or safe) to take a mouse, rat, reptile or amphibian out of the wild; but sometimes, by fate, a stray cat, dog, or even rabbit finds you when you least expect it.

tear here

alpha
books

The 12 Commandments of Pet Keeping

1. Thou shalt regard thy pet as family, whether it wears fins, feathers, fur, scales, or slime.

2. Thou shalt not leave thy sense of humor at the door when thou carriest thy new pet over the threshold.

3. Thou shalt prepare thyself ahead of time with proper education and supplies for the arrival of thy pet of choice.

4. Thou shalt supervise all children's handling of and interaction with the pet, and ensure that the animal's care is entrusted to an individual of the adult kind.

5. Thou shalt do all in thy power not to breed thy pet.

6. Thou shalt feed thy pet the food designed for its palate and resist all temptation to overfeed.

7. Thou shalt provide thy pet with the proper shelter and commit to keeping that shelter clean.

8. Thou shalt provide thy pet with appropriate mental stimulation and physical exercise each and every day.

9. Thou shalt acknowledge that animals, too, think, feel, and deserve respect—and that each has its own unique language which its owners are honorbound to study and understand.

10. Thou shalt get thy pet to the veterinarian in the presence of emergency, and practice sound preventive care in the meantime.

11. Thou shalt not take in more pets than thee can properly house, care for, and shower with love and attention.

12. Thou shalt commit to thy pet for the long haul.

Pet Families

The Mammals: These furry, warm-blooded critters—the dogs, the cats, the rabbits, the pigs, the rodents, and such—are available in every size and shape. They require daily care, and most thrive best with regular human interaction.

The Birds: Feathers and flight are the two most outstanding characteristics of this winged, and rather demanding, group of pets, who also require daily care and attention from the people with whom they bond.

The Reptiles: Most snakes, lizards, turtles, and tortoises can live quite contentedly without a close, personal relationship with their owners, but they do require heat and light to warm the body and fuel the metabolism. Only knowledgeable caretakers need apply.

The Amphibians: "Look but please don't touch" is the adage shared by the slimy, sensitive, meat-eating frogs, toads, and salamanders of the amphibian family. A damp, cool, sheltering environment and plenty of live prey is all they ask for.

The Fish: An aquarium, fresh food, and filtered, well-oxygenated water are the greatest gifts you can offer these undemanding critters, who in return soothe our frazzled nerves and whisk us away to another world.

The Arachnids: Yes, certain members of the spider family—many tarantula species, to be exact—can make great pets, perhaps taking the prize for least demanding of the bunch, assuming of course you can stand feeding your pet live prey.

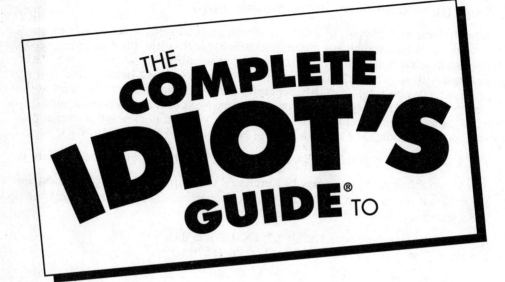

THE COMPLETE IDIOT'S GUIDE® TO

Choosing a Pet

by Betsy Sikora Siino

alpha
books

A Division of Macmillan General Reference
A Simon & Schuster Macmillan Company
1633 Broadway, New York, NY 10019

Macmillan Publishing books may be purchased for business or sales promotional use. For information please write: Special Markets Department, Macmillan Publishing USA, 1633 Broadway, New York, NY 10019-6785.

International Standard Book Number: ISBN 0-87605-341-X
Library of Congress Catalog Card Number: 98-46579

01 00 99   8 7 6 5 4 3 2 1

Interpretation of the printing code: the rightmost number of the first series of numbers is the year of the book's printing; the rightmost number of the second series of numbers is the number of the book's printing. For example, a printing code of 99-1 shows that the first printing occurred in 1999.

Printed in the United States of America

Contents at a Glance

Contents

Part 6: In a Class by Themselves   289

21 Feisty Ferrets   291

22 Tickly Tarantulas   307

Foreword

A book telling you how to choose a pet? How could that be? How can someone possibly explain to you how to go about picking an animal companion—one who will share your daily life and become a part of your emotional being? After all, choosing and bonding with a pet is an intensely personal experience, almost as unique and individual as finding a spouse. How can something as impersonal as the pages of a book tell you how to find the right creature for this relationship, and then tell you how to go about fostering that bond?

It seems like an impossible task. Except that it isn't. Not with Betsy Sikora Siino as your guide. Only a very special writer could take on such a big challenge and pull it off. Only a writer with an intense spiritual and emotional connection to animals would dare attempt this. Betsy is that writer.

Since Betsy was a child, she has been deeply attached to animals. Dogs and horses were her early obsessions, although she has since broadened her passion to include just about every animal in the world. Her empathy for all creatures in the animal kingdom and her deep and intuitive understanding of each domestic species is what led her, many years ago, to write about animals.

Given Betsy's depth of knowledge and astounding insight into companion animals, there is no better person to hold your hand as you begin your journey into pet ownership. The creature you ultimately choose to bond with, the one you will allow into your heart, will be the one whose essence is most compatible with yours. With this book, Betsy will help you decide who you are in the world of pet ownership, and will show you which of the many animals out there is the one that will most easily blend with your soul. Sure, it's a personal decision, but who better to be your guide than someone who understands the profoundness and spirituality of the steps you are about to take?

In this book, Betsy guides you through all the steps necessary to find that future companion. She does so with great thought, feeling and insight, not only into the animals she writes about, but also into the human mind. If you read her words and take them to heart, you'll not only find the right pet, but you'll enjoy your companion throughout its lifetime in a very special way.

Audrey Pavia

Audrey Pavia is a professional animal writer and a contributor to numerous pet publications. She is a former editor of Horse Illustrated and AKC Gazette.

Introduction

For more than a decade now, I have been writing about all kinds of animals, from dogs to dolphins, from cheetahs to chickens, from horses to hermit crabs. I imagine that is why this book has been such a delight for me to write. Embracing so many different animals within the covers of a single book is not only a culmination of the work I have done for a good part of my life, but also a unique addition to the types of books available out there to would-be pet owners.

What you are about to embark on is a journey through some of the planet's most popular pets—the key word here being *pets*. You will find plenty of information on the so-called exotic pets (reptiles, amphibians, tarantulas and such), but you're not going to find advice on housing wild animals (wolves, lions, raccoons) or any animal that is illegal to keep (unless you happen to live in an area where ferrets, gerbils or hedgehogs are still illegal). I'm talking mainstream here.

I'm also talking about the goal of seeing that these animals who, through little choice of their own, come to share our human households, are happy, sane, and healthy. That's really an amazing concept when you think about it, and it's quite a responsibility for us to live up to. I'm hoping this book will help us all live up to that responsibility handsomely—and have fun doing it.

The key to success is to make wise choices in the beginning. Get educated and informed before you take the plunge—just as you would before making the big commitment to a prospective spouse. It's really not all that different with pets. So regard this book as your own personal in-house matchmaker, and maybe, just maybe, it will help your pet-owning experiences become some of the most enjoyable and most rewarding in your life.

How to Use This Book

Start thumbing through this book, and you'll notice a pattern. As I've discussed, it covers an entire menagerie of animals—21, to be exact—and each is afforded its own chapter where it is celebrated for the unique individual it is.

That individuality is important to me. As a species, we humans tend to assume that some animals are more "worthy," more valuable than others. Sometimes this is a matter of money: That which costs us more, we offer a higher level of care. But you're not going to find much mention of price tags in the pages that follow. Where pets are concerned, you don't always get what you pay for. A higher price tag does not necessarily guarantee a healthier or in any way "better" pet; a lower price tag doesn't mean a pet should be viewed as disposable.

But even beyond that, as far as I am concerned, every pet is priceless, whether it's a goldfish you win at a county fair, a hamster you buy for five bucks at the local pet supply store, or the $800 purebred puppy you obtain from a top-notch dog breeder. They all deserve the finest care that we can offer, and they all have the potential, if given the chance, enrich our lives.

To help you compare different types of pets, each chapter begins with a chart that rates the pet on nine categories, such as how much time they require, how well they get along with children of different ages and how expensive they are to keep. Each category is ranked from one to five, with one being the least and five the most. And to help you compare apples to oranges, or fish to mice, or cats to dogs, Appendix D puts all the charts together into one big one. You'll also find charts in each chapter that tell you what equipment you need to buy along with each pet, the general cost of upkeep and what the critter eats.

In honor of pet individuality, each chapter offers an introduction to a particular member of the animal family that we are exploring. You'll spend a day in the life of a tarantula, a cat, a gerbil or a goldfish. The intent is to see life through the eyes of these animals, and to understand how you can help to ensure that life is as positive and fulfilling as it can be for the animals you bring into your home. From there, you'll learn about the character of the animal, choosing a healthy pet of that species or family, and how to care for it properly.

Obviously, I'll be covering a lot of ground here and presenting a lot of rather diverse information. Caring for a gecko, for instance, is quite different from caring for a hedgehog or a potbellied pig. So as not to confuse the issue, and to help you make reasonable comparisons when you're doing all that necessary research on choosing a new animal companion, I have divided the book up into parts, arranging the animals into the following groups:

➤ **Part 1: So Many Pets, So Much Love**

Before we dive in and get to know the 21 animals that are at the heart of this book, let's explore why we live with animals, how we pursue this vocation, and how we can help to ensure we make wise choices.

➤ **Part 2: The All-Stars**

Here you'll get to know what are undeniably the world's most well-known, if not always properly cared for, pets: dogs, cats, rabbits, guinea pigs and hamsters.

➤ **Part 3: The Small and the Furred**

Live in an apartment? A small condo? A rented room? You may just find the pet of your dreams in this section, for here you'll find the classic rodent collection: mice, rats, gerbils and chinchillas.

➤ **Part 4: Fine Feathered Friends**

Here, you'll look at two quite irresistible birds that are relatively easy keepers: budgies (you may know them as parakeets) and cockatiels.

➤ **Part 5: Scales and Slime**

If your interests run in the realm of the reptiles and amphibians, this is the section for you. Get ready to meet lizards, snakes, turtles and tortoises, frogs and toads, and salamanders.

➤ **Part 6: In a Class by Themselves**

If you just can't resist the unusual and your intentions are pure (meaning you're in this for more than just obtaining a conversation piece or an attention getter), then come on in and meet the ferret, the tarantula, the hedgehog and the miniature potbellied pig. Oh yes, and the goldfish, as you've never seen her before.

What About All Those Little Boxes?

As you begin your journey through this universe of pets, you will notice a collection of boxes scattered throughout the book. It might be worth your while to check them out, if I do say so myself. Here's why:

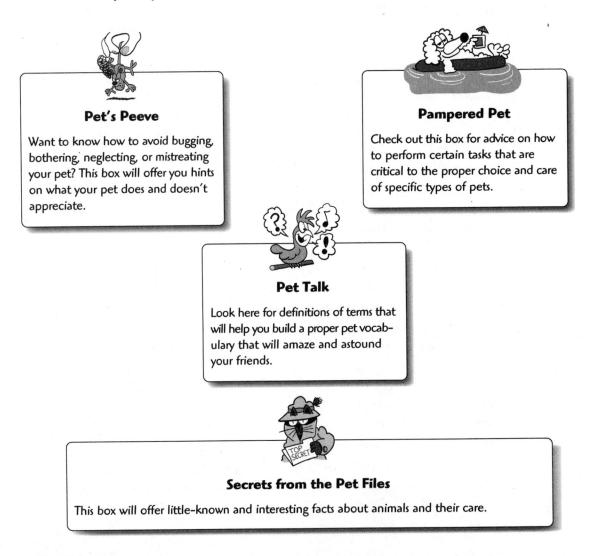

Pet's Peeve

Want to know how to avoid bugging, bothering, neglecting, or mistreating your pet? This box will offer you hints on what your pet does and doesn't appreciate.

Pampered Pet

Check out this box for advice on how to perform certain tasks that are critical to the proper choice and care of specific types of pets.

Pet Talk

Look here for definitions of terms that will help you build a proper pet vocabulary that will amaze and astound your friends.

Secrets from the Pet Files

This box will offer little-known and interesting facts about animals and their care.

Acknowledgements

Thanks, thanks, thanks to the hundreds of people and animals through the years who have inspired, contributed to, and supported my quest to see that each and every companion animal is handled with tender loving—and knowledgeable—care. Through my work I have had the wonderful fortune of meeting the most dedicated, most educated, most experienced people in animals that we animal lovers might possibly imagine. The animals of the world are better off for their efforts.

As for the writing of this book, which occurred while I was moving from one end of the country to the other, I couldn't have done it without the assistance of "the Harvey girls" in Orchard Park, New York—delightful Sarah and Erin and their lovely mom Rita—who so lovingly cared for my little Christopher while I haunted the library. My same gratitude goes to my editor at Howell Book House, Beth Adelman, who was so very supportive and infinitely patient with me throughout the process of producing this manuscript.

Thanks, too, to Howell executives, Dominique DeVito and Sean Frawley, who several years back entrusted me with the awesome responsibility of writing about entire menageries of animals, and started a ball rolling that has resulted in this latest addition to the fine family of Idiot's Guides.

And finally, Michael and Christopher: I stand speechless at your endless, even saintly, almost supernatural, patience and support.

Part 1
So Many Pets, So Much Love

For thousands of years, people have been living with animals: dogs, cats, ferrets, mice, and goldfish are some of the earlier species to agree to domestication. Now such animals as gerbils, budgies, iguanas, and tarantulas have been added to the mix, and you'll be meeting all of them in the pages ahead.

But before we get down to the details—the character, choice, and care of these specific animals—let's take a little time to explore the whys and hows of pet keeping. Living with animals is one of the most universal human activities. It's something we humans feel compelled to do, something it seems we were meant to do. And something we are apparently always trying to do better.

As you're about to see, pet keeping is essentially an art form that has changed dramatically in recent years, and only seems to be getting better. So join us as we take a journey back in time to the first pets, the animal gods, the literary muses, and the cultural symbols. Then we'll move forward in time to contemporary pet ownership: the trends, the responsibilities, and the family commitments.

Chapter 1

Why We Live with Animals

We think it was a dog—that first pet. In fact, given the archeological data, the carbon dating, and the fancy DNA testing, we are pretty sure of it. The first animal to agree to give up its wild ways and form a partnership with people was a dog.

That dog began, of course, as either a wolf or a shared ancestor of both the wolf and the dog, depending on which theory you wish to embrace, but this simple act of agreeing to become family to our species would change the course of history. Of course, we didn't recognize the significance of the deal at the time, but we would soon realize the obvious merits of the arrangement. So profound were they that we would set out to domesticate other animals, as well. And the rest, well, it has become history.

An Ancient, Devoutly Pious Bond

It should come as no surprise that our current pet-keeping practices and the accepted niche pets occupy throughout the world did not come about overnight. We have for centuries . . . no, make that millennia . . . been working on the relationship we have today. It's often been a bumpy road—with humans invariably to blame for the troubles along the way. For a proper understanding of all this, a brief history lesson is in order. First stop: Back to a time when animals ruled the earth.

Secrets from the Pet Files

Sometimes animals need pets, too. Racehorses, for example, can often be calmed only by the presence of their own companions, typically goats or cats. And Koko, the legendary gorilla who speaks so fluently in sign language, is rarely without a pet cat—a tradition begun with her first beloved kitty, Ball, whom Koko named herself.

Four-Legged Deities

In the beginning, animals were gods. They weren't companions. They weren't our equals. They made the rain fall. They made the sun shine. They sacrificed themselves for our sustenance when we proved ourselves deserving. And when early representatives of our species were fortunate enough to fell an antelope or a bison, they gave thanks to the animal gods for looking after them, for considering them worthy to survive.

We pride ourselves today on our progressive attitudes toward animals, our concerns for their well-being, our exhaustive research into their health and nutrition. But 20,000 years ago when primitive artists didn't have a whole lot of free time on their hands, they chose animals to grace the walls of their caves. That they paid a type of homage to non-human creatures is virtually unfathomable to our modern-day sensibilities.

Animal Gods Throughout the World

Elevating the animals to gods was an almost universal phenomenon. Some of the earliest humans looked to the animals around them, admired and learned from them, and evoked their spirits in their religious rituals. Nature was the mother. The animals were her children on earth. Such a world view was common in Europe and among most native peoples of North America, as well. A respect for the animals—the bears, the wolves, the bison—was inherent to the Native Americans' lives. Native Americans viewed the animals as their equals in the natural world, regarding each species as an independent nation no different in status from their own.

Animal gods also ruled the ancient Egyptians. Among this fascinating group was sun goddess Bastet, a cat who was both virgin and mother (a precursor to Mary, perhaps?); Anubis, the jackal-headed physician to the gods who also held the secrets of the afterlife; and Sirius, the

Pampered Pet

When you choose to live with animals, you will inevitably discover that the best way to preserve your sanity is to keep a healthy, even self-deprecating, sense of humor about you.

dog star, guardian and protector of the earth. Even the oft-vilified snake was respected by the Egyptians, who considered it a symbol of immortality because of its habit of shedding its skin and emerging reborn. So highly esteemed were animals in Egypt that those who didn't happen to be gods, but rather pampered pets, often followed their owners into the afterlife, buried and/or mummified upon the deaths of their owners so they could accompany them into the next world.

Religion Fights Back

In 1912, playwright George Bernard Shaw wrote in *Androcles and the Lion,* "I really don't think I could consent to go to Heaven if I thought there were to be no animals there." Were he to have said that several hundred years earlier, he would have been branded a heretic.

In the early days of the Christian Church in Europe, church leaders did not particularly care to share the spotlight with a bunch of god-like animals. Though many within their own ranks were avid pet keepers and breeders, reveling in the company of dogs, cats, monkeys, and birds, the public belief in animal deities would not, could not, be tolerated. People who held such beliefs were punished, and those who kept pets were viewed with suspicion.

Secrets from the Pet Files

Pet owners in 16th- and 17th-century England had to be especially careful that they were not suspected of harboring a witch's *familiar,* an animal that helped facilitate the witch's secret powers. When hunting witches, investigators would determine whether a suspect had an affectionate relationship with an animal. Dogs, cats, ferrets, toads, lambs, hedgehogs, rabbits, and mice were all implicated at one time or another. If such a relationship was discovered, it was deduced that the animal must certainly be the witch's familiar.

Legend of a Greyhound Saint

One example of the Church's quest to quash the animal gods is found in the story of Saint Guinefort. This particular saint, you see, was a Greyhound. The legend holds that hundreds of years ago, a French nobleman returned home to find his beloved Greyhound, Guinefort, covered in blood and standing beside the baby's overturned cradle. In a rage, the man destroyed his dog, only then to discover the baby alive and healthy under the cradle but surrounded by remnants of a now-dead serpent. Guinefort had saved the baby's life.

Full of grief and remorse over what he had done, the nobleman buried the dog and built a shrine to his memory, which would ultimately inspire the cult of Saint Guinefort in the 13th century. The Church eventually stepped in to destroy the monument and renounce all beliefs in the dog's alleged healing powers, but the tale has persisted through the centuries as testament to the value, and the power, of animals in an age long ago.

From Gods to Pets

We have a pretty good idea of just how certain species of animals traded in their god-like status for a more, shall we say, earthbound existence. Why they did it, well, that's one of those secrets for the ages. We must just be thankful that they did, and try to repay the favor whenever possible.

Wolf Becomes Dog

We often fantasize about that fateful moment. The scene: A band of freezing, starving, scantily clad hunter-gatherers shiver helplessly around their meager Ice Age fire, lamenting the lack of food and furs. Then, into their midst strides a most benevolent wolf, bearing in his jaws a freshly killed deer. "Follow me," his body language seems to say. "There's more where that came from, and I will share with you all my most treasured secrets of the hunt." And so the legendary partnership is born.

Sorry to burst any bubbles here, but that is probably not at all how it happened. Interestingly, it was probably the companionship aspect that preceded any work partnership we would eventually forge with the canine species. Those early Stone Age types, you see, had to eat whatever they could get their hands on, including wolves.

Every once in a while those primitive people, in their constant quest for food, would stumble upon a litter of wolf pups, which they would bring into camp. And every once in a while, one of those pups—the friendliest and most affectionate of the bunch, no doubt—would charm his captors into sparing him from the stew pot. Canid and human got acquainted, word spread, more pups joined the fold, and eventually, the wolves that would ultimately become dogs began to join the hunting parties—but not until after they had become friends and family.

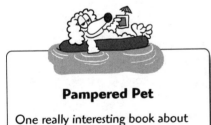

Pampered Pet

One really interesting book about how dogs became a part of our lives is *Man Meets Dog*, by Konrad Lorenz.

An Epidemic of Domestication

When the hunter-gatherers adopted a more stable, agrarian lifestyle about 10,000 years ago or so, the dog's role in the family expanded beyond that of hunting partner. Soon dogs were guarding and herding the sheep, protecting the household, pulling the sled, managing the fishing nets—you know the story. And so, too, began the rudimentary selective breeding practices that would result in the hundreds of distinctive dog breeds we know today.

Meanwhile, domestication had worked out so beautifully with the dog that humans began to experiment with other animals. The dog was followed by goats and sheep, then cattle and pigs. Then along came horses and domestic fowl, and then, finally, the cat, chosen for her innate skills as four-legged rodent exterminator—and no doubt also for her purr.

Domestication of the dog and those animals that followed did not happen overnight. But it did occur throughout the world. And along the way, the animals became mortal. We no longer viewed them in awe. We possessed them. They now revolved around us. In trustworthy hands, that might be okay, but we humans . . . well, we tend to let power go to our heads. While domestication would mark the dawn of pet keeping as we know it, we would stumble mightily along the way.

Pet Styles of the Rich and Famous

While companionship opened the door to domestication, work set it in stone. But throughout it all, that element of companionship remained a fixture in the bond between people and their pets. From the early Greeks, Chinese, and Romans who kept birds, monkeys, fish, and small dogs, to the Japanese shoguns who kept 100,000 dogs and taxed the farmers to finance their care, to Mary Queen of Scots' small dog who allegedly followed her to the gallows, pet keeping through the ages has entered some fascinating realms.

Aristocrats and royals have long draped themselves in the status of pet ownership. Nowhere has this been more prevalent than in the British Isles. Britain's royal families have always sponsored the breeding of dogs and other animals, including Charles I and his descendants, Queen Victoria (who seems to have owned virtually every known breed of dog), the reigning monarch Elizabeth II, and just about every ruler in between. Throughout the world, wherever the high-born congregated, there were animals. It seems that pet keeping was part of their station.

Secrets from the Pet Files

Pet keeping among the aristocracy may account for the rise of the lap dog—a dog that has no particular work to do and will sit comfortably for hours as both fashion accessory and beloved companion. Only the wealthy could afford to keep an animal whose sole job was giving pleasure.

Contemporary Humans and Animals: Not Always Pretty

From the most primitive of tribes to the most opulent palaces of wealth, the desire to live with animals, to invite them in to become members of the family, is probably one of the most universal, most democratic, compulsions on earth. Through the ages pets of various species have been buried—or mummified—with loved ones (an honor, really), elevated to official court positions by admiring royals, pampered in the most outrageous fashion, and just plain adored by just plain folks.

But despite the great sacrifices animals have made for us through the ages, both as gods and as companion/partners, we humans have frequently stumbled along the way. Animals have been exterminated *en masse,* tried for murder, regarded as despised symbols of wealth, and blamed for every plague, climatic aberration, and pestilence in the world. Yep. It's been a hard road.

It would seem that we have had trouble handling all that power we assumed when we domesticated the animals. So what else is new? Nevertheless, the animals have stuck by us. They haven't given up on us—yet.

A World Without Animals: Perish the Thought!

What a cold and dreary place the world would be without the animals, both those in the wild and those that live in our homes. There is something about living with animals that we just can't get from another human being. Our need to live with animals is as powerful today as it was thousands of years ago.

Our pets bring nature into our homes. They fill a spot in our souls that we contemporary types long ago traded away in exchange for our position as the supreme species. Yet with our pets, we can forget all about that pact and return to our roots, acknowledging the common thread that runs through all living creatures. As Chief Seattle so eloquently asked, "What would man be without the beasts?" It's scary to even think about that one. Instead we may ask ourselves, why do we live with animals? Because we need them, that's why. And we need them much more than they need us.

The Writer's Muse

Writers of all nations, cultures, and eras have focused their attentions on animals, often enviously. Walt Whitman, in his immortal *Song of Myself,* wrote, "I think I could turn and live with the animals, they are so placid and self-contain'd. I stand and look at them long and long. They do not sweat and whine about their condition. They do not lie awake in the dark and weep for their sins." Dostoyevsky wrote that we must "Love the animals: God has given them the rudiments of thought and joy untroubled;" while according to George Eliot, "Animals are such agreeable friends—they ask no questions, they pass no criticisms." Even Shakespeare added his two pence with, "Nature teaches beasts to know their friends."

Animal Emotions: Do They or Don't They?

Do animals have emotions? Do they think? Of course they do. But were you to make such proclamations, oh, say, 300 years ago, we won't even contemplate what horrible fate might have befallen you. How, we can't help asking, could animals go from all-powerful deities to unfeeling automatons? The answer: They didn't. We just went insane for a while and refused to see the truth.

Though he was certainly not alone in his thinking, 17th-century French philosopher René Descartes single-handedly performed a great disservice to animals everywhere when he decided to pontificate on the subject of their minds. He let it be known to all who would listen—and many did—that animals had no emotions, no sensitivity to pain, no thoughts. They were machines. Apparently, Descartes had been drinking so much of that fine, rich burgundy of his homeland that he failed to notice the response when you mistakenly step on a cat's tail, or the unmistakably emotional welcome-home greeting from a dog. His opinion: pure hogwash. But viewing animals in this way makes it far easier to exploit them, doesn't it?

Fortunately, times have changed. Beginning in the 19th century, perhaps because pet keeping became more commonplace among the common people, the British, and then the Americans, began to reevaluate yet again their treatment of animals. A new concern for animal welfare arose. The 20th century dawned with a new promise of humane treatment of animals, complete with laws to prosecute those who would defy this—laws that would ultimately be used for the protection of children, as well. My, wouldn't Descartes be disappointed!

Secrets from the Pet Files

In the beginning, veterinarians were trained only in the care of livestock, as these were the bread-and-butter animals. But during the second half of the 20th century, companion animals earned an official status of their own, becoming valued members of society. So an entire branch of veterinary medicine has emerged dedicated to the care of dogs, cats, reptiles, amphibians, ferrets, and rodents.

Pets As Substitute People

Through the years, pet keeping, a seemingly benign and pleasant pursuit, has been the subject of great debate. The common refrain from the critics has been, "Pets are nothing more than substitutes for people," or "If you care about animals too much, then you won't care enough about people." Such foolish comments were made 150 years ago, and they're still being made today. You can just hear the whiny inflections, can't you?

But pet owners know the truth. Yes, some people do get carried away, treating their pets like children; showering them with gifts, birthday parties, and first-class plane tickets; and "hearing" them speak in human tongues. But that is not how most of us live with animals. We do not shut ourselves off from both reality and the rest of the world in order to spend our every waking hour with Binky or Fluffy. Besides, what makes us think animals would want to be people anyway?

Secrets from the Pet Files

Mark Twain described the differences between animals and people best when he wrote, "If you pick up a starving dog and make him prosperous he will not bite you. This is the principal difference between a dog and a man."

No question, we are lucky to have animals around. And we're lucky that they aren't people. Pets, you see, set a good example for us. Because we must see the world through the eyes of a creature not of our own species—a dog, a cat, a hedgehog, a guinea pig, an iguana, a cockatiel—we become more tolerant, compassionate people. We are healthier inside and out, blessed with a quiet confidante who listens to our problems without judgment or argument. Pets bring out our natural desire to nurture, and they allow us to be touchy-feely. In a nutshell, pets make us better people. And what, all you whiny complainers out there, is wrong with that?

The Modern Bond: Back to the Past

Whatever it is that draws us to animals simply cannot be explained or even identified via the scientific method. It is magic—a magic that is today manifested culturally in the minions of animals of all shapes, sizes, and species who have taken center stage in movies, on greeting cards, in toys and collectibles, in our artwork, on our televisions, and in our literature. Those 20,000-year-old cave paintings were just the beginning.

The bond begins when we are infants, when the first toys we find interesting are plush, big-eyed stuffed animals that elicit in our still underdeveloped minds the infamous "cute response." In that instant of recognition, we claim the legacy of our ancestors. We succumb to the impulse to cuddle, to hug, to seek comfort with these creatures. And they willingly comply.

As we grow, we come to realize, to our delight, that those stuffed toys are modeled after real live animals. And some of these animals can actually live with us in our homes. Certainly there are those among us who will betray the trust and regress to treating animals as our unfeeling subjects. But most of us, millions of us, actually, will crave a close relationship to animals. Like those hunter-gatherers of eons past, we will invite creatures of another species into our homes and treat them with the respect they deserve, viewing them not as gods, but as companions and members of the family.

The Positive (and Documented) Effects of the Human-Animal Bond

Pet Talk

It's no coincidence that so many baby animals share similar infantile characteristics: large heads, large eyes, short snouts, and fluffy body cover. All this facilitates the *cute response*—the ability of baby animals to elicit nurturing and protection from their elders. It's a survival tool.

Stone Age humans revered the animals for keeping them alive. Today, contemporary folks often make similar claims about their pets. These claims are rooted in what is known as the human-animal bond. A bond that cannot quite be explained, but that is one of the most powerful forces on the planet—and obviously always has been.

Bonding with animals is not reserved solely for specific cultures. It is an age-old phenomenon that set the pet-keeping idea in motion in the first place. It is why we seek out the sympathetic ear of an animal when times are tough. It is why many people and cultures keep pets long after the march of progress has rendered the animal's original vocation obsolete.

Just look at the Native Americans. Many tribes were known to regard their dogs with higher esteem than their horses and livestock, even though the dogs served no practical purpose other than companionship. James Herriott, author of *All Creatures Great and Small,* made similar observations about his clients, the farmers of Yorkshire, England, who would keep and pamper dogs who performed no known useful function on the farm. And what of all those cat owners out there who have never seen a mouse in the house to justify keeping a feline companion? There's something else at play here, and we need not be ashamed to admit it.

Real, Honest-to-Goodness Health Benefits

As humans, we require companionship, just as we require food, water, and air. We know this instinctively, just as those Stone Age hunters-gatherers obviously did. And when we have that companionship in our lives from a pet, well, we just may live longer. It's true. In general, people who live with pets in a positive, nurturing way are healthier and live longer. It has been documented again and again.

Consider, for example, the magic pets wield over the human heart and circulatory system. Study after study after study—so many studies that you wonder why they even bother to keep studying this—have shown that for most people their blood pressure decreases when they pat their pet or hold it in their arms. People recovering from heart

11

surgery also have an easier time when they are pet owners, and they have a superior survival rate, too.

Therapeutic Vocations for Animals

The profound effects animals have on people of all ages are simply too numerous to contemplate, let alone list. Pets are our confidantes, our teachers, our protectors, our comforters, and members of our families. Within these exalted parameters, they have the power to comfort and heal those in need: lonely old folks, abused children, confused adolescents, people suffering from illness or injury, or just a member of the family who has had a bad day. This is no new revelation, but how lovely that believing it is no longer grounds for capital punishment!

Pet therapy is no novelty. Though animals have been enlisted for centuries to assist in human healing and rehabilitation, the term *pet therapy* was first introduced in 1969. It was coined by child psychiatrist Boris Levinson, who realized that the children he counseled invariably seemed more comfortable, more forthcoming with the information vital to their healing, in the presence of Levinson's dog Jingles. For the first time, pet therapy was being discussed in a scientific context. It has since gained the acceptance it so richly deserves, evident in the millions of people who have been helped by pet therapy when nothing else would work.

Secrets from the Pet Files

Today there are non-profit organizations whose sole purpose is to help pet owners, such as senior citizens and people living with AIDS, keep their pets. They provide financial support, grooming, even dog-walking services for those who just can't do it themselves. For many such people, their pet gives them a reason to get up in the morning, and losing it would be devastating.

Today service dogs assist the blind, the deaf, the ill, and people in wheelchairs, while therapy animals visit all types of patients in all kinds of places. It is not unusual to find dogs, cats, rabbits, and guinea pigs in convalescent hospitals, prisons, centers for abused and abandoned children, children's hospitals, cancer centers, and school classrooms populated by troubled teens. Time and time again, miracles occur.

An elderly man in a nursing home, who hasn't spoken in years, musters the energy and the courage to greet verbally a gregarious tabby cat who has come for a visit. An abused child confides her pain to a soft, brown bunny, and a troubled urban youth finds a new direction in life thanks to the presence of a friendly mixed-breed dog in his classroom.

When someone cannot be reached in any other way, it is an animal that unlocks the door. It is an animal that is the conduit to a new life. An animal is the miracle worker. And that is why we live with animals.

Various organizations throughout the country evaluate, test, and register would-be therapy animals. To prepare your pet for such a high calling, start early. Socialize a young animal to a variety of people, places, and experiences. Train your pet to behave properly in social situations, and attend obedience classes regularly if your prospective therapy animal is a dog. And vaccinate and groom your pet regularly.

Pet's Peeve

Just any animal can't automatically be a therapy animal. There are liabilities when you are taking an animal into health facilities and schools. This is why most such facilities will accept the services only of those animals that have been registered.

Where Do You Fit In?

Wow! It's really kind of awe-inspiring isn't it, this long and illustrious tradition of pet keeping? All those animals and all those people have brought us through the millennia to where we stand today. So what about you? Are you ready to become a part of this grand and glorious tradition?

The first step toward becoming a successful pet keeper is to accept the realities of the mission. Living with animals can be a hassle. It can be expensive. Guaranteed it will be messy. It can take up much more of your time than you ever expected. But it can also be one of the most rewarding undertakings of your life. All are welcome, but success doesn't come easy.

Whether you have lived with animals since childhood or are making your first attempt as an adult, you are in for a surprise. Animals enrich us. Animals make us more interesting. Animals make us whole. Each species, each individual animal is unique. And each has the power to change a life. Magic, remember?

Proving Yourself Worthy

As we have seen, the human desire to live intimately with animals is almost as old as humans. And the arrangement has changed dramatically through the years. From our position today, we look back in wonder at how far we've come, and look forward to see how far we have yet to go. That's where you come in.

Not everyone wants to live with animals. Not everyone should. But those who do are in a position to become a part of living history and to make a difference. When you choose to invite an animal in to share your home, you are no different from that primitive man or woman who did the same thing with the wolf cub tens of thousands of years ago. The responsibility is no different. Whether you choose a lizard, a cat, a dog, a mouse, a gerbil, or a goldfish, you must do so with honorable intentions. The fact that domestic animals exist among us today, the result of an arduous process and intensive commitment on the part of the people involved, is testament to the fact that primitive people, and so many individuals since, did it right. And we must now take the baton and do the same.

Secrets from the Pet Files

Service dogs once had to fight for every square inch of public access they received. This all changed in 1990 with the passage of the Americans with Disabilities Act. It mandates that all registered service dogs—guide dogs, wheelchair assistance dogs, hearing dogs, seizure alert dogs, and so on—must be allowed free access to public buildings and other venues.

Doing the Pet Thing the Right Way

In this era of self-help books and introspection, we are far more likely than our ancestors were to evaluate why and how we do the things we do. And that is exactly what we must do when contemplating pet ownership. Far too many people make the mistake of jumping in impulsively—the easiest recipe for failure. We owe some forethought on the subject to the pet keepers who came before, we owe it to the animals they kept, and we owe it to our own prospective pets.

A lifetime commitment is what this is. And that means the lifetime of the animal, even if that animal happens to be a large parrot or a tortoise who could very well outlive you. When you acknowledge the lifetime commitment part of the arrangement, you prove your noble intentions. Then consider the mechanics of that commitment. Whether you long to take in your first pet, or add a new one to an existing pet household, ask yourself some key questions. Why do I want a new pet? Why do I want this pet? What do I expect from this pet? What will I do if the relationship doesn't work out?

The chapters ahead will help you answer these questions honestly and logically, and make you a better pet owner, too. In the meantime, welcome to the monkey house. Oops! Strike that. No monkeys here (wild animals, you know). Make that the rabbit house . . . or the dog house . . . or the budgie house . . . or . . .

The Least You Need to Know

➤ Before they were companions, animals were regarded as gods and similar religious deities all over the world.

➤ The wolf or other wild dog was the first animal to become a companion; the process was long and gradual and would ultimately extend to other animal species, such as cats, mice, and ferrets.

➤ Throughout history, humans have viewed animals as both soulless creatures incapable of pain and emotion, and as indispensable companions that we cannot live without.

➤ It's a scientific fact that our bond with animals can help us to live longer, healthier, more emotionally fulfilled lives.

➤ Living with animals brings with it incomparable rewards, but it is a lifetime commitment that requires a great deal of time, energy, and money.

Chapter 2

How We Live with Animals

In This Chapter

➤ Changing trends in pet ownership

➤ An introduction to the pet industry

➤ Let your personality guide your choice

➤ Pets in the classroom

Mahatma Gandhi once said that we may judge the morality of a culture by how it treats its animals. So just how does Western culture measure up? We're doing okay, although we could do better. And we are trying. Every year we acknowledge the power of animals in our lives. Every year pet ownership becomes a more accepted part of daily life. Every year society as a whole lends more credence to the magic of the human-animal bond. And every year the public demand for high-quality pet products—food, toys, even clothing—burgeons.

Of course, all is not rosy. We still have plenty of problems to solve. Animals are still abandoned, still relegated to animal shelters, still euthanized for lack of homes. But more and more pet owners are striving to do better at the job. Someone's out there buying all those new pet products, the number and variety of which surely rival the number of baby products sold each year. And more and more people than ever before are willing to read books like this one to help them prepare for a new pet and commit to that animal for the long haul.

We might even venture to say that we are entering a golden age of pet ownership, made even more symbolic with the promise of the new millennium. Sure, everyone these days speaks of the millennium as a momentous occasion. But somehow, when speaking of pet ownership, a vocation that has been around for many, many thousands of years, the whole millennium significance just seems to make sense, doesn't it?

The Contemporary Ark

We have already explored the world of the earliest pet owners and the profound contributions they made not only to our own pet-owning styles but also to the types of pets we live with today. Needless to say, things have certainly changed. And most of those changes have been for the good of the animals. While there are certainly exceptions to the rule, all in all we can say that today we are more kind to animals than we have been in the past. We acknowledge freely and publicly that, just like us, animals feel and think. And most of us really do go out of our way to make life as comfortable and rewarding as possible for the animals in our care.

Pet's Peeve

It's scary to think how many pregnant women have been advised to get rid of their cats. The fear is that cats can transmit illnesses such as toxoplasmosis. But it is cat feces, as well as dirt from a garden, that carry the spore. Just wear gloves when cleaning the litter box, or, better yet, delegate the dirty work to the father-to-be.

In Olden Days

In days past—and we're talking only 30 years ago or so—pet ownership was anything but the vocation it is today. We would just own pets. Most of us loved our pets and all, but it was no big deal. And we all just automatically knew how to take care of whatever animal we might happen to live with. We assumed it was some inherent knowledge we were born with, certainly nothing we would need to consult a book about.

Small animals and birds were kept in cages with some seeds thrown in for food. Cats and dogs spent their lives running loose in the neighborhood or alone in the backyard, were fed some generic type of pet food, and perhaps were bathed now and then when the kids felt like pursuing some novel project. Fish swam around and around and around endlessly in bowls. Reptiles . . . well, we'd probably rather not even think about their sad lot in life, and that goes for frogs and salamanders, too.

The 21st Century: A Golden Age?

The times are a-changing for pet owners. And for pets. And much for the better. If this truly is a golden age of pet ownership, that is probably because we know so much more about the various animals we keep as pets than we did those 30-odd years ago. And we have made a conscious effort to increase our collective knowledge.

Veterinary medicine, for one, has made huge strides, as has nutritional information on individual species. We have also taken the time to research how the various pets would live in their natural states. Dogs, for example, prefer living with their families, outdoors *and* in. Fish, even goldfish, need aquariums with air pumps and filtered, circulating water. And chinchillas prefer two-story cages and a nocturnal existence. Armed with this information, we have tried our darnedest to satisfy our pets' individual needs. The result has been longer-lived, more contented pets and an all-around more rewarding experience for owners and animals alike.

Secrets from the Pet Files

The late British dog trainer Barbara Woodhouse once declared, "Animals are so much quicker in picking up our thoughts than we are in picking up theirs. I believe they must have a very poor opinion of the human race."

All signs point to the fact that we will only learn more as time passes and will keep using what we learn to make life better for our pets. Just look at all the pet-oriented Internet sites now on the World Wide Web and the many pet-care books released each year—and all the people who are taking advantage of them. This, then, is the landscape of 21st-century pet ownership: Leaps in understanding and information, combined with a contemporary desire to return to nature. It can only bode well for the animals we invite into our homes.

Urban and Suburban Living

How we live and where we live determine how and where we live with animals. So when society makes a dramatic shift, in this case moving from the rural life to the more urban and suburban kind, it is definitely our pets' business. Today more and more of us live in the closer quarters of the suburbs and the city, and our pets have had to adapt. Fortunately, that is their forte. Most domestic pets—and that is all we are concerned with here—are highly adaptable. They can go from rural to urban and back again, as long as they live with trustworthy people who acknowledge their pets' needs as well as those of the human members of the family.

Within this increasingly urban and suburban pet environment, we find all manner of pet owners. Sure, there are the typical family units and their typical collections of dogs, cats, and various and sundry small animals. But we also find single people; college students; elderly, perhaps homebound, folks; and even homeless people living happily and intimately with animals, all of them reveling in the very real benefits that come from living with creatures of other species.

The Challenges of the City

Despite our pets' adaptability, urbanization has nonetheless presented pet owners with some significant challenges. Dog bites, for one, are on the rise, thanks to too many ill-trained, under-exercised dogs living too close to other people and dogs. The remedy? Easy. Get the dog into obedience classes and make sure he is exercised each and every day.

Cats, too, are affected. An outdoor cat is at risk in a suburban or urban environment, a potential victim of cars, cruel pranksters, and even displaced wild predators. As a result, more and more people are providing indoor-only accommodations for their feline pets, and that's a good thing. It's all part of the transition.

Pampered Pet

Molting or skin shedding is a way of life for many reptiles, birds, and tarantulas. Your job is to ensure that they are not stressed or injured by the experience, and that feeding and temperature protocols are observed to the letter, no matter where you live.

The Rise of the Exotics

Related to the urbanization trend has come the increased popularity of the so-called exotic pets. Lest you think this refers to such non-pets as lions and tigers and bears, let me set the record straight. The term "exotic" might better be defined as the smaller, quieter, less-demanding pets. Specifically, this includes (among many others) rabbits, mice and rats, hedgehogs, amphibians, reptiles, fish, and even birds.

Urban living or no, dogs and cats remain the classic, most populous pets, a position that will probably never be upset by, say, geckos or tarantulas. But the smaller, more convenient pets allow even frequent travelers with latchkey households to revel in the company of animals. The challenge is that many people smitten with the exotics bug have had no experience in caring for them. They must then be willing to learn.

What Pets Do Americans Own?

Dogs	37%
Cats	32%
Freshwater fish	11%
Birds	6%
Small mammals	5%
Reptiles	3%
Saltwater fish	0.6%

Source: American Pet Products Manufacturers Association

They must also be willing to choose their pets with an eye on the bigger picture. Given the increase in the demand for exotic pets, we have witnessed a related increase in the number of breeders who are concentrating on small mammals, reptiles, and amphibians. Such efforts, assuming they are undertaken with care and compassion for the animals, are good for a species. As we will see in the chapters to come, captive-bred animals are far superior to their wild-caught counterparts when it comes to accepting the role of a pet.

The Pet "Industry"

Money makes the world go around, and is therefore one way to tell that this is indeed a golden age of pet ownership. It's a simple lesson in supply and demand. Both the supply of and the demand for pet products—general, specialized, and absolutely frivolous—have increased phenomenally in recent years, catapulting the pet industry into a multi-billion-dollar entity. And that is something that cannot be ignored.

Pet's Peeve

Each year, millions of wild reptiles and birds are captured from their native habitats and absorbed into the pet trade. Many die, and most are never content as pets. It is kinder and more practical to choose a captive-bred bird, reptile, or amphibian as a pet.

Secrets from the Pet Files

Dog owners spend an average of $300 a year on their pets. Cat owners spend $220. Fish owners spend just $35. Bird owners spend $60, as do owners of small mammals. And reptile owners spend $80. That's just for maintenance, and doesn't include the price of the pet and any start-up equipment.

What We Buy

Attend a pet industry trade show sometime and you'll no doubt be flabbergasted by the array of products you find there. Virtually every pet species and every possible product for those species are represented—sweaters for hamsters, snow boots for dogs, first-aid kits for guinea pigs, training treats for fish. The list would fill volumes. So would the names of people who are buying. Both sides of the supply-and-demand equation are fully operational.

Every year the market grows by leaps and bounds. Pet food companies, based on their extensive ongoing research, come out with healthier, more nutritious pet foods. Dog

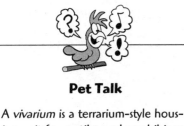

house manufacturers design houses with superior insulation that are also easier to clean. Reptile product companies introduce safer heating elements for snakes and lizards. And the world of cat toys and scratching posts? Goodness! Given the variety, a cat should never need to hang on the living room draperies again.

How We Buy

Needless to say, what we buy has changed dramatically in the past few decades, and so has how we buy it. America's pet shop network is currently undergoing some dramatic transitions of its own. Small, independently owned mom-and-pop shops are being squeezed out by the enormous pet-supply superstores.

Though painful to the smaller operations, the superstores bode well for the pet owners because they offer such a wide variety of products, generally at the best prices. The animals also benefit because most superstores do not offer puppies and kittens for sale (one of the industry's most damaging controversies). Many work with local animal shelters instead, providing high-visibility space for them to adopt out their homeless charges. What's in it for the store? The adopters will probably shop there for their pet-supply needs.

A Revolution in Services

Equally dramatic is the increase in the variety of services now readily available to the pet owner. Veterinary medicine has made giant strides. Just 20 years ago, for example, a cat owner might have laughed out loud at the suggestion that he or she take a lethargic cat to the veterinarian. Now there are entire, and very successful, animal hospitals devoted solely to the care of cats. Birds, too, are enjoying a level of health care their owners never dreamed possible two or three decades ago, as are the various members of the rodent family, rabbits, hedgehogs, ferrets, reptiles, and the amphibians.

The quality of nutrition, vaccines, dental care, medications, and even anesthesia for just about every imaginable pet species has all improved significantly, and continues to do so each and every year. Groomers, pet-sitters, boarding kennels, trainers, and behaviorists are enjoying a renaissance of their own, and more and more pet owners are not hesitating to call in the experts. Pet care has become serious business, both for the providers of services and for the pet owners in need of those services.

What Does It All Mean?

The benefits of the pet industry's widespread success are obvious. The wide availability of a wide variety of products make caring for pets easier and more efficient. At the same time, manufacturers are motivated to learn more and more about proper pet care,

Secrets from the Pet Files

Purebred dogs have become phenomenally popular—often and unfortunately because they appear in popular films and television shows (does *101 Dalmatians* ring a bell?). In the United States, purebred dogs are registered by the American Kennel Club and the United Kennel Club. Not to be ignored, however, is the lovable mutt, who now has several registries of his own that not only register mixed-breed dogs but also sponsor shows and activities around the country where a purebred pedigree is not required for participation.

information that is subsequently, via their products, passed on to pet owners. The result? Better care for our animals.

The democratic nature of the industry is also of great benefit. Today, no pet species is left in the cold. All are created equal. Products, services, nutrition, housing, and general care information are out there not only for the most famous dog breeds but also for the least-famous species of amphibian. All a pet owner needs to do is ask.

You no longer need to mistreat a pet accidentally to learn from your mistakes while you ultimately master the art of keeping, oh, say, tortoises, tarantulas, or tree frogs. How to keep them content and healthy is no longer a mystery. The industry has enhanced the quality of our animals' lives, evident in the longer life spans so many pet species now enjoy.

Pet's Peeve

If an animal is worth living with, it deserves veterinary care when needed. That care is now readily available for most, if not all, of the animals people keep as pets. Even ill or injured fish can be helped by new medications.

But there are drawbacks to the pet industry, too. One of them is derived from the very fact that we refer to it as an industry. When we regard animals as a business, the high calling of pet ownership is overlooked, and they somehow lose their souls. With dollar signs in our eyes, it's too easy to lose sight of the fact that these are living, breathing creatures.

Inspired by the industry's promising profits, for example, too many people may be motivated to breed their pets in order to get their own pieces of the pie. This often turns into the sad lesson that all those young animals cannot be placed in good and permanent homes. The remedy here is to return to the real reason why we choose to live with animals in the first place. And that has nothing to do with money.

A Multi-Cultural Calling

In Chapter 1 I discussed the worldwide appeal of animals. People rich and poor, rural and urban, young and old all share the same desire to live with animals, and all have the potential to be great (or not-so-great) pet owners. We can consider pet ownership a genuinely cross-cultural pursuit.

But there is also a kind of multi-culturalism at play. You see, the pet world is made up of many little pet worlds, each devoted to specific species, and each boasting a distinctive set of protocols, vocabulary, and even famous personalities. In this way, each of these individual worlds becomes a culture of its own—each appealing to different folks.

Pet Talk

Puppy raisers are dedicated individuals who volunteer to raise service-dog puppies for the animal's first one or two years of life. Needless to say, this is one of the most emotional, yet rewarding, roles a dog lover can take on.

Sorting Through the Stereotypes

Dog people. Cat people. Snake people. Frog people. We seem to have a stereotype for all of them. The tweed-jacketed, shotgun-toting, pipe-smoking dog guy. The crazy cat lady who lives with 37 cats and dresses in brightly colored cat-motif clothing and jewelry. The leather-clad, tattooed snake owner who accessorizes his outfit with an eight-foot python around his neck. The eight-year-old frog lover, a little boy with dirty hands and three small amphibians in his pocket, looking like a refugee from a Tom Sawyer movie.

Obviously, we all know pet owners who are nothing like these stereotypes, but there is a grain of truth to the concept. Certain personality types are drawn to certain animals. This hinges more on the nature of the animals. Snake enthusiasts, for example, can include everyone from our tattooed, leather-clad friend to a clean-cut 10-year-old girl with a fascination for reptiles and baseball to a young urban professional with a heavy travel schedule who wants a quiet, easy-care pet.

Pet Talk

A *zoonosis* is an illness people can catch from animals. The most common animals that carry zoonoses tend to be reptiles and birds, so great care must be taken by both healthy and at-risk individuals in handling these animals.

Instead of looking at someone and trying to figure out what kind of animal person they might be, look instead to the animals. They'll tell you everything you need to know, both about yourself and about all the pet owners you see out there every day.

Matchmaking for Pets and People

How about a budgie (known to many as a parakeet)? Budgie qualities: friendly, beautiful, not too noisy, social, somewhat messy, requires daily feeding and attention, suited to city or country life. The right owner for this pet would be someone who wants interaction with their pet but who may not have the time or inclination to engage in heavy outdoor exercise. Someone, perhaps, with limited living space, but who wants a friendly, sociable animal companion that requires daily care. Oh, and this person doesn't mind performing minimal housekeeping chores every day, either.

Obviously people of any age, gender, social class, taste in clothing, or profession can fit this profile. See how it works? The next time you see a kindly, gray-haired grandma walking a potbellied pig on a leash, or a muscle-bound body builder carrying a tiny white Maltese dog in his arms, you'll think differently about the scene, won't you?

Pet's Peeve

Please don't ever choose a pet based solely on its appearance. Make sure you understand what kind of care it needs *before* you make the commitment.

Playing Matchmaker for Yourself

Now try this little matchmaking exercise on yourself. Think you might be interested in a rabbit? Here you have a quiet, soft, warm, fluffy animal that is best suited to indoor living. Owner interactions are a must, as is time spent out of the cage each day. Housing doesn't take up too much room, feeding is easy, and cleanup is not too rigorous. Oh, and rabbits also need to gnaw. That new Berber carpeting could be in danger. Now evaluate your own qualities. Do you have the time to play with your rabbit every day? Is your house full of valuable antique furniture? Are you a rabbit person? If not, there are plenty other pets out there.

All in all, we just need to be like the primitive people who looked to the animals for signs. They trusted the animals to know what was best, and we can, too. When you feel that ancient longing to share your home with an animal companion, the animals hold the answers to which pet is right for you. Different pets for different people. That's the beauty of the multi-cultural pet world.

Pets in School

It is not at all unusual to find small pets in elementary school classrooms, and indeed they can provide children with a wonderful introduction to the animal world. Unfortunately, though, these animals, surrounded by crowds of young children each day, don't always receive the care and consideration they require, even under the leadership of the most well-meaning teachers.

To make life more pleasant for classroom gerbils, guinea pigs, rats, hamsters, and the like, teachers should assume all responsibility for the animals' care, all handling should be done with strict adult supervision, and the animals should be provided with comfortable hiding places into which they may duck from the attentions of the adoring kids whenever they feel the need.

Also, it's really not fair to allow different kids to take the animal home every weekend. This is a source of great stress. A teacher who invites an animal into the classroom must take on the role as primary caretaker, weekdays and weekends.

The Least You Need to Know

➤ Contemporary times have seen profound changes in pet ownership, with animals being regarded as family members, pets and their owners adjusting to a more urban existence, and a dramatic rise in the popularity of the so-called exotic pets.

➤ Pet owners spend billions of dollars each year on their animals' housing, food, veterinary care, grooming, toys, and every imaginable type of product, all resulting in all-around better pet care.

➤ To ensure success in the pet-owner relationship, you must take great care to choose your pet carefully and honestly, and to avoid the impulse buy.

➤ Pets make great additions to a classroom, but only if the teacher commits to the total care of that pet.

Chapter 3

It's a Family Affair

In This Chapter

➤ Pet-keeping commitments

➤ Evaluating how suitable your home is for a pet

➤ Establishing who will care for the family pet

➤ Avoiding the pitfalls of pet ownership

Whether yours is a family of 1 or a family of 12, the moment you bring a new pet into the fold, the number goes up a notch. Now you are 2. Now you are 13. When we think of this in terms of family, a most sacred word, we endow the idea of pet keeping with the respect and honor that is its due.

Now imagine for a moment that you are a 10-year-old dog who has lived all your life with a family that you loved and trusted. Then one day, the family decides to move many miles away. Oh, dear! What to do with the dog? Too much bother. Off to the shelter he goes. Imagine yourself as that dog.

Unfortunately, this is not uncommon. Every day animal shelters must deal with animals who have essentially been betrayed by the people they regard as family— people who may not have properly considered the significance of the commitment they made to their pets eight weeks, eight months, or even eight years ago when they invited them to join the family.

To approach this mission half-heartedly, on impulse, or out of a misplaced quest for ego gratification is to invite heartbreak for everyone involved. And inevitably it will be the animal who suffers the brunt of it all. On the other hand, approach this vocation with enthusiasm, honesty, and a thirst for as much information as you can possibly collect, and you arm yourself with the most effective tools for success. Enter the relationship with a clear vision and realistic expectations of what lies ahead, and accept freely the trust that animals so desperately want to believe we deserve.

The Commitments (Yes, There Are More Than One)

The definition of pet keeping: A lifetime responsibility, a potentially expensive commitment, a potentially time-consuming prospect, all for the health and enrichment of human life.

Wow! Living with animals is pretty serious business. Viewed in this light, you can see why it's so important to think about it a bit before you succumb to the charms of a pair of big brown eyes and a cherubic expression that seem to beg, as only young animals can, "Take me home. Oh, please, take me home." Deciding on a whim that you simply must obey those pleading eyes really isn't taking into account all that will be entailed in that critter's care for the next 13 to 15 years.

That puppy or kitten may indeed be begging you to take it home, mustering all its wiles to elicit the famed "cute response" upon which so many baby animals have relied through the ages. But for the good of that little animal, we must muster the common sense that is *our* species' birthright. I do not intend here to promote the idea of disposable pets. So before you take so fateful a step, it's wise to first take a deep breath and use your head instead of your heart to understand just what it is you're getting into when you feel yourself falling for an animal's charms.

Pampered Pet

Even responsible owners sometimes lose their pets, so it is very important to make sure that your pet wears identification, if it can. Proper I.D. can be collar tags, tattoos, microchips, or, for birds, leg bands.

Pampered Pet

One way to enhance your experience as a pet owner is to join a club. In addition to groups for cats, dogs, and canine activities, there are also groups for owners of turtles and tortoises, rats, rabbits, ferrets, and just about every other pet species imaginable.

Open to Learn

We gaze enviously at the quiet bond that exists between an aging dog and his master as they sit beneath a tree watching the ducks on a spring day, or even the intelligent trust in the eyes of an iguana as she sits perched on her mistress' lap. That bond, that trust, do not come about by magic. They are the products of years and years of carefully choreographed interspecies communication and experience. And it all begins with learning.

You can never know all there is to know about a particular animal and its unique view of the world. To assume that you've already learned all you can is a sad, potentially fatal, mistake. There are plenty of dog owners out there, for example, who are stuck in the negative, force-based training techniques that they observed back in the 1950s. Their unwillingness to learn negates the volumes and volumes of insight animal researchers have gleaned since that time. With no understanding of the contemporary focus on positive reinforcement and a dog's natural pack-driven desire to please, the dog's resulting confusion and the owner's resulting frustration (and, no doubt, sore muscles) strains the relationship unnecessarily.

If only we would open our minds up to the realization that perhaps there is something new under the sun! Of course, many people today are happily basking in that light, and with great results. This ongoing quest for knowledge and the expertise it so naturally brings are part of the commitment an owner makes to his or her pet. How energizing it is to witness the joy of revelation in a dog's eyes when, even after years and years of trust and companionship, she realizes that her owner really does understand what she's telling him. The communion in that moment must be experienced to be believed.

Pet Talk

Herpetology is the study of reptiles and amphibians. *Herpetoculture* is the practice of breeding and raising these animals. Those who study and keep reptiles and amphibians are called *herpetologists,* and they refer fondly to their pets as *herps.*

Money, Money, Money

For the most part, pet ownership is not an inexpensive proposition. There is a price tag on doing it the right way. When people complain about the high cost of well-bred, properly socialized ferrets or hedgehogs these days, or lament the $50 adoption fee at an animal shelter for a cat, well, my friends, remember that this is only the beginning.

This is not to suggest that keeping a pet is a pursuit reserved solely for the wealthy. Hardly. But it is important to remember that even an inexpensive pet needs expensive upkeep. High-quality food, whether it's a dog's commercially available dry kibble or a cockatiel's daily ration of fresh seed and veggies; a small pet's housing unit and accessories; a goldfish's aquarium and all the necessary filters, thermometers, and furnishings; an iguana's heating element; and even the dust for a chinchilla's bathtub—all cost money.

This does not even take into account the cost of veterinary care—and all pets, even small pets, deserve veterinary care. Grooming, too, whether done at home or by a professional, must be considered in your pet-keeping budget. And what about when you travel? Who will take care of your pet(s) then? Better add pet-sitters and boarding kennels to the spreadsheet. The moral of the story, then, is don't jump in without thinking the economic factors through completely. They do make a difference.

It Takes Time

Have you thought about the time commitment involved in pet keeping? Nag, nag, nag. But this, too, is a critical element of pet care. It takes time to feed a pet, to clean a pet's cage or enclosure, and to groom a pet. And some pets require more time than others.

Dogs, for instance, will require far more attention than a snake, a mouse, or a fish. So if it's a dog that's occupying the top position in your wish list, consider the time element very, very carefully. Will you have time to play and exercise with your pooch every single day? And attend obedience classes? And practice your obedience lessons at home? No? Then perhaps a dog (or a ferret or a potbellied pig) isn't your perfect pet match.

Pet's Peeve

The number-one drawback to pet ownership cited by both dog and cat owners is finding pet care when they are away.

Perhaps you'd live happier ever after with a hamster, a rat, a guinea pig, or even a cat, all of whom might be better suited to your daily routine. But even those animals are not ornaments. They need your care, and they need your attention. Better to think about this now than to realize you've made a terrible mistake after you've installed a big, strapping German Shepherd in your home.

Evaluating Home Sweet Home

Okay, so you've given great thought to the financial and time demands of living with animals, and you're closer to deciding what kind of pet might be right for you—or might not be. Now it's time to evaluate your home, the place that will ultimately house both you and your pet (just throwing your pet out into the backyard simply will not do, unless you are designing an elaborate outdoor estate for a potbellied pig; more on that in Chapter 25). Your home, and your own comfort within your home, will be affected by the presence of an animal, so you must decide just how much of your private space you're willing to share. The following questions will help you evaluate this honestly.

Must It Be "House Beautiful?"

Look around your home. Have you put a lot of time and money into the decor? Warning, warning! If so, this must be a major factor in your choice of a pet. That antique velvet couch? Hmmm . . . You can train a dog to stay off of it, but a cat, no way. Is that new plush carpeting on the floor? Oh, dear! A rabbit or a guinea pig could make fine work of that—and of those first-edition Hemingways, too. My, what a lovely loft! Where do you intend to install the budgies' bird cage? You know birds can make a mighty mess at mealtimes, don't you? Something to think about.

You must be honest with yourself. How important to you is a spotless, sanitized home with everything in its place? Long-time pet owners tend to find comfort in a stray white hair on the couch or a feather by the front door. Such discoveries make them smile. Would they make you smile, or would they raise your blood pressure? If the answer is not a smile, perhaps for you a tarantula or a fish would be a better pet than a furry animal or one that requires a messy bedding material.

Pet's Peeve

Some (make that most) pets bring a whole new set of cleaning challenges into the house: dirt, mud, insects, fleas, ticks. How do you feel about that?

Assuming you can tolerate some changes to the perfection you may have become accustomed to in your home, there are steps you can take to accommodate both your pet and yourself. On rainy or snowy days, for example, keep some towels by the door to help clean off a dog's feet when he comes back in after an outdoor romp. Designate a corner for the bird or rabbit cage that you don't mind seeing littered with food and bedding, and carpet the floor beneath with layers of clean newspaper that will allow for quick and easy cleanup. Use your imagination. Maybe all you need to do is vacuum more often. Any small changes you make would certainly be worth the effort.

Is Your Home Right?

While most pet owners can figure out a way to keep their house relatively clean, some issues cannot be so easily tackled. A "no pets" policy in a rented apartment is one. The good news is that such policies usually target only cats and dogs (though it's easier to find a rental that accepts cats than dogs), and will overlook such small, silent types as rats, guinea pigs, gerbils, reptiles, salamanders, and the like. No wonder these quiet easy-care wonders are growing so popular every day, especially among apartment and condo dwellers.

Some pets can benefit from living in a home with a yard: dogs obviously (though they should not be relegated exclusively to the yard) and, as you will see, tortoises, too. Both of these animals enjoy spending time in the great outdoors, the dog to stretch his legs, the tortoise to soak up some much-needed rays. Just make sure the yard is securely fenced, safe, and escape-proof, and you're in business.

Pet's Peeve

Some pets can be pretty noisy. When evaluating a particular species, be realistic about the dog's bark, the bird's screeches and chatter, the ferret's hisses and screams, a frog community's chorus of croaks, and the chinchilla's nightly bleats, purrs, and whistles.

Even without a yard, though, you can work out acceptable alternatives. Just look at all the dogs who live with New Yorkers in high-rise apartments. Rain or snow, those pups need to go outdoors to relieve themselves several times a day. The remedy? Dogs who learn to relieve themselves on concrete, and owners with warm coats, thick waterproof boots, and sturdy umbrellas.

Do You Have a Family Consensus?

You must also consider the needs and opinions of all the people who will be living with the animal you propose to bring into the family. You certainly can't bring a snake into a family where someone is absolutely terrified of snakes, or a feline companion into a home where cat hair triggers asthma attacks. Nor is it fair to bring a Rottweiler into your home if your wife is intimidated by large dogs. The dog will pick up on this instantly, and your wife will find herself relegated to a subordinate position. Investigate these potential problems early, and you'll prevent the heartache of dealing with a hopeless situation after the pet has already joined the family.

Assuming that a particular species and, where appropriate, breed receive everyone's vote of approval, make sure this pet will not be seen solely as a novelty. In evaluating the family consensus, ask questions and seek honest answers. Is everyone enthusiastic about the new addition? Are all committed to the pet's care? How about some extra housecleaning? And what about other pets in the household? Are you prepared to do what you must to introduce newcomers to the fold, while maintaining the existing pets' emotional and physical well-being? Are you prepared to keep the pets permanently separated if they just can't get along?

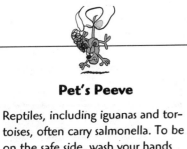

Pet's Peeve

Reptiles, including iguanas and tortoises, often carry salmonella. To be on the safe side, wash your hands thoroughly with anti-bacterial soap before and after handling reptiles, and thoroughly clean any surfaces the animals come into contact with.

Promises, Promises

It's like a first crush—that flush of excitement when we bring a new pet home. And as happens with that first crush, the initial excitement will inevitably fade, only to be replaced, we hope, by a more real and enduring affection that will be the foundation of the bond between pet and owner for years to come.

An Adult Responsibility

"I promise I'll take care of him." How many children through the years have whined, pleaded, and cajoled, begging their parents for a puppy, a kitten, a hamster, or a snake? How many have made that same passionate promise that they and they alone solemnly swear to feed, water, walk, bathe, and brush the new pet every single day, day in, day out, for as long as they both shall live? And how quickly is that promise forgotten when the new pet's luster fades?

It happens so often that this is what you must expect. Adults must accept, with or without the promise, that pet keeping is a job for an adult. Period. We cannot, in good conscience, delegate the care of a living, breathing creature to an eight-year-old child—even one who has made heartfelt promises. If your child promises to do the dishes, and then doesn't, you can let them pile up in the sink. But it's cruel to leave a pet without care just to teach a child a lesson.

Pet care is an adult's job, so if you do not have the stomach to feed pinkie mice to a snake or live insects to a salamander, exert your parental authority and make yours the deciding vote on what type of pet the child will have.

Secrets from the Pet Files

One of, if not the, most successful animal families is the rodent family. Credit their opportunistic natures, their phenomenal adaptability and their efficient reproduction rates. For millennia they have lived, uninvited, in close contact with humans, sharing our food and our homes, and deflecting famously our attempts to eradicate them. Little wonder, then, that rats, mice, gerbils and guinea pigs have thrived so stunningly as pets—and that so many owners have inadvertently found themselves midwives and nursemaids to large families of rodents.

The Beautiful Bond Between Children and Pets

Of course I do not for a moment wish to suggest that children cannot help out with the care of a pet, or that they must be kept separated at all times from the animals in the family. There is a natural bond between children and animals, one that begins when a baby makes friends with his or her first stuffed bear, bunny, or cat. From then on, the die is cast. Children discover that these stuffed critters, and then the equally soft and quiet genuine articles on whom those toys are modeled, can be the most delightful, most trustworthy companions imaginable.

So yes, the children should help out with the care of the family pet(s). Only this way will proper pet-care attitudes and practices be carried on into future generations. Pets are excellent teaching tools, instructing children in the fine and noble art of responsibility and compassion. In getting personally acquainted with animals (with supervision, of course), in learning that animals, too, can be hungry and sleepy and playful, children learn to respect life. They also gain their first sense of their own place in the broader scheme that is the animal kingdom.

Lifestyle Considerations

A pet's care also hinges on the nature of his owner's lifestyle. Is this a latchkey home where the animal is left alone during the day and owner interaction is restricted to mornings, evenings and weekends? That's fine for many pet species—rodents, rabbits, even some cats—and it is especially peachy for the nocturnal critters such as hedge-hogs and chinchillas. Dogs, however, could have a tough time with it, since most must go outdoors to relieve themselves several times a day, and their unfulfilled need for social interaction can result in chronic separation anxiety and destructive behavior. Such dogs require lots of quality time and attention when their owners are home, and lots of daily exercise to release that problem-causing stress and excess energy.

Secrets from the Pet Files

The typical pet owner is married, with children. They own their own home, and are some-where between 25 and 45 years old.

Demanding travel schedules can also interfere with responsible pet ownership, espe-cially if you own potbellied pigs, ferrets, some birds, cats and, of course, dogs. Even if your pet is amenable to frequent separations (mice, snakes, and fish, for example), who will care for your animals while you are away? It certainly doesn't hurt to think about this while you are deciding just which pet species is right for you.

What Every Pet Needs

I've said plenty about what you should look for in a pet, but how about what your pet wants from you? All any animal asks for is a clean, spacious, comfortable home with a cozy bed or nest into which she can retreat and hide; clean water and fresh food; and an environment that is appropriate in temperature and humidity to her species.

Toys, daily attention, and family interaction are critical to some species, and all pets—fish, reptile, rodent, or whatever—whether they realize it or not, expect affection from their owners. From that affection springs respect, and from that respect comes the ani-mal's realization that she can depend on you. In that realization lies the security that every pet craves when she takes up residence with a human family.

Avoiding Pesky Pitfalls

When you join the ranks of the illustrious pet-owner club, you truly enter a whole new world—and a rather emotional world, at that. The bond you share with your pet can pack quite a wallop, inspiring you to learn even more (a good thing) and to get even more deeply involved in the fabulous world of animals—another good thing. But you must keep your head about you. What follows are four traps that even loving, well-meaning pet owners can find themselves falling into.

Just Say No to Breeding

"We're breeding Bambi because we want the kids to experience the miracle of life." Oh, if only they would retire that tired old cliché once and for all! You may be further motivated because friends are always commenting on Bambi's friendly disposition or lovely white coat. But given the health and vitality of the pet industry these days, and the many breeders, responsible and otherwise, who are producing more than enough animals of all kinds to supply the demand, we are not today suffering some drastic shortage of pets. Quite the opposite, actually. You do not need to jump on this bandwagon to duplicate your sweet pet and offer the kids a biology lesson at the same time.

There are plenty of pets out there from which to choose, and there are plenty of excellent books and films these days that will teach kids about life and birth—without creating a passel of creatures that may never find loving, permanent homes. That old miracle-of-life lesson becomes a nightmare for the entire family. Instead, why not direct your energies toward teaching the kids about the importance of spaying and neutering—one of the greatest gifts you can give your pet. In accepting the role of responsible pet owner, you'll wind up with a healthier pet, a better-adjusted pet, and perhaps a longer-lived pet. And what an excellent example to set for the kids!

Pet's Peeve

According to the Humane Society of the United States, 8 to 12 million animals are sent to the nation's animal shelters each year. Sadly, 30 to 60 percent of the animals in shelters are euthanized. Spay or neuter your pet, and be responsible both to your animal companion and to the animal world at large.

Just Say No to Overfeeding

The simplest way to kill your pet with kindness is to overfeed him. And, unfortunately, this behavior has reached a fever pitch in recent years. The epidemic of obesity is now public enemy number one for our pets. An obese pet, whether a hedgehog, a dog, a cat, a rat, a ferret, a rabbit, or a potbellied pig, is not a healthy animal.

But it's so fun to feed animals! The excitement, the enthusiasm your pet exhibits when you dangle a favored morsel in his face—what a joy to behold. And pets are so appreciative of food—most are, at any rate. But if you want that pet to remain with you for as long as is healthfully possible, you must curb your habit of offering rich, wholly inappropriate foods to your beloved companion.

So table scraps, be gone. Out with the fat-riddled but oh-so-yummy treats. Go ahead and treat your pet when treats are in order (training time, for one), but only with healthy treats made for animals, and only in conjunction with appropriate exercise and a diet designed for your particular companion. Your pet's health is in your hands. So ignore his pleading. You know what's best. And your pet, even if you're stingy with the between-meal snacks and table scraps, is gonna love you anyway. I promise.

Secrets from the Pet Files

According to the American Pet Products Manufacturers Association, cats have overtaken dogs in terms of population. America is host to 66.2 million cats and 58 million dogs. This breaks down to 2.1 cats per home in 31.5 million cat-owning households, and 1.6 dogs per home in 36.4 million dog-owning households.

Just Say No to Collecting

It starts innocently enough. You take in one pet and oh, how wonderful it is to have that critter in the house. Gosh, you declare, if one is good, two must be better. And yes, it is. Then it's, well, why not three? Four? Five? Twelve? You can never have enough pets, can you? Yes, you can.

People who live with more pets than they can properly house, care for, and in most cases, afford, are known as *collectors*. For most, it's a case of simply being addicted to the company of animals, coupled with a desire to provide a home for every animal in need. That is a noble goal, but an impossible dream. The result is a house full of animals, all of whom end up suffering the effects of limited resources and attention.

Just how many is too many pets? Well, that depends, not only on the size of your home and bank account, but also on the number of hours in a day. Even if you have enough money and property, no one has unlimited time. And as you have seen, pets place great demands on your time. So evaluate your situation honestly and make honest choices, no matter how desperately you wish to save them all. We all do. In the meantime, harden your heart, be practical, and keep only the number of pets that will fit reasonably in your home, that you can care for properly, and that you can afford.

Just Say No to Abandonment

One of the ugliest phrases in the pet world is, "We had to get rid of him." Yet it is also one of the most used. Granted, sometimes, even with careful forethought and love, the pet-owner relationship just doesn't work out. It would be unfair and deceitful to suggest otherwise. But far too many people are willing to throw in the towel prematurely. Were they to look into the situation a bit more carefully, perhaps they would find out that the cat's sudden failure to use the litter box is the result of the new baby in the house, or the unbearable stench of the ferret's enclosure can be remedied by having the animal neutered and cleaning his home weekly rather than monthly. Sometimes just a minimal adjustment, and a little creativity, is all we need.

And sometimes not. If an animal is vicious or uncontrollably aggressive, then the relationship probably must end. And it really isn't fair to send a pet and all its problems on to another owner. In such cases, euthanasia is really the kindest remedy, but one that many pet owners simply do not want to consider.

Regardless of why you decide a particular pet may no longer stay within your home, treat that animal with dignity. We simply cannot tolerate those who would abandon animals—and this means *any* animal, large or small, scaly or feathered, furred or slimed—on the side of the road to fend for themselves.

Pet's Peeve

Never release an unwanted animal into the wild. It may be ill-equipped to survive. It may also survive all too well, eventually endangering the native wild animals.

The Least You Need to Know

➤ When you decide to live with an animal, you must commit to providing for that animal with investments of both finances and time for the duration of your pet's life.

➤ When contemplating pet ownership, you'll have to evaluate whether you can deal with a home that is not as clean as you might like, whether your home is appropriate for the pet you're considering, and whether you have a family consensus on the responsibility of caring for an animal.

➤ Kids and pets are a classic combination, but pet care is an adult responsibility.

➤ Just say no to breeding, overfeeding, abandoning, or collecting too many pets.

Choosing the New Family Member

In This Chapter

➤ How to use this book

➤ Where to look for your new pet

➤ How to look for your new pet

➤ Preventing pet-choice problems

If you haven't guessed it by now, deciding when, if and how you choose a pet is a pretty big deal. When you place a high value on animals and the joy, comfort, and companionship they so generously bring into our lives, they are not to be dealt with frivolously or on a whim. They deserve respect and dignity. And respect and dignity come from thoughtful choices.

Thoughtful choices are what this particular chapter is all about. Having read this far, you have explored the illustrious traditions and history of pet keeping, your own motivations for joining in this age-old vocation, and the realities of just what living with animals entails, both physically and emotionally. This, my friend, is only the beginning. Now it's time to get down to brass tacks: the guidelines for making a decision that involves bestowing a creature of another species with the title "family member." After that, you will get a little better acquainted with some of the animals you may be meeting as you consider your decision.

How to Use This Book to Your Best Advantage

Before I go any further, it's time to explain just how you can use this book in your quest for a new animal companion. In this so-called "golden age" of pet ownership, animal lovers may at times feel they are being inundated with choices—choices in products and choices in pets. You may find yourself dizzy and confused, and wind up either foregoing pet ownership altogether, or closing your eyes, eeny-meeny-miney-moing it, and choosing an animal that is entirely inappropriate for you.

Indeed there are many more mainstream pet species out there these days than there were 20 years ago, and many of them are quite fascinating. There is every chance you might be interested in, say, a cockatiel, a chinchilla, a miniature potbellied pig, or a tarantula, but have little or no experience in or knowledge about caring for them. No problem. Read on. This book will help.

Pet Talk

A *tame* pet is not the same as a *domesticated* one. A wild animal—a wolf or a raccoon, for instance—can be tamed, but it will always be a wild animal. Domestication, on the other hand, is the result of decades or even centuries of selectively breeding generations and generations of animals.

What This Book Is

With so many people out there these days longing to live with animals, we who love and care about animals hope and pray they will make wise choices. This book seeks to help in that mission.

Within these pages (all under one roof, so to speak), you will meet, in detail, a variety of different animals. Some of these may be new to you (the hedgehog perhaps), just as they may also be new to the pet world. Others are old friends: dogs, cats, goldfish. All belong here, for while there may be widespread confusion about the new kids on the block, there have also been many misunderstandings about the care and character of some of the old favorites (keeping goldfish in bowls, for example). This book will help clarify some of that confusion and rectify those misunderstandings.

What This Book Isn't

You may have noticed that the phrase "perfect pet" has not been used up to this point, and after this paragraph it will not be used again. You will explore the fact that some pets are better suited to some people than others, but perfection is altogether different. There is no perfect pet. To imply that any animal should, or even can, meet such exalted expectations would be unfair to every pet owner and, of course, unfair to the animal.

You will see the word "exotic" used to describe certain pets in this book, but that applies only to those so-called exotic animals that are part of the mainstream pet world (no alligators, bears, monkeys, or big cats here, thank you very much). Nor should you assume that I especially advocate any of the animals highlighted here, exotic or no. While I want to celebrate the animals, I don't want them winding up with people who aren't right for them, or vice versa.

This is also not a breeding manual. My concern here is for the well-being of animal companions and their success as members of the family. My concern is *not* how people may make thousands of dollars breeding Dalmatians or hamsters or rabbits. Where appropriate, you'll find information on how to prevent your pets from breeding—almost every mammal species can be safely spayed and neutered these days—but you will not find a guide to pet reproduction.

This book is also not meant to be the final word on the pets discussed, but rather a detailed introduction to the world's favorite pets. The idea is to help you decide just what type of pet might be right—not perfect, but right—for you. And what type might be a disaster.

Pampered Pet

Once you decide what kind of pet is right for your family, you'll need to get another book that goes into the details of care and training for that pet. We've learned a lot about animals in recent years, so please make sure you take advantage of that knowledge.

Who This Book Is For

Perhaps you've wanted a dog all your life but are only now, as an adult, getting the opportunity to make your dream come true. Or maybe you're looking for some type of reptile or small furry pet for your child, or you're pursuing a pet as part of a communal family project. Maybe you've always lived with a variety of animals but find yourself enamored of something new. However you're approaching this adventure, regard this book as a textbook and confidence builder, a one-stop source of information to guide you through the twists and turns of the vast pet world and all the various animals waiting there.

How the Book Is Set Up

In the pages to come, you will meet 21 different species or families of animals, with a chap-ter devoted to each. The information within these chapters is the product of all the varying, sometimes heated, sometimes even violent opinions and theories on who these animals are and what they do and don't need to thrive.

Each chapter begins with "A Day in the Life" section, that allows you to spend a day with a specially chosen representative of the featured species or family and get a glimpse into what living with it might be like. From there you'll explore the character and background of the animal, then what is specifically involved in choosing one as a pet, and finally, an overview of the critter's care. Easy!

Where to Find Your New Pet

Like the number of pet species available today, you'll also find a seemingly endless array of sources where you might purchase or adopt your new pet. Just what you needed—more confusion! But it need not be confusing—assuming, of course, that you are willing to invest the necessary time to investigate. What follows are some brief discussions about the pros and cons of the various places where you can get pets (you'll meet them again in the upcoming animal chapters, too).

Pet's Peeve

Resist the temptation to jump on the trend-pet bandwagon. You may genuinely long to live with a Dalmatian, a hedgehog, a potbellied pig, or a Jack Russell Terrier, but evaluate your motives carefully. Too many people buy before they think, and the result is thousands of discarded trend pets that simply weren't able to meet the impossible expectations of star-struck, ill-prepared owners.

Breeders

Breeders can be excellent sources for almost every animal you will find in this book. The trouble is, not every prospective pet owner has easy access to a breeder, especially if you are seeking something like an unusual species of snake or a tarantula. Many breeders remedy this by shipping animals to their buyers—with money-back guarantees, of course. But many buyers aren't comfortable with mail-order pets because they can't take a look at the breeder's operation or even their prospective pet ahead of time.

To find breeders, ask local veterinarians, check out listings in the various animal magazines, and, if possible, attend shows. The best places to find a group of breeders all assembled under one roof are dog, cat, bird, or reptile shows, and county and state fairs (the fairs often feature rabbits, potbellied pigs, and most of the rodents). Then, if at all possible, visit the breeder's facility. You want to see a place with clean, uncrowded living conditions for the animals, fresh food and water, and, where appropriate (as with dogs, ferrets, hedgehogs, potbellied pigs, and cats), attention to proper socialization. Just because someone hangs out a shingle and starts breeding animals does not mean that person is ethical, reliable or even qualified.

Pet Shops

In the pages to come, you will find some criticisms of purchasing certain kinds of pets from pet shops. This is not meant to discredit this typically very convenient source of pets, but it is a warning to proceed with caution. Some pets are simply not appropriate "products" for the pet-store environment. Given their intensive socialization needs (not to mention the genetic problems in purebred dogs), dogs, cats and potbellied pigs top the "not appropriate" list. Those with a passion for snakes and ferrets would, no doubt, join this chorus and add their animals to the list.

There are some good pet shops out there that are clean, and have intelligent employees, proper animal housing and happy, healthy animals. These might be fine sources for such animals as rodents, fish, budgies and cockatiels, and some reptiles and amphibians. There are even shops these days that specialize solely in the sale of reptiles and amphibians, many with stellar reputations. Just be careful. Too many heartbreaking stories have emerged from the pet-shop doors—primarily stories about dogs and cats. Let's try to make sure that your experience won't become another sad tale.

Newspaper Advertisements

The first thing many would-be pet owners do when they decide to get a pet is open the newspaper. Here you will probably find columns and columns of available pets, both from breeders (ethical and otherwise) and from people attempting to get rid of pets that they've decided are just too much trouble (pets that could well be your diamond in the rough).

As for the breeders' ads, they run the gamut. You will find the most ethical show breeders who are experts in their species or breeds, who live and breathe their animals and want only the very, very best for them. But you will also find the so-called "backyard breeders" who typically breed an animal on a whim in the false hope of making a buck or of teaching their kids about where animals come from.

If it's a dog you're looking for, the quickest way to tell the serious breeders from those of the backyard variety is that the serious ones will refer to the mom dog as a "bitch" and will never use the phrase "he has papers and everything." All genuine and ethical breeders should discuss genetic problems, contract guarantees, and spaying and neutering, and grill you about your intentions and your lifestyle. This book's position on pet owners who become breeders has already been made perfectly clear, but again: Don't do it. And for you potential buyers out there, buying from a backyard breeder may not only result in a less-than-healthy pet for you, but it may also encourage these individuals to breed more.

Pet's Peeve

When you begin to read the advertisements in the newspaper for available pets, you'll notice many animals offered "free to a good home." This places the animals in danger, because people do not always value what is offered free. Disreputable types frequently answer such ads, offering promises of loving homes and care, only to turn around and sell the animals to unacceptable owners or research laboratories, or use them for other cruel purposes.

Secrets from the Pet Files

Real breeders who do it right don't make much, if any, money. Prenatal and postnatal veterinary bills, the necessary vaccines, appropriate housing, top-notch nutrition, and, for some species, all that time invested in socializing the young animals adds up—as does the ethical breeder's guarantee that he or she will take the animal back at any time if there are any problems. These individuals are guided not by a desire to rake in the big bucks, but by a deep passion for a particular species or breed and a desire to strive for perfection. They may charge more than the backyard breeder, but you usually get what you pay for.

Rescue Groups and Animal Shelters

As you have seen so far, and as you will see in the pages to come, far too many discarded animals end up in animal shelters each year. And shelters aren't just for dogs and cats anymore. You're also likely to find iguanas, snakes, rabbits, rats, and even tarantulas. Many of these homeless animals have the potential to be fabulous pets, but because of a lack of commitment or know-how from their original owners, they haven't had the opportunity to claim their birthright. Who knows? You may just be the one to make that animal's dreams come true—and vice versa.

Virtually every community has at least one animal shelter. Shelters can be run either by the local government or by local animal-welfare organizations. Also growing more visible every year are rescue groups that target all sorts of animals, from single breeds of cats or dogs, to ferrets, to turtles and tortoises, to amphibians, to rabbits, to pot-bellied pigs, and everything in between.

Rescue groups are typically comprised of a network of individuals with a shared desire to keep their breed's or species' discarded creatures from falling through the cracks. They provide foster homes for them, rehabilitate them if necessary, and place them in what this time they hope to be permanent homes. Both rescue groups and shelters require nominal adoption fees from their adopters, to help defray their costs. And because they don't want to see the animals coming back again, they make sure those adopters' motives and intentions are honorable.

The Moment of Truth: Choosing Your New Pet

At last! Here you are. The research, the homework, the self-evaluation have been exhausting. The soul-searching grueling. But you have emerged educated to doctoral proportions. You are now prepared to welcome a new pet, confident that you can choose wisely and commit for the long haul. Let's take a look at how you should go about making this momentous decision.

Secrets from the Pet Files

There is much debate about whether talking birds understand what they are saying. The fact that birds in households with cats will call, "Here kitty, kitty" to the family feline could probably be used as evidence by those who believe birds only mimic. After all, why would a bird invite a predator to come by? But those from the other camp claim that this obvious show of humor is just another facet of the extraordinary avian intellect.

Timing Is Everything

When the time comes to choose your new companion, it must not be any old time. Even this seemingly simple element of choosing a pet involves some forethought. But you should be used to that by now.

First, don't take an animal from its mother before it's ready. Now, for animals that are not raised by a mom—frogs, for example—this isn't an issue. But for some animals, premature separation from mom can have lasting effects on the poor baby's personality and your relationship with it. So take this seriously when your pet of choice is a dog, cat, ferret, potbellied pig, rabbit, hedgehog, budgie, or cockatiel. Keep in mind, too, that for some of these animals—the birds, for example—"mom" could be the breeder, who is taking great pains to socialize the animal to humans. Be patient. It's worth the wait.

Think long and seriously about just when you will bring your new pet home, too. As a rule of thumb, try to wait until the beginning of a weekend or a vacation. That way, you can get your pet installed into its new abode, and you won't have to run out again right away to go to work or school or any of your other weekday commitments. You can use those first few days to get acquainted and to begin to convince your new pet that you are a person to be trusted.

Preparing Your Mind, Heart, and Home

Bringing a new pet into your home will disrupt the current rhythms of the household. The extent of this disruption will vary, of course, depending on just which pet you decide to welcome into the family. You are wise, then, to prepare for the animal's arrival ahead of time. This will prevent the stress of happily carrying your new puppy, kitten, mouse, rabbit, ferret, or frog over the threshold, only to discover that it has nowhere to sleep, nothing appropriate to eat, no feeding and water supplies, and no bedding. Now what kind of a welcome is that?

No, your new companion deserves better than that. Although animals don't take offense the way people do, your pet will certainly be more content if it is brought into this new environment, rife with strange smells and prying eyes, and placed within a cozy, secure home where it can, at its leisure, become familiar with you and its new surroundings. Preparing ahead of time will also give you the opportunity to think about your new responsibilities and the changes it will make in your own life. Remember, this is a major change for you, too.

Pet Talk

Although they are often labeled "cold-blooded," reptiles and amphibians are actually *ectothermic.* This means their bodies are warmed and cooled (and their appetites stimulated) by their exterior temperature. This explains why reptiles need to bask in the sun or another heat source, why amphibians are constantly seeking shelter from the sun to protect their skin's natural insulating moisture, and why the proper care of these animals is downright scientific.

The Big Decision

Choosing a pet can be a pretty emotional endeavor. And frankly, it should be. We're talking family here. That is why it's so very important to keep the emotions in check and do all you possibly can to choose your new companion with your mind as well as your heart. The two must work in tandem.

In the pet chapters to come, you will find, in detail, what you should look for in terms of physical condition and temperament when choosing a new pet of a given type or species. There are, however, certain characteristics that are fairly standard markers of a healthy animal (even the human animal). The ideal for most species is:

➤ Clear, bright eyes

➤ Nose, ears, and eyes that are free of discharge

➤ A lively attitude

➤ A good appetite

➤ Abrasion-free skin, covered by a uniform coat of hair, scales, or feathers

➤ Clear, unlabored breathing

Pay attention to the environment, as well. Look for clean, uncrowded living conditions for the animals, and diligent attention from their caretakers. Is the water clean and the food fresh? How about the other animals? Evaluate the overall health of *all* the animals, not just your prospective pet. Your new pet's cage mate may have a highly contagious illness that won't make itself known in your pet until several days after you take it home.

Pampered Pet

No matter what kind of animal you're talking about, there are certain signs that indicate veterinary attention is in order. Loss of appetite; a drastic change in behavior; discharge from the ears, eyes and/or nose; lethargy; diarrhea or constipation; stiff or un-comfortable movement; and/or con-gested breathing all warrant a call, and probably a visit, to the vet.

With these intellectual evaluations behind you, now is the time to allow your heart to be your guide. If there's one particular animal that seems to be healthy, has a good disposition, and has, for some indefinable reason, captured your heart, that is probably the pet for you. Best wishes to you both!

Preventing Problems

A variety of problems can emerge during your relation-ship with an animal—too many, actually. Many of these are rooted in the ethics involved in taking a creature of another species into your home as a companion. This very act might seem a recipe for disaster, and sometimes it is. But you possess the power to prevent some of these ethics-related problems—a heroic act you can perform both when you choose a new pet and when you welcome that animal into your home.

No Impulse Buys

Sometimes pets come to us when we least expect them. Stray cats, for instance, are often rescued from a destitute life on the street, they move in and they never leave. Bravo! But such exceptions aside, if you have read the previous section about preparing for your new pet with accommodations and supplies before bringing it home, then you know you won't be seeing any support for the romantic impulse buy here. Purchasing or adopting a pet on a sudden whim hardly meshes with all that pre-planning stuff, does it? It also doesn't allow a would-be owner much time to gather up the information so vital to a successful long-term pet-and-owner relationship. Please think about that before you leap.

No Pity

Perhaps more difficult to avoid is the pity buy: the kitten that's a bit too old in the pet shop; the rabbit that is destined to be snake food if someone doesn't buy it in an hour or so; the runt of the litter. Of these three, the first two animals may actually have what it takes to be wonderful pets. But the last one, the runt, may not. Every day people purchase animals like this. They feel sorry for the pitiful creatures, and even though they hadn't intended on getting a new pet right now, they come home with one anyway.

The trouble is, these kind-hearted souls, who we may be proud to claim as members of our species, may just be asking for trouble. Choose the runt because the little guy was being bullied by its siblings and you could wind up with a fearful, shy pet with health problems and a tendency to bite first and ask questions later. Or not. Maybe all will work out beautifully. Hope so. But even if it doesn't, you can't be faulted for your kind heart.

Pet's Peeve

More and more dog owners are having their dogs debarked. This is a surgical procedure in which the veterinarian makes an incision in the dog's vocal chords. In most cases, this turns an incessant bark into an incessant whisper, and the bark usually returns with time. Debarking must never be used to hide the fact that someone is keeping dogs illegally, or without an owner first trying to control the barking through training and behavior modification. Sometimes a little more exercise each day is all a barking dog needs.

Wild-Caught Pets versus Domestic

You will notice as you begin to peruse the pet chapters of this book that some animals are missing: wolves, squirrels, chipmunks, monkeys, bears, raccoons—in other words, wild animals. No, you won't be finding them here. You will, however, find some pets within these pages that do technically qualify as wild—the birds, reptiles, and amphibians, for instance. These animals are established, accepted pet species, and those promoted here have been bred in captivity.

I'll come right out and say it: I absolutely do not approve of taking wild animals as pets, or taking pets from the wild. Even if properly housed and fed, wild-caught pets are, for the most part, never truly contented, for their hearts remain with their wild roots. They can also be downright dangerous, carry disease and parasites, and, to top it all off, illegal.

Which brings us to yet another ethics question, one of the most devastating and controversial of the animal world. When you accept a pet that has been involuntarily removed from its natural environment, you are supporting the wildlife trade, much of which is illegal. While many within this "market" are trading in legal species, millions of the targeted animals are killed each year during capture and transit. Some of these same traders may also be poachers and financiers of poachers, so any way you slice it, this is not a decent option for an intelligent and ethical pet owner.

Pet's Peeve

When designing your menagerie's homestead, remember not to mix rodents, meaning don't house rats with mice or guinea pigs with chinchillas or hamsters with gerbils. Respect the differences. Most of these animals (except for mice) prefer to live solo anyway.

Careful Introductions

You have been lectured at length about when to bring your new pet home (at the start of a weekend or a vacation). Now we'll look into *how* you should go about it. Animals, even well-socialized animals, can be terribly stressed by the upheaval of coming into a new home, so be sensitive. You may mean well, but those first few days are not the time to hold some big "Welcome Pet" party. It should be just the family. Quiet. Peaceful.

If you're adding a new frog, tortoise, cat, or bird, for example, to a household that already hosts one or more of these animals, quarantine the newcomer for a few weeks before exposing the others to it. Do what you must do to allow your new pet to adjust, even if that means leaving a snake or a tarantula alone altogether for a few days, or convincing the kids that no, the puppy can't sleep in bed with them on its first night in its new home. Just be patient. It may take time. But do it right, choose wisely, prepare diligently, and before you know it, you won't even remember what it was like before this animal came into your household and made life so much warmer and friendlier.

Secrets from the Pet Files

When choosing your pets, don't mix predators and prey. The reasons for this should be obvious. We don't even want to think about what can happen to a rabbit in the presence of a ferret, or a mouse that is a designated playmate for a snake or a cat.

The Least You Need to Know

➤ This book is a guide to help would-be pet owners choose animals that are best suited to their personalities and their lifestyles; it's *not* a breeding manual or a promotional vehicle for individual pet species.

➤ This book explores 21 types of pets, each chapter beginning with a "Day in the Life" of the featured animal, followed by an overview of that animal's character and care.

➤ Pets are available from breeders, pet shops, animal shelters, rescue groups, and private parties, but not all are appropriate sources for every type of pet.

➤ Prepare for your new pet before you bring it home.

➤ When choosing, pay attention to your prospective pet's health as well as its appearance.

➤ Avoid problems by resisting the impulse or pity buy, choosing domestically bred rather than wild-caught animals, and introducing your new pet carefully to its new home.

Part 2
The All-Stars

Okay, so you now have a sound foundation in the vocation that we call living with animals. You understand that it's not something that can be taken lightly, that it's an issue of family, and that it involves some very serious soul-searching and commitments. So here we go. Time to meet the animals.

In this section, you will be meeting the animals that are typically considered the most popular, the most populous, the most well-known and traditional pets. The animals we all know and love: the dogs, the cats, the rabbits, the guinea pigs and the hamsters. But it may be surprising to learn that some of us don't know as much as we should about choosing them wisely or taking care of them once we bring them into our homes. The chapters ahead will remedy that.

Darling Dogs

In This Chapter

➤ A day in the life of a dog

➤ Understanding dogs and the way they live

➤ Choosing wisely, choosing permanently

➤ A short course on caring for canines

We call the dog man's and, not to be sexist, woman's, best friend. There is a reason for this. The dog was probably humanity's first four-legged friend, and thus has, in time, become our *closest* four-legged friend. The relationship was forged thousands of years ago when the dog unselfishly agreed to help a rag-tag group of primitive folks find food and keep warm on those frigid Ice Age nights. Ever since those initial introductions, the dog has endured within the human heart. First loves always do.

Given the illustrious relationship our two species has shared, why is it that so many people have such difficulty in making contemporary dog-human relationships last? Chalk it up to human impulse. Chalk it up to human ignorance. The dog would certainly deny culpability if we were to ask his opinion on the matter. And the dog would be justified in doing so. Let's see what we can do to help prevent the impermanence that so often plagues what is meant to be a legendary partnership.

Secrets from the Pet Files

Most so-called canine behavior problems are simply natural canine behaviors that are not being properly directed. For instance, dogs need to chew. Offer them an ample and varied supply of chew toys and they won't chew on your things. Digging, too, can be a doggie's delight, so designate an area of the yard where the pup is welcome to indulge. Incessant barking is often a symptom of loneliness or boredom. A little more daily attention and exercise could remedy the situation handsomely. Just think like a dog, and you can figure out the problems together.

Dogs As Pets

	light	1	2	3	4	5	heavy
Time commitment						✔	
Grooming						✔	
Feeding				✔			
General cleanup					✔		
Suitable for kids age infant to 5			✔				
Suitable for kids age 5 to 10				✔			
Suitable for kids over 10					✔		
Sociability						✔	
Expense of keeping						✔	

A Day in the Life

There is no typical day in the life of a dog. For some dogs an average day means leaping out of bed at sunup to bring the sheep in from the upper pasture. For others, it involves assisting their blind or wheelchair-bound owners through their daily activities. For others it means accompanying police officers in patrol cars or customs officers looking for drugs. And for some, it means lounging on satin pillows, munching on liver-flavored bonbons while mumsy and daddy dote on them.

Such variety is the spice that makes up canine life—evident in the vast number of breeds of all shapes, sizes, colors, temperaments, and even natural instincts. Through the centuries, we humans have sculpted this species into whatever we wanted or needed it to be at a given moment. From the Golden Retriever to the Maltese to the Irish Wolf-hound to the Rottweiler to the Poodle, there is a breed (and every imaginable mix of breeds) to fit every need, every whim, and to complement every lifestyle, regardless of the nature of the days that make up that lifestyle.

But when we ponder the awesome challenge of choosing one of these animals as a pet, we need to look beyond the species' specialized skills to an average day in the life of an average pet dog. Let us consider a typical day in the life of a Border Collie named Davey for a brief glimpse into what responsible dog ownership entails (although plenty of examples exist, we are not interested here in what irresponsible dog ownership entails).

Morning

You awaken at dawn (sleeping in with a dog is as unlikely as sleeping in with a toddler in the house), and rain, shine, or snow, you get Davey outside for the morning walk.

This walk must be long enough to help your pup expend the physical and emotional energy that, left unchecked, can lead to such behavior problems as digging, chewing, and barking. Make sure to bring poop-scoop implements along to ward off those nasty stares that neighbors justifiably reserve for those who don't clean up after their dogs.

You and Davey have breakfast, and then it's off to work around the house. Whether that includes cleaning the garage, raking leaves, or finishing up a small household construction project, it will also include the attentions of Davey, who will insist on being at the heart of the action.

Pampered Pet

The simplest poop-scoop instrument is a plain old plastic sandwich bag. When presented with one of your dog's calling cards, place your hand into the bag and grasp the object of your attention in your sandwich-bag-protected hand. Turn the bag inside out, and there you have it: a fully contained, relatively odorless bundle that you may now discard without ever having touched the contents directly.

Noon

Lunchtime. You resist Davey's pleadings for table scraps and offer him a healthier treat instead, a carrot stick or a dog biscuit. After lunch you drive to your pup's obedience class. Sure, he knows the basics, but at age three he, like most dogs, could use a refresher. Once class is over, you take him to the dog park to run and play with his buddies and burn off some energy. On the way home you stop at the pet supply store for a refill on dog food.

Now, if you're lucky, Davey is ready for a nap, but don't hold your breath. Because you did your homework before choosing this particular breed, you are well aware that there is a good reason why Border Collies have the reputation of being such tireless, fiercely intelligent dogs in constant need of activity. With that nap idea nixed, the kids step in to save the day. They invite Davey to participate in a rousing game of in-line skate hockey. Davey accepts the position of goalie and successfully prevents the opposition from scoring.

Pampered Pet

Bring along plenty of extra sandwich bags when you go to the dog park, which you may graciously offer to fellow dog owners who conveniently "forget" to bring along cleanup tools of their own.

And Night

After dinner (remember that dogs are most comfortable when their daily rations are divided into two or three meals a day), you realize that Davey is a bit itchy and scratchy. Time for a quick bath. After a thorough scrubbing in the bathtub, Davey gives a good shake and saturates the bathroom with water. Then, to prevent Davey from catching a chill, you bring out the blow dryer, set on warm not hot.

The evening tends to be many a dog owner's favorite time. You are no exception. You sit together as a family. Davey at last is resting, yipping and twitching as he snoozes at your feet, reliving the day's adventures in his doggy dreams. Then, just before bed, one more trip outside for Davey to relieve himself, and everyone falls into bed exhausted.

Canine Social Studies

Dogs are amazing. They habitually save Timmy from the well, retrieve the animals we hunt, herd our livestock, guard our homes and streets, and lower our blood pressure with their mere presence. (Really, they do. It's been documented scientifically). In return we owe them proper care, attention, affection and exercise. We also owe society at large our efforts to be responsible in our dog ownership by cleaning up after our pups; obeying leash laws; vaccinating, spaying, and neutering our pets; and ensuring that they don't bark incessantly. Add this all together, and you find yourself with a rather large commitment on your hands.

The key to living successfully with a dog is forging a strong relationship with your pup as soon as possible. Although our interspecies relationship seems to have come about almost miraculously, your bond with your own pet will not form so divinely. It requires much time, effort, consistency, and even clairvoyance on your part. You must learn each others' languages if you are to achieve that communion we all envy in those who cohabitated with the likes of Lassie and Old Yeller.

Secrets from the Pet Files

Beware of wolf-dog hybrids. Or rather, beware of those who would sell you wolf-dog hybrids. They will promise you that these animals, which are part wild wolf, part domestic dog, are the most extraordinary pets ever invented—and invented is exactly what they are. What they probably won't mention is that most wolf-dog hybrids cannot be trained or housebroken; that they will tear up a couch in a matter of minutes; that they are dangerous to children because of the wolf's predatory instincts and the dog's unpredictable nature; and that they are fundamentally confused and miserable, trapped between two worlds.

Who's the Boss?

Your first decision when inviting a member of the canine species into your home is to determine who will be the boss. Relinquish this position to your dog, and you'll find yourself living with a monster whose every wish is your command.

You'll soon discover that friends and relatives would rather change the air in their tires than visit a home with a resident dog who bites, barks constantly, and performs a rather unpleasant dance on the legs of anyone who ventures to cross the threshold. You'll wear a clothespin on your nose because of the carpet stench that only the unhousetrained dog can create, and your furniture will look like it fell into a wood

Pet's Peeve

Avoid sending mixed messages. If, for example, you don't want a full-grown, profusely coated, 110-pound Alaskan Malamute sleeping on your bed or fine antique couch, don't allow the animal to do so when he is a soft and cuddly, irresistibly adorable 10-pound puppy.

chipper. You'll find yourself sleeping on the couch because the dog has claimed your bed as his and his alone. Incredible, you say? Highly improbable? It happens every day. And it's not a pretty sight.

Now those canine movie idols—Lassie, Beethoven, Hooch, and the like—they knew when to follow their instincts, but they also knew who was in charge. They shared a meeting of minds with the men, women and children in their lives, and all thrived from the mutual respect. These dogs were not beaten into submission, nor should you believe for an instant that any dog requires such a heavy hand in order to establish your leadership. May patience, understanding, and consistency be your guides. Only by learning how to communicate with your dog in a language he understands, and remaining steadfast in what you expect of him during the daily routine of playing, grooming, and working, will you establish your leadership and reap the rewards of a legendary dog-owner partnership.

Mutual Learning

Most folks believe that when they embark on the grand mission of dog training, they are training their dogs to behave. Sounds reasonable. And simply because they've attended a canine obedience class or two, many fancy themselves instant experts in the field. Overnight they become unofficial Ph.D.s in canine behavior.

But can you keep a secret? Dog trainers everywhere, and the dogs they work with, know that while the dogs do benefit from obedience class, it is the owners who are the primary targets of the lessons. Without divulging this secret, good trainers gently instruct their human students in the art of consistency and the nuances of communicating with their dogs. They encourage the owners to practice their new-found skills at home each day. The result? A well-trained dog owner, and hence a well-trained dog.

Training Magic

"Oh, I don't believe in training. It takes away a dog's freedom." Unfortunately, many misguided souls out there believe that training is cruel and unusual punishment for the deep and sensitive soul that is the dog. Indeed, training can be cruel when it is grounded in physical punishment and aggression, but find a trainer who subscribes to the philosophy of positive reinforcement, and training is a joy for everyone involved. Commit the entire family to dog training, begin as early as possible, and avoid creating that canine monster we spoke of earlier.

Secrets from the Pet Files

Mom dogs start training their pups as soon as possible. You can too. Puppies as young as three months of age can participate in formal puppy kindergarten classes available now in most communities. These use training methods that acknowledge a puppy's short attention span and give youngsters a head start on obedience training. Most kindergarten classes also involve play sessions in which young puppies, as they wrestle and tumble with others of their own age, learn that they need not fear larger pups, nor use smaller ones as chew toys.

The philosophy of positive reinforcement is really quite simple. It emphasizes reward and trust, rather than fear and punishment. The dog sits, stays, and comes when called. He is rewarded with treats and/ or praise. The dog learns that his bathroom is outside, not the living room carpet. The dog is rewarded. The dog sits quietly as you clip his nails or brush his tail. He is rewarded. And you are rewarded with the satisfaction of knowing that you have worked together for this very positive communion.

Pampered Pet

Beware the myths surrounding spaying and neutering. Male or female, an altered dog, with proper exercise and diet, will live a longer and healthier life. Free from the influence of unbridled and unnecessary hormones, the dog will be more attuned and attached to its owner, and will never contribute to the population of unwanted pets.

Whether you're talking basic obedience commands, grooming tolerance, housetraining, or social skills with other dogs and people, positive training lies at the heart of it all. Cruel? Hardly. A dog's wild ancestors were part of a pack, and dogs are used to the idea of a hierarchy. A dog feels more secure and happier when someone he knows and trusts is in charge. A well-trained dog is a free, and usually much-loved, dog.

A Blueprint for Finding Your Pup

All dog people seem to do is preach. Take your time. Do your homework. Avoid the impulse buy. Don't just take the first pup you see. Annoying advice? It is if you are one who enjoys the thrill of spontaneity. But spontaneity has no place in inviting a new dog to join your family.

In keeping with that Yoda-like advice from the experts, you must start out with a blueprint for success. Were the wee Jedi master to guide you, he would no doubt instruct you to hit the books and attend dog shows and dog activities to glean as much information as you can about dogs in general, and about your chosen breed in particular.

Whether you are seeking a puppy or an adult dog, try, try, try to draw on all you have learned when it comes time to choose your canine companion. Steel your heart from melting at the sight of that warm and wonderful ball of fluff that greets you as though you are some long-awaited deity returned to earth. Choose with your intellect and common sense as well as your heart.

Where Not to Look

And just where, oh where could your little dog be? You will find yourself discussing your quest *ad nauseum* with friends, relatives, and perfect strangers. The wise souls among them will advise you to forego the pet-store pup that may have been commercially produced without regard to genetic health, temperament, and proper care.

These puppies, products of what are referred to as "puppy mills," lie at the heart of one of the dog world's most heated controversies. By choosing from another source, you steer clear of this controversy, and perhaps help future canine generations by reducing the demand for pet-shop pups. Your choices do make a difference, both for you and for the entire family of dogs.

What Does a Dog Cost?

The purchase price of a dog can vary widely. However, the average dog owner spent $216 for their small dog, $163 for their medium dog and $203 for their large dog.

The average dog owner also spends per year:

$196	Dog food
$138	Non-surgical veterinary services
$104	Grooming
$49	Other supplies
$36	Flea and tick products
$30	Toys

Better Alternatives for Dog and Puppy Buying

Opt instead for puppies and dogs from good, ethical breeders whose motives are guided not by the almighty dollar, but by an abiding passion for a breed and the desire to seek perfection in that breed. You will find these breeders at dog shows and in dog magazines. You can also contact trainers, kennel clubs, and veterinarians in your area, as well as the American Kennel Club for referrals to breeders who specialize in your chosen breed.

Other potentially excellent sources you might be wise to investigate are breed rescue organizations and animal shelters. Both specialize in offering second chances to dogs, both purebreds and mixed-breeds, whose previous homes just didn't work out, usually because of owner ignorance and negligence. Breed rescue is typically a network of fanciers of a particular breed, often breeders themselves, who rescue the animals, rehabilitate them if necessary, and then take great pains to get them placed properly and permanently. Both shelters and rescue groups charge nominal adoption fees and demand, for good reason, that the dogs they adopt out be spayed and neutered.

Pampered Pet

If possible, meet a puppy's mom and dad to see what character traits they may be passing on to their progeny.

So check out all the possibilities. Once you start looking, wherever you look you'll find dogs who want nothing more than to devote themselves to pleasing you. There are no guarantees in dog choosing, but you can increase your odds of finding a friendly canine companion by observing several temperament guidelines. Look for a pup or older dog that is friendly, bright-eyed, and outgoing, and resist the temptation to rescue the shy and retiring runt, who may not hesitate to bite you and other family members out of fear. And finally, pay attention to that intuition that just seems to draw some pups naturally to some people, and vice versa. Perhaps you knew each other in another life.

The Canine Inquisition

When you decide to choose a new canine family member, questions—hundreds of questions—must be answered. The first of these must be directed toward you. Am I ready for a dog? What kind of dog? Large or small? Mixed-breed (some of the world's greatest dogs are mixed-breed dogs) or purebred? Puppy or adult? Longhaired or shorthaired? Athlete or couch potato? Polka dots or hairless?

When evaluating pet prospects, riddle the breeders or shelter workers in charge of those prospects with questions about the dogs' health, breeding, genetic background, training history, and temperament. Is he good with cats? Children? Gerbils? And expect to be riddled with questions in return. Be very, very suspicious of a breeder or shelter employee who does not grill you about your dog ownership background, your lifestyle, and your housing situation. Don't be offended by such questions. You need to prove that your intentions are honorable. The inquisition just means that someone cares about that dog and wants to make sure he finds a permanent, loving home.

Secrets from the Pet Files

Ideally, a puppy really should not leave his mom until he has reached seven or eight weeks of age. This gives the pup ample time to benefit from his mother's incomparable lessons on how to be a dog, after which he will be ready emotionally to transfer his attentions to his new human parents, who will now be responsible for his ongoing education and care.

Papers and Everything

Want to know how to make a veteran dog enthusiast's head explode? Just boast that a particular dog "has papers and everything." As the veterans know, those who make this statement typically do not understand that the papers of which they speak so proudly—American Kennel Club registration papers—are not the papers that really matter to the health and well-being of the dog, and the longevity of the dog-owner relationship. They merely certify that the dog is a purebred, and that the fact has been recorded with the AKC. The AKC itself will tell you it is no guarantee of quality.

The papers that count are the papers that certify a puppy's parents have tested clear of hip dysplasia (a painful and all-too-common malformation of the hips presumed to be genetic), eye problems, and other genetic maladies that may afflict a particular breed's family tree. If the dog you are purchasing or adopting is allegedly spayed or neutered, ask for documentation to prove that, too. You get the picture.

Pet's Peeve

You must choose a dog or puppy not because his coat color complements your home's interior decor, but because his size and nature complements your lifestyle and your family's activities.

The other vital piece of paper you should seek is the sales or adoption contract. If you are purchasing a dog or puppy from a breeder, that individual should prove his or her merit with a contract that guarantees the health of the dog and demands that the pup be returned to the breeder should you find you cannot keep him somewhere down the line. You, in turn, prove your mettle by vowing that you will abide by certain care guidelines, and spay or neuter a dog that will not be shown or bred. A similar contract, an adoption contract, should follow a rescue or shelter dog into his new home.

Room and Board

So, you took the plunge and there you stand with a cuddly puppy nestled in your arms. He looks up adoringly at you for guidance. Now what?

Don't panic. You did everything right. In your wisdom, you prepared ahead of time. You did not go to the mall to buy a mattress pad, only to come home with that doggy in the window. Oh, no. You made the conscious decision to invite a dog into your home. You did your homework and chose not only the best breed or mix of breeds for your lifestyle, but also the best individual candidate for the job. And then, before you brought the pooch home, you prepared for his arrival. You assembled the supplies: the bed, the food, the dishes, the leash and collar (and ID tag, which your dog will wear at all times, right?), the chew toys for relieving stress, the grooming tools. . . .

Secrets from the Pet Files

Choose a dog as a pet, and from that day forward that animal will forever dictate where you will live. Dogs require more room and attention than many other types of pets, and can be more prone to trouble, so they are often unwelcome in rental accommodations. To combat this, prepare a rental résumé for your dog. Present in writing your dog's qualities (good with kids, quiet, and clean) and accomplishments (obedience titles, heroic tendencies, favorite pastimes). Complete the package with reference letters from friends, relatives, and others who know him well. A prospective landlord may be willing to bend the rules simply because you have made such an effort to prove your dog's worth as a tenant.

As those first few weeks and months pass, you'll notice that the demands of dog ownership have reduced your bank account balance, your free time, and maybe even your waistline, now that you have dedicated yourself to exercising your pet every day. Before you know it, your pup is thriving in the new routine, and you won't even remember what life was like before you heard the pitter patter of little puppy feet trotting down the hall.

When You Get a Dog, You'll Also Have to Get These

Leash	Chew toys
Collar	Play toys
Food dish	Crate or pen with bedding
Water dish	Dog license
Dog brush	Flea control products
Nail trimmer	Care and training book

What Every Dog Needs

What every dog needs is a routine. Your pooch needs to know that you are the boss and he is a beloved and trusted, though subordinate, member of the family pack. But he also needs to know that he will be fed at certain times of the day, that his walks will occur within a certain time frame in the morning and evening, that he will be groomed regularly, and that the kids will be home from school to play when the sun occupies a specific position in the sky.

Nothing pleases a dog more than predictability. Sure, some changes in plan are exciting from time to time, but in the routine there is security. So stick to it. Don't try to keep your dog guessing.

Establishing the routine begins gently. You bring your new pet home just before a week-end so you can get acquainted. You allow your new pet to adjust to his new surroundings, and avoid inviting the entire neighborhood over to celebrate his arrival and completely terrify the poor dear. As the days pass, you help your pup understand what is expected of him within the structure and rhythms of his new household. The dog, in turn, should reward you with a deeper trust and adaptability. These gifts will make him a joy to travel with and an easy keeper, both at home with the family and in the boarding kennel when his family is away.

Pet's Peeve

Do not punish your dog for accidents. If you catch him in the act, startle him with a whisk-away action, and then take him to the appropriate place. It is totally useless and also cruel to "rub the dog's nose in it." Remember, positive reinforcement is all.

Routines are a must for housetraining. After all, what goes in on schedule comes out on schedule. In fact, housetraining need not be a trauma. As with all training, it simply requires consistency and patience. Whether training a puppy or an older dog, designate an area outside as bathroom. Periodically during the day, particularly after the dog's meals and whenever you see him sniffing about suspiciously, whisk him away to the designated bathroom, offer a command and praise the pooch profusely when he complies.

When you are not at home or cannot watch him, confine your pup in either his dog crate or a similarly enclosed corner of the house, perhaps a canine exercise pen in the kitchen that is his sanctuary, so he can learn that the home at large is not his bathroom. As your dog learns control, you can increase the areas of the house where he is allowed free access.

Let Sleeping Dogs Lie

Sleeping arrangements are critical to a dog's routine. This begins with puppies, who will play tirelessly, only to plop down suddenly in midstride and fall fast asleep wherever they may be.

Your job is to let that pup know there are certain areas of the house where he may take those naps in peace. This may be a confined area of the kitchen, laundry room, or master bedroom. It may be in a dog's crate, which can be a valuable housetraining tool as well as a comfy den-like bed. Wherever it is, make sure the dog understands, first, that he has a safe haven from which he can escape the noises and commotion of the household; and second, that he cannot have free run of the house when you are not at home (such freedom only leads to household destruction and canine danger).

And don't just automatically assume that big dogs sleep outdoors and small dogs sleep indoors. Wherever the family is, the dog wants to be there too. Indoors or outdoors. Size is insignificant. Regardless of where you live, whether house, condominium, apartment, or farm, assuming the dog receives his required exercise, which will vary between, say, a Pekingese and an Australian Shepherd, he will be content to be where you are. Period.

Pet Talk

If dogs were allowed to breed freely, every dog in the world would exhibit similar characteristics. This *natural dog*, as it is called, would be medium-size, 35 to 40 pounds or so, with a curled tail, short brown hair, erect ears, and a pointed muzzle. That is the base model from which all other breeds have diverged so dramatically.

To Health

Would you like your dog to live a good long time? Of course you would. Your pet probably won't outlive you, but even if this is your first experience living with a dog, you can help ensure that your pet reaps the full and healthy life that should be his birthright. This has everything to do with prevention.

Pay close attention to your dog's health, inside and out. Feed him only high-quality, commercial dog food, preferably two or three times a day, and never directly before or after vigorous exercise (the combination of which can cause the deadly condition of canine bloat). Don't allow your pup to indulge in table scraps or inappropriate treats, and resist your own temptation to offer them. You need not bribe your pet.

What Does a Dog Eat?

Premium-quality dry commercial dog food

Low-fat treats for dogs (sparingly!)

Low-fat people food treats (sparingly!)

Pampered Pet

Beginning at about six weeks of age, puppies should receive a series of four vaccines spaced several weeks apart for parvovirus, leptospirosis, canine hepatitis, distemper, parainfluenza, and coronavirus, followed by boosters every year thereafter. Rabies cannot be administered until the pup reaches four months of age, followed by boosters either yearly or every three years, depending on the vaccine and the laws in your area.

Groom your pup regularly—brushing, combing, nail clipping, tooth brushing, bathing when necessary, and so on—and when doing so watch for lumps, bumps, and parasites on the skin that could signal trouble. Make sure he gets plenty of exercise, too. Attention to the dog's psyche, internal organs, and nutrition will manifest in a dog's healthy coat, sparkling eyes, and a cheerful disposition.

Also critical to your dog's health is establishing a good relationship with your pet's veterinarian. Regular veterinary visits for booster vaccines, fecal parasite checks, and routine checkups are on every healthy pet's agenda. Your veterinarian will rely on you to keep an eye out for signs of budding health problems that are most successfully treated in their earliest stages. You, in turn, will rely on your veterinarian for his or her clairvoyant sixth sense that will spot the slightest, most subtle signals of trouble from a possibly uncooperative, terrified, and thus aggressive patient that cannot speak or tell the doctor where it hurts. Simple.

The Least You Need to Know

➤ Because of the vast personality and vocational differences between breeds of dogs, there is no typical day in the life of a dog, just as there is no typical dog.

➤ Because dogs are so keenly aware of pack order and the family hierarchy, they require consistent leadership, training, and socialization throughout their lives.

➤ All dogs need training; the well-behaved dog enjoys far more freedom than his ill-behaved counterpart.

➤ It's best to get a dog from an ethical breeder, shelter, or rescue organization, and to ask plenty of questions about the dog's health, genetic profile, background, and temperament.

➤ Most dogs are happiest when they are offered indoor-outdoor living arrangements with a predictable routine, plenty of attention and exercise, and high-quality food.

Charismatic Cats

You either love them or hate them. There is no in-between with cats. Few animals evoke at the mere mention of their names such heated bursts of emotion from us opinionated humans. Indeed, few animals are shrouded by the rich body of folklore that festoons the cat—and, thus, the baggage that comes with it: the misunderstandings, the old wives tales, the superstition. Affectionate and loyal. Cold and distant. Sultry and beautiful. Frightening and evil. Together, these words illuminate the many faces of the cat we humans have conjured up through the ages. But how can such disparate notions really portray the same animal? Because the cat, by its very nature, is full of contradictions.

Somehow this only seems to enhance the cat's allure as a pet. But be warned: As much as we find ourselves enchanted at the thought of living with cats, we don't choose cats as pets. They choose us. I'll do my best here to show you how you might make yourself a worthy candidate for the exalted position of cat caretaker (we will forego the word "owner" so as not to offend our feline readers). As for you cat haters out there—and you know who you are—you, too, are urged to read on. Cats commonly worm their way into the hearts of people who have professed a lifetime hatred of everything feline. Should you find yourself in this unexpected position, you'll need to be prepared to take on your new responsibilities.

Secrets from the Pet Files

When I say a cat chooses you, I am not exaggerating. Unlike any other type of pet, 49 percent of pet cats are acquired as strays.

Cats As Pets

	light	1	2	3	4	5	*heavy*
Time commitment				✔			
Grooming					✔		
Feeding			✔				
General cleanup			✔				
Suitable for kids age infant to 5		✔					
Suitable for kids age 5 to 10				✔			
Suitable for kids over 10				✔			
Sociability					✔		
Expense of keeping					✔		

A Day in the Life

Once upon a time, cats were gods. They were honored hunters of the realm. Few societies have so adored the cat as the ancient Egyptians. Beginning sometime around 3000 BC, they recognized the cat as an ideal candidate to keep their granaries free of rodent infiltrators. The cat was thus highly regarded and even deified for its efforts. It was also not unusual for an Egyptian ruler to consult a cat when it was time to make important decisions, and to kill or injure a cat was an offense punishable by death.

The mummified bodies of cats have been discovered lying beside those of deceased kings and queens. The cats were obviously so beloved that they were invited to accompany their noble caretakers into the next world.

Cats were also the mystic familiars of witches, and hence symbols of the coven. And so they found themselves the scapegoats of medieval European people, who sought redemption in the destruction of the mysterious animals that seemed somehow privy to our species' deepest, darkest secrets.

Secrets from the Pet Files

The idea that bad luck will come when a black cat crosses your path is one of the oldest and most universal of all superstitions. It probably began with the Greek myth about a young woman named Galenthias, who was turned into a cat and became a priestess for that patron saint of witches, Hecate. The association stuck. Despite the cat's exalted position among the ancient Egyptians, thanks to its somewhat supernatural appearance, the black cat would forever be seen, even today, as a symbol of witchcraft and bad omens.

Needless to say, the typical day in the life of the typical pet cat has changed dramatically since then. Cats are now rarely called upon to be the conduit between humanity and the heavens. Their quintessential hunting skills continue to evoke images of their wild cousins, yet a diet of barn mice is hardly considered ideal for today's healthy feline pet. Although they are still preyed upon by those who mean to make cruelty to animals an art form, such activities are no longer sanctioned. The bottom line: For the most part, the cat's lot in contemporary life, now far more grounded in reality, has improved dramatically. Let's take a look at the day in the life of one contemporary kitty.

Good Morning, Kitty

Welcome to Fluffy's house. Sure, two humans pay the mortgage, but that is a formality. Fluffy is queen around here.

And when the sun rises, this queen expects her due. She demands that breakfast be served up in a timely manner and that she receive a formal invitation to snuggle into that cozy corner under the covers next to her mistress, should her feline majesty decide to sleep in this morning. When she does emerge from her warm nest, she stretches with a dramatic flourish, attends to a tiny spot in need of grooming on her toe, and then it's off to survey her domain.

Midday Whims

As the day progresses, Fluffy prefers the freedom of spontaneity to the restrictive rigors of a routine. Plans and schedules are for dogs. Cats just don't operate that way—except where mealtimes are concerned. Fluffy and her mistress have had their disagreements from time to time over this freewheeling philosophy, but it shouldn't take you long to guess who inevitably emerges victorious. The queen's subject never harbors hard feelings. It comes with the territory.

You never know what might strike Fluffy's fancy at a given moment. She may desire a quick bout of chase-the-catnip-mouse. Or maybe she won't. A brief game of hide-and-seek with mom might be nice. Or maybe not. Perhaps she'll ac-cept mom's invitation to go out on the lawn on a leash. Are you kidding? How about a snooze in the sun at the bay window? Definitely!

Secrets from the Pet Files

Cats spend about 70 percent of their day sleeping and 15 percent grooming. This is not only true for domestic cats. In the wild, a lion will sleep 20 hours a day.

An Evening Distraction

It's 6 p.m. The doorbell rings. Fluffy runs to investigate. She has never been one of those ridiculous creatures who hides under the bed at the first hint of excitement. A man and a woman walk in the door. The man spots Fluffy in the hall. She recognizes instantly the benign smile on his face, the uninviting position of his arms, the stiffening of his spine. "I really don't care for cats, thank you very much," his silent messages reveal to this cat's watchful eye. "I intend to change all that," Fluffy seems to say.

Fluffy steers clear of the annoying baby talk emanating from the woman visitor—talk allegedly designed to lure Fluffy into the arms of someone who obviously already admires cats. Where's the challenge there? No, it is the man who must be conquered. And this is just the cat who can do it.

Fluffy summons her most convincing whiles. She rubs up against the man's legs (a gesture that marks him with her scent, claiming him as Fluffy's own). She dons her softest, most charm-

Pampered Pet

Even a cat that spends her life indoors should wear a properly fitting collar and current identification tag at all times. You never know when your beloved might slip silently out the front door without you knowing. You can further ensure your pet's safety by engraving the message "If I'm outside, I'm lost," on the flip side of the tag.

ing gaze that tells the man she has eyes only for him. And finally, the big gun: the purr. Before the man even knows what has hit him, a fluffy, rather smug-faced feline is sitting in his lap. He is taking great pleasure both in the rhythm of her purring and the irresistible softness of her fur. "My, what a lovely animal," he remarks. Then, just as suddenly, she is gone. Fluffy's work here is done.

The Feline Mystique

Few societies have been able to resist the allure—and the mystery—of the cat. Superstition aside, we cannot deny the innate power obviously embodied within the graceful feline physique, a power that artists have long attempted to capture in their works. In more contemporary times, this has extended to the media of film and television, where nary an alley is featured without the screech of a cat in the background.

Cats have played good roles and bad. Si and Am in *Lady and the Tramp* were star villainesses, and Lucifer the cat was one of poor beleaguered Cinderella's countless nemeses. On the other hand, think of Pywacket in *Bell, Book and Candle* and Gepetto's sweet and gentle pal Cleo in *Pinocchio,* and we once again find examples of the dual role the cat takes on in the human mind.

Secrets from the Pet Files

Cats have delightful habits. Purring, of course—that way the cat has of imitating the soft hum of an engine—is a favorite of both cat owners and non-cat owners. Kneading too, is rather delightful. This is what we call it when a cat actually imitates the act of kneading bread with her front two paws. Behaviorists believe this is related to behaviors of young kittens nursing, but, as one writer put it, kneading may also be simply "a private demonstration of serene ecstasy."

What a Cat Is . . . and Is Not

You may not be able to train a cat to do all the tricks a dog can, but this is undeniably an extremely intelligent animal. Too intelligent, say the cat's many fans, to succumb to the arbitrary bidding of a species it considers to be its inferior (us). Yet the cat is not a little person in a furry package. In fact, a cat might take such a notion as an insult.

No, a cat is perfectly content with being a cat, an animal that inspires great devotion from its followers. Unlike a dog, which wears its every thought and emotion on its collar, the cat embodies dignity and stoicism (thus proving a diagnostic challenge to veterinarians). Never one to wallow in self pity, neither is a cat likely to shower you with affection for a small act of kindness. No, a cat is typically more comfortable with more subtle exhibitions of her affections, such as sleeping next to you in your bed, or allowing you to play with her, or allowing you to spend time petting her in the evening.

The Pet of the New Millennium

Surveys show that each year the cat is gaining in the pet popularity contest, and for good reason. As living situations become increasingly urban, the cat emerges an ideal pet for apartment- and condominium-dwellers. With indoor-only living arrangements considered the safest for cats these days, older folks can benefit from the presence of this warm, soft, purring companion, and never need worry about taking her out for long daily walks in the ice and snow.

Pet's Peeve

Please don't buy into the myth that cats don't need your love and attention. They do! They crave your time and affection as much as any pet. They just prefer it on their own terms.

If you travel, again, a cat could be your ideal companion. Indoor cats do get bored and depressed if left alone for long periods of time, but because they don't require a lot of walks and are self-cleaning, it is a lot easier to find someone to look after your cat when you're away. Clean, quiet, easy to care for: What more could you ask for?

If you long for a pet that will hang on attentively to your every word and obey your every command, a cat is not for you. You will certainly be able to find some games to play with your cat, and you might even be able to coerce her into walking on a leash from time to time, but that is entirely up to the cat. Most cats would rather perish than obey a string of commands. Save yourself some grief, and don't enter into this relationship with unreasonable expectations.

Getting Chosen by a Feline Companion

Obtaining a cat is no great challenge. Cats are everywhere. In fact, there are too many cats and not enough homes for them all. Take an informal poll of cat owners and you'll find a collection of heartbreaking and humorous stories worthy of a Pulitzer Prize. Cats can come into our lives from the most unexpected places—grocery store parking lots, deserted buildings, the neighbor's barn—and when you least expect them. Sure, we would like to believe that we make a conscious decision to bring a cat into our life, but the fact remains that it is usually the cat who does the choosing. And we have no choice but to go along for the ride.

So what's a body to do? Just sit back and wait for a cat to walk by and pick you out of the crowd? Well, no. You must take an active role, even when your prospective pet is feline.

The Breeder's Cat

If you covet a pedigreed cat—say, a sinewy Siamese or a fluffy Persian, a breeder of purebred cats may be your safest source for a pet. A reputable, ethical breeder is attentive to genetic health and temperament as well as that all-important appearance.

73

Attend some cat shows, peruse breeder listings in cat magazines, and ask local veterinarians for advice about good breeders in your area.

You might also find your breed of choice offered at a local pet shop, but you take your chances there. Just like purebred dogs, purebred cats can fall victim to a variety of genetic maladies that result from sloppy gene-pool management. The same risk accompanies the purebred kitten who has been bred by inexperienced pet owners—"backyard breeders" they are called—who breed their cats and offer the kittens through the newspaper. Serious breeders, on the other hand, guarantee their kittens for health and temperament, agree to take them back at any time if need be, and do all they can to produce the finest animals possible—and to ensure they are placed in proper homes.

The Rescued Cat

Pampered Pet

When adding a new cat to a household that already hosts a resident feline pet, have the newcomer examined immediately by a veterinarian and keep the kitties separated for a few days. This trial separation will serve as a health quarantine period.

Most cats come into their owners' lives from animal shelters, off the streets as strays, or through some other type of rescue situation (a family moving, an unwanted litter, a child who becomes allergic to cats, and so on). Regardless of kitty's birth, all are equally deserving of love, affection, and respect—and proper attention to their health and well-being.

Although a robust species, the cat is prone to a variety of infectious illnesses for which she must be properly tested and vaccinated as soon as you strike your agreement to cohabitate. In the case of the stray, a good bath and deworming will also help ensure a comfy new start for the kitty. You may even discover post-bath that the wayward orphan you believed was smoky gray is actually a dazzling white.

Whether you purposely visit the shelter to evaluate prospective pets or simply cross paths with a homeless animal who at first glance realizes she is fated to spend the rest of her life by your side, you get acquainted and before you know it, the cat has installed herself in your home and claimed it as her own. She has adjusted to the comforts of domestic life and its dependable supply of food and warmth, and you cannot remember what life was like before this soft, fuzzy purring machine made herself at home in your home.

Solid Preferences, Pleasant Surprises

Of course you can't just take in every stray cat you meet. Do that and you'll become the crazy cat lady or crazy cat guy. You must make choices—and do it with a good shot of common sense.

Bright eyes, healthy skin and coat, a clean disease and vaccination record, an even bite: Beyond these basic prospective pet evaluation factors, you will no doubt have conjured

Secrets from the Pet Files

According to the Humane Society of the United States, a single female cat and her offspring can be responsible for producing 420,000 cats in seven years. Multiply that by the more than 66 million cats in American homes today, not to mention the millions of strays, and you have, well, a nightmare. Given the sad plight of the many homeless cats that populate the nation's streets and animal shelters, the message is clear: Be kind, honor the feline, and spay or neuter your cat.

up in your mind your vision of the ideal feline pet. For some this means a longhaired tabby, for others a cat with folded ears, and for still others this means (believe it or not) a cat with no hair.

For you, there may be no cat but a longhaired cat, while the question of male or female is inconsequential (both should be spayed or neutered, after which both make equally fine pets). But what about age? You may decide that nothing but a kitten will do, only to find yourself face to face at the shelter with a four-year-old shorthaired calico who you just can't get out of your mind. That's it. Don't fight it—you have been chosen.

So sure, go ahead and think about what you would like in a cat. But remember, the cat is an animal of many surprises. Don't be shocked if you wind up with a cat that is nothing like the animal you envisioned in your mind's eye. Once you make the fateful step, another inevitable discovery awaits you: Cats are extremely addictive. Succumb to that age-old feline spell, and you may just find your one-cat household become a two-cat household and ultimately a three-cat household, each new cat a unique and vital addition to the fold. Just don't overdo it. There is such a thing as too many cats. And besides, cats don't like crowds. They need their space.

Pampered Pet

Some cats like to be "only" pets, while others love a companion. When you get a second cat (or a third, or . . .), don't expect a miracle. The two may become fast friends, or they may simply tolerate one another's presence. Either outcome is acceptable.

A Proper Feline Home

Just when you thought there was nothing more you could possibly do to prove yourself worthy to your cat, there emerges the issue of housing. Cats are pretty persnickety about the quality of their digs and, considering how they have sacrificed the wild ways of their majestic big cat cousins to live with us, they have certain opinions regarding what constitutes a proper home.

For one, that home must be amply stocked with the necessary supplies. To save your cat any inconvenience, these should be gathered before your new pet crosses her new threshold. Stock the kitty pantry with only fresh, high-quality commercial cat food and treats. Purchase grooming supplies (kitty nail clippers, shampoo, flea comb) for those occasions—bath time and nail-clipping time, for example—when you will be treated to a potentially deafening demonstration of your pet's vocal range. Collect a variety of toys in hopes that at least a few will appeal to your pet's sense of fun. And finally, prepare a soft comfortable bed for your cat, knowing full well that your little darling may never set foot on the thing. *Your* bed may prove far too enticing to your pet, but frankly, what's the harm in that?

When You Get a Cat, You'll Also Have to Get These

Food dish	Litter scooper
Water dish	Cat litter
Cat brush	Scratching post
Nail trimmer	Cat tunnel/tree
Toys	Cat carrier
Bed	Care and behavior book
Litter box	

The Secret of Successful Cat Keeping

Keep kitty indoors. That's the secret. Simple, isn't it? Granted, there are some cats who thrive in an indoor-outdoor living situation—say, cats who have found sanctuary from a cruel world as resident barn mousers, and those kitties that high-strung racehorses cling to like security blankets within the crazed environment of a racing stable. But cats who spend their lives inside live longer and are safer, healthier, and saner than those allowed to wander the neighborhood streets free and unsupervised.

The indoor cat does require exercise and mental stimulation, however. You need not release mice into your abode to hone her hunting skills, but you can try installing a bird feeder outside a window that can provide the resident feline with hours of viewing pleasure. Toys, too, can provide that much-needed exercise, but kitty will have strong opinions on which toys she deems acceptable and which are the ultimate bore. And toys, by themselves are no fun at all—even ones that move on their own. Cats need *you* to play with them.

In addition to offering kitty a fine selection of toys, you may try your hand at decorating your home with a nod to feline sensibilities. Go out and see what's available. Perhaps you'll choose treehouse-like scratching posts and tunnel sets that provide tubular explorations. But don't be surprised if you present these to your cat, only to have her glance at them, sniff, turn and leave the room. Then don't be surprised when you return later and find her enjoying a rollicking good time with the new trees and toys, just because she thinks you're not looking.

Declawing cats is a common practice these days, typically done to protect furniture and window coverings from those sharp kitty claws. But it is a rather gruesome procedure that can have short-term effects on the cat's psyche and long-term effects on her safety. A cat without claws cannot climb to avoid an attacking dog, nor can she defend herself in an altercation with another cat. Even if you're sure these situations will never come up with your indoor cat, claws and all the things a cat does with them—scratch, knead, groom, and mark territory—are part of being a cat.

Pampered Pet

Cats also scratch to stretch their spines. Be sure to buy a scratching post tall enough that your cat can reach way up and get a good stretch.

Some sessions with a feline behaviorist and a trip to the pet supply store for a scratching post are more humane alternatives for dealing with a cat who loves to scratch and hang on the draperies. Use catnip to encourage your cat to scratch in the right places. And make sure to trim her claws regularly. Your veterinarian can show you how.

What Does a Cat Cost?

The purchase price of a cat can vary widely. And because most cats were received as kittens, strays, or from friends, 78 percent of cat owners did not pay for their cats. Of the ones who did, the average price was less than $100. Purebred cats can be much more.

The average cat owner also spends per year:

$165	Cat food
$87	Non-surgical veterinary services
$48	Other supplies
$31	Grooming
$26	Flea and tick products
$19	Treats
$18	Toys

Cleanliness Is Next to Catliness

Cats are incredibly, fastidiously, obsessively clean. They spend a great deal of time cleaning themselves, contorting their bodies into unbelievable Gumby-like positions to attend to every single one of those hard-to-reach nooks and crannies. Of course, you will have to step in and assist from time to time. The delightful chore of clipping the claws, running a soft brush and a flea comb through kitty's fur, and the dreaded bath time all fall on your head. No doubt you'll come up with some amazing contortions of your own to get out of some of these duties, but they are all part of the commitment you made the day you invited a cat into your family.

Feline bathroom habits, too, are some of the cleanest in the pet world. Provide your pet with a litter box and clean litter, and your cat should take it from there. Natural instincts, you know. Your job is to keep the box clean each and every day, and to provide several litter boxes for the resident cats when yours is a multi-cat household.

The litter box must be scooped at least once a day, and the entire box emptied, scrubbed, and refilled once a week or so. New types of clumping litter will extend the time between litter changes, but there is no such thing as a litter box that never needs daily scooping or regular cleaning.

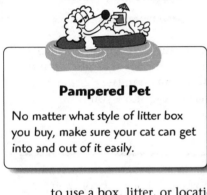

Pampered Pet

No matter what style of litter box you buy, make sure your cat can get into and out of it easily.

Cats are very fussy about their litter boxes, and with good reason. Their noses are thousands of times more sensitive than ours, so if you think the box seems a little "ripe," imagine how it smells to them! Plus, they're walking in it. Think about that the next time you're feeling a little too lazy to scoop.

There are all kinds of litter box styles, from plain pans to covered boxes with doors. Your cat will let you know which one she prefers, and will also make her litter preferences known. She does this by refusing to use the box if it's not to her liking. Please, don't force your cat to use a box, litter, or location that she finds unacceptable. You won't win the battle, and you both will be miserable.

And a final word of warning: There are some litter boxes on the market today that advertise themselves as never needing cleaning. This is a myth. If you're not prepared to scoop daily and scrub regularly, a cat may not be the right pet for you.

What's for Dinner?

'Tis a puzzlement. Cats—quintessentially carnivorous animals who fare best on a diet of high-quality commercial cat food—are renowned for their finicky palates. Yet obesity has reached epidemic proportions among today's feline population. How can that be?

Well, historically a cat's diet consisted of whatever she could catch on her own—a profoundly unhealthy and unsafe proposition in this day and age. Perhaps today's more sedentary feline lifestyles are responsible for current weight-gain trends, but it would seem this is a secondary cause. The primary cause is simply too much food. As more and more cats are enjoying a life of luxury, more and more owners seem to be equating that lifestyle with a feline need for calories and fats.

It's a safe bet kitty is playing a pivotal role in this, of course. The allegedly finicky eater convinces her guilt-ridden owner that if she is not offered a steady variety of rich, high-calorie foods each day, she just might starve to death. Or perhaps your crafty feline has mastered the skill of extracting treats from each family member one at a time throughout the day. She munches treat after treat from morning to night—and soon she is svelte no more. At this point, a family meeting is in order to halt everyone's cat-treating habits. After that, a trip to the pet supply store to buy a low-calorie, low-fat commercial diet food for cats is in order. Kitty, you're going on a diet.

Pet's Peeve

Obesity is a major cause of health problems in cats, so please keep an eye on your cat's weight. A controlled diet and plenty of exercise are the best ways to keep your cat svelte and healthy.

What Does a Cat Eat?

Premium-quality dry commercial cat food

Low-fat treats for cats (sparingly!)

Low-fat people food treats (sparingly!)

A Most Challenging Patient

Beloved Yorkshire veterinarian James Herriott, author of *All Creatures Great and Small,* prided himself on his ability to restrain cats and treat them with little trauma to himself, his patient, or his patient's owner. To acknowledge this gift was extremely progressive, because when he was practicing, pre– and post–World War II, most cats didn't get any veterinary care. Most cats owners thought of them as self-maintaining.

We now accept that cats are deserving of veterinary care, but our cats still tend to resist such attentions. A veterinarian who shares Herriott's skills is worth his or her weight in gold. They start by reading the mysterious mind of a stoic patient who refuses to acknowledge that she is ailing. Then they ignore the otherworldly shrieks and howls that only a protesting cat can emit. The routine feline booster vaccines (for leukemia, FIP,

Pet's Peeve

Although cats are natural-born hunters, it is a myth that domestic cats can fend for themselves. To release a pet cat into the wild is down-right cruel. While there are successful feral cat colonies populated by street-smart kitties, the pet cat lacks the skills necessary to protect herself from starvation, exposure, and the dangers of unknown people and animals.

FUS) are administered on schedule, and the annual or biannual examination for suspicious signs (lumps, bumps, small wounds, parasites, and the like) that may indicate health problems proceed without a hitch.

Despite your cat's protests, the annual trip to the vet is good for her. Love her responsibly, which means not always giving her *exactly* what she wants.

The Least You Need to Know

➤ Cats are accustomed to dictating their own daily activities rather than abiding by the whims of their owners.

➤ Because of the mystery and independence of cats, people typically either love them or hate them, and have for centuries.

➤ Cats need almost as much love and attention as dogs. They just prefer it on their own terms.

➤ Cats are clean, intelligent animals ideally suited to an indoor-only living arrangement, which is also the safest, healthiest situation for a feline pet.

➤ While some owners do purchase cats from breeders and adopt them from shelters, it's very common for unsuspecting people to find strays on the street and discover that they have suddenly become cat owners.

Robust Rabbits

In This Chapter

➤ A day in the life of a house rabbit

➤ The coexistence of rabbits and humans

➤ Choosing the right rabbit for you

➤ Rabbit room and board

Look around. You'll see them. Rabbits are everywhere: in our backyards, on our golf courses, in our gardens. On our television and movie screens. In our Arctic tundras, in our children's books, in our gift shops, and on our greeting cards. Rabbits are also in our houses.

Rabbits boast one of the world's most pervasive animal images, reproducing, well, like rabbits, whether in the media, on stuffed-animal assembly lines (especially at Easter time), in the wild, or in unsuspecting pet households. Yet with such mass appeal comes the misfortune of an "oh-anyone-can-own-one" reputation that blinds people to the need for research on a rabbit's care. I'll do the rabbit a favor here and try to dispel some of the misinformation that plagues so many of them who share our lives. A glimpse into the day in the life of an average, everyday, very much loved pet bunny is a good place to start.

Rabbits As Pets

	light	1	2	3	4	5	heavy
Time commitment				✔			
Grooming				✔			
Feeding				✔			
General cleanup				✔			
Suitable for kids age infant to 5		✔					
Suitable for kids age 5 to 10				✔			
Suitable for kids over 10					✔		
Sociability				✔			
Expense of keeping				✔			

A Day in the Life

When taking a peek at a day in the life of a pet rabbit, we must first decide just which type of rabbit we'd like to observe. Traditionally, rabbits were not kept in the style to which they have become accustomed in this century. When kept at all, it was typically for meat and fur, and this legacy followed the rabbit into her first experiences in the pet world. Rabbits were fine pets—cute, cuddly, and all that—the accepted theory held, but they belonged outdoors.

Times have changed for the pet rabbit. We now speak of the "house rabbit," a pet that, like a cat or dog, spends most of her time indoors with her family. The contemporary domestic rabbit has found this house-rabbit stuff much to her liking, and has easily embraced the joys of human companionship and a domestic lifestyle. Yes, some pet rabbits still reside outdoors, ideally in spacious hutches sheltered from sun, cold, wind, precipitation, coyotes, and mischievous children, but the rabbit whose day we will be exploring here is a house rabbit. There is no better life for a bunny.

Pet Talk

The quickest way to offend a rabbit is to call her a rodent. She shares many characteristics with rodents—a quiet disposition, teeth that never stop growing, a penchant for gnawing on anything in her path—but a rabbit occupies her own unique niche in the animal kingdom. Refer to the rabbit as a *lagomorph,* and earn her undying respect.

Bunny in the Morning

Morning. The house is bustling as the family members prepare for their day. Resident bunny BeeBee tumbles out of the cozy bed of straw in her enclosed nest box she calls home. She nibbles upon a breakfast of rabbit pellets, clean romaine lettuce, and carrot tops, then takes a hefty drink of fresh, clean water. The kids did the feeding and watering this morning, but mom supervised to make sure they didn't fall down on the job.

After breakfast, BeeBee visits the litter box. Then time for a nap. For now, she remains confined within her private abode, a large wire, well-ventilated, cage made especially for her. The family is at work and school right now. To allow BeeBee to run freely through the house unsupervised would be irresponsible, wouldn't it? BeeBee doesn't think so, but her opinion carries no weight here.

Bunny at Midday

Yay! The kids are home. They head straight for BeeBee's enclosure. She accepts their invitation to play. She hops out of her cage and stretches those long back legs. The kids run to the kitchen for a snack. This is her chance. She hops at rabbit speed over to the corner of the living room. Mmm! This new carpet has been calling to her for days. Then, mom walks in. BeeBee freezes mid-gnaw. Mom scolds the kids for their negligence and whisks BeeBee up into her arms. So much for that activity.

Pampered Pet

Rabbits are intelligent, social creatures, and they will form complex relationships with other rabbits, people, and other animals.

Having now found herself abruptly placed on the rabbit-proof tile in the kitchen, BeeBee looks around. Mom has put out some of BeeBee's toys, and it's time for a nice game of bat the ball. BeeBee bats it in circles, then chases it across the floor.

Is that the dog BeeBee spies at the door? He seems to be in need of a little grooming. She hops over and tends to the region at the back of the pup's neck. My, how BeeBee loves to knock all that predator-prey stuff on its head! Especially since mom is right nearby, watching.

Bunny in the Evening

With the setting sun, BeeBee's instincts tell her it is time to slow down. Time for dinner. A new selection of pellets and fresh greens are presented for her dining pleasure. After dinner, the family heads out to the backyard. BeeBee, in harness and leash, joins them. Secure in knowing that one of the kids holds the other end of the leash, she explores the grass and the ladybugs, nibbles on a dandelion or two, and enjoys the company of her clan.

The day's not over yet. Back indoors, BeeBee jumps up to her usual perch on mom's lap. Mom as always uses this opportunity to check BeeBee's ears (BeeBee is a lop-eared rabbit, and those moisture-trapping floppy ears can be prone to infection). She runs a soft brush gently through BeeBee's hair, and then strokes that coat with her fingers, enjoying this quiet time at the end of the day just as much as BeeBee does. At 10 p.m. BeeBee is returned to her cozy home, grateful for the comfort it offers, and satisfied with the life that the rabbit fates have dealt her.

Secrets from the Pet Files

Sure, rabbits enjoy the company of their own kind, but sometimes they enjoy it too much. A male and a female housed together will soon become a bunny family, leading to stress in the household and among the bunnies when you realize you don't have the time or the accommodations to care for so many bunnies responsibly. Then you discover that placing all those baby bunnies in new homes is downright impossible. The joy of rabbit ownership quickly deteriorates into a rerun of "The Trouble with Tribbles" episode on *Star Trek*. So think ahead: Spay and neuter your pets, and make sure you know the sex of any animals you buy.

Unexpected Pet Pleasures

Soft, silent, those ears, that little pink nose—how can you resist? You can't. One glance and you're hooked. "I'll just run out to the corner pet store and get one," you say. Wait just a minute! You have a little research to do on the subject. We may *think* we know rabbits, but no one is born knowing what rabbits require to help them live the good life to a ripe old age of 10 or 12.

Rabbits in Legend and Lore

The first stop in our journey to meet the *real* rabbit is understanding the rabbit's role as a cultural icon. Call her rabbit, call her bunny, but please don't call her dinner (many cultures do, including our own, but we don't want to bring that up now, do we?). Regardless of name, the animal of which we speak is a delightful little critter that, depending on the breed, can curl up in the palms of your hands, or at least rest comfortably in your arms. Unfortunately for the bunny, she also boasts the most well-known coat of fur on earth, but we won't go there, either.

Though keeping rabbits as pets is a relatively new phenomenon, the rabbit's appeal has been celebrated for centuries by writers who have chosen her to tell us stories about ourselves. The rabbit's featured appearances have included, among others, Aesop's pompous hare, who loses a race to a tortoise; the rabbits of Richard Adams's *Watership Down,* who provided a mirror in which we might discover our own humanity. Bugs, Peter, Thumper, Alice's manic white friend—all are immortal. And all are here to tell us something about ourselves.

Pampered Pet

Nowadays more and more small animal veterinary clinics have expanded their scope to include rabbits. While a periodic trip to the veterinarian may stress your pet momentarily, it will only enhance the bunny's long-term quality of life.

The Essence of Bunnyhood

The problem with using the rabbit to understand ourselves is that we fail to understand the rabbit. It's a charming animal, but rabbit behavior can also suggest a paranoid streak. That's not an insult, it's nature. If you were a prey animal, particularly a small prey animal sought after by predators ranging from ferrets to mountain lions to humans, you, too, would have a hard time trusting those that are bigger, badder, and have larger weapons than you.

Self-preservationists or no, rabbits are also social butterflies at heart. They may appear quiet and unassuming on the surface, but because they don't make noise or beg for attention, boredom is a chronic problem that too many pet rabbits face every day.

Stimulating normal rabbit activity is a must in the daily routine of the healthy, well-adjusted, properly-cared-for bunny, as is an owner who is willing to learn to understand her needs and messages.

Beware of Bunnies at Liberty

Your rabbit may wish to wander throughout your home, and frankly, she should be allowed some free time out of her pen. But beware of what might happen if you don't prepare for and monitor the situation carefully. The rabbit may be cute and cuddly, but beneath that fluff beats the heart of a world-class destroyer. Her primary weapon? Her teeth and her natural inclination to chew.

Electrical cords, computer cables, antique furniture legs, the new Berber carpeting, an entire library of first-edition books: All are irresistible to the rabbit on the prowl. So be kind to your bunny and don't allow her to cut a wide path of destruction through your inattention. This will only lead to hostile feelings on your part, and a potentially fatal injury for your pet.

Handling Your Rabbit

True or false: A bunny's ears are built-in handles for quick and efficient bunny lifting. False. A bunny's ears are amazingly constructed, acutely sensitive (and very cute) organs designed to protect this prey animal from the dangers in her environment. You can help alleviate her fears by lifting the dear animal properly.

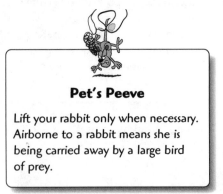

Pet's Peeve

Lift your rabbit only when necessary. Airborne to a rabbit means she is being carried away by a large bird of prey.

Because rabbit sizes range from two pounds into the double digits, choose your method accordingly. You may lift a small rabbit by firmly grasping the loose-skinned nape area at the back of her neck, while simultaneously wedging your other hand under her rear end. Lift and nestle the rabbit securely like a football beneath your arm.

For a larger rabbit, first wedge one hand beneath the rabbit's midsection, supporting the rib area between her forelegs with your hand and arm. Support the rear area with your other hand, lift up, and, again, hold her like a football.

In both instances, once the rabbit is securely tucked in, rest your free hand on her back and provide your pet with the support, security, and confidence she so craves.

Communing with Bunnies on Their Own Level

Throughout your dealings with your pet rabbit, even a rabbit who trusts you implicitly, you are wise ever to remember your bunny thinks like a prey animal—and to remember that you belong to the most dangerous predator family on earth. Place your pet's home in a quiet location where she can find peace and sanctuary from a noisy household, and pay attention to your bunny's signals.

If your bunny flattens her body to the ground, she is frightened and is trying to make herself invisible. If she seems to shake her head at something or someone, that signal is universal: She is just saying no. If she kicks, screams, grinds her teeth aggressively, stomps her feet or hisses . . . well, those signals are pretty universal in meaning, too. Your goal is to care for your bunny so responsibly that she rewards you daily with purrs, licks (rabbit kisses), and a relaxed, squatting body position. Just imagine how nice that will make you feel.

Secrets from the Pet Files

Rabbits simply cannot be rendered extinct. Various cultures throughout the world have tried through the ages—typically rural people frustrated at the ease with which a resident wild rabbit population can decimate a crop—only to discover that this species is simply meant to be. Humanity has yet to devise an extermination method that can beat the rabbit's phenomenal reproductive rates and survival instincts.

Rabbits and Kids

Although the kids may vow that they will provide the necessary play time and activity, and promise just as vehemently to take good care of the family bunny, an adult must be the ultimate overseer. Just like boredom, unintentional neglect can, to put it mildly, impair a pet bunny's quality of life.

Relegate a rabbit's care to a child, and you will probably end up with a malnourished, dehydrated bunny in a less-than-pristine cage. Fail to supervise interaction between the bunny and her young caretakers, and you may not notice that the youngsters have been attempting to lift their charge by her ears or tug continually on her cottony tail. The result: a bunny with personality defects not at all of her own making.

Rabbits and Other Pets

Similar dangers can occur when a rabbit is left to fend for herself among other pets in the household—especially when those pets are of the predatory kind, such as cats and dogs. Rabbits can get along famously with such animals (as our opening story implied), but they must be introduced gradually, preferably when both are very young, and from that day forward their interactions must be supervised carefully. Your oh-so-trustworthy Golden Retriever who looks up at you oh-so-innocently as he licks the pet bunny may actually be *tasting* the bunny—and awaiting his golden opportunity. Then, as soon as you turn your back: Chomp! So mind the troops at all times.

Finding and Choosing a Rabbit of Your Own

Every color, every size, every shape, and even every temperament: Envision in your mind a portrait of what you deem to be the ideal rabbit pet, and you will probably be able to find it. Chalk this up to this particular pet's widespread popularity. But this popularity also means that you must tread cautiously to ensure you end up with the healthiest pet possible.

The Rabbit of Your Dreams

Rabbits of old were typically a rather generic-looking species. But things have since changed dramatically. Human tampering with rabbit genetics has resulted in more than 40 breeds of rabbits in all colors of the animal rainbow and with all kinds of markings. Add the rabbit's speedy reproduction rates to this equation, and you should have no trouble finding the bunny of your dreams.

This does not free you from doing your homework ahead of time. There are more than enough bunnies out there to choose from; that goes without saying. But a supply of pets that far exceeds the demand does not diminish a bunny's right to a long-term commitment from her owner. Attention to health and temperament and a commitment to responsible care are the primary ingredients for forging a successful long-term relationship with this legendary critter.

Avoid the Easter Rush

It's March. Winter is receding and spring is beginning to blossom. You're at the mall shopping for drapery hooks when you spot the most adorable creature you have ever seen: a tiny white rabbit that couldn't be more than a few weeks old. Easter decorations abound. The inspiration hits you: Wouldn't it be cute to have a real live Easter bunny for the holiday?

You have just joined the minions who entertain that very notion every spring, leaving in Easter's wake herds of rabbits that, with their decorative value now obsolete, are in need of homes that just aren't available. So resist that temptation. Choose a pet rabbit wisely and with forethought—and try celebrating Easter with a plush stuffed bunny instead. The real thing won't mind a bit.

Where to Get Your Bunny

When choosing a pet bunny, think first about what you are looking for and check out the options. Regardless of the source you choose, look for a facility that is clean and has knowledgeable personnel that are compassionate to their charges.

Is it a purebred show bunny you are seeking? If this concept sounds outrageous to you, then probably not. Nevertheless, an entire purebred rabbit and show breeding community exists within the rabbit world, dedicated to preserving the various rabbit breeds humankind has concocted through the decades.

Secrets from the Pet Files

The best way to learn the fine art of rabbit showing, and to learn just when and where the shows are held, is to join the American Rabbit Breeders Association. ARBA sponsors shows around the United States and governs the registration of eligible rabbits. Call them at (309) 827-6623. Younger rabbit lovers should also look into their local 4-H groups.

These rabbit breeders are most easily located at county and state fairs and rabbit shows, where they congregate to show off their stock. At these shows, you will be able to locate rabbits that may not be so easily found in the general rabbit population: a Dwarf Hotot, for example, a Himalayan, or perhaps a Mini Rex.

While purchasing a puppy from a pet shop may be a ticket to heartbreak, you should fare fairly well when choosing a rabbit from a reputable, ethically run establishment. Many pet shops obtain their bunnies from reputable rabbit breeders, they house and display their stock in a stress-free manner, and they are concerned about placing their rabbits in capable, loving hands. You might even find some purebreds among the available bunnies, perhaps the ever-popular Netherland Dwarf (the smallest member of the domestic rabbit family) or one of the equally popular lop-eared breeds.

As our Easter tale tells, overpopulation is a sad scourge of the rabbit world. The indiscriminate and unintentional breeding of pet rabbits has led to a dramatic increase in the census figures of homeless rabbits, and many an animal shelter has stepped in to help. Also providing a safety net (though, like their shelter counterparts, facing an essentially no-win situation) are rabbit rescue societies that try to place as many homeless rabbits as they can with responsible owners. Whether you are seeking a generic pet bunny or a purebred, shelters and rescue groups are excellent sources for locating healthy, loving rabbit pets of all ages.

What Does a Rabbit Cost?

The purchase price of a rabbit can vary widely, but the average is $19.56.

The average rabbit owner also spends per year:

$66	Non-surgical veterinary services
$60	Rabbit food
$32	Other supplies
$17	Grooming
$11	Toys

The Big Decision

When choosing your new pet, do so with an eye toward health and temperament. A rabbit with a quiet, even disposition and bright-eyed curiosity, for example, is probably being cared for and socialized properly. You may expect a natural tendency toward caution on the part of the rabbit during first introductions, so don't label this a sign of some past and insurmountable abuse or torment.

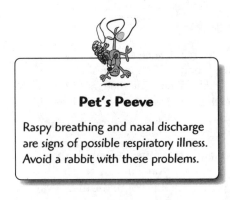

Pet's Peeve

Raspy breathing and nasal discharge are signs of possible respiratory illness. Avoid a rabbit with these problems.

On the other hand, if a rabbit screams, thumps her feet wildly, flattens herself to the ground and seems to equate you with a rabid wolf slobbering at the door of her cage, that rabbit is not quite as well-adjusted to a domestic lifestyle as she should be.

A rabbit's appearance is an excellent indicator of overall health. There are no guarantees, but bright eyes; clear breathing and a discharge-free nose; an even bite; and a shining, vibrant coat are what you should look for in a potential pet. Examine the animal's housing situation, too. If the rabbits are kept in crowded or unclean quarters, and if some of the animals don't appear healthy, it's probably best to look elsewhere.

Rabbit Room and Board

A rabbit in the wild: What a delightful sight! There upon the grass you spot the twinkling dark eyes; the adorable long ears that twitch and sway; the variegated brown coat that serves as camouflage; the rocking-horse way of hopping; and that nose that never stops twitching. And to think, this animal—its domesticated cousin, that is—could be living in your home, reserving its delightful nose-twitch greeting just for you.

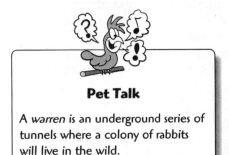

Pet Talk

A *warren* is an underground series of tunnels where a colony of rabbits will live in the wild.

In the wild, rabbits enjoy a rather utopian lifestyle (*sans* the predators, of course), classically characterized by a colony of rabbits that cohabitates happily in their warren. Needless to say, re-creating such accommodations for your pet really isn't practical, nor does your pet expect you to go to such extremes. No, all your rabbit asks for is a spacious, well-ventilated, appropriately furnished enclosure that is kept clean and well stocked with ample food and water. Simple.

Rabbits in Our Homes

In the wild, rabbits live peacefully side by side as long as their basic needs are met. The same may be said about the pet rabbit living among us humans in our own native habitats. Meet your rabbit's basic needs, treat her with respect, and find yourself rewarded with a quiet, clean, gentle companion whose care shouldn't break you financially. In addition, a rabbit will take great pleasure in meandering freely through your home like a pet cat or dog, assuming of course you have litter-trained your pet and properly rabbit-proofed the abode for the protection of both the bunny and your belongings.

A House of Many Rabbits

Do be careful should you find yourself addicted to this species. Rabbits enjoy living with other rabbits, but territorial tiffs can result from communal rabbit housing. Each bunny should be provided with her own domain. There is also that pesky rabbit reproduction problem to think about. So regardless of your pets' genders, house each rabbit separately, supervise all time spent out of the cages, and have all your pets spayed and neutered. This way, management of the multi-rabbit household will be more of a joy than a chore.

Pet's Peeve

Don't troll the pet stores if you don't have enough room for another bunny in your household. Stories abound of rabbit lovers whose homes are at rabbit capacity, but who just couldn't resist saving an older bunny who was about to become snake food. Sad as their plight may be, you can't save them all.

The Rabbit's Luxury Accommodations

As we have seen, in these more progressive rabbit-keeping times, indoor accommodations are now considered superior to an outdoor hutch for the rabbit pet. But regardless of location, the rabbit's home—preferably a cage designed especially for rabbits—should have proper solid flooring and thick bedding to protect those soft little feet that have inspired so many bunny slippers.

When You Get a Rabbit, You'll Also Have to Get These

Rabbit cage	Flea comb
Food dish	Litter box
Hay rack	Litter scooper
Water bottle	Litter
Bedding material	Rabbit carrier
Chewing blocks	Harness and leash
Toys	Care and behavior book
Grooming brush	

In addition to its rabbit resident, the cage should also house a cozy enclosed nest box (complete with a carpet of fresh, clean hay bedding), a litter box (complete with clean litter), safe chew toys (a must for that chewing compulsion), a hay rack, and a clean set of food and water dishes. All of these must be kept squeaky clean, meaning daily washing of food dishes; daily removal of soiled bedding, flooring, and litter; and weekly cleaning of the cage.

Cleanliness leads to a contented, friendly, well-adjusted rabbit pet who spends time tending to her own grooming needs as well. The well-groomed animal will also be better equipped to fend off the respiratory illnesses that can plague many bunnies.

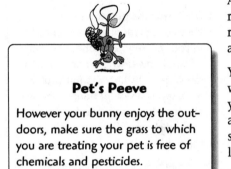

Pet's Peeve

However your bunny enjoys the outdoors, make sure the grass to which you are treating your pet is free of chemicals and pesticides.

Attend to each of her common-sense care components regularly, and you will end up with a minimum of rabbit-related odor and a more pleasant household all-around.

Your indoor rabbit will enjoy some time outdoors, as well. You can satisfy this in two ways. First, try training your pet to walk on a leash . . . well, not really walk, but at least wear a harness, graze in the grass, and sniff the spring flowers while you hold on to the leash and keep a lookout for dogs and other predators.

The second method is to place your bunny out on the grass in a spacious wire cage with a secure top and no floor. The lack of flooring allows the bunny to graze and the secure caging allows her to enjoy the fresh air in safety.

Pass the Carrots

Despite what Bugs Bunny says, rabbits cannot live by carrots alone. The optimum rabbit menu includes three items: commercial rabbit pellets, fresh greens, and hay—the ultimate vegetarian feast!

What Does a Rabbit Eat?

Commercial rabbit pellets
Fresh greens
Hay
Fresh fruit or commercial treats (sparingly!)

The one overriding guideline that governs rabbit feeding is that every dietary component must be served up fresh, fresh, fresh. To keep a rabbit robust and healthy, and to promote the long life span that every rabbit deserves, feed your pet twice a day.

The daily ration should include two fresh servings of pellets and greens, one offered in the morning and one in the evening. This should be supplemented by a handful of fresh hay, from which the bunny may nibble all day, served in the cage hay rack.

As for the bunny's dessert menu, reserve the treats for training and special occasions to prevent obesity—enemy number one of a long life span. Restrict treats to a bite or two of fresh fruit or commercial morsels designed just for rabbits. Either should be offered only once every few days. To forego the calories altogether, you might try offering your pet a branch from an organically grown (pesticide-free) fruit tree for a change of pace in her quest to satisfy her gnawing needs.

Pet Talk

Cecotropes are soft pellets that are produced within a rabbit's large intestine. In her wisdom, Mother Nature has endowed the rabbit with the natural ability to produce this material, which is an amazing nutritional supplement that the rabbit instinctively knows to ingest.

The Least You Need to Know

➤ Fortunately for rabbits, they are now more likely to be kept as companions rather than food animals.

➤ Rabbits can be delightful, quiet companions, but be sensitive to the fact that they can be easily frightened and quite destructive if allowed to roam the household unsupervised.

➤ There is a vast variety of rabbit breeds and mixes of breeds available from breeders, pet shops, and even animal shelters and rescue groups.

➤ The healthiest pet rabbit is the "house rabbit," her accommodations including a secure, clean cage or hutch; a cozy nesting box; plenty of fresh water and good food; safe chew toys; and supervised time outside of her cage.

Chapter 8

Gregarious Guinea Pigs

> ### In This Chapter
>
> ➤ A day in the life of a guinea pig
>
> ➤ The guinea pig, past and present
>
> ➤ Choosing a healthy guinea pig pet
>
> ➤ An overview of guinea pig care

Way back when, cute, furry, cylinder-shaped animals trundled along the mountains of Peru. They were sweet little critters, with a penchant for squealing and squeaking, and they lived in colonies within networks of underground burrows that kept them safe from harm and loneliness. When not playing together or looking out for each other in their own variation of Neighborhood Watch, they fed on the rich green vegetation that grew so abundantly in their home territory, and led what might be described as a pastoral existence.

These little animals were what we call guinea pigs, or, as they became known in England, cavies (pronounced *kay-vees*). They still lead that life of mountain splendor in their South American homeland, but the population has decreased some. Their fortunes, you see, have changed through the years. From that mountain existence, and various incarnations in between, they today occupy a prominent position in the pet world, offering warmth and companionship to people who want to share their lives with creatures molded by an almost fairy-tale existence.

Secrets from the Pet Files

In their natural state, guinea pigs live in groups called *herds*. We might, however, be more inclined to call these groups packs, for their composition is similar to that of a wolf pack. Presiding over each herd is a dominant male and a dominant female, and all follow protocols of guinea pig language and behavior that help to ensure the survival of the herd.

Guinea Pigs As Pets

	light	1	2	3	4	5	heavy
Time commitment				✔			
Grooming				✔			
Feeding				✔			
General cleanup				✔			
Suitable for kids age infant to 5		✔					
Suitable for kids age 5 to 10				✔			
Suitable for kids over 10					✔		
Sociability				✔			
Expense of keeping				✔			

A Day in the Life

The guinea pig has come a long way from his native territory below the Equator—in geography as well as role. Guinea pigs were "discovered" as pets in the 20th century, but we humans didn't take this responsibility very seriously until recently. We regarded them as easy-care blobs that were fun to look at but didn't require much input from us. Fortunately for those so-called blobs, we have since learned the error of our ways.

Although it has taken us humans a while to come around and understand just what these cute creatures require for a satisfied and contented captive lifestyle, we seem finally to have figured it out. Let's take a look at a day in the life of one lucky guinea pig and see just how this formula works to our collective advantage.

A Guinea Pig Morning

The sun peeks in through the window. It's Georgie the guinea pig's alarm clock. Like the people in his native land, he wakes with the sun and retires with the moon, asking only for fun and an active day in between.

He expects a morning meal, which is cheerfully served up right on schedule by his mistress. She speaks quietly to Georgie as she fills his ceramic food dish with guinea pig pellets, fills the water bottle with fresh water, and checks the sipping tube for a free flow of liquid. Then she places a handful of fresh hay in the hay rack.

She reaches her hand into Georgie's cage and picks him up for a snuggle. He, in turn, offers the greatest gift a guinea pig can give his owner: He gurgles. His owner smiles. She knows this means he is content, relaxed, and most appreciative of the life he leads. She also knows that the gurgle is reserved only for those people who have earned most-favored-owner status.

Pet's Peeve

Like all pets, guinea pigs can easily become bored if you do not make the effort to stimulate their minds with toys and attention. A bored guinea pig will chew on his own fur. Let the first sign of fur chewing be a warning that you have some work to do.

In the Afternoon

Georgie knows the routine. Morning is usually a low-activity time for him, a high-activity time for his mistress. Translation: He must be content to wait patiently while she does the household chores. Fine with him. He knows his time will come.

His time comes after noon. He hears his mistress approach the cage. He hops around in anticipation. She opens the cage door, and he is happy to come out into the world. The room is properly pig-proofed so that Georgie's innate rodent desire to gnaw won't get him into trouble (electrical cords—a favorite—can be very dangerous).

Today he's in for a real treat. His mistress takes him out into the backyard and places him in the "special" cage: a spacious wire cage with four sides and a secure top, but no floor. She says this gives Georgie a chance to play horse—to graze. He loves to nibble on the fresh grass (which is free, of course, of pesticides). He also enjoys the soft rays of the sun diffused through the trees.

Ain't We Got Fun

What a glorious guinea pig day it has been! And it's not over yet. Georgie's mistress knows that guinea pigs love to play. After evening feeding time, he's game for more.

Although tired by the day's activities, Georgie gets a second wind when his owner places a brown paper bag on the floor. He waddles over. He waddles in. What's this? A surprise inside! A grape. She thinks of everything.

Now exhausted, Georgie is grateful to be lifted gently into the air by those trusted hands. He is transported over to his familiar cage with its familiar scents and furnishings. Before his mistress places him inside, she holds him a minute and pets him. This, too, is part of the evening ritual, as is his response: the goodnight gurgle.

Guinea Pigs Past and Present

Decide to take a guinea pig into your home, and you become a part of this interesting animal's long and illustrious history as pet and companion. Of course, many who take this step don't quite realize the tradition this very popular rodent pet is steeped in. If they did, they might be a little bit intimidated.

Although they are neither pigs nor from Guinea (or even New Guinea), stretch your imagination a bit and you may be able to see a slight resemblance between pigs and the small furry rodents that share their name. As with pigs, the male guinea pig is called a *boar* and the female a *sow*. The guinea pig boasts a pig-like body shape that is somewhat uniform in diameter from front to backside, and the animal's head is quite large in relation to that husky form. His ears are shaped similarly to those of a pig, and both use squeals and gurgles in their vocal repertoires. And finally, as those who love both species already know, the guinea pig, like the pig, is far more intelligent and fun-loving than the general public cares to give him credit for.

So where did the name *guinea pig* come from? Well, no one knows for sure. The animal hails from Peru, although one theory holds that perhaps "guinea" was meant to be a derivative of Guyana, where guinea pigs were traded in the early days. Or perhaps it was a name bestowed by the Dutch, some of the first Europeans to bring guinea pigs home for the pet trade, in honor of either their boats or their money. Take your pick. As for "pig," that probably came from the animal's resemblance to the pig in body shape and vocalization (the squeals). England's word "cavy" no doubt comes from the animal's scientific name, *Caviidae porcellus,* although that, too, is a subject of debate.

Another Similarity Between Guinea Pigs and Pigs

This brings us to another alleged, and rather unpleasant-to-ponder, similarity between pigs and guinea pigs that is linked directly to the rodent's rather fascinating past. Some claim the guinea pig got his name because he tastes like a pig. And some of these people would know. You see, for thousands of years guinea pigs have been cuisine in their native Peru.

Secrets from the Pet Files

The guinea pig occupies a hallowed place in human folklore in its native Peru. Legend holds that guinea pigs are mystical beings that can heal an ailing body and assist dying people from the world of the living to the great beyond. Yet another reason to make them comfortable within your home!

Long before the rise of the Inca civilization, native Peruvian people considered guinea pigs a prime source of nutrition. They still do, and guinea pigs have yet another thing in common with pigs: They are raised as meat animals.

An Exotic Guinea Pig Past

We are not, of course, interested here in guinea pigs as dinner, and we trust that is not your intent, either. But the guinea pig also has a long history as pet and companion. It begins, we think, when the Incas domesticated guinea pigs both for livestock and as religious icons around 5000 B.C. Then, sometime around the 1600s when Dutch traders arrived, they discovered that these unusual critters were not at all adverse to taking a long ocean voyage to the other side of the world.

Cooperative as they were with such dramatic changes in geography and lifestyle, guinea pigs proved how equally amenable they were to being kept as pets. Soon the guinea pig was all the rage. Queen Elizabeth I became enamored of this sweet little animal, and, in keeping with the adage that as goes Elizabeth, so goes the rest of Europe, the upper crust followed her lead. They invited guinea pigs into their homes and obviously found them to be not only delightful critters but also quite adaptable genetically. Not content to own a guinea pig that looked just like the guinea pig in the castle down the road, many of these early European guinea pig fanciers began breeding their pets furiously in attempts to conjure up new and unusual guinea pig strains. The guinea pigs of many colors, patterns, and coat types we see among us today were their legacy to us.

Will the Contemporary Cavy Please Sit Up?

We have compared guinea pigs to pigs, and our comparisons really weren't all that outrageous or illogical, were they? But in terms of care, guinea pigs are a lot more like rabbits. The tenets of care for both are virtually identical.

Granted, rabbits are larger than guinea pigs. Rabbits tend to be calmer and cooler in the head than guinea pigs, and they are less vocal. Guinea pigs are also not quite as reliably littler-box trained as rabbits. But there are plenty of similarities. Both animals share a penchant for hay and need the same diet. Both are prey animals ever on the lookout for predators; they have the same grooming and housing needs; they both need attention, play, and affection every day; both are most responsibly and comfortably kept indoors; and, yes, both are raised as food animals.

Pet Talk

Of all the rodents commonly used as subjects in research laboratories, it is the guinea pig whose name has become synonymous with experimental subjects. While guinea pigs are no longer so popular in labs, the name remains.

Guinea pigs and rabbits also enjoy time spent out of their cages every day—supervised by their loved ones, of course. The guinea pig at liberty can be a guinea pig in the kitchen, exploring the ridge beneath the cabinetry for dropped morsels of food, or out back in a secure floorless wire cage that permits the resident guinea pig to graze on the sweet spring grass without risk of encountering a hungry dog or even a ferret.

The Social Life of a Guinea Pig

It should be rather obvious by now that despite any past impressions his docile disposition may have given, the guinea pig is anything but an apathetic ball of fluff. He needs some excitement in his life. He may not be the Olympic athlete of the rodent family, and he may not enjoy running around and around and around on the exercise wheel like, say, his hamster cousins, but he enjoys games and activity, just as he would if he roamed the mountains of Peru with his wild brethren.

Fun and Games

As our friend Georgie demonstrated, guinea pigs enjoy being out and about—with supervision, of course, to ensure they don't choose a live electrical cord or poisonous plant as the latest and greatest chew toy. Use your creativity in designing fun, safe games for your pet, and you will help to bring out the comedic spirit that lies within the heart of so many guinea pigs.

A playful guinea pig will delight in a variety of toys. A paper grocery bag with a special surprise waiting inside can satisfy the guinea pig's inherent love of burrowing, hiding, and discovering. Other favored paper products include cardboard toilet-paper or paper-towel rolls, and cardboard boxes that can be arranged as a guinea pig condo. Just remember that cardboard toys probably won't last long. As much as guinea pigs love to play with the stuff, they also love—and need—to gnaw. There are few materials more delectable—or safer—than cardboard.

Secrets from the Pet Files

Pet-sitters are people (preferably bonded and licensed) you hire to come into your home when you are away and care for your pets. Small animals such as guinea pigs are perfect candidates for such care because, unlike dogs, they do not believe that the presence of the pet-sitter and the absence of their owner mean they have been abandoned forever. When interviewing a potential pet-sitter, ask for qualifications and references, and do the necessary checking.

The Human Family

We have plenty to learn from the guinea pig's wild past, one lesson being that he craves companionship. Without other guinea pigs to offer this, you must step in as substitute pig. This means working toward your Ph.D. in guinea pig language—the intricate network of squeals, gurgles, body positioning, and such that guinea pigs use to communicate with each other and with the people in their lives.

In many a guinea pig's life, some of these people are kids. Kids and guinea pigs are a natural combination, but only as long as the kids are carefully taught how to conduct themselves properly around a small animal they could squash with a single step. Instruct children to be quiet around and respectful of your pet, and teach them proper handling techniques. And remember that every pet must have an adult caretaker. Please don't let your pet suffer so your kids can learn a lesson about responsibility.

The Non-Human Family

Some of the creatures in a guinea pig's circle of friends might be others of the non-human kind. Other guinea pigs, for example. Guinea pigs enjoy the company of their own kind—it makes them feel at home—but it is usually safest to house each animal separately, and allow them to play in neutral territory.

Guinea pigs are herd animals, but be careful with introductions. They also have a tra-dition of dominance and submission within their herds and fierce gender competition.

Pampered Pet

Although females have been known to live happily together, the ideal buddy combination is considered a spayed female and a neutered male.

Introduce guinea pigs to each other gradually—and on neutral territory—and remember that spaying and neutering can preempt most problems that might arise between guinea pig pets.

Take care to prevent the arrival of little guinea pigs, too. Spaying and neutering will obviously ensure against this, so make that appointment with a veterinarian experienced in small animals *before* initiating guinea pig social hour.

What about other pets? In all likelihood, those other pets will be of the predatory kind—namely, cats and dogs. Yes, some cats and dogs can learn to interact safely with guinea pigs—which are prey animals, remember—but this must be approached with great care. Introductions are best conducted when the animals are young. Regardless of age or outcome, every minute of such interactions must be carefully supervised, and if the guinea pig shows the least sign of fear, abort the mission and accept that the two may never live in harmony. And that's okay.

How to Find and Choose a Guinea Pig

Four hundred years ago, Dutch traders may have just loaded a bunch of guinea pigs onto their ships and sailed across the ocean to dispatch them to a society of aristocrats waiting for the hot new pet. You, however, will need to put a little more thought and care into this. A guinea pig could share your home for a decade or more, and become quite bonded to you and your family during the process. It's wise, then, to approach your choice with a healthy dose of common sense.

So Many Colors, So Many Styles

Their shapes and sizes may be fairly uniform, but when it comes to cosmetics, guinea pigs run the gamut. Some guinea pigs have short hair, and some have long hair. Some have smooth satiny coats, and some are covered with cowlicks—referred to in guinea pig circles as whorls and rosettes. Guinea pigs are tan and brown and peach and black and white and brindle and spotted and banded and masked. Guinea pigs are everything anyone wants them to be, bred for centuries for a vast variety of colors, patterns, and coat lengths that can make it almost impossible to choose.

You know what's next, don't you? You need to decide just what type of guinea pig you would like. If you are simply seeking the friendliest, healthiest companion you can find, then perhaps choosing short hair over long, or vice versa, is sufficient screening. But if you're looking for a particular color, pattern, or coat type, you have your work cut out for you. Your job is to find a guinea pig that is not only friendly, healthy, and well bred but is also blessed with those external characteristics you admire. And that can be a bit more of a challenge.

Breeder, Pet Shop, or Shelter?

Most people automatically assume that the pet shop (the clean, knowledgeably staffed pet shop with uncrowded small-animal enclosures, of course) is the most logical place to find a pet guinea pig. Guinea pigs are hardly rare pets, but in pet shops they are not carried as often as, say, rabbits, rats, or mice. If your intention is to make the rounds of the pet shops and evaluate a variety of guinea pigs, make some calls first. Find out if a particular shop carries guinea pigs in general, and the type you prefer in particular, and save yourself some time.

You might also want to check with your local animal shelter to see if any guinea pigs are available there for adoption. Today, more and more shelters are taking in small animals for adoption, especially animals such as guinea pigs and rabbits that can, with proper care, enjoy long, healthy lives.

Another option—and one that might sound a bit surprising to newcomers—is the guinea pig breeder. Breeders, most of whom specialize in specific types of guinea pigs, can be excellent sources if you're seeking a particular breed of guinea pig, perhaps a Coronet or an Abyssinian. Breeders are not as difficult to locate as you might think. You can contact your local 4-H organization or the American Rabbit Breeders Association, which sponsors rabbit and guinea pig shows and governs the registration of both animals.

Pampered Pet

When looking for guinea pig breeders, ask local veterinarians. In a culture that deems the inexpensive guinea pig to be a disposable pet, a breeder with a regular vet believes that guinea pigs deserve medical care. You may have to pay a bit more, but it will be worth it.

Time to Choose

When it comes time to choose your new guinea pig pet, arm yourself with as much information as possible. Know what to look for: clean, twinkling eyes; a smooth, even coat and healthy skin; clear breathing that indicates there are no respiratory problems; a clean bite that permits proper chewing of food; and perhaps curiosity about a newcomer in his midst. This last characteristic may not be evident until later, after you two get acquainted, so don't hold a lack of courage against an animal upon the first meeting.

Then be ready to ask questions. The ideal matchmaking session involves you, the prospective owner, asking questions about the guinea pig's background and care. Does the seller guarantee the health of their stock? What have the animals been fed up until now? Are they socialized? The breeder, shelter volunteer, or pet-shop employee should then return the volley with questions to you, to determine if the guinea pig will be going to a proper, deserving home. Will you be keeping your pet indoors? Do you have children? Neither side should take offense at the questions. If anyone—say, the breeder—is insulted by your inquiries or won't guarantee the health of their stock, then perhaps you'd best look elsewhere.

Preparing for a Guinea Pig Pet

How difficult could it be? He's a guinea pig. What's so hard about taking care of one of those? Well, anyone with this approach to guinea pig keeping had best not let their pet hear them. Those delicate animal sensibilities could be permanently damaged—as could his health and well-being in the care of a lackadaisical owner. A guinea pig may remind many of a stuffed animal, and far too many guinea pigs have been treated as such in the past. But as we have seen, guinea pigs require quite a lot more care.

Secrets from the Pet Files

For young people interested in guinea pig showing, a great place to start is 4-H. The name stands for Head, Heart, Hands, and Health, and the mission is to help young people learn to pursue the traditions of farming in a responsible manner. We'd be hard pressed to come up with a critter more fun to share these lessons with than the guinea pig.

A New Guinea Pig in the House

While you're in the process of learning all the innermost secrets of the guinea pig that lead to his optimum care, here's one more: Guinea pigs appreciate routine. They are most comfortable knowing exactly how many times a day they will be fed (twice is best), when they will be fed (morning and evening), where their home will be at all times (a nice quiet corner of the house out of direct sunlight or drafts), who their family members are, and what will be expected of them from one day to the next. But in order to implement and follow this routine, you must supply your pet with the correct equipment, housing, and diet.

What Does a Guinea Pig Cost?

The purchase price of a guinea pig can vary widely, but the average is $14.39.

The average guinea pig owner also spends per year:

$68	Guinea pig food
$58	Non-surgical veterinary services
$54	Grooming
$32	Other supplies
$17	Toys

Housing: Interior and Exterior Decorating

You need not create a series of underground burrows in which to house your guinea pig, but you should keep your pet's natural tendencies in mind when designing his home. A wire, gnaw-proof cage is the best choice for a well-appointed guinea pig domicile. Make sure it has a secure door and lock mechanism and a removable, solid floor. This kind of floor is the easiest to clean, and it won't trap those cute little guinea pig toes and feet.

Within the cage you should install a private nest box, complete with bedding of clean, dry hay; a litter box (placed at the end of the cage opposite the nest box and dining area); and several toys, which you can rotate periodically to keep life exciting for the resident guinea pig. Carpet the floor of the cage with three inches or so of dry, clean bedding—preferably non-cedar wood shavings or shredded paper products designed especially for rodent housing.

Guinea pigs, like rabbits, can be litter-box trained, but they don't tend to be as reliable in this as their long-eared friends. You can encourage them to use the box by making sure it always contains clean litter, and by placing boxes strategically wherever the guinea pig may wander: in your pet's cage and in various corners of whatever room he may be exploring at a given moment. Just don't expect perfection, and you'll be pleased with just how brilliant your little pet can be.

When You Get a Guinea Pig, You'll Also Have to Get These

Guinea pig cage	Grooming brush
Food dish	Flea comb
Hay rack	Nail trimmer
Water bottle	Litter box
Nest box	Litter scooper
Bedding material	Litter
Chewing blocks	Travel carrier
Toys	Care and behavior book

Keep the cage in a quiet corner of the house, sheltered from direct sunlight or drafts, and keep it clean. The quickest way to lose your guinea pig pet's respect—and to contribute to the onset of serious illness—is to neglect your housekeeping duties. Follow a schedule, which includes daily removal of soiled bedding and litter, and daily cleaning of food and water receptacles. Follow this up by changing the bedding completely, and scrubbing the cage structure with water and mild soap every week (twice a week if you can). Of course, the resident guinea pig will have to clear out for the wholesale cleaning, so be sure to have a holding cage or travel carrier for this purpose.

Food, Glorious Food

Three important furnishings that no self-respecting guinea pig home can be without are the feeding dish (a ceramic dish with a weighted bottom to prevent tipping), the hay rack, and the water bottle with sipping tube. In addition to fresh water in the water bottle, guinea pigs require daily rations of fresh food, preferably offered once in the morning and once in the evening.

The optimum guinea pig diet includes two servings daily of pellets made especially for guinea pigs, coupled with a handful of fresh hay and a serving of fresh greens. Where the veggies are concerned, the darker green, the better.

The guinea pig is unable to manufacture vitamin C, and the greens, along with the pellets, will provide the nutrition your pet needs.

What Does a Guinea Pig Eat?

Commercial guinea pig pellets

Dark-green vegetables

Hay

A guinea pig cannot live on pellets alone, or hay alone, or veggies alone. Each of the elements in the guinea pig's diet is critical to overall guinea pig health. Where the guinea pig diet and health are concerned, balance is all.

One of the greatest threats to a guinea pig's (and to so many other pets') health is obesity. Perhaps it's that "pig" name that inspires owners to feed them like hogs in the barn, or simply the fact that it's just so darn fun to lavish these sweet creatures with rich treats. The reason is irrelevant; the consequences can be deadly, or certainly terribly uncomfortable, for a tiny animal that has trouble getting around and suffers from obesity-related illnesses. There's nothing fun about that.

The Least You Need to Know

➤ Guinea pigs once roamed the wilds of Peru, but they have adapted beautifully to a domestic pet environment by way of the research laboratory.

➤ Guinea pigs enjoy time spent out of their cages, but without proper supervision or sensitivity to their prey-animal roots, they can be easily frightened or injured.

➤ Whether seeking a longhaired or a short-haired guinea pig from either a breeder, shelter, or pet shop, choose your pet based on overall health, temperament, and the cleanliness of the environment in which he is being housed.

➤ Guinea pigs thrive best with a predictable routine, indoor housing, plenty of attention from their owners, and a fresh supply of food and water.

Chapter 9

Heavenly Hamsters

> ### In This Chapter
>
> ➤ A day in the life of a hamster
>
> ➤ Understanding the hamster point of view
>
> ➤ Choosing a healthy hamster
>
> ➤ A short course on hamster care

If you ache to live with animals and consider them vital to your very survival, but your lease states that under no circumstance can you pursue such a heinous hobby, the hamster may be just what you need to satisfy the emptiness that only an animal in your life can fill.

There really are no famous hamsters to speak of, nor are they lauded for heroic acts, but hamsters can bring much magic into the home. The hamster, you say! That little blob of fur back in first grade that ran around and around (and around and around and around) on the wheel in his cage? Come on along and see for yourself just how they work their magic. See how a hamster may be the salvation that those with an undeniable longing for a pet are looking for.

Hamsters As Pets

	light	1	2	3	4	5	heavy
Time commitment				✔			
Grooming			✔				
Feeding				✔			
General cleanup				✔			
Suitable for kids age infant to 5		✔					
Suitable for kids age 5 to 10				✔			
Suitable for kids over 10					✔		
Sociability			✔				
Expense of keeping				✔			

A Day in the Life

Hamster owners know the secret. The revelation often comes by accident. In a typical scenario, mom and dad tell the kids that no, they cannot have a dog; too much work, too much trouble. They reach a compromise: a hamster. The parents throw each other a wink. Trouble has been averted. The kids walk away thinking, "Well, at least it's something."

A pleasant surprise awaits this family. No, their new pet won't be catching any Frisbees, but he's cute, friendly, and fully equipped to satisfy those animal longings. After only a short period of time, the family is delighted, not to mention amazed, at what wonderful companions these little guys can be. Take a look into a single day in the life of one of these critters, and you'll see why.

Good Morning, Hammy

Hammy is a golden, a.k.a. Syrian, hamster—the classic short-haired hamster with large rounded ears and chubby cheeks that has shared so many human households during the last half of the 20th century. Were Hammy a wild hamster living in his native Middle Eastern desert, sun-up would signal bedtime. Nocturnal by nature, after a night of traveling far and wide in search of food, he would return to his underground burrow, snuggle in, and bid the world good-night.

But our friend Hammy, while still for all practical purposes a creature of the night, lives by a rather different time clock—and has far fewer challenges to his daily existence. In

Secrets from the Pet Files

A nocturnal desert existence in the wild endowed the hamster with large, luminous eyes and acute senses of hearing and smell. The result is a very sensitive little eavesdropper who will be alert to all that transpires in the household.

traditional hamster fashion, he has adapted famously to the rhythms of his human household and left the dangers of the desert behind (although he does tend to awaken occasionally in the night for a snack and a short workout).

Hammy's morning, then, means rising and shining with the family. He greets each family member individually, recognizing their voices and scents as those of people he can trust. Morning greetings complete, Hammy munches on a fresh serving of veggies and hamster pellets, and takes a spin or two on the hamster wheel. (Joke if you must about the pea-brained futility of this activity, but remember that joke the next time you mount the treadmill or the stair-climber.)

Into the Evening

Hammy spends his midday hours much as his wild counterparts would. Answering that instinctive call that protected them from sun and predators by driving them underground during the day, he burrows into the bedding of his cage, curls into a ball and takes a nap. He must be fresh for the return of his family. He emerges occasionally for a snack and a sip of water. He may even, at times, stash a cheekfull of grain in a far corner of his cage. A hamster never knows when the food supplies might dry up. Then back to his snooze.

Pet's Peeve

Hamsters are a delightful bunch, but we face one important drawback when living with them: Like many of their rodent brethren, they just don't live that long. Two to three years is about all you can expect.

Once the key enters the latch on the front door, Hammy, the ideal latchkey pet, sits in his food dish (a favored perch), ready to play. He knows this is usually Hammy-at-liberty time. He relishes the time he spends each day out of his cage, but he has no idea how carefully his owners watch out for his well-being when he is free. Heating vents, the clothes dryer, and such are all forbidden territory to Hammy. Visiting neighbor kids are also treated with caution. There will be no teasing of Hammy or rough handling of any kind. House rules.

After playtime and dinner, Hammy, now back in his cage, tends to his evening grooming ritual. His owners never tire of the spectacle of their pet washing his face and ears with his tiny hands—a routine that means a hamster feels safe, content, and secure. They never tire, either, of watching him scamper across the kitchen floor inside his clear plastic hamster ball, run the wheel, take small treats from his owners' hands, or just leap spontaneously for joy. Who knew that living with a hamster could be like this?

Hamster Social Studies

The quickest way to understand the hamster in your house is to look back into his wild past. This can be rather challenging, because much about this wee creature remains a mystery. Because of his rather clandestine, wild lifestyle that kept him beneath the desert sands by day, when most naturalists were snooping around, few even knew that the hamster existed until about the middle of the 20th century.

There aren't many hamsters in the wild anymore, but the few survivors are still nocturnal. They have to be. To survive they must steer clear not only of the searing daytime desert sun but also the minions of rodent-hungry predators that view hamsters as their own fast food.

Combine the natural survival instincts of desert life with the hamster's small size, and you have a pet ready made to suffer the fear and confusion of captivity. But these natural inclinations are balanced by another of this tiny pet's gifts. He is profoundly adaptable—an unfortunate gift, really, in that it originally spurred the demand for hamsters as laboratory animals. The hamster's research lab experience, while hardly a positive stage of his life on earth, also served to teach us a great deal about the care of hamsters. And this makes us better able to keep him in his present role as a family pet.

Secrets from the Pet Files

Though reports of so-called tailless desert mice surfaced sporadically prior to the 20th century, Professor I. Aharoni, a zoologist from Jerusalem, is credited with "discovering" hamsters. It all began when he found a female hamster and her 12 babies in the Syrian desert in 1930 and took them home with him. That's when he found out they weren't mice after all, but a unique rodent species. Sadly, only three of these hamsters survived. But today it is believed that the entire pet population of golden, or Syrian, hamsters are descendants of those original three.

Pocket Pet with a Sweet Disposition

The hamster has thrived in domestic life. We have taken to him not just because he is small, cute, clean, quiet, and surprisingly affectionate and interactive but also because he has no tail. It's true. Rats also make lovely pets, but that hairless tail is just too much for many people. The alternative? A hamster, of course.

In exchange for his adorable, tailless physique, you owe it to the hamster to give special consideration to his nocturnal sensibilities, his obsessive attention to cleanliness, his small size amid a world of predators, his need for daily exercise—you get the picture. Yet, in addressing these issues, many a well-meaning owner has made a serious mistake. Upon realizing what a sweet-natured little creature the hamster is, those owners just naturally assume the sweet little thing needs a roommate. They assume wrong. This could be a recipe for disaster.

Alone and Loving It

Look to the wild, too, for clues to a hamster's social sensibilities. Survival is tough for the wild hamster. Finding enough food for one hamster is hard enough. Finding enough for a whole clan would be downright impossible. The result? Hamsters are solitary critters who really aren't all that crazy about others of their own kind (except at mating time, of course). In the wild, they'd be competing for food, water, and shelter. In the pet household, we're talking about competition for an owner's attentions. Old habits die hard. And they can lead to some messy, even bloody, quarrels.

Pet Talk

The hamster was named for his ample cheek pouches. In these chubby cheeks he can store food that he may then stash in a hidden cache. Hamster is derived from the German *hamstern,* meaning "to hoard."

If you would like to live within a multi-hamster household, go ahead. Just make sure each of your little darlings is afforded his own individual domicile. Enjoy, too, the natural birth control separate housing provides to a population of animals that typically have trouble controlling themselves in the area of procreation.

True to the traditions of the rodent family, hamsters can reproduce with phenomenal speed—leaving you wondering how you are going to care for all those little hamsterlets, let alone get them placed in responsible homes. Separate housing will prevent all that and keep peace in the household at the same time. Enough said.

Where and How to Find Your Hamster

While hamsters are rare in the wild, they are just about as plentiful as they can be in the modern-day pet market. Decide a hamster is for you, and you will find hamsters readily available in almost every pet shop in every town. This includes the pet-supply superstores that specialize in the sale of products and only carry a few live animals. Such availability is actually to the species' detriment because it conveys the message that hamsters are somehow disposable pets, unworthy of much care or consideration. But of course that's not your approach to this pet, is it?

Your first mission is to determine just what type of hamster you would like. As you will see, there is more to the hamster world than simply the classic golden. Your next responsibility is to evaluate the hamster stock available to you and choose the best candidate for a long and healthy life as a pampered companion. You must evaluate, too, how the pet shop or breeding operation passes muster as halfway house for hamsters en route to new homes. Clean enclosures, spacious housing, fresh food and water, and a knowledgeable staff are what you should find at the place where you purchase your hamster.

Secrets from the Pet Files

Various hamster species have existed around the world, the largest member of the family being known simply as the *common hamster.* A classically wild hamster, this animal, native to Russia and Central Europe (where he has long been despised for his appetite for agricultural crops) is an object of obvious fascination to hamster enthusiasts. He is, however, a poor candidate for life in captivity and has no intention of ever changing his mind on this.

Goldens and Teddy Bears and Satins

Once upon a time, there was but one pet hamster. That would be the golden, or Syrian, which you have already had the pleasure of meeting. As hamsters have become more popular pets, the types of hamsters available for that role have multiplied. The golden remains the favorite, but even he has proven quite versatile in satisfying the desires of hamster owners.

In addition to the classic golden, there are a large number of variations on this theme—a phenomenon, really, when you consider that only a few short decades ago we hardly knew that the hamster even existed. Thanks to some manipulation by human breeders, the golden has evolved to include within his clan the teddy bear, a longhaired hamster; and the satin, whose name speaks for itself. Though many insist the original gold is the most genetically healthy color expression, also represented on the family tree is a variety of "engineered" colors and patterns—characteristics that would spell immediate annihilation in the hamster's desert homeland. If you find yourself longing for one of these unique critters, you may need to seek out a hamster breeder.

And the Adorable Dwarfs

While you're out there scouring the landscape for a new hamster pet, you will no doubt encounter a rather unexpected candidate: That would be the dwarf hamster, a relative newcomer to the hamster world who is taking that world by storm. Typically only half the size, if that, of his larger golden cousin, the dwarf is most accurately described as a ball of fur. He enchants admirers with his soft coat of earthy grays and browns, the dorsal stripe that runs down his back, and the adorable portrait he presents when rolled into a ball for a nap.

What Does a Hamster Cost?

The purchase price of a hamster can vary widely, but the average is $8.74.

The average hamster owner also spends per year:

$34	Other supplies
$31	Hamster food
$15	Non-surgical veterinary services
$13	Toys
$4	Grooming

Keepers claim that the dwarf's reputation for indifference to his human handlers, a flighty nature, and a brain size commensurate with that of his physique is undeserved—but they need not worry. The dwarf hamster is a force to contend with, a pet with a much-deserved and ever-burgeoning fan club.

Choosing a Healthy Hamster

The more you know about rodents, the better equipped you will be to choose a healthy hamster. "I never dreamed I'd want to learn more about rodents," you might be thinking to yourself right about now. Okay, okay, but here you are considering living (voluntarily) with a rodent, so what better time to educate yourself about this fascinating family.

Pet's Peeve

Beware of stress, the greatest threat to a hamster's health. Kids and other pets, particularly pets of the predatory kind, can be chronic stress producers.

Although they have an undeserved association with filth, rodents are, as a whole, clean little creatures who take great pride in their appearance and great pains to keep their coats and skin presentable. Their teeth are also of great concern both to the animal and to those who care for it. A rodent's incisor teeth never stop growing. Rodents must thus gnaw continually throughout their lives to keep those teeth sharp and honed (hence your need to supply your toothy pet with acceptable chew toys). You must therefore choose a hamster with a proper bite and ensure that your pet will not suffer from bite-related malnutrition and pain.

Indeed, most of your guidelines for choosing a hamster pet are rooted in hamster health. "Take me to your hamsters," you instruct the young clerk at the pet shop. You peek into their enclosures (there are several, of course, because this shop, a good one, doesn't want to overcrowd the dear animals). The animals appear healthy, the accommodations clean. A particular golden hamster with lovely white markings captures your fancy. His ears and nose are clean; he breathes clearly; his dark eyes twinkle; and his coat is smooth, even, and lustrous. He appears to be curious and content, and he sits up on his hindquarters to greet you. See that! He likes you. Go forth with this one and prosper.

Home Sweet Hamster Home

Part of welcoming a new hamster into your family is ensuring that you have educated yourself on the basics of caring for the newcomer, and stocked up on the supplies he will need to feel comfortably at home in his new domicile.

In all probability, you won't go into debt when gathering these supplies. But it's wise not to skimp, either. A cardboard shoe box, for example, may provide a fine temporary home to a tarantula, but it will be shredded instantly by a hamster—and cause great stress to the critter at the same time. Do your pet proud and care for him the right way from day one.

When You Get a Hamster, You'll Also Have to Get These

Hamster habitat	Chewing blocks
Small holding cage	Exercise toys
Food dish	Climbing toys
Water bottle	Grooming brush
Nest box	Care book
Bedding material	

Something Out of Hamstertectural Digest

When you bring your new pet home, you have to have somewhere to put him, somewhere that is all his own. In other words, have his permanent habitat ready ahead of time, and he will be eternally grateful.

There are various hamster housing options. Poll several devoted owners, and you'll no doubt hear some swear by the traditional wire cage for the ventilation it offers. Others will cast their vote for the aquarium-style glass enclosure that is easy to clean and offers ample burrowing capacity. And still others wouldn't dream of housing their hamsters in anything but an endless tube setup that mimics the underground tunnels of a hamster's native habitat.

Of course all options have their critics as well as their proponents. The glass enclosure, for example, is accused of restricting ventilation, and the tube setup is described as a nightmare to clean.

Regardless of the style you choose for your pet, make sure the interior offers separate areas for sleeping, feeding, hiding, and eliminating. Remember, too, that cleanliness is of paramount concern to a hamster. (Just count the number of times in a single day that your hamster washes his face, and you'll understand. Does the word "compulsive" mean anything to you?) Add "thorough hamster habitat cleaning" to your weekly calendar and stick to it. That clean environment, coupled with the properly divided living space, will keep stress at bay and help ensure that the hamster never succumbs to the effects of respiratory illness that can be so deadly to this rodent.

Pampered Pet

To accommodate your hamster's semi-nocturnal rhythms, place his habitat in a quiet, low-traffic area of the house, and make sure the location is out of direct sunlight and drafts, both of which can be detrimental to hamster health.

While hamsters do not hibernate in the classic sense, they can drift off into a state of dormancy when the mercury dips below levels the hamster is accustomed to. If you notice during a particular cold snap that your pet, even though he is housed indoors as hamsters should be, begins to slow down, sleep more, and lose his usually hearty appetite, you may need to warm the room up a bit. This is most safely accomplished with a ceramic space heater (no direct heat or sunlight on the hamster's habitat, please). Allowing the hamster to succumb to dormancy could prove dangerous to his long-term health.

The Accouterments

What you fill your hamster's habitat with is just as important as what you choose to house your hamster in. Remember first that the hamster is a burrower, and supply him

Pet's Peeve

Avoid cedar shavings for bedding. While they may smell great to you, the aroma is too intense for small rodents. Choose pine or aspen instead.

Pet's Peeve

A hamster should not spend the day endlessly running in an exercise wheel, becoming exhausted and dehydrated. Hamsters need a variety of games and interaction to keep them healthy and happy.

with several inches of bedding under which he may hide when he feels so inclined. Wood shavings are the favored bedding material, although some owners prefer shredded paper and products made from vegetable materials. For the safety of your pet, make sure that whatever you choose is a product made specifically for the care and housing of small animals.

The same holds true—and safest—for the other habitat furnishings. You will need to supply your pet with a nest box and/or hiding places, food and water receptacles, and that steady string of toys and chewing items that make life worth living for a hamster. You might also try rotating the toys every few days to keep life exciting for your pet. Because pet care has become such a mega-industry in the past decade or so, you will find more toys than you can possibly imagine at any well-stocked pet supply store.

The saddest, and most chronic, problem to afflict the modern hamster pet is boredom. He's too much of a gentleman to complain, but within that tiny package beats the heart of a world-class athlete, a physical consequence of those years in the desert traveling great distances each day in a quest for scant supplies of food. To keep a hamster happy (and healthy), supply him with a wide variety of hamster toys: a hamster wheel, a hamster ball (a clear ball in which the hamster runs and propels himself, ball and all, forward), and an ample selection of safe gnawing items.

Formal Introductions

Your hamster's first moment within his new home is no time to invite everyone you know over to meet the family's new pet or to allow your son to cart him off to show-and-tell for his first-grade class. Your hamster is no rocket scientist, but he understands the stress of transition, and will require a few days to adjust to all the new sights and scents in his environment. So take it easy. You'll have ample time for the one-on-one quality time you so crave with your pet.

Once your hamster seems comfortable in his new digs, you may begin some more personal interactions. During those first few days, you have set the groundwork for this simply by removing soiled bedding from his enclosure and offering him fresh food and water—actions that subtly accustom your charge to your scent. When it's time to become more brazen, open the door and simply (and quietly) rest your hand in the bedding. Allow the hamster to approach and investigate. This too may take time, but soon you will earn the tiny creature's trust, and both of you will look forward to the time you spend together.

Secrets from the Pet Files

Depending on their species, hamsters can range in size from the tiny dwarf hamster at approximately two to three inches long, to the large, wild common hamster, which measures in at a whopping eight to twelve inches. Somewhere in the middle lies the classic golden, or Syrian, hamster, who is about five to six inches long and weighs in at three to five ounces.

How to Hold a Hamster

It's amazing that a creature as tiny as a hamster can be so trusting of human handling. Earn this trust, and you will find that your pet enjoys his perch in your hand.

Because of the hamster's small size, lifting him up is no great challenge. Simply reach down, grasp his cylindrical little form firmly but gently (and certainly securely) in your fingers and against your palm, and lift. Offer extra support to the animal by putting your other hand underneath him, and you're set.

Holding a hamster is simple, yes, but maintaining the trust that permits it means you must make sure children handle the hamster only under careful supervision—and always over a table or other raised surface to prevent the little animal from taking a deadly dive to the floor. And while we're talking about this, resist the temptation to allow the hamster to run loose on that table or other raised surface. You may be thinking you're offering your pet a fun moment of freedom, but it just invites disaster should your hamster not realize that Columbus was wrong and you *will* fall off the edge of the world when you come to the end of the table.

How to Feed a Hamster

The hamster is a classic vegetarian, and his diet is just about as simple as simple can be. In keeping with the tenets of basic rodent care, he should have his food available to him at all times, and it should be fresh. The basis of his daily ration is a commercially prepared food. Seed mixes are popular, but a pelleted or block-type food mix are superior because they prevent the hamster from choosing only the ingredients he likes and perhaps sabotaging the complete-and-balanced nature of his diet.

What Does a Hamster Eat?

Commercial hamster pellets or block food

Seed mixtures

Fresh vegetables

Pet's Peeve

Do not feed your hamster canned or frozen vegetables, uncooked beans, green parts of potatoes and tomatoes, or sprouting potatoes.

Hamsters cannot, however, live by seed mix alone. Complement this with a modest helping of fresh food each day—some broccoli, some shredded carrots, perhaps a few peas—and a constant supply of fresh, clean water.

The hamster's water should be offered in a water bottle mounted on the side of the enclosure with a stainless steel sipping tube. The animal's food, with the exception of seed mixes that hang along with the water bottle on the side of the enclosure, should be served up in dishes that are squeaky clean. Ceramic dishes with weighted bottoms tend to be the easiest to clean and to anchor securely in the bedding, plus they can withstand a hamster's chewing ambitions. They can also withstand that classic hamster habit of sitting in the food dish—and tipping a flimsier receptacle over.

Cleanliness and Caches

For the health of the hamster and his habitat, change the water and dispose of uneaten fresh food each day. And keep on the lookout for stashed food. Remember the cheek pouches for which the hamster was named. Don't underestimate your pet's desire to follow his ancient callings to save for a rainy day. Cached within the bedding of his cage could hide the day's ration of fresh veggies—and soon, once decay sets in, it will make itself known in rather unpleasant ways. So respect your pet's natural instincts, but remember that you're not obliged to maintain his home as a storage unit for old food.

The Least You Need to Know

➤ Many people are surprised to discover that a typical day in a hamster's life includes spending time playing and enjoying attention from a trusted human.

➤ Hamsters are nocturnal, solitary creatures (without tails) that were discovered for research and companion purposes only a few short decades ago.

➤ Golden (the classic), teddy bear, satin, and dwarf hamsters are readily available from pet shops and breeders, but choose carefully for health and temperament.

➤ Hamsters are best housed solo, with hiding places within their cages as well as clean, safe bedding material thick enough for burrowing; and chewing materials to accommodate the need to gnaw shared by all members of the rodent family.

Part 3
The Small and the Furred

Welcome to the realm of the rodents. Here you will meet pets, some beloved culturally (gerbils and chinchillas), and some maligned (mice and rats—especially rats). All have fur, but each is as unique and as fascinating as a pet can be. And in most cases they are ideal for people who live in small condos or apartments—even when such residences (and you didn't hear this from me) forbid the keeping of pets.

The animals in this group can pretty accurately be described as "easy-care" pets. But that doesn't give us license to be negligent in their care, or to shirk our responsibility to learn all we can about their characters and their needs. That will all be covered in the pages ahead. So come on. Let's get to know some rodents.

Chapter 10

Modest Mice

In This Chapter

➤ A day in the life of a mouse colony

➤ Exploring the many faces of the mouse

➤ Choosing a mouse, or mice, of your own

➤ Mouse care and keeping

Aren't mice sweet? Aren't they adorable? Sure, that's what we say—until we spot one in the kitchen, and then you'd think Godzilla had come to earth intent on devouring every human on the planet.

How could such fear and loathing be leveled against a tiny creature that weighs virtually nothing; sports the tiniest, pinkest, softest little ears; and looks up at you with the most darling bewhiskered little mug you ever did see? When you look at it this way, the mouse is not so bad. In fact, it seems that although she has much in common with her larger cousin, the rat, the mouse has a much better time of it. It's the cuteness factor. Humans are ever suckers for a cute face. We just don't want a mouse popping out at us unexpectedly from the pantry before we've had our morning coffee.

We want control of the situation. We want the opportunity to welcome mice into our homes as pets. They, in turn, probably do not care to have their eardrums split by our screams when they enter uninvited. Yes, it's the invitation that is the key ingredient. This permits us to prepare for them, to gather the necessary supplies, to choose the healthiest, and yes, the cutest little mousie we can. And when we do this, we realize that this is probably the easiest of all pets to live with.

Secrets from the Pet Files

People have always been inspired by the cute mug of the mouse. For centuries writers have immortalized the wee creatures, forming a fan club that includes William Shakespeare, Geof-frey Chaucer, and Henry David Thoreau.

Mice As Pets

	light	1	2	3	4	5	heavy
Time commitment			✔				
Grooming			✔				
Feeding				✔			
General cleanup				✔			
Suitable for kids age infant to 5		✔					
Suitable for kids age 5 to 10			✔				
Suitable for kids over 10					✔		
Sociability		✔					
Expense of keeping			✔				

A Day in the Life

When investigating a day in the life of a mouse, we might logically be inclined to compare the mouse to her rodent cousins, like the rat, the gerbil, and the hamster. While there are certainly some similarities, a more accurate model for mouse society might be an aquarium. It's true. Mice are the quintessential homebodies, and, like fish, safe within their home is where they prefer to be.

Also like many fish, they prefer to live in groups. For this reason, we will be exploring the day in the life not just of one mouse, but of several. The star of our show will be a tiny gray mouse named Twinkle, but Twinkle is not alone. She has a family. Turn your attentions to Twinkle's day, and you must include the contribution of her tiny roommates.

Twinkle, Twinkle, Little Mouse

Twinkle is a tiny eight-month-old female mouse. Her weight would hardly register on a scale, and she measures approximately two inches from the tip of her nose to the base of her tail. Like most mice, Twinkle is cute. You know: the tiny wriggling nose, the twinkling black eyes, the long twitching whiskers. She reminds most who meet her of a cartoon character. (Now there's a novel idea!)

All of the mice who live with Twinkle share her mouse cuteness. They are also all female. Their owners don't care to turn their home into an experiment in mouse overpopulation, which is what happens practically overnight in mouse houses with both males and females.

It's morning within the cozy enclosure that Twinkle shares with her three sisters. Unconcerned about what is occurring beyond their home—a glass enclosure the size of a 20-gallon fish tank—they rise with the first rays of the sun. Twinkle greets each of her pals individually. Then they move over to the dining area—a section of the enclosure that is separate from their sleeping area, and separate from the area they have designated as their bathroom. Their caretakers, so reliable, have

Pet Talk

Like the rat, the hamster, and the guinea pig, the mouse is a rodent. Its family name is taken from the Latin word *rodere*, which means "to gnaw."

already served breakfast: a fresh serving of commercial mouse feed and some dry wheat bread for a treat. Then on to the water bottle on the side of the enclosure for a drink. Time to start their day.

Life of Leisure

All day our four little mice truly lead a life of leisure—quite different from their wild cousins who must spend their days finding their own food and bedding materials, hiding from neighborhood cats, and evading traps. To satisfy their voracious appetites, designed to fuel the speedy mouse metabolism, Twinkle and company nibble all day on the food that was left by that benevolent hand in the morning. They eat, they drink, they groom, they nap.

And they play. Those who care for these mice know that although mice are shy, quiet, and undemanding, they can suffer from boredom just like any other pet. They also understand that the best recipe for preventing this is not to spend time with their mice themselves, but to provide them with a variety of toys that they can enjoy on their own and with each other. PVC piping is fun for hiding. So is a cardboard toilet-paper roll that provides both a hiding place and a chew toy. Twinkle's owners also understand what a delight it can be to observe and admire their little mouse community from afar—just as they would an aquarium.

Behind-the-Scenes Routine

Despite the hands-off approach, those understanding owners can't remain completely uninvolved. Behind the scenes they are quite busy ensuring that all goes smoothly within the mouse house. For example, on this particular day, afternoon is cleaning time. Twice a week this occurs because, you see, mice demand the squeakiest clean environment possible. These mice are accustomed to the routine. They trust the hands that enter their domain, because those hands have never given them reason to react with fear.

Twinkle is especially amenable. For her it is a game. When the hand comes in each day, she approaches it gingerly, knowing that it probably holds a treat—a grape slice or perhaps a sunflower seed. On most days, the hand simply removes soiled bedding, which Twinkle is glad to be rid of. But on this day something is different. Sensing this,

Secrets from the Pet Files

We have tried for ages to exterminate mice—to no avail. Mother Nature has armed the mouse against such efforts with a phenomenal reproduction mechanism. A female's fertility kicks in at about two months of age. Nineteen to 21 days later she can deliver her first litter, and from then on, watch out! A veritable breeding machine, a healthy female can conceive again about 24 hours after she has given birth, and theoretically can have as many as 16 or 17 litters in a single year. Still think you'd like to put a boy and a girl together?

Twinkle hops up on the hand and is rewarded with a treat. She is removed from her safe haven—a little scary, yes, but only temporarily. She is placed into another enclosure, one far less luxurious, but clean and dry. Soon she is joined by her three sisters.

Back in their clean home again, our little mouse friends settle in for the evening. They nibble on an evening meal. More grooming. More play. A spin on the exercise wheel. Then two snuggle in together in the enclosed nest box. Two more opt to curl up into the bedding on the floor of their home. All settle in for a good night's sleep.

Mouse Social Studies

The mouse goes through life with her own unique world view—a world view that makes it clear why the word "mousey" means "timid." When you're as small as a mouse, it's only logical, isn't it? But the character of the mouse runs much deeper than simply a shy, scared little critter that does all she can to keep out of our view. Indeed, mice can live right under our very noses in our homes, adept at keeping their presence a secret for weeks.

The Many Faces of the Mouse

When the casting director phones a mouse, it is usually to offer it a role in some beloved family film. The Disney studios have held a particular fondness for the mouse, no doubt because of Mickey, who started it all. Mickey, rather un-mouse-like in his gregarious nature and outgoing ways, spawned an entire dynasty of Disney mice, including the charming little heroes who help release Cinderella from her stepmother's bondage, to the Rescuers, who, well, do lots of rescuing.

Indeed, these little objects of our extermination efforts have had much exposure in the arts, from inspiring such beloved children's books as *Stuart Little*, to fables about country mice and city mice, to cherubic images on greeting cards for all occasions. The faces we choose for the mouse within our culture are testament to our admiration for her kind.

Mice, Wild and Domestic

The real mouse is quite different from the one we have imagined. Seen in the hard, cruel light of reality, there are just two faces of the mouse: the wild mouse and the domestic mouse. The story began, of course, with the wild mouse. Approximately 10,000 years ago, this savvy critter realized that those odd two-legged giants had begun to grow and store grain. With stealth-like finesse, she moved in to investigate, and, impressed with the seemingly endless supply of food, she decided to stay.

This is not to say that all mice moved in and decided domestication was the way to go. We all know that is not the case. But time passed, and as humans throughout the world became acquainted with the tiny, oh-so-cute creatures, the mouse evolved to become one of our first established pet species.

Secrets from the Pet Files

Were it not for the mouse's decision to cohabitate with humans, there's a good chance the cat never would have been domesticated. When the mouse volunteered herself to live amid human food supplies, the cat was pressed into service to keep the mouse at bay.

On a lark, we began to breed those we chose to keep as pets and realized we could breed all colors and patterns, and even various body shapes—and breed them very quickly, at that. These mice became the mice that today are our laboratory subjects and our pets. Unlike their wild cousins, these domestic strains have thrived in captivity, and, as we learned from Twinkle's example, do even better in our care today because we have continued to learn more about their unique view of the world.

Cozy in a Crowd

When you decide to invite a mouse to join your family, you must respect your new pet's wishes. This is only fair with any pet, but especially a pet that's so tiny, so timid, and has such a rich history of extermination attempts.

There are two points you are wise to remember: Mice are easily frightened, and mice don't want to be alone. They also don't really want to be with us. They want to see us occasionally, and they want us to feed them and provide for them as we have been doing for the past 10,000 years, but most mice don't want to curl up with us for a nap or play in our laps or our living rooms.

Pampered Pet

If you do choose to keep males, you'll have to clean the mouse house more often. While males mark territory, they still like things squeaky clean.

No, mice are quite opinionated about whom they wish to be with—and that is other mice. Perhaps they feel there's safety in numbers. Mice are extremely social with each other, but be careful here, too. We've already discussed the dangers of housing males and females together, but you confront a different challenge when housing several adult males together. Because they are quite territorial and prone to scent marking, a male domicile can be a bit more, shall we say, stinky than a house full of females. That territorial nature can also lead to some pretty nasty quarrels—no, make that fights—between the resident males. A colony of females, then, tends to be the most peaceful to manage, while males are best housed separately.

Respecting Your Mouse

The greatest favor you can do for your mouse pet is to keep the handling of her to a minimum. Unlike various other members of the rodent family, mice do not enjoy being cuddled. Some handling is necessary, particularly when it's time to clean the cage and move the mouse into a holding cage, but you need not make handling a daily occurrence. Your mouse will appreciate this.

You may be wondering about now just where you fit in to this picture. Don't be offended by your mouse's seeming indifference. She is simply heeding her nature. She does need you in her life. Really she does. In her own way, she even appreciates you. She just asks that you respect her and her instincts. Do so, and she will let you know in her own special way and in her own time that you have earned her trust.

A Child's Role in Mouse Care

Your mouse will also appreciate your standing guard between her and the kids. Kids can be noisy and boisterous, but they can also be quite attracted to the cute mouse in the cage. Go ahead and allow the kids to be part of your pet's life, but only under supervision. As assistant caretakers, children can learn lifelong lessons about pet responsibility and care. Allow the child to help feed and give water to the mouse, but don't allow screaming, yelling, or other disrespectful behaviors that lead to mouse stress.

It's also best to leave handling of the mouse to the adults. A child who holds a mouse, even carefully, is likely to drop the animal should it become frightened and start wiggling. A child who insists on "playing" with the mouse presents the same danger. When a tiny mouse wriggles, for whatever reason, a child's first impulse may be to squeeze—and, well, that is the end of the mouse.

If the child drops the mouse and the mouse falls to the ground, she will become either an injured mouse or a runaway-never-to-be-found mouse. Their brains may be no bigger than a petite pea, but mice have been around a long time and they know danger when they see it. Mice are not easily convinced to return to a situation, even a comfortable one, that left them hurting.

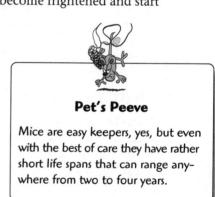

Pet's Peeve

Mice are easy keepers, yes, but even with the best of care they have rather short life spans that can range anywhere from two to four years.

Mice and Other Pets

And what about pets other than other mice? Can they befriend a pet mouse? That's an easy one to answer: no. Mice and other pets just don't mix, especially if that other pet is a predator such as a cat, a dog, or a ferret. Can you imagine being a tiny mouse, and having the cat peering into your cage smacking her lips for hours and hours at a time? It will stress your tiny pet, perhaps to death.

Mouse Stress

Beware of the effects of mouse stress. Stress is not healthy for any pet, but this is particularly true for the mouse. Mice are highly susceptible to stress, which can, in turn, lead to illness and death. Keep stress at bay, and save your pets' lives, by keeping their handling to a minimum; placing their domicile in a quiet, low-traffic corner of the house; and keeping other pets, and children, away.

Pet's Peeve

It's foolish, not to mention cruel, to believe all the animals in a household menagerie need to live happily side by side like a scene out of *Dr. Dolittle*. All the animals under one roof is fine, but keep them separate, sane, and safe.

Respecting your mouse will keep her healthy and happy and will extend her short life span as long as possible. You can help to keep a pet mouse as healthy as possible for as long as possible by observing religiously the following guidelines:

➤ Keep stress to a minimum.

➤ Make sure food and water are fresh and available at all times.

➤ Keep the mouse's house and bedding as clean as possible.

➤ Provide the mouse with a variety of toys and hiding places for mental stimulation.

➤ Provide a home that offers the resident mouse ample ventilation to prevent respiratory problems.

➤ Don't overcrowd the cage.

Choosing a Healthy Mouse Pet

It should be fairly obvious by now that mice are cute, readily available pets. It should also be obvious that you should never take a wild mouse, which can be aggressive and carry disease and parasites, as a pet. There's no need. Mice are also inexpensive, and there are all kinds to choose from.

What Does a Mouse Cost?

The purchase price of a mouse can vary widely, but the average is $4.06.

The average mouse owner also spends per year:

$29	Mouse food
$20	Other supplies
$11	Toys

A Tale of Two Mouse Buyers

The most logical place to buy a mouse is the pet shop. Even large superstores that specialize in pet supplies rather than live animals usually sell mice, and they usually have plenty available. There's a reason for this—a sad reason. As you probably know, mice are sold in abundance not just as pets, but also as food for another pet I'm going to talk about in this book. That pet is the snake.

Imagine the scene. After much thought and preparation, you finally walk into the neighborhood pet shop to choose two new pet mice. The shop is clean and responsibly staffed, of course, and the mice are not overcrowded in their display cages. You stand there evaluating the animals for twinkling eyes, the clear breathing that indicates a lack of respiratory trouble, an even bite, and a smooth, healthy coat that is the sign of overall good health.

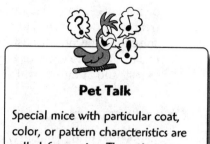

Pet Talk

Special mice with particular coat, color, or pattern characteristics are called *fancy* mice. The satin mouse, with its silky, shiny coat, is a fancy mouse.

Then, some guy stomps in and asks an employee to fetch two mice for his snake—any mice. As you'll read in the chapter on snakes, a responsible snake owner protects their snake by feeding only frozen mice. But not every snake owner is that responsible. So what do you, the fledgling mouse owner, do when you see this sad scene? Just carry on with your plan. Two lucky mice will be going home with you.

Buying from a Breeder

Another option for acquiring a mouse—and one where you're not likely to rub elbows with someone shopping for a snake's dinner—is a breeder. Today there are dedicated folks out there who are upholding a hobby begun centuries ago. They strive to breed perfect specimens of special mice of all coats, shapes, colors, and patterns. Those enthusiastic folks who breed and care for these mice are pleased when would-be owners seek them out for fine and fancy pets. You can find these people at county fairs and pet fairs, and at shows specifically sponsored by fancy rat and mouse breeder organizations.

Making a Mousey Home

You've brought a mouse (or mice) into your house. You've installed this quintessential homebody in her cage, which is positioned in a quiet corner of the house, and for the next few days you intend to keep things quiet as your new pet adjusts to her home, and to the scents and sounds of the people who live there. Interrupt her sanctuary only to remove soiled bedding and to feed her and provide clean water.

When it's time to introduce yourself formally, your hand is the most likely ambassador. Open the cage door and just rest your hand in the bedding. Keep your hand still and keep yourself quiet. The mouse may come forward to investigate, or may not. Just be patient. Follow the same ritual for a few minutes every day—perhaps even lay a treat (a sunflower seed or a piece of a grape) in your palm to bribe your pet. Eventually she should become accustomed to your hand and learn to associate it with the generous people who every day make her house a home. And watching your mouse at play, at rest, and at dinner will soon become a favorite, most relaxing time of your day.

The Mouse House

Before you bring your new pets home, it's wise to have their home within your home already set up. This prevents pandemonium. There are two classic mouse house styles from which to choose: the traditional wire cage and the glass aquarium-style setup.

For years, many an experienced mouse keeper has sworn by the aquarium style with a tightly fitting screen top (to allow air in and keep the family cat out), but now many of these people are turning to the wire cage with a solid, foot-friendly, easy-clean floor. The reason? Ventilation: a critical component in mouse keeping, presumed to prevent the respiratory problems that so often plague small animals.

When You Get a Mouse, You'll Also Have to Get These

Secure mouse cage	Bedding material
Small holding cage	Chewing blocks
Food dish	Exercise toys
Water bottle	Climbing toys
Nest boxes	Care book

Whichever setup you choose, secure and it must be escape-proof. That means a door and a locking mechanism for a cage, or a tight-fitting top for an aquarium-style abode. The enclosure must not be made of wood, which, while attractive, will be shredded in days by a resident rodent who so loves and needs to gnaw.

Pet's Peeve

Rodent incisors continue growing throughout the animals' lives. To keep them healthy and honed, mice must gnaw constantly on a variety of surfaces. Fail to provide them with ample materials, and the animals will be unable to eat. They will suffer great pain, and ultimately death.

And the Rest of the Necessities

The properly appointed mouse house also includes three inches or so of bedding on the floor for soft footing and cozy burrowing. To prevent health problems, this should be commercially available bedding material specifically designed for small-animal housing. Aspen wood shavings or shredded sanitary paper are safe choices for mice (no cedar, please—the aromatic oils in cedar can irritate the respiratory system). A handful of fresh, clean hay will also be most appreciated by the resident mice as bedding material.

And while we're on the subject of bedding material, don't forget the nest boxes. Mice love to hide, and they appreciate having their choice of a variety of hiding places. The collection can include a commercially available plastic nest box, an empty oatmeal cylinder or cardboard toilet-paper roll (also safe gnawing items), or clean PVC piping. Remember from Twinkle's example that toys are also important furnishings. A variety is available for your mouse's playing pleasure.

Housekeeping for Mice

As we have seen, the mouse's enclosure and everything in it must be kept clean. Soiled bedding should be removed daily, the food dishes and water bottle must be cleaned daily. The entire cage or tank should be cleaned with plain old soap and water (and rinsed thoroughly) weekly or twice a week. A bit of advice: A scent-marking male's domicile may require the twice-a-week regimen—at least. Following this plan religiously will help to keep your mice content and healthy, and help you feel more intimately involved in the care of these very natural pets.

Mice are naturally clean animals who groom themselves daily both to keep their coats pristine and to vent stress. They really don't need your help in this (surprise, surprise), but even a clean, well-groomed mouse can attract external parasites. Here is an area where your mouse does need you—and she needs you desperately for both diagnosis and treatment.

At the first sign of fleas or mites, contact the veterinarian immediately for his or her recommendation of a parasite-eradication product that is safe for mice (stronger products designed for larger animals could kill your little friend). Signs of these pests include itching or hairless patches on your mouse. You may also see the nasty little critters. While treating the mouse, or mice, as directed, clean her cage and all its components completely, and discard the bedding and uneaten food. You need to start all over again with your now-parasite-free, and thus stress-free, pet. Your pet will feel better, and so will you.

Pampered Pet

Don't forget to include all your mouse's toys in your cleaning regime.

Pet's Peeve

Throwing food in from the top of the cage encourages begging and biting. Always place your pet's food in the food dish.

How to Feed a Mouse

Rounding out the accouterments of your mouse's house are the feeding dish and the water bottle. The feeding dish, preferably a ceramic dish with a weighted bottom to prevent tipping, should be cleaned daily, as should the water bottle with a sipping tube that hangs on the side of the mouse's enclosure.

When not being cleaned, that feeding dish must be filled at all times with a fresh serving of commercial mouse pellet mix or block-type feed. The block feed has a hard texture that helps maintain the proper edge on these gnawers' incisors.

What Does a Mouse Eat?

Commercial mouse pellets or block food

Fresh vegetables

Cooked sweet potato

Whole-wheat bread

Seeds (sparingly!)

Nuts (sparingly!)

This diet should be supplemented every few days with something more exciting—some morsels of clean, fresh foods, such as broccoli, cooked sweet potato, or whole-wheat bread. As for treats, you might try seeds and nuts, but offer these sparingly as they can be too rich for the tiny and oh-so-sensitive mouse digestive tract.

Pet's Peeve

Never take a mouse from the wild for a pet. Wild mice can carry disease, are aggressive, and will spend their lives trying to escape your clutches.

What About Wild Mice?

Wild mice do not make appropriate pets, but that does not mean that if a wild one invades your household you need capture it with cruel traps or poison it. Instead, try a humane trap. With this device, a bit of food lures the tiny invader into a cage-like enclosure, triggering the door to close without injuring the inhabitant. The mouse may then be set free in a field or similar venue more accepting of mouse residents.

After you liberate the mouse, go home and make sure all the foods in your pantry, including pet food and bird seed, are stored in airtight containers. You thus remove the welcome mat inadvertently set out for more mice.

The Least You Need to Know

➤ A mouse is most content spending a day within her clean, spacious cage with an endless supply of food and in the company of other mice.

➤ Best compared to aquarium fish, pet mice are easily frightened and should be handled only when necessary.

➤ Mice are available (inexpensively) from breeders and pet shops. Never take a pet mouse from the wild, as her temperament is ill-suited to domestic life and she could carry disease.

➤ Make sure a mouse's bedding is clean; of a safe, non-aromatic material; and deep enough (approximately three inches) for burrowing.

➤ Offer a mouse water in a traditional water bottle, and food in heavy ceramic dishes that cannot be tipped over or chewed.

Chapter 11

Rational Rats

In This Chapter

➤ A day in the life of a rat

➤ Exploring the myth of the rat

➤ Choosing the ideal rat for your home and family

➤ Rat care made easy

Sit back and relax. Now close your eyes. Conjure up in your mind your image of the ideal pocket pet: small enough to snuggle into the palm of your hand; soft fur and an adorable mug; cute little ears; expressive eyes; a penchant for play; charming; funny; intelligent; affectionate; and anxious to immerse himself in every family activity. Ah, the pet of your dreams!

Well, guess what? That pet of your dreams does exist. And what's more, at this very moment he is waiting at the pet shop down the street—waiting to come home with you and make your household his own. That animal, that prospective new family member, is none other than . . . are you ready? . . . don't be shocked now . . . okay, here goes . . . you New Yorkers may need to call your therapists for this one . . . it's none other than *the rat.*

Okay, pull yourself together. Yes, you heard correctly. The rat, as in "you dirty rat," "don't rat on your friends," and "what a rat!" And to those who know him on a highly personal basis—the only basis the pet rat will tolerate—one of the greatest pets humans have ever invited into our homes.

Secrets from the Pet Files

If it weren't for rats, men would never have walked on the moon. Long before people went into space, rats did, just to make sure everything would be okay for us. The rats did well in early space flights, clearing the way for Yuri Gagarin, Alan Shepard, Neil Armstrong, and the rest.

Rats As Pets

	light	1	2	3	4	5	*heavy*
Time commitment				✔			
Grooming			✔				
Feeding				✔			
General cleanup				✔			
Suitable for kids age infant to 5		✔					
Suitable for kids age 5 to 10				✔			
Suitable for kids over 10					✔		
Sociability					✔		
Expense of keeping				✔			

A Day in the Life

I know what you're thinking. A day in the life of a rat: Scavenging for heaven-knows-what along the tracks of the subway. Raiding your pantry and devouring the oatmeal, and the pasta, and the rice, and everything else he can get his little paws on. Infecting everyone with a horribly contagious plague that will wipe out half of the world's population. We all share these kinds of images, and frankly, they are based in truth.

But the rat I speak of here, and a particular day in that rat's life, are quite different. I speak here not of the wild rat, whose quest for survival makes him an entirely undesirable pet, but of the domestic and rather pampered pet rat.

So let's be fair to the rat. Let's give him a chance to demonstrate his virtues—a task at which he is quite talented. Those who pay attention with an open mind inevitably end up touched, and charmed, by what they discover.

Good Morning, Jimmy the Rat

The sun pops up over the hill, and Jimmy the Rat is ready to go. This is when his family awakens, so, by gosh, he will too. Innately adaptable as he is, he would be just as willing to follow a nocturnal schedule. Either one is fine with him. Life is good.

Jimmy sleeps in a quiet corner of the family room in a well-appointed, multistory cage that offers him ample variation in both scenery and accessories. As nice as his accommodations are, though, a rat can't stay cooped up all day. Time out in the great big world is critical to his contentment. Jimmy's family knows this. And Jimmy knows they know. Nowhere in his psyche is there any idea that he should be cautious around the people who share his home. Nowhere does he have even the most remote inkling that people might be dangerous to him or compete with him for food and housing.

Nope, Jimmy's people are family. And the feeling is mutual—evident the minute the kids spill into the family room at sunup. How thrilled they are to see their pet! He greets them through the bars of his cage with a wiggling nose. He is set free to join the family for breakfast, perched up on a shoulder for a panoramic view and close proximity to the noisy morning babble.

Midday Adventures

Something's different today. After breakfast, when everyone takes off for work or school, Jimmy typically returns to his cage for a nap, a snack, and a few solitary activities. But today, Jimmy is loaded into his travel crate and off to the car he goes.

The mystery of just where Jimmy might be going is solved when he finds himself removed from the crate and held up in front of a second-grade classroom. Shrieks ring out from the back. Exclamations of disgust, too. "Gross," says a teacher's aide. "No, listen," insists Jimmy's young handler. Some in the audience do. There is much to learn. Jimmy in the meantime, does his part. He is friendly. He is fun. He begs for their affection. He succeeds. Within 15 minutes, the room is his.

Pampered Pet

Rats are *really* smart. How smart? You can teach a rat to come when you call his name, to sit up, or to jump through a hoop.

"I want to hold him." "Me, too." "So do I." Jimmy is his most charming. He even climbs up the arm of one little girl who seems willing. She giggles. Jimmy revels in the attention. Sure, there are some kids who aren't impressed—but you can't convince them all, now can you?

Goodnight, Jimmy

Evening may be Jimmy's favorite time. Everyone's home; Jimmy is rested. A quick dinner for all, after which Dad needs to finish assembling that new mountain bike. He's having some trouble. The instructions seem to be written in Egyptian hieroglyphics. Perhaps Jimmy can be of assistance. He stands nearby on his hind legs and leans forward every so often, investigating with his long, sensitive whiskers. Dad still doesn't get it. Bored, Jimmy hops up to Mom's shoulder. What's on TV? *Seinfeld*. And one of his favorite episodes! Jimmy watches from beginning to end, snuggling into Mom's neck.

Time for bed. Jimmy isn't tired, but he complies. There's plenty to do in his cage: wheels, chew toys, and tubes. And of course, a treat of a fresh peach. What a day! "Every rat should try living with people," we might imagine Jimmy thinking as he snuggles into his cozy nest box for a quiet and private night's sleep. Many do, although not all are invited in.

The Social Life of the Rat

Estimates place the worldwide rat population at somewhere around 5 billion. And among those, we find a multifaceted character that combines an undeserved negative reputation; an indestructible family tree; a much-maligned soul; an indomitable spirit; and even the bubonic plague (it was the fleas, darn it!)—all in one tidy little package.

Extermination companies may do big business in targeting rats, but the rats are still here. If aliens were to visit our planet in the wake of a nuclear holocaust, they'd no doubt return to the mother ship with reports of a planet populated only by rats and cockroaches.

Secrets from the Pet Files

About 40 percent of all mammals are rodents, making them the largest order of mammals. Found all over the world, rodents have learned to adapt to just about every terrain and climate. In the process, they have learned that humans possess much that might be of value, such as food and shelter, and the rodents, particularly rats, have learned to take advantage of this proximity. The result: an ageless struggle for dominance.

The Curse of the Tail

Okay, so the idea is starting to grow on you. Maybe this animal is a wee bit misunderstood. Maybe he could make a nice pet. Maybe he would be fun to have around the house. But then you see that long, hairless, kind of scaly looking tail. And it's not just any tail. It's the biggest, thickest tail you could ever imagine on such a small animal.

Why bring up the tail? Because many a would-be convert to rat ownership has bailed out at the last minute—all because of that tail. It appears the rat has quite a few cards stacked against him when it comes to convincing human beings that he really is a sweetie. But the rat, like all those rats who came before him who have survived all manner of disaster and eradication attempts, has prevailed.

Contemporary Culture and Rats

A decent discussion of the social life of the rat, and the ample gifts in this area that he brings to his relationship with his human family, must begin with a look at the rat in our popular culture. And in that department, the rat is in need of an image consultant.

When Tramp, of *Lady and the Tramp*, risks his life to rescue the resident baby in the Darling's house, what is the troublemaking creature that sparks the episode? You guessed it: a rat. And what was the Pied Piper hired to get rid of?

In the movies, rats have repeatedly terrorized Indiana Jones and his action-hero friends in various and sundry action-adventure flicks. Rats have played serial killers, pets to the quirky or demented kids on the block, and interlopers in a yuppie's newly purchased, soon-to-be-renovated penthouse. And they are a commensurate part of the scenery in every dark alley scene ever shot.

To the rat's credit, in a backhanded compliment sort of way, never is he painted as dim-witted or lazy. In the movie *Titanic,* when those locked in steerage see the rats running in a pack down the corridor, they know that following the rats is the quickest and surest way to safety. And some literary rats have been shown as the intelligent creatures they truly are. Think of Ratty in *The Wind in the Willows,* who always gets his impulsive friend Toad out of trouble. And do you remember Templeton, the friendly, helpful rat in *Charlotte's Web*?

Secrets from the Pet Files

Rats were first domesticated for research and have unselfishly helped us conquer devastating illnesses and learn much about the nutritional needs of our bodies. But animal lovers are pleased to see that some effort is being made to reduce the number of rats used that way.

Rats Just Want to Have Fun

As some of the world's most adaptable creatures, rats have lived side by side with us, even in our own homes for centuries—and they have taken notes. If given their druthers they choose to live where we live and eat what we eat. And while meeting their basic survival needs at our expense, they have noticed out of the corners of their beady little eyes that our games and activities are pretty appealing, too. The pet rat will insist upon joining in.

Pet's Peeve

Rats do enjoy handling. But never, and we mean *never,* lift a rat by his very prominent tail.

Any game is fair game to a rat. He will watch intently to understand the rules, and then jump in. It's your job to make sure this doesn't go too far. The rat may be savvy and smart, but he is not indestructible, so you must help him to understand his limits. Don't assume, for example, that a friendly dog will just naturally take kindly to him and that it's OK to leave the dog and the rat alone to get acquainted. Don't assume the rat can be passed through the hands of all the neighborhood toddlers without anyone suffering injury. Don't allow a rat free, unsupervised run of the house, either, or you may end up with an electrocuted rat or a kitchen full of shredded cabinetry. Manage your rat's activities with common sense.

So Where Does This Leave Us?

If you are seeking a pet that wants to be alone, don't get a rat. If you are seeking a pet that is most content to remain out of the flow of family traffic, don't get a rat. And if you are seeking a pet that is terrified at the mere suggestion of leaving the security of his cage routine for the unpredictability of family activities, a rat is not for you. In fact, if you're seeking a shrinking violet of a pet and that is just what you expect from little rodents, a rat just might outsmart you and soon be the dominant creature in your household.

When the subject is rats, we are wise to pay attention. Although I am making a valiant attempt here to dispel the negative image of the rat and prove his merit as a pet, that does not mean we should ignore his role as troublemaker.

Pampered Pet

To lift a rat, attract your pet's attention with a treat, and he may just step up into your hand. If he is not so amenable, wrap both hands around the sides of his body to hold him safely and securely, then lift.

What you'll learn early on is that there is good reason rats have been chosen for study of the human psyche: running those mazes, for instance. It's no secret that rats are highly intelligent critters. Some owners and researchers believe their smarts even rival that of dogs. So if it's a smart, fun-loving pet you're looking for who doesn't mind being the center of attention and even seeks that position out, then overlook your natural prejudices and give a rat a chance. You will be amply rewarded. Thousands of rat pet owners can't be wrong.

Where and How to Find a Pet Rat

It's hardly a challenge; rats are everywhere. No, not the rats in the sewer. Not the rats in your attic. Pet rats. The choice can sure pull on your heartstrings, though. Imagine walking into a pet shop and finding an ample collection of rats for sale, only to hear that some of them will be sold to snake owners. Yikes!

Should you just save them all? No, you can't do that. What you can do, or at least try to do, is harden your heart, decide just exactly what kind of rat you're looking for, and go out and look for him. Unfortunately, you may have to put blinders on to the fate that faces some of the rats you will find along the way.

Different Rats for Different Folks

Wild rats do not exactly come in a rainbow of colors, but the domesticated rat is an entirely different story. There's the classic white with either black or pink eyes, the plain wild brown, the dusty gray, and, of course, the shiny black whose glowing eyes are all that may be seen in the dark. But there is much more to this animal than color. Much more.

Years ago when rats agreed to be pets, their human handlers began fiddling with their pets' genes. They may not have quite understood what they were doing at first, but in time their efforts, enhanced by the rat's speedy reproduction rates, resulted in the many rat colors and types we see within the domestic rat population today.

Go out shopping for one of these animals, and you'll find a vast selection of colors, patterns, and coat textures—even hairless rats. Many of these are referred to in rat circles as *fancy rats*. See a collection of such animals draped in long tresses, silken coats, or vibrant pastel patterns, and the images of sewers or subway tracks couldn't be further from your mind. Satin pillows and crystal—that's more like it.

What Does a Rat Cost?

The purchase price of a rat can vary widely, but the average is $4.06.

The average rat owner also spends per year:

$29	Rat food
$20	Other supplies
$11	Toys

One, Two, or More?

The next question you must answer is how many rats should you acquire. Rats are small, fun, easy-care pets. Why not take several into your home? You can, but be careful. This can be dangerous. First, male rats who were not raised together may be quarrelsome when asked to share their home. And then there is that pesky rat reproduction rate. In addition to his many other talents, the rat has mastered the fine art of light-speed procreation. House a male and female together, and soon you'll come to understand yet another reason why the rat has survived the ages so handsomely. Rat rule of thumb: Never let your population dwindle.

While a multi-rat household may be fun for all parties involved (assuming, of course, that you do not turn it into a breeding compound), remember that a rat can be perfectly content as an "only" rat. Perhaps even more content. Just take a look at a single-rat household, and you'll see why. The resident rat gets all the attention, all the toys, and all the play. Solo housing is also just peachy for this animal, who, in truth, will probably be more social with his owners if he is the only rat in the house.

One Sad Drawback

Perhaps the major drawback in living with a rat is the animal's short life span. Rats typically only make it to two or three years of age, which is quite sad when you consider how deeply they bond to their families. That's just the way it is. They live fast and die young. But those few years can be packed with fun and memories that it would be a shame to miss.

Short life span or no, you are honor-bound to choose your pet with care and consideration. Once you have realized this, your mind will surely boggle with the many choices you have to make. First, where should you get your new pet?

Wherefore Art Thou, Rat?

The pet shop is the most likely option. Consider only those establishments that are clean, well-managed, and staffed by people who share your admiration for rats. But the pet shop is not the only game in town. Even animal shelters may have rats come their way from time to time.

Should you find yourself enamored of one of the fancy rat varieties, a pet shop may or may not carry it. You may have to seek out a breeder who specializes in that particular type. Now, your head may be spinning at the concept of a rat breeder, but our sweet, fun-loving domestic rats have to come from somewhere, don't they? And where better than from someone who loves and understands rats and wants to see them raised in homes by those who share their sentiments.

Secrets from the Pet Files

Rat clubs also rescue pet rats (or former lab rats) that, for one reason or another, have become homeless. Adopting a needy rat is a very nice thing to do. Rat shows are a good way to find rats clubs and rescue rats. You can also ask at your local animal shelter.

As for where to locate such a breeder, well, the fancy rats figure prominently at rat shows. (Rat shows? Now your head is really spinning!) Rat shows are held either independently or as part of county and state fairs, sponsored by the various rat and mouse organizations across the country. Once you start looking, you'll find the resources everywhere—and be amazed that you never noticed them before.

A Word of Warning About Wild Rats

Rats are not expensive pets, but some potential owners may wish to save even more money by getting a rat pet from the wild. Big mistake! First, it can be downright impossible to capture a rat alive from the wild (ask any exterminator). Every day rats handily evade our traps, humane and otherwise.

If you were able to capture a rat, you are just asking for trouble. An animal of such phenomenal survival abilities is not typically one with a gentle and benevolent nature. The rat is a fighter. To force a wild rat into a living situation designed for a domestic

Pet's Peeve

It is cruel to release a pet rat into the wild. Your little pet is ill-equipped to survive life's rigors and compete with the big, bad wild rats for food.

rat will only ignite the wild animal's survival instincts. He will bite. He will not play. He will be terrified and aggressive at the same time. His every breath will be directed toward seeking escape. He may also carry disease. So spend the money. Set the proper foundation for success.

The Moment of Truth

And now, the final decision. Which rat? There are so many. You have found a pet shop, breeding facility, or shelter that fills the bill, that is clean, and that doesn't overcrowd the available rats. Time to choose. Remember what the rat is supposed to be, and choose accordingly.

Anything but shy and retiring, most of the rats you meet will stand up to greet you and literally beg you to take them home: "Me, me, pay attention to me!" That's a good sign. You want a friendly rat, a charming rat, a rat who likes you and enjoys life. But while you're reveling in the attention of all these potential pets, ask those all-important questions:

- ➤ Do the rats in the enclosure look healthy?
- ➤ Are their eyes bright, their bites even, their ears clean?
- ➤ Do they breathe clearly, to indicate an absence of respiratory illness that is the scourge of small rodents?
- ➤ Are their noses free of discharge?
- ➤ Do they sport healthy, even coats?
- ➤ Is their skin free of blemishes?
- ➤ Do the rats seem to have been properly socialized to humans?

And finally, is there one particular rat that just plain seems to like you? Do you like him? Well, there you go. A match made in rat heaven.

Rats at Home

Rats have long shared the human home, but as pets (invited guests, if you will), they require their own home within your home, both for their safety and to preserve your house. As we will see, however, there is a reason the rat is considered an easy-keeper.

Rat Room

Rats are best housed in cages or enclosures designed especially for them. For example, rats generally enjoy climbing. A multistory domicile is thus a fine choice for your pet, ideally a cage with gnaw-proof bars that offers various levels for playing, snoozing, or just sitting and enjoying the view. An added bonus to this setup is that toys and nest boxes can be placed on various levels to keep the rat interested.

Some keepers opt for a glass aquarium-type setup, but this is limiting in the mental and physical stimulation it can provide its rat resident. Critics claim it limits proper ventilation, as well, which is a critical element in warding off the respiratory illnesses that are the greatest risk to pet rat health.

When You Get a Rat, You'll Also Have to Get These

Secure multilevel cage	Nest box
Small holding cage	Chewing blocks
Food dish	Exercise toys
Water bottle	Climbing toys
Bedding material	Care book

Make sure the cage doors and, if applicable, the top of the glass tank are rat-proof: infallible hardware in the former case, and a tight-fitting, wood-framed screen in the latter. A flimsy, rip-riddled screen draped across the top of a glass enclosure may provide ventilation, but it will be history in a flash—as will your pet. The same holds true for a cheesy latch on a cage door. The rat is a wizard at escaping, whether challenged by a particular type of hardware or a tiny hole at the base of a glass enclosure.

The good news is that even if he does escape, your rat's goal will probably be to find you and join in whatever you're doing at the moment.

Pampered Pet

If you can't find your rat, just hold out some favored treats and call his name. He should answer the call in no time.

Home Furnishings

Furnish your rat's home with a variety of nest boxes and/or hiding places for sleeping and playing (cardboard paper-towel tubes, and PVC piping are favorites for playtime). Toys, too, must be present. The rat is a world-class gnawer, so make sure the toy box includes safe chew toys—and be ready to replace them when they have been demolished by those phenomenal incisors that never stop growing.

Bedding, too, is a great concern. Carpet the floor of the cage with a layer of bedding thick enough for the rat to burrow into. Use only products—typically wood shavings (no cedar, please, it irritates your rat's respiratory system) or shredded paper—made

Pampered Pet

Thanks to all of the rat's time in the laboratory, much has been discovered about rat health. And your pet deserves veterinary care if you see signs of injury or illness.

specifically for small animal housing, and keep that bedding clean. Remove droppings and soiled areas as soon as possible, and look out for food caches while you're at it.

Believe it or not, rats are neat freaks. Relatively odorless pets, they will remain that way only if their owners commit to routine cage cleaning. This means cleaning their food dishes and water bottles daily, changing the bedding every few days, and cleaning the entire cage every week or, if possible, twice a week. Keep a temporary cage handy to house your pet comfortably during cleaning.

Rat Food

Feeding a rat is much like feeding a pig—or at least that's how it's popularly perceived. We view both as animals that will eat anything, so we might as well just offer them our leftovers and they'll be fine. Well, needless to say, they won't be fine. We must offer them only good, fresh foods appropriate to their dietary needs that will foster their health and well-being throughout their lives.

A rat has a high metabolic rate that must be sustained with seemingly constant eating. Your lesson from this biological fact? Make sure your pet has food available at all times. That's easy enough.

What Does a Rat Eat?

Commercial rat pellets or block food

Grain mixture

Cooked sweet potato

Whole-wheat bread

Cooked pasta

Fresh fruit

Nuts (sparingly!)

A rat will thrive best on a diet comprising primarily a commercial pellet mix or block-style food designed especially for lab rats. The block form does double duty as tooth-maintenance device—its hard texture helping to keep the rat's ever-growing teeth honed and sharp. This simple diet may be supplemented every other day or so with a ration of high-quality grain mixture for small animals, or a serving of fresh food, such as a couple of grapes, dry whole-wheat bread, cooked sweet potato, cold cooked pasta, or banana.

How to Feed a Rat

The key word in feeding rats is freshness. Leave the food, whether commercial grain mix or a grape, within the cage for no longer than 24 hours. The simplest schedule is to feed the rat in the morning, perhaps offer a supplement in the evening, and don't forget the power of the treat (healthy treats only) during your daily activities when you are playing with your pet outside of his cage. Then, next morning, remove any left-overs and start all over again.

And finally, don't forget the most important nutritional component: water. Make sure the rat has access to fresh, clean water every minute of every day. Experts in the rat field recommend the traditional water bottle with a stainless-steel sipping tube for this. The bottle hangs on the side of the cage, where the water will remain safe from contamination. Change the water daily, keep the bottle clean, check the sipping tube daily for clogs, and you will be following the ultimate recipe for rat health.

The Least You Need to Know

➤ Despite their wicked reputation as vermin, rats are some of the most social, most intelligent, most easy-care pets you could wish for—as long as you can overlook that tail.

➤ Rats are very social animals, but are best housed alone because of their territorial tendencies and staggering breeding rates. Their social needs must then be met by their owners, who should be willing to play with their pets outside of the cage each day.

➤ Choose a healthy rat from a reputable source—a breeder, a well-run pet shop, or a rescue group—and not from the local field, alley, abandoned building, or subway.

➤ Although they are resilient animals, pet rats deserve clean housing, hiding places within their enclosures, ample chew toys, fresh food and water, and plenty of respect and attention from their owners.

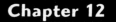

Chapter 12

Gentle Gerbils

> **In This Chapter**
>
> ➤ A day in the life of a gerbil
>
> ➤ Gerbil social studies
>
> ➤ Choosing a friendly, healthy gerbil pet
>
> ➤ Gerbil care in a nutshell

We typically meet them when we are children—often in our classrooms during our formative years. That tender introduction may be our first encounter with a pet that isn't a dog or a cat—assuming, of course, we grow up in a state where these small animals are legal.

Legal? Yes, this animal is banned in several states. She must be pretty ornery. She must be rather dangerous. Well, maybe not. In fact, she weighs less than a pound and can fit into the palm of your hand. Her teeth are used not for decapitating victims, but for gnawing on wood and seeds, and her roar is best described as a soft squeal. She is—oh, horror of horrors—the gerbil.

How could that be? Apparently, some of the folks in charge believe that if the general public is entrusted with the responsibility of caring for these tiny rodents, they might escape into the wilds, and roving packs of gerbils will wreak havoc on our precious agricultural resources. Of course, we would be hard pressed to find evidence of a similar phenomenon—say, herds of escaped hamsters perpetrating such an atrocity— but we can't be too careful now, can we?

But the gerbil is not illegal everywhere, and that is why we are privileged to discuss her here. Of the more than 80 species of gerbils that call various desert-type regions of Africa, Asia, and Europe home, the gerbil at the heart of this discussion is the classic pet gerbil, the Mongolian gerbil. This critter that strikes such fear in the hearts of so many state agriculture departments is a lovely little animal that once encountered is rarely forgotten.

Gerbils As Pets

	light	1	2	3	4	5	*heavy*
Time commitment				✔			
Grooming			✔				
Feeding				✔			
General cleanup				✔			
Suitable for kids age infant to 5		✔					
Suitable for kids age 5 to 10				✔			
Suitable for kids over 10						✔	
Sociability					✔		
Expense of keeping					✔		

A Day in the Life

In the wild, the gerbil is a denizen of the desert, digging endless networks of underground tunnels to accommodate her vast extended family. And while Gracie, the pet gerbil we will be meeting, has come a long way from life in the desert, those natural instincts, and thus what she demands of life in captivity, remain intact.

Dawn's Early Light

Gerbils are quite willing to do whatever it takes to fit into our human households. Take Gracie, for example. An alarm clock rings in a distant room. Time to get up. Fine with Gracie. Snuggled into the hay bedding in her nest box, she rolls over to awaken Pearl—together they are the Yin and Yang of the gerbil world. Both emerge from the nest box, sniff the air (nothing new there), and hop on over to the dining section of the cage to see what is being served for breakfast.

Right on schedule, the cage door opens, a hand enters, and the food dish is filled with a fresh serving of pellets. Yum! A few nibbles and then some water. Then Gracie is off for a spin on the exercise wheel. Then it's Pearl's turn. The two enjoy their morning, taking turns with the toys, at the water bottle, and on the wheel. They play hide-and-seek in the length of PVC pipe in their cage. They spend some time gnawing on the delectable apple tree twigs that appeared in the cage this morning. Finally, they burrow into the bedding of their spacious, well-ventilated stainless-steel cage and cuddle up together for a nap.

Pampered Pet

A wild gerbil would usually not be out and about in broad daylight. But the ever-accommodating gerbil will adjust herself to your schedule.

Taking Care of Business in the Afternoon

The gerbil sisters awaken, ready for more of the same: play, a nibble or two of lunch, kind words from an owner, perhaps another nap. But today is different. The trusted hand returns to the cage. Neither occupant would ever dream of greeting it with anything but friendly curiosity. Each one willingly hops aboard, and before they know it, that curiosity has found both of them relocated in a holding cage. It's cleaning day.

While they wait out the procedure, that trusted hand enters once more, this time bearing some special treats: a couple of quartered grapes and some chopped greens. When cleaning time is over, it's back to the security of their now-pristine abode. The two sniff around and take inventory to make sure everything is there and as it should be. All checks out a-okay.

Winding Down at Evening

As the household slows down, the gerbils, adapting their rhythms accordingly, wind down too. They share a light dinner, and then Gracie enjoys a short trip out of the cage. She willingly hops on that trusted palm, the scent of which always means either new adventure or food, and settles contentedly into it. Another hand comes down across her back and holds her gently in place on her magic carpet ride.

Gracie feels no urge to jump away—an impulse typically reserved for moments of fear, which is a rather foreign concept to Gracie. She has it made—the ultimate gerbil life! Her cage is always clean, her bedding is always thick enough for burrowing, her sister is the best roommate any gerbil could ever ask for, and her caretaker knows to approach her pets with a soft voice and overall manner.

Pet's Peeve

Be gentle with the gerbil's tail. Rough handling or lifting the tiny animal by the tail can result in a painful loss of hair and skin. Respect that tail, and make sure everyone who handles your pet does the same.

She uses that wonderful, soothing voice at bedtime when she bids Gracie and Pearl good night. "Sleep tight, my darlings." They snuggle in, huddled together so close that it's impossible to tell which tiny gerbil foot and which furry brush-tipped tail belongs to which gerbil. They have slept this way since they were tiny, naked baby gerbils napping next to mom. They will always sleep this way. Family—it's the gerbil way.

The Social Life of the Gentle Gerbil

While all rodents share the same fundamental characteristics—the ever-growing incisors, the adaptability, the quick reproduction rates—each rodent family approaches life from a unique perspective. The gerbil is no exception. Though gentle and quiet, once installed in a human household she exerts a distinctive personality that for many small-pet enthusiasts makes her the most delightful rodent pet of all.

Secrets from the Pet Files

A rodent's incisors are true miracles of Mother Nature's engineering. These two prominent front teeth continue to grow throughout the rodent's life. They are also equipped with their own internal sharpener, thus ensuring that the teeth remain razor sharp throughout the animal's life.

Wild Gerbils Underground

One of the most efficient avenues to take when exploring the world of the pet gerbil is to first explore the world of the wild gerbil. From her we may deepen our understanding of just why gerbils behave as they do in our homes, and what they require to live a long and happy life.

Wild gerbils are community-minded critters. They live in large family groups in compounds that consist of well-organized underground tunnels and burrows. Rather xenophobic in nature, they usually do not openly welcome newcomers into their kingdoms, but get along famously with those of their own clan. What we then learn from this is that gerbils are among the most social of the rodents, and thus are best kept in pairs and groups in captivity.

Pampered Pet

A captive gerbil can live to a ripe old age of four or five years. Not bad for a small rodent!

Because of their burrowing tendencies, gerbils will tolerate wide-open spaces only as long as they trust their caretakers and are shielded from loud noises and sudden movements. In a gerbil's mind this means a large hungry bird is swooping down, a sensation that will send her running for cover, never wishing to venture out from the safety of her cage again. Old genetic instincts die hard.

Gerbil Family Values

As you have seen, *familia* is quite important to gerbils. They harbor deep loyalties to those with whom they have bonded—an honored group that you, if you prove yourself worthy, may be invited to join. They thrive best with other gerbils, but remember, you must provide the little family with plenty of space to prevent the fighting that can erupt in overcrowded conditions.

And another warning: House a male and a female together, and you will indeed see just how deeply rooted those family values are. Gerbils tend to be monogamous, and the very progressive dad will often help care for his kids. But because it's unfair to produce litter after litter of animals that may have difficulty finding homes, perhaps it's wisest to keep the sexes separated and stick to same-gender pairings. Make these decisions when the gerbils are young, however, because as they mature and grow set in their ways, gerbils do not tend to tolerate the introduction of newcomers into their family groups.

Gerbil Character and Disposition

This very communal nature has made the gerbil what she is today. Though she can be a bit timid (you would be, too, if you were only a few inches long and your only means of defense was your the ability to kick sand in someone's face), she is not inclined to bite unless she's mistreated, frightened, or in pain. Her whole character has been sculpted by the fact that she has traditionally shared such close quarters with her fellow gerbils.

In deference to her compatriots, the gerbil has evolved into a very polite little critter: quiet, clean, relatively odorless, naturally robust, and healthy. Just an all-around sweet little girl. The ideal roommate. The ideal pet.

A Natural Leap: Gerbils As Pets

Given the gerbil's abundant pet qualities, it only makes sense that we would be anxious to invite her into our homes. Add "easy care" and "inexpensive" to the equation, and the gerbil would seem to have it all. Indeed, her many fans believe she does.

For yet another perspective on what life is like with this adorable rodent, let's compare her to some of the other popular rodent pets: the rat, the mouse, and the hamster. In a nutshell, the gerbil falls somewhere in the middle of them on the scale of smarts and personality. Intellect-wise, the gerbil and the hamster stand somewhere between the rat and the mouse. The gerbil, when properly respected, is more comfortable in the company of humans than are the mouse and the hamster. Yet, like the mouse, the gerbil likes having her own gerbil buddies around. The hamster is more of a loner. The rat, on the other hand, is the social butterfly of the rodent family. Few animals, rodent or no, are as brazenly gregarious as the rat.

The Prey and the Predators

While we're at it, let's compare the gerbil to the dog and the cat, too. The comparisons between them can be summed up in three words: oil and water. They simply do not mix.

Sure, you'll hear the stories. "Oh, my gerbil gets along great with my cat. She never even lets out a squeak when they're together." That's obviously because the gerbil is scared frozen. She can't squeak. The poor dear is petrified. Why do that to this tiny prey animal? There is no need. Go ahead and own other pets, but maintain the peace of mind of all, and keep them separate. It's only fair.

Secrets from the Pet Files

What is it with humans and rodent tails? Many of us blanche at the thought of living with a rat because of that long, thick, oh-so-naked tail. The mouse's tail is naked, too, but it's not quite so large. Enter the gerbil. Yes, she has a long tail. But *voilà!* That tail is also covered with hair, often with a delightful little brush on the tip. Ah, now we feel better!

Choosing a Gerbil Companion

In those states where gerbils are not contraband, they are readily available. So go forth and find your new companion. Just make sure you do so with the usual tools of the mission: common sense, a sharp eye, and an understanding of how the gerbil views the world around her.

Initial Introductions

When meeting a prospective gerbil pet for the first time, honor the simple protocols from the gerbil book of manners written for just these very moments. This will set the stage for your interactions for the rest of your days together, and help convince the gerbil from the get-go that your intentions are honorable:

➤ Keep your voice low.

➤ Avoid startling or frightening the gerbil with sudden, quick movements or threatening gestures.

➤ When you hold the gerbil, hold her gently and securely.

Handling a gerbil is an important act that can make or break the relationship. Don't force the issue. Begin by simply placing your hand, very still and quiet, in the gerbil's cage, and allow her to come and investigate. Let her get acquainted with your scent. In the presence of a typical, well-adjusted gerbil, you need not fear a bite or any other aggressive behavior.

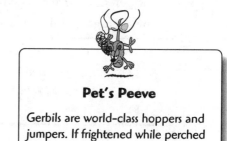

Pet's Peeve

Gerbils are world-class hoppers and jumpers. If frightened while perched in your palm, your gerbil will gone in a flash.

If the gerbil hops up on your hand to investigate further, very slowly cup her carefully into your hand, lift her slowly to you, and then place your other hand over her back to provide even more security. And remember: Those hind legs of hers can be deceiving. Think kangaroo and you'll get the picture. If she could, she would kick sand in the face of the individual who had the gall to frighten her, but in the absence of sand, escape will do just fine.

Making the Choice

While there are gerbil breeders about these days who, as part of the so-called gerbil fancy, breed for show and to conjure up new colors and types, this group is still not quite as large as those in the guinea pig, rabbit, mouse, and rat worlds. Consequently, you will probably be purchasing your gerbil from a pet shop, and you are probably safe in doing so. This is assuming, of course, that you go only to a well-run establishment

Pet Talk

The enthusiasts of a particular animal—the ones who like to breed and show their pets—are called the *fancy*.

that is clean, and that the animals are not kept in crowded conditions that can lead to health problems in the available stock.

You take your chances when you answer a pet owner's advertisement in the newspaper for the sale of whatever type of baby animals she or he has brought into the world—including gerbils. However, the gerbil is one animal that is less risky to purchase this way. Just make sure you choose only a healthy-looking animal of at least four or five weeks of age from a clean, well-maintained environment. Evaluate the temperament of the entire gerbil family and how they have been handled by their human family. And while you're at it, you may also want to gently inform the "breeders" that you have no intention of breeding your pet because you know how difficult it can be to place the babies in decent, permanent homes. In other words, hint, hint, perhaps this should be their last litter.

What Does a Gerbil Cost?

The purchase price of a gerbil can vary widely, but the average is about $9.

The average gerbil owner also spends per year:

$34	Other supplies
$31	Gerbil food
$15	Regular veterinary care
$13	Toys

Pet Talk

Agouti isn't just for gerbils. It's a color combination in which each individual hair alternates with light and dark bands of color, and you can find agouti hairs on many types of animals.

Most of the gerbils you encounter in your quest, if not all of them, will resemble each other very closely in color and build. Most gerbils are *agouti-colored*, an earthy combination of browns, black, yellow, and white, a natural camouflage designed by Mother Nature to protect her little gerbils in their desert homeland. While you may find some variations on this theme—say a gerbil that is solid black or brown—and indeed it might be fun to own a gerbil of a different color, your primary concern when choosing your pet should be health and temperament. What fun is a coal-black gerbil if she wants to bite you in a very un-gerbil-like manner every time you approach her cage, or exhibits a runny nose or an uneven bite?

Any health problems you do spot in a collection of potential gerbil pets are probably caused by stress or poor hygiene, rather than anything inherent in the gerbils themselves. These are hardy little animals, and, when properly kept, they will stay that way. Bright-eyed and bushy-tailed is the gerbil you want to take home with you, as well as clear-nosed, properly jawed, and uniformly coated. Throw in a dash of well-adjusted and curious, and call it a match.

One Gerbil or More?

When you are choosing your new gerbil pet, remember that gerbils are happiest in pairs. The time to ensure your gerbil's happiness is right when you choose your new pet. As you have seen, it is safest to choose two gerbils who already consider themselves family. In other words, just take two, and you'll be providing your pets with gerbil companionship—one of the most important priorities for the gerbil psyche.

If, somewhere down the line, you decide that these pets have become rather addictive and you would like to add more to the mix without breeding them yourself (a responsible position to take), accept the fact that newcomers will probably have to be housed separately from your original animal(s). And that's okay. You can try placing the respective cages side by side to allow the residents to adjust to each others' scents and voices, and maybe eventually they will defy the odds and agree to more personal interaction and even cohabitation. Just don't force the issue. Separate gerbil housing is hardly a sin. And it may mean salvation in the multi-gerbil household.

Pampered Pet

Stick with same-sex pairs, unless you want your home transformed into a major gerbil-breeding operation within a few months.

Home Sweet Gerbil Home

In the wild, gerbils are fastidious animals, probably understanding instinctively (as the vast majority of animal species do) that a filthy home can lead to health problems. Gerbils carry this concept further by designing their digs much as we design ours. Visit a wild gerbil abode, and you will find a separate sleeping area, a separate dining area, and even a separate bathroom area. And we thought we originated this architectural concept! "Ha!" says the gerbil. "We've been doing it this way for ages, back when you all were living in one-room caves."

Regardless of who pioneered the architectural concept, your job is to institute it in the design of your pet gerbil's home. Fill this abode with the proper furnishings, make your darling gerbil comfortable physically, mentally, and, of course, gastronomically, and she will be most pleased by your attempts to earn her affections.

All the Bells and Whistles

Your choice of cage for your gerbil is second in importance only to the choice of the gerbil herself. So think again about your pet's background: an underground maze of tunnels and lots of room to move around. Let that be your guide. Yes, you can attempt to mimic this domicile by housing your pet in one of those setups that is sold as a series of tubes and compartments, but you need not go to such extremes. A simple stainless steel rodent cage or an aquarium-type tank will suffice nicely, as long as they are well-appointed, clean, and big enough for the resident animals (we will assume you will be housing two).

Pampered Pet

Commercially available wood shavings (not cedar—it irritates your gerbil's respiratory system), shredded paper, or pellets are safest for your pet's bedding.

Regardless of the type of gerbil house you choose for your pet, make sure the door and its locking mechanism are secure, opt for a solid floor over a wire floor (for your pet's foot comfort), and check periodically for sharp edges or surfaces that can cause injury. Carpet the floor with three inches or so of bedding so the gerbils can satisfy their natural inclinations to burrow.

As for furniture, forget the Ethan Allen. A simple enclosed nest box/bed, a selection of safe toys, and a clean food dish and water bottle will suffice. Position these items in such a way as to separate the dining area from the bedroom from the bathroom from the play area, and you're in business.

When You Get a Gerbil, You'll Also Have to Get These

Secure cage	Chewing blocks
Food dish	Exercise toys
Water bottle	Hiding and tunneling toys
Bedding material	Care book
Nest box	

Where is the best place for the gerbil cage? This is not a decision to be made carelessly. Your choice could affect both your pet's health and her mental well-being. Gerbils, as you have seen, do not appreciate noise or lots of household traffic. They also don't tolerate humidity (they are, after all, desert animals), which can cause respiratory problems. Add all of these conditions together, and you will not have a hard time figuring out where *not* to place your gerbil's abode. Once you've eliminated all those places, see what's left in your house.

It's not unusual for people to purchase small pets on impulse, but this isn't doing the animal any favors. To prevent the stress that can result from such an impulse, once you decide to purchase a gerbil, prepare for your pet ahead of time. Purchase the cage, the exercise wheel, the bedding, and all the other accessories, and have your pet's new home prepared before you bring her into her new environment. Then, when she does cross the threshold, she can make himself right at home. This is a great favor you can do for your new pet, and gerbils don't often forget a kindness.

Remain ever vigilant to the types of materials to which your gerbil is exposed. Anything is potential gnawing material to a rodent, even if it happens to be a live electrical cord. So keep anything delectable but inappropriate out of the teeth's way. To satisfy those toothsome urges, supply your pet with a variety of safe gnawing items, such as chew toys specifically made for rodents, and fresh twigs from fruit trees that are free of pesticides or other chemicals.

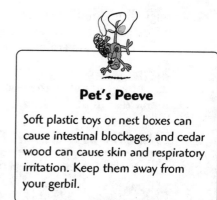

Pet's Peeve

Soft plastic toys or nest boxes can cause intestinal blockages, and cedar wood can cause skin and respiratory irritation. Keep them away from your gerbil.

Keeping House

As with all rodent pets, gerbil health can be maintained only within a clean environment. The cleaning regimen for a gerbil's domicile, which you take on when you accept the role of gerbil caretaker, follows the formula well-suited to every rodent pet.

Although your gerbil is a relatively odorless pet, every day soiled bedding, feces, and leftover food should be removed from the cage and bedding. The food dishes and water bottle also require daily cleaning. You should clean the entire cage or tank—a complete change of bedding and scrubbing all cage or tank surfaces—once a week. Following such a schedule not only results in a happier, healthier gerbil, but also a happier owner who has successfully kept any potential gerbil-housing odors at bay.

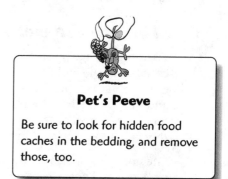

Pet's Peeve

Be sure to look for hidden food caches in the bedding, and remove those, too.

Being a desert mammal, the gerbil's internal system, right down to each and every cell, is extremely efficient in its conservation of water. You will find evidence of this in the relatively low quantity of urine the small animal excretes, and thus the relative lack of odor in her cage. Do not for a moment believe, however, that this means you may offer your pet water only every once in awhile. Every pet, including the gerbil, requires fresh, clean water, 24 hours a day, 365 days a year.

The Well-Fed Gerbil Pet

Gerbils in the wild are, by necessity, opportunistic feeders. That's typically the case with desert dwellers who don't have much of a choice of what they eat or when they might find dinner. Like most rodents, their tastes lean toward the vegetarian, satisfied by foraging for seeds, leaves, and roots. They probably wouldn't turn down a passing insect or worm in a pinch, either.

Forcing a pet gerbil to forage for her own food will quickly lead to malnutrition. You can, however, follow the lead of the wild gerbil when deciding what to feed your pet: simple diet in the wild, simple diet in captivity. It's as simple as that.

What Does a Gerbil Eat?

Commercial gerbil pellets or block food

Cooked sweet potato

Whole-wheat bread

Cooked pasta

Fresh fruit

Fresh, leafy greens

Seeds (sparingly!)

That simple diet consists of a high-quality commercial rodent diet, available in either pellet or block form. Two daily servings of this gerbil staple will suffice. You will also find seed mixtures marketed for gerbils, but these can be a bit too rich for the gerbil digestive tract. You can round out your pet's diet with moderate servings of fresh fruits and greens, and perhaps occasional helpings of whole-wheat bread or cooked pasta. Just don't overdo it. A fat gerbil is not a happy gerbil, nor is she a healthy gerbil.

Get Thee to the Gerbil Doctor

Twenty years ago, even 10 years ago, you would be laughed out of the room, perhaps even out of the building, were you to tell someone you were taking your pet gerbil to the veterinarian. But fortunately for the gerbil, times have changed. The care of exotic and small animals is finding more and more acceptance within the veterinary curriculum, and pet owners are more and more willing to seek the necessary care when their tiny pets show signs of illness.

The notorious signs that indicate an ailing gerbil are fairly easy to spot by observant owners who know their pets well. If you see any of the following symptoms, make a note of them and get your pet to the veterinarian. And ignore anyone who would laugh at you for doing so.

➤ Loss of appetite

➤ Change in the color and/or consistency of her feces or urine

➤ Listless or lethargic behavior

➤ Sudden aggressiveness when you approach

➤ Heavy breathing or panting

➤ Discharges from her eyes or nose

➤ Lack of interest in grooming herself

➤ Dull, unkempt coat

➤ Lesions on her skin

Kids and Gerbils

A gerbil is traditionally thought of as a child's pet, but it is a big mistake to relegate the animal's well-being to the sole care of a child. All pet care is an adult's responsibility.

Indeed, living with such a sweet, gentle little animal offers a child a wonderful opportunity to get acquainted with the ins and outs of responsible pet care. But all of that should be done under the watchful eye of the adults in the family. Far too many small animals have suffered from the passionate promises of youngsters who are inspired by pets when the animals first join their household, only to have the luster fade with the start of Little League or soccer season.

If your child promises to do the dishes every day, you can let them pile up in the sink in order to teach Junior a lesson about responsibility. But it is cruel to make an animal suffer just to make a point to your child. By all means give your child some responsibility for the family pets, but it is ultimately your responsibility to make sure all is right with your gerbils.

Pampered Pet

The gerbil is the quintessential classroom pet. But teachers should remember that classroom animals deserve proper care and respect—including minimal handling and the care of an adult.

The Least You Need to Know

➤ Gerbils are probably the sweetest, most gentle members of the rodent family, yet keeping them as pets is illegal in some states.

➤ In the wild these social animals live in large family groups within networks of tunnels. Pet gerbils thrive best when housed with others of their kind and are offered ample areas for hiding and burrowing.

➤ Gerbils can live as long as four or five years, but like all pet rodent species, they are highly susceptible to respiratory illnesses that may be prevented with a clean environment.

➤ As desert animals, gerbils are very intolerant of humidity. Keep the gerbil cage in a quiet, secluded location and away from moisture, direct sunlight, or drafts.

Chic Chinchillas

Your grandmother may have had a chinchilla, but chances are she didn't keep it as a pet. Chinchillas as pets are a pretty recent phenomenon; chinchillas as coats go way back. You see, chinchillas are native to the high rocky peaks of South America's Andes Mountain range, one of the coldest, driest regions of the planet. Though some might consider this region less than lovely, it is home to this adorable animal who is graced with one of the densest, most beautiful coats of fur in the animal kingdom.

In addition to his lush coat, the chinchilla's native habitat has provided him with one of the stranger habits in the animal kingdom. Here is the chinchilla, residing in a land of unbearably frigid temperatures in a hostile environment where water is scarce enough for drinking, let alone for bathing. He knows his key to survival is that lustrous coat on his back, which he must keep groomed and clean. What's a chinchilla to do? How can he keep that lustrous coat so lustrous?

Learn how to bathe in dust, that's how. Yes, I said dust. Soft volcanic ash, to be exact. Chalk it up to yet another miracle of the animal kingdom. Wherever they live, animals from all branches of the animal family tree have proven themselves capable of evolving and adapting to whatever survival challenge their skilled sculptress, old Mom Nature, deigns to throw their way.

Pet's Peeve

Accustomed as they are to life in high rocky mountain peaks, chinchillas do not tolerate heat well. They will thrive best in temperatures below 75°F, the ideal being somewhere around 68°.

A Day in the Life

Much to the chinchilla's relief, the demand for his coat has diminished somewhat through the years. Yet we remain enamored of this animal that is probably the closest we will ever find to a living, breathing stuffed toy. We can't help but revel in the sensation of that indescribably soft coat between our fingers, and melt when the wearer of that coat snuggles up to us when we hold him.

Today our fixations on this animal are focused not on the commercial uses of his pelt, but on his care and personality. Sure we love that rich coat of fur, but most of us prefer to stroke it while its original owner is still wearing it. And when we do, we realize what a charmer that original owner can be. Let's take a quick look at a day in this small gray critter's world, and see how he works those legendary chinchilla charms.

Chinchillas As Pets

	light	1	2	3	4	5	*heavy*
Time commitment				✔			
Grooming					✔		
Feeding				✔			
General cleanup					✔		
Suitable for kids age infant to 5		✔					
Suitable for kids age 5 to 10				✔			
Suitable for kids over 10						✔	
Sociability					✔		
Expense of keeping				✔			

Charlie Chinchilla at Dawn

Meet Charlie, an 18-month-old gray chinchilla. Charlie is quite round, because that is how chinchillas are built, and he views the world through two equally round black eyes that gleam like obsidian. Were Charlie a wild chinchilla (which are rarely found these days), those eyes would be open when ours are closed, and he would tuck himself into bed at sunrise. Chinchillas, you see, are nocturnal, although most, like Charlie, are not fanatics about this.

Charlie, like most of his kin, has learned to defy those natural callings. An adaptable nature is the hallmark of the chinchilla family—and the rodent family at large—and Charlie does whatever he must to fit in with his family and their daily rhythms. They don't always recognize this, but that's okay. They treat him well, and that's what matters.

Pet Talk

Nocturnal animals are active during the night. *Diurnal* animals are active during the day. *Crepuscular* animals are active at dawn and dusk.

Just look at this morning. They rise and visit him first thing, just as they have for the past 15 months. Then it's breakfast for all. Cereal for the family and a modified version of that for Charlie: rodent pellets and some chopped greens and fruit—and fresh water instead of mom's and dad's coffee.

Charlie Chinchilla at Dusk

Charlie tends to enjoy snoozing, snacking (on the good, healthy food in his food dish and the hay in the hay rack, of course), and relaxing in the morning and during the day. No problem. His family respects his routine.

But when afternoon rolls around, so does Charlie's sense of adventure. Time to go out and play. Fortunately, his owners know this about Charlie, and they are ready to answer the call. Charlie enjoys the interior of his classic two-story chinchilla condo, complete with ample hiding/napping areas and a nice, big exercise wheel to accommodate Charlie's largish size. But nothing quite compares with time spent out of the cage.

Charlie is, of course, supervised constantly while he is at liberty, and all access to delectable electrical cords and potentially poisonous plants is denied. No debate there. No debate about the other pets, either. When Charlie is out and about, the dog and the cat remain in the other room. Period.

Secrets from the Pet Files

Yes, the chinchilla is a rodent—beautiful cousin to the rat, the mouse, the guinea pig, the hamster, and the gerbil. Although they vary dramatically in appearance and intelligence levels, all are vegetarians, all are compelled to gnaw because of their ever-growing incisor teeth, and all are tough little animals.

Charlie Chinchilla: Night Owl

Nighttime is when Charlie's blood really starts pumping. This particular evening, however, he's in for a special surprise. Two trusted hands reach into his cage and deposit a familiar square-shaped container. Then Charlie sees the dust. It's bath time! He jumps in and starts spinning. What a spectacle. Imagine a tiny tornado where once there stood a small, furry animal. That fine gray powder starts flying, and Charlie is rendered invisible within the eye of the storm. Then, just as quickly, it is over. Charlie emerges from the dust, refreshed and clean. The hands return to remove his unique bathtub.

Pet's Peeve

As for snakes and ferrets, a chinchilla should not even know that such animals exist. These animals are the chinchilla's mortal enemies.

Now clean and well scrubbed from his dust bath, Charlie trundles out of his cage to share some quality time with his family. He sits on a comfortable lap to watch a little television before bed. His mistress strokes his back, tickles him behind his ears—the usual routine of mutual tactile relaxation therapy. His owner can't imagine anyone preferring an inanimate version of the chinchilla coat (that is, a fur coat) to petting the living breathing animal—so warm and gentle and affectionate; such a delight.

Lights out, but not for Charlie. Those large button eyes of his will help him navigate in the dark. Sure he'll sleep some, but then he'll get up and take a spin on the exercise wheel. Then a nap. Then time for a snack. Then a leap up to the second floor of his cage, back down to the bottom, and back and forth, back and forth. That's what chinchillas do. They pretend they're back in the mountains—whether they have ever been there or not.

A New Perspective on Chinchillas

It used to be that when the subject was chinchillas, the subject was also invariably fashion—and caviar and champagne and all that luxury stuff. But that has changed over the past few years, thanks to successful anti-fur campaigns supported by such high-profile celebs as the late Princess Diana, who have declined to wear coats that rightfully belong to small animals.

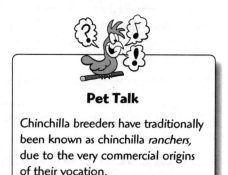

Pet Talk

Chinchilla breeders have traditionally been known as chinchilla *ranchers,* due to the very commercial origins of their vocation.

While the chinchilla's life as coveted fur animal is certainly not one to be envied, it has provided one unexpected and very positive offshoot. The commercial management of chinchillas in captivity has led to a wealth of knowledge among veterinarians, breeders, and would-be pet owners of chinchilla health, behavior, and general care. We never would have gleaned such information if our only experience with them was watching them forage for food among the rocks in the Andes. So it would appear that every cloud, like the silver sheen of the chinchilla's coat itself, truly does have a silver lining.

That Gorgeous Coat

The chinchilla's coat is one of, if not the, thickest, softest, most gorgeous on the planet. It is not only breathtaking to the eye and the touch, but is also a miracle of engineering. The density arises from the fact that as many as 60 hairs can sprout from a single hair follicle.

The protection the coat offers its wearer includes insulation from frigid temperatures, but that's not all. In the high peaks of the chinchilla's native homeland, survival is a constant struggle with the elements and equally determined predators. Should a predatory bird swoop down to hoist an unsuspecting chinchilla into the air, it would end up, if those follicles are working properly, with nothing but a beakful of soft, gray fur. That fur, you see, is engineered to be released with relative ease at just such critical moments. Mother Nature thought of everything!

Although gray and its various shades are the classic chinchilla colors, these animals may also be found in blond, black, and beige. Each hair, which can grow as much as an inch in length, is typically darker at the base, lighter in the middle, and darker at the tip, resulting in an almost metallic sheen.

Pet's Peeve

If you're a light sleeper, it's best to keep the chinchilla cage in a more secluded corner of the house, or you'll be awakened periodically throughout the night by your chinchilla's nighttime activities.

The Ideal Latchkey Pet

It didn't take long for those who originally decided to get to know the chinchilla, for whatever purpose, to realize just what quiet, gentle creatures these animals are. You don't have to be a trained field biologist to recognize the chinchilla's nocturnal habits and to realize this just might make a wonderful pet.

And so they do. Chinchillas are now finding themselves more and more in demand as companion animals. This is especially true if the humans seeking companionship work long hours, which might not be so great for a more demanding pet species. Although they are generally quiet and docile, chinchillas do require daily interaction with their owners. But the morning and evening hours are ideal for that interaction—a perfect match for owners with busy work schedules.

A Creature of Habit

While they are amenable to a life in captivity, chinchillas can be persnickety little critters that are demanding in certain areas. Incredibly sensitive, they do not tolerate extremes of any kind, whether it be noise, temperature, or spontaneous changes in their routine. These are quintessential creatures of habit, and demand that their daily routine be followed to the letter each and every day. Deviations can result in neurotic behavior, such as fur chewing, refusing to eat, and even serious illness. Call this the ultimate type-A personality pet.

So consider yourself warned. You must do your best to feed your pet at the same times every day (preferably morning and evening); to clean the cage of feces, soiled bedding, old food, and other debris; and to play with your pet outside of the cage. All play sessions should be conducted under careful supervision of a responsible adult and only in chinchilla-proofed rooms. Dust baths, too, must be offered regularly. Chinchillas are not only sensitive, but they hold grudges, too. Their expectations are quite demanding, and their trust is easily broken. Remember that, stick to the routine, and you should all be fine.

The Felix Unger of the Rodent Family

If there were a big rodent family reunion, the other members of the family would probably chastise the chinchilla for his obsession with cleanliness. "How vain can you be?" they ask him. "We're clean, too, but this is ridiculous."

It's not ridiculous to the chinchilla. Nor is it vanity. It's a matter of life and death. What else would have driven this animal to learn to bathe in volcanic ash? The chinchilla knows instinctively that in his native land a filthy coat can mean exposure to the elements and, subsequently, death. Whether wild or domestic, he therefore spends a great deal of time tending to the health of that coat.

One important component of this is the dust bath. He coats his fur with the dust provided in the dust bathtub, which sops up the excess oils and dirt that can catch in the dense growth of hair covering the chinchilla's body. Then the chinchilla gives a tornado-like shake to rid the hairs of that dust, just as other animals shake off excess water after a bath or a swim. This leaves the chinchilla fresh as a daisy and ready to face the world again with confidence and health.

Pampered Pet

Remove your chinchilla's dust bath when it's not in use to prevent him from using it as a litter box or a playpen.

A chinchilla will thrive on two or three dust baths every week. If you notice a rather unkempt appearance to the fur, you may need to increase the frequency a bit. If, on the other hand, the skin appears dry and the chinchilla is scratching obsessively, then perhaps he is overdoing it a bit. If your chinchilla goes on a dust-bath strike—which is probably your fault for violating the routine clause of your pet-owner contract and neglecting to offer the bath for a few weeks—you can help by brushing your pet with a soft brush. In the meantime, keep offering the dust bath periodically to entice him back to his natural habits. He may or may not comply. Few animals hold grudges like a chinchilla neglected.

The chinchilla extends these same expectations to his environment. It's only obvious, isn't it? Clean environment, clean chinchilla. It's all part of the picture. While the chinchilla will handle most of the bathing duties on his own (you must provide the supplies, of course), it's your job to keep the rest of his house in order. Remove soiled bedding, feces, and leftover food daily; keep the food and water receptacles clean; and change the bedding and clean the cage weekly. The result? A chinchilla who is healthy in mind, body, and spirit.

Pet's Peeve

Never bathe a chinchilla with soap and water! It will strip out all the coat's natural oils and make your pet susceptible to illness.

Choosing a Chinchilla Pet

Chinchillas, with proper care and housing, can live to the ripe old age of 8 to 10 years. That's pretty good for a rodent. But there's another clue to be gleaned from this fact: Inviting a chinchilla into your home is a long-term commitment. So choose wisely, choose with common sense and sensitivity—and with that long-term commitment in mind.

Mind Your Manners

We have spent much time and effort exploring the nature of the chinchilla, but what about the nature of the chinchilla owner—that individual best suited to life with this furry little critter? You are, after all, the other side of the equation of the successful relationship between our species and this beautiful beast.

The chinchilla is most comfortable in the company of someone not unlike himself— or someone who can at least play the part. This sensitive soul will recoil at aggression or noise, and perhaps never offer his trust again after it has been violated. In the chinchilla's eyes, then, the ideal human companion is quiet and considerate. He or she knows that a chinchilla will not tolerate rough handling, which will result both in a shy, distrustful pet and in the loss of clumps of hair. This critter enjoys interaction, but in a comfortable, controlled environment, free of sudden movements or earsplitting noises that are offensive to the chinchilla's large and sensitive ears.

The rewards are ample for the owner who agrees to exercising this decorum. Hold the soft, round form of a chinchilla next to your heart, and you'll understand. His warmth alone is heaven, as is the soft kiss of that legendary fur against your neck. Your chinchilla may purr in response. He may cuddle up closer. But if you are truly worthy of his affections, he may just reach out and nibble a bit on an available finger. Then, my friend, you have achieved the highest honor that a chinchilla can bestow. Be proud.

The best way to lift a chinchilla takes into account his history as a fur animal (the need to protect the coat and delicate skin with minimal handling), and his own security and comfort. While you must never raise the animal into the air by his squirrel-like tail, the tail can provide a secure handle for the initial liftoff. With one hand, grasp the tail at its base and lift the chinchilla's hind end up just a little bit. Slide your other hand in underneath the chinchilla's body, and with this secure support, lift him up and off the ground.

Cradle him quickly to your body with both hands for optimum security, and hold him securely against you. Enjoy his natural inclination to cuddle, his warmth, and the gentle rhythm of his heartbeat (you won't get that from any fur coat).

Pampered Pet

You can find chinchilla ranchers at county fairs or pet fairs, where chinchillas are inevitably displayed.

Where to Look

With the rise in the popularity of chinchillas as pets, these animals have become far more visible in a variety of locales. You probably need not look far when you decide to invite one into your home.

You can begin, of course, with the pet shop. Work only with a shop that is clean, properly and compassionately staffed, and houses the available chinchillas in proper, spacious accommodations. A good sign is a shop that requires all would-be owners to wash their hands before handling the animals.

It's also helpful to deal with a shop that stocks a wide variety of chinchilla and rodent products. A shop that offers cages, feed, and toys especially for chinchillas, as well as that all-important dust for bath time, will be a valuable resource in the months and years to come. Whoever is stocking the store also obviously realizes that chinchillas require their own unique brand of care.

What Does a Chinchilla Cost?

The purchase price of a chinchilla can vary widely, but the average is $378.33.

The average chinchilla owner also spends per year:

$60	Chinchilla food
$50	Non-surgical veterinary services
$72	Other supplies
$20	Toys

If you are able to locate a chinchilla breeder or rancher, survey the premises of the breeding operation carefully. Value that individual who won't let young chinchillas leave their mothers before six to eight weeks of age, who runs a clean operation, who is concerned about the life you will provide your new pet, and who stresses the importance of gentle handling and proper socialization. Deal with such an individual, and you will probably end up with a healthy pet with a stable temperament.

Smart and Friendly Chinchilla Choices

When it is time to choose your chinchilla pet, evaluation can be tough. Chinchillas, you remember, are nocturnal, and you will no doubt be doing your evaluation during the day, when the animal is at its lowest energy level. That's okay. Just keep this in mind and don't hold it against the chinchillas. A docile, even lethargic, demeanor in a chinchilla at high noon does not necessarily mean he is ill. He's probably just sleepy.

Pampered Pet

For the best evaluation, try to meet pet prospects first thing in the morning or late in the afternoon.

Don't hold a cautious attitude against a potential pet chinchilla. Shy and rather demure with strangers, a chinchilla might back away from you during the first moments of your initial meeting. Begin, then, by simply placing your hand into the cage, or, if the chinchilla is outside of his cage, offering your hand in a nonthreatening greeting. Hold your hand very still (perhaps place a raisin treat in your palm), and allow the animal to come up and investigate. When he sees that you mean no harm, he should allow his curiosity to win out and come forward to evaluate you. If, however, your peaceful gesture is greeted with an attempted bite and an aggressive charge, the chinchilla either has not been properly socialized or is carrying some negative psychological baggage from past relationships. Proceed with caution!

Signs of a Healthy Chinchilla

Finally, the common sense part of your mission. You want to choose the healthiest chinchilla pet possible. This means the chinchilla who has bright twinkling eyes, a properly structured jaw (critical for rodents), clean ears, and a lustrous, fluffy coat. The coat is a barometer of health, and a chinchilla that is properly devoted to coat care also tends to be balanced and even-tempered. Don't be alarmed if the adult chinchilla you are looking at has orange-colored teeth. That is normal for a chinchilla. Strange, but normal.

While furriers have, for decades, fixated on the chinchilla's fur for the profits it represented, it is also the best indicator of overall internal health and nutrition. There is no greater way to evaluate your pet—with the exception, perhaps, of the feces. You should examine both daily for changes that could indicate internal health problems. Look for bald patches in the coat or an overall unkempt appearance, and watch for changes in feces consistency (the most notable being diarrhea), and bathroom habits (such as constipation). At the first sign, get your pet to a veterinarian skilled in rodent care immediately.

Room, Board, and Dust

While chinchilla owners have been known to house their pets outdoors, your chinchilla's homestead is best kept an indoor establishment. Excess heat, humidity, light, and precipitation can be dangerous to chinchilla health, and only indoors can you properly control the elements that affect a chinchilla's overall health and well-being. Our emphasis, then, will be on this ideal environment—for that should be what pet owners wish to provide for their pets.

When You Get a Chinchilla, You'll Also Have to Get These

Multilevel cage	Exercise toys
Food dish	Play toys
Hay rack	Dust bath
Water bottle	Dust
Nest box	Litter box
Bedding material	Clumping litter
Chewing blocks	Care book

Two-Story Traditional with Master Bedroom

Providing the optimum accommodations for a chinchilla does not mean you must re-create a mountain habitat for your pet. Hardly. But we can take some clues from that existence and modify them for the contemporary human household. Manufacturers have graciously acknowledged this desire and have made available a variety of excellent products.

The chinchilla cage is one such product. Chinchillas are most comfortable in a two-story cage that helps them view the world from different levels and hop like a kangaroo from one floor to the next. While it's not the Andes, a deluxe chinchilla cage provides all the necessary chinchilla accouterments: a dust bathtub with cover (to keep the resident rodent out when bath time is over), a secluded bed/hiding place, a built-in chinchilla exercise wheel and hay rack, and perhaps even a litter box. All of these are positioned in separate areas of the cage. Chinchillas, type-A critters that they are, like to keep their beds and dining areas far from the litter box, and they prefer separate play areas, as well.

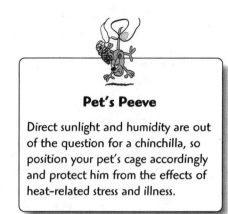

Pet's Peeve

Direct sunlight and humidity are out of the question for a chinchilla, so position your pet's cage accordingly and protect him from the effects of heat-related stress and illness.

Being Creative with Chinchilla Housing

If your pet's cage is missing any of these standard chinchilla components, it is your job to supply them. Every chinchilla deserves access to a cozy bed, complete with clean hay bedding, at all times. As for the bathtub, that can be placed in the cage only at bath time and removed after the bath is over. The safest bathtubs and beds are made of stainless steel or cardboard. Plastic and wood can be shredded by those rodent incisors. Cardboard can be, too, but it won't cause intestinal obstructions.

A similar eye on safety applies to anything within your chinchilla's cage, whether that's toys or the caging material itself. Check the cage periodically, ideally during your weekly heavy cleaning sessions, to make sure there are no exposed or sharp edges on the corners or cage bars. Examine the security of the door lock and its hinges, too, whenever you take your pet out for his daily romp.

Interior Decorating

In addition to the structure of the cage, you must also think about those important little accessories that make a house a home. Bedding, for one. A chinchilla will be most comfortable on a solid floor: It offers superior security when compared with wire flooring. Carpet this floor with several inches of bedding: wood shavings or a shredded paper product made especially for rodents. As for the litter box, a clumping-style litter will be the easiest for removing the urine which is typically the only odor-causing agent in a properly maintained chinchilla cage.

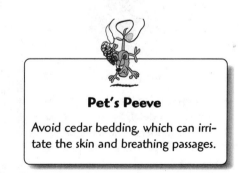

Pet's Peeve

Avoid cedar bedding, which can irritate the skin and breathing passages.

And finally, what about that infamous bathtub dust? You need not make a trek to the Andes to collect volcanic ash from your pet's native homeland. That can be dangerous and quite expensive. Simply fill the tub with commercially available chinchilla dust. This is ideally suited, both in consistency and sanitation, to meet the dust-bath needs of a chinchilla.

If you think you can save a few bucks by filling the tub with dirt from your backyard or sand from your toddler's sandbox, banish that idea from your mind immediately. Such things can be riddled with parasites, and they are not of the proper tornado-producing consistency. They are an affront to the sensibilities of a chinchilla pet and a violation of your contract with this animal. The proper dust is inexpensive, and it can be reused for several weeks, as long as you restrict your pet's access to it between baths.

A Natural Diet

Just as we must consider the chinchilla's homeland when designing his domicile, so must we remember how that environment shaped his digestive tract. Needless to say, a sparse diet of grasses, bark, roots, and berries, does not make for a constitution tolerant of rich foods.

What Does a Chinchilla Eat?

Commercial chinchilla pellets or chow
Alfalfa
Timothy hay
Fresh green vegetables

The contemporary pet chinchilla, a classic vegetarian with simple tastes, is best sustained with a simple diet of high-quality chinchilla pellets or chow (offered twice a day, preferably morning and evening), and a handful of fresh alfalfa or timothy hay served up once each day in the hay rack to provide roughage. You can supplement this with occasional (moderate) helpings now and then of some fresh greens, but just remember that simplest is best. Simplest is most natural. Just keep it fresh and keep it available.

Pampered Pet

In keeping with the chinchilla's fixation on schedules, try to serve breakfast and dinner at the same times every day. You know how chinchillas can get . . .

A chinchilla must also have access to fresh, clean water at all times. No need to duplicate the scarcity of water in the animal's homeland. To do so is to shorten your pet's expected life span. A good old-fashioned water bottle with a sipping tube is the most efficient way to supply your pet's water. Just make sure that, like the feeding dishes, it is cleaned daily, and watch for obstructions in the sipping tube. Abide by these simple guidelines each and every day as part of your normal household routine, and your pet should live to a ripe old age in lustrous splendor.

More Than One?

Chinchillas like to be alone—to a point. They are solitary critters in the wild and prefer to remain so in captivity, as well. Now don't take this personally. We're talking about other chinchillas here. Although they do usually like to know that other chinchillas are about—in the wild it was comforting to know that a chinchilla was hiding behind the rock next to yours—a single chinchilla housed solo in his own bachelor pad is far more content than one in a more communal housing situation. Communal housing can lead to stress-related illness and territory-related aggression, especially among males once sexual maturity kicks in.

Chinchillas can be rather addictive, however, so if you would like more than one, make sure that each has his own private cage, his own private territory. You can place the cages side by side so the two can regale each other with the bleats and purrs of the unique chinchilla language, but keep them separate and keep them content.

The Least You Need to Know

➤ Chinchillas are nocturnal creatures who are most interactive with their owners during the morning and evening hours (and may stay up playing noisily all night).

➤ Native to the mountains of South America, chinchillas are accustomed to a cool, dry environment, and thrive best in temperatures around 68°F.

➤ Chinchillas do not tolerate rough handling, filthy living conditions, unnecessary household noise, or deviations from their daily routines.

➤ A chinchilla is best housed indoors in a two-story cage with a sturdy food dish, a hay rack, a water bottle, a secluded nest/bed, and a bathtub for dust bathing.

Part 4
Fine Feathered Friends

Once upon a time, we thought of birds as ornamental pets that sat in cages, maybe sang or talked a little, and picked at a cup of seed. But times have changed. Today we know that birds need a more varied diet, time out of their cages, and a stimulating environment that addresses their surprisingly high intelligence.

We have long been fascinated with birds, perhaps envying their ability to soar above us and their fantastic array of plumage. But it's only recently that we've learned how to truly care for them in the way they need and deserve.

Here we'll look at two of the most popular avian pets: budgies and cockatiels. Either one will work its way into your heart faster than you can say "tweet."

Chapter 14

Bold Budgies (a.k.a. Parakeets)

> ### In This Chapter
>
> ➤ A day in the life of a budgie
>
> ➤ Getting to know the budgie
>
> ➤ Choosing a budgie, or two or three or four . . .
>
> ➤ Budgie care for beginners

The budgie is a bird of many colors. You may know this bird as the budgerigar or the parakeet, but they are one and the same. The budgie is the world's most popular pet bird, and also one of the most colorful. Within the budgie family, you can find birds of virtually every color in the avian rainbow: yellow, blue, green, turquoise, lavender. Who wouldn't want such vibrantly colored creatures in their homes?

But the budgie is more than merely an object of beauty, which is, as we all know, only feather deep. The budgie, you see, is as beautiful inside as she is outside. This is a small parrot that is sweet, friendly, affectionate, and mellow, and one of the easiest birds to care for, too. In other words, she is an ideal choice of avian companion for the first-time bird owner—an excellent introduction to the complex, and often rather quirky, world of birds.

But before we look at the budgie, let's just settle this name question. The *budgerigar,* as she is known officially, is a bird of two names. One name, and by far the most festive, is *budgie,* a shortened version, of course, of budgerigar. But these delightful little birds are also known to the masses as *parakeets.* Purists will point out, however, that "parakeet" refers to a variety of birds hailing from different regions of the world. The parakeet we are discussing here, and the one that comes to most minds at the mention of the word, is the friendly, colorful little bird from Australia, the budgie.

Budgies As Pets

	light	1	2	3	4	5	heavy
Time commitment				✔			
Grooming				✔			
Feeding				✔			
General cleanup					✔		
Suitable for kids age infant to 5		✔					
Suitable for kids age 5 to 10			✔				
Suitable for kids over 10				✔			
Sociability				✔			
Expense of keeping				✔			

A Day in the Life

A budgie in the wilds of Australia is most likely to spend her days socializing in the trees with great flocks of her kind, swooping down for a meal here and there, preening, gossiping incessantly about the latest budgie affairs, envying the vibrant blue breast of the bird on the neighboring branch, comparing notes on how the chicks are doing—you know the drill. In captivity, she's likely to pursue her own version of exactly the same activities.

But while a pet budgie may follow a similar path, she is still a pet budgie. You should do your best to help her satisfy those wild longings as best you can within a domestic environment. If you do, a pet budgie can thrive beautifully in virtually in house, apartment, or condominium. For a better understanding of how you transform your home into a reasonable facsimile of Australia, we'll follow for a day a sprightly, well-adjusted yellow budgie named Katie.

Pet Talk

Budgerigar was reportedly translated from a phrase in the Australian Aboriginal tongue that means "good to eat."

Morning

Katie is a single budgie. She has no flock, so, as happens with birds, she has bonded deeply with her human caretakers. She's quite an attractive bird, but that is of no concern to Katie. You see, Katie is on a mission. Her job, which she takes very seriously, is to initiate her owners—first-time bird owners—into the grand scheme of responsible bird care.

How busy they keep her, morning, noon, and night. Yesterday morning they suffered from some sort of temporary insanity and failed to notice that although her seed dish looked full, it was actually filled with empty seed hulls and she had nothing to eat. Katie set them straight. They won't be making that mistake again, if they value their eardrums.

Secrets from the Pet Files

Birds are popular pets—and are becoming more so every day—but the budgie's popularity is downright phenomenal. Almost half of the pet birds in the United States are budgies, and those figures are mirrored in other countries throughout the world. What can we learn from this? The budgie's beauty and personality cross all cultural boundaries.

Hoping for a fresh start today where they can do their bird proud, Katie's owners remove the sheet cover from her cage (it's so much easier to sleep when she's sheltered). They also removed the soiled paper from the bottom of her cage, and put in a fresh sheet. Katie greets the sun and her family with a song, just as she would in the wild. She hops from perch to perch inside her cage in a charming dance that is part of her morning ritual, and bounces over to feast on seeds and fresh veggies.

Noon

At midday, a solo budgie might be lonely having spent a day without the company of other budgies. But not this bird. In keeping with the routine upon which every budgie thrives, Katie knows that now is playgym time.

Pet Talk

A *playgym* is a miniature playground for birds, furnished with toys and games for special out-of-the-cage fun.

Katie climbs the playgym ladder, takes a swing on the swing, and jingles a few bells with her beak, always looking to her owners to make sure they are watching to see how brilliant and adorable she is. This always occurs, mind you, in a safe, budgie-proofed room with closed doors and windows and covered mirrors. We don't want an escaped or injured budgie, do we? Katie's owners may be absent-minded at times, but they never fail to protect their pet's safety this way.

After playtime today, Katie receives a special surprise: a shower. How she loves this! She perches on her owner's hand and revels in the warm mist from a spray bottle. She's never been to the native homeland of the budgerigar, but this experience takes her back to those wild genetic memories that all budgies share of basking in the drops of a surprise downpour in the Outback.

And Nighttime, Too

Sometimes in the evening, Katie's owners conduct voice lessons. They repeat phrases over and over again, hoping Katie will follow suit. She never has. It's not that she can't talk; she simply chooses not to. No problem. Her owners did not choose Katie with the idea of immortalizing themselves in the record books for some kind of budgie vocabulary record.

While Katie is free to choose just how and when to vocalize, she has no such choices where her safety is concerned. Tonight it is time for wing and nail clipping. She used to visit the veterinarian for these procedures, but her owners took the time to learn from the doctor the proper way to clip Katie's flight feathers (and thus prevent a flight-related household tragedy) and her toenails (to prevent tearing and foot injuries).

Shortly thereafter, it's time for bed—again, all part of the routine. Katie is pleased to return to her clean, comfortable cage. She cocks her head as the cage cover sheet is draped over the bars, and she drifts off to sleep on her favorite perch, as safe and secure as any bird deserves to be.

Budgie Social Studies

Imagine you are stranded in the Outback of Australia, surrounded by nothing but barren land and scrubby vegetation. Then, suddenly, on the horizon you spot a tree.

From that tree emanates the most lovely music you have ever heard. And on its branches are ribbons of color: green, yellow, and blue. An oasis? No, budgies.

Budgies are native Australians that embody in bird form the charm, simplicity, and rugged spirit of their homeland. Though they have been favored additions to a more domestic existence for centuries now, they still retain that wild spirit. The budgie's two worlds collided in the mid-1800s, when European naturalists and traders on a southern route began to discover this best-kept secret of England's notorious penal colony continent at the bottom of the earth. Those budgie charms could not be kept secret for long, however, and soon all of Europe, and eventually America, was keeping and breeding budgies.

Pet Talk

There are *American budgies* and *English budgies*. American budgies are typically smaller and a bit more high-strung than their counterparts in England, where the breeding of budgies has been a veritable religion since the mid–19th century.

Destined for Pethood

As time passed, those original wild budgie greens, yellows, and blues would blossom into a rainbow of colors, always complemented by the signature stripes that presumably served as camouflage for those wild outback birds. The budgie's ever-growing legions of fans soon discovered that although this bird could nicely accent a room's decor, so could she also brighten the spirits of the people with whom she lived. Such discoveries only continued to fuel the passions of allegiance that the budgie has so long enjoyed. As addictive as budgies can be, many a keeper past and present has felt compelled to re-create the bird's tradition of living in large wild flocks by establishing their own wild flocks in captivity.

There is no shortage of budgies available as pets these days. That's a good thing, because wild budgies may no longer be taken from their native home—also a good thing. However, there is often a shortage of know-how among fledgling owners on the proper care of these popular pets. Far too many people still consider them merely part of the furniture, without need of much attention or anything to eat other than seeds. As we know today, behaviorally, nutritionally, and morally, this is entirely the wrong outlook. Those who first pioneered keeping budgies as pets had a good excuse for not giving their birds what they needed: They didn't know any better. Today, we do.

A Little Human in a Bird Costume?

Many an animal expert has chastised those who would anthropomorphize their birds— that is, endow these winged creatures with human qualities. But it's easy to do with such an intelligent animal that wants nothing more than to interact with you. After talking to a flock of bird owners, you are likely to come away thinking birds must be part human—or humans must be part bird.

Secrets from the Pet Files

As birds continue to grow in popularity, so does the availability of proper avian veterinary care. This is a highly specialized field of veterinary medicine, and as a budgie owner you must commit to finding such a specialist. Not just any vet will do.

And budgies, well they are just ripe for human comparisons. They insinuate them-selves into our lives and demand our attention. Budgie busybodies, ever hungry for social interaction, crave company. Their natural instincts tell them that the best com-pany is another budgie, but their hearts tell them that in the absence of fellow budgies, that awkward stork-like creature that fills the food dishes each day will do just fine.

In case you hadn't guessed, *you* are the stork-like creature. So be prepared. Before you dive into budgie keeping, remember that birds can be messy (although a seven-inch budgie should be less so than a two-foot cockatoo), birds can be noisy (although the budgie's sweet voice is far less shattering than the voices of her larger cousins), and birds can really demand your attention. Of course, the fact that they want you in their lives is the very reason you're considering a bird as a pet, right?

Preventing Budgie Boredom

You should also be aware that birds are smart, I mean *really* smart. Researchers believe the smartest birds, such as African Grey parrots, are about as smart as dolphins and chimpanzees. While your budgie won't be quite that sharp, she will prove to be smarter than you think. And that means you need to give her things to do and toys to play with, to prevent her from growing chronically, dangerously bored.

Given the budgie's long history coexisting most willingly with humans, we have a pro-found heritage to uphold when we invite one of these lovely creatures into our homes. If you're not up to the challenge of providing your pet with both the proper care, mental stimulation, and lots of attention, then perhaps you should look elsewhere.

The budgie is the ambassador of the pet bird world. First-time bird owners most often begin with budgies, and they prove to be delightful companions and hardy, easy-care pets. Before they know what has hit them, those first-timers are inspired to try larger, more complex birds, and the rest is avian history. In fact, the more you learn about birds in general and budgies in particular, the more you come to understand that our species' desire to live with these fascinating creatures transcends our simple envy of their ability to fly.

In return for the budgie's enrichment of our lives, we must offer her an understanding of what she requires, and a commitment to providing that. In short, we owe her a daily routine, fresh food and water, a collection of safe and exciting toys, and full-fledged family status.

Secrets from the Pet Files

Latchkey budgies need attention, too. While budgies, even single ones, left home alone all day can fare just fine with a dependable schedule and owner attention, it may be easier for them with some background noise. Try leaving the radio or television on during the day (not too loud, of course) to provide that comforting din, and see how your pet likes it. If your bird's a talker, perhaps she'll help keep you up to date on the daily soaps or the breaking news each evening when you return home.

Choosing a Healthy, Perky Pet

Let's get this out of the way right now: Go ahead and think about what color budgie you would like, but don't allow that to be the sole factor in your choice of a bird that could be living with you for 15 years or longer. That is akin to buying a puppy because of his adorable appearance with no thought to his personality or health. Choices based on appearances alone do not make for a healthy pet-owner bond. A variety of factors contribute to this complex relationship, and most are far more important than the color of a bird's feathers.

When You Least Expect It

You don't need to go to Australia to find your new pet. There are plenty of budgies to choose from here in the United States. Once you begin your search, you'll spy them everywhere—perhaps even in the tree outside your window.

Pet's Peeve

Unfortunately, most escaped budgie stories do not end happily. Many die at the hands of predators, or from cold or starvation. Protect your little pal!

You may know someone who found his or her budgie this way. It's a common story. The bird is a refugee from an apparently nurturing if not sufficiently attentive home, where a window or door was left open. Once is all it takes. Flying free (Oops! Forgot to clip those wings, too!), the bird soon finds herself lost and takes up with a new family that she has chosen for herself. Meanwhile, you're out minding your own business, not thinking about birds at all. The budgie swoops down, showers everyone with her charm and charisma, and that's it. The family is hooked. The bird has a new home.

The More Conventional Approach

We must also include the pet shop as a source of budgies. While the pet shop—the clean, properly run pet shop, of course—can be an excellent source for those who do plan ahead, it may also serve to attract those who never planned to get a bird when they went out to buy some dog food. But while they were in the shop browsing through the bird section of the store, they just couldn't resist the dazzling color, the sweet tweet, and the economical price tag that greeted them as they walked by the budgie display.

Much worse are the large department stores that sell birds as part of a limited pet section. In that scenario, you go out to buy underwear and come back with a bird. Please, don't buy your budgie on a whim. Think about it carefully, plan what you'll need, and then look for the healthiest, best-socialized bird you can find.

Another option for locating a healthy budgie pet is the budgie breeder. Both aristocrats and those of less than blue blood have been breeding budgies for centuries. And they still do. Just visit a local bird show, and you'll be amazed at the number of breeders represented and the variegated beauty of their birds.

The bird show is an excellent place not only to learn all about budgie keeping from the experts, but also to find a lovely new pet. Although you will no doubt be inspired by the happenings at the show, resist the impulse to purchase a bird from a breeder who seems more interested in money than in ensuring that his or her birds go to proper homes, or someone who is willing to sell a young bird that is less than six weeks of age. Resist the impulse, too, to come home with an entire flock.

Secrets from the Pet Files

We've all seen the photos of a bird sitting on a dog's nose and the cat pawing at the bird cage. In these adorable portraits, the bird always looks stoic. But it's a defense mechanism to hide her panic. Putting a bird near a natural predator is cruel and unusual punishment. Such interactions are dangerous for the bird, and can create potentially fatal stress. Is it worth it?

One, Two, or More?

This brings us to an important question: How many budgies should you buy? Yes, budgies are social butterflies who enjoy other budgies, but what does this mean for you? Assuming you have the room, the time, and the resources, there are benefits to keeping a pair or more of budgies.

A flock of budgies can coexist contentedly as long as you provide them with ample space and food, and understand that they can get territorial with newcomers. If you are purchasing, say, a pair that has already shared a cage, this really shouldn't be a problem. But when adding a new bird to an existing cage, it's best to gradually help the birds get acquainted by placing them in separate cages that may stand side by side for a while. Perhaps eventually they will be able to share the same cage. Perhaps not. Perhaps they will remain in separate housing but agree to play together outside of the cage, where territory is not such a hot issue. Perhaps not. Regardless of the multi-bird management style you adopt, a multi-bird household provides the natural avian company that budgies crave—and hours of entertainment to their observant owners.

However, many owners have found that birds within multi-budgie households tend not to bond as deeply to their human handlers. Why? Well, it's obvious, isn't it? If a budgie has a bird flock, she doesn't need a human flock. However, without her own kind, the budgie must choose a substitute. The beauty of budgies, and a reason they have become such immensely popular birds, is the seamless ease with which they are able to transfer this loyalty. Wings or no wings, cere or no cere, everyone is family to the budgie.

Pampered Pet

Before you begin the get-acquainted phase, a new bird should be in quarantine in another room for a few weeks to make sure it is not bringing home any parasites or diseases.

Evaluating the Flock

When it comes time to choose your new pet, look for the healthiest, most robust budgie you can find. This means a bird with a clean cere—a vital indicator of respiratory health. Look, too, for healthy, even feathering that indicates the bird has not been picking at her feathers; clear eyes; a plump, expansive chest area; and a fabulous attitude.

Budgies are meant to be gregarious, fun-loving, and curious. You should be able to tell right away which of the birds that you are evaluating fit this

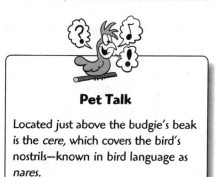

Pet Talk

Located just above the budgie's beak is the *cere,* which covers the bird's nostrils—known in bird language as *nares.*

mold. You'll see it in how they treat each other and in how they treat you. They aren't shy about it, and you should not be shy about setting a sound foundation in your budgie-owning experience by choosing your new pet with common sense and an eye toward health and personality.

Life in the Bird Cage

There is no way for us to understand just what it must be like to live in a bird cage, but we do know that a pet budgie can enjoy this rather artificial environment as long as it is properly furnished and cleaned. And as long as the bird is offered ample time outside the cage for fun and interaction. Perching in a cage 24 hours a day, 365 days a year is no life for a creature born and bred to soar toward the heavens, so you must do your best to make your budgie's more earthbound existence enjoyable.

Bird keeping will vary from one budgie household to the next, primarily because some will house one budgie and some will house several. As you have seen, birds in either situation can thrive. While the basic tenets of care apply regardless of how many birds occupy the cage, it is the single-bird accommodation we will concentrate on here.

Pampered Pet

When choosing a cage for your budgie, steer clear of "guillotine-style" doors that can slam down on a bird. If you *must* buy such a cage, always keep a clip handy to clip it open securely.

Avoiding the Gilded Cage

Safe, roomy, and clean. This is your budgie's heart's desire as far as her cage is concerned. It's not too much to ask for, and it's the least you can do to supply it. Once you begin looking for your bird's cage—which, for obvious reasons, is best done before your new pet joins the family—your head will spin at the countless possibilities.

To get through the maze of choices, think like a bird. If you were a budgie, what would you like in a cage? Sure, you'll most likely be flightless because of wing clipping, but even a clipped bird can fly some and would like a cage that offers an opportunity to spread her wings a bit.

A cage with both vertical and horizontal cage bars might be fun for climbing—especially if the bars are close enough together to prevent trapped feet or heads. And finally, there simply must be ample space for toys and a variety of perches at varying heights. If another budgie will be sharing your domicile, then everything goes double.

Choose a cage with a removable tray on the bottom for easy cleaning. Cover this with clean newspaper *every day* to catch food spills and budgie droppings, but don't expect the tray to catch all of it. The surrounding floor will certainly catch its fair share. Acrylic cage bars will make for easier cleaning.

What Does a Budgie Cost?

The purchase price of a budgie can vary widely, but the average is $53.90.

The average pet bird owner also spends per year:

$68	Bird food
$36	Other supplies
$26	Toys

The Importance of Perches

Imagine having to stand barefoot on the same hard substance all day, every day, and you'll understand why good perches are so important. Most cages come with a perch or two, but they aren't always the right diameter for your budgie. The tips of your bird's toenails should go about two thirds of the way around a perch. If the front and back toenails touch or almost meet, the perch is too thin, and your bird will have trouble standing up straight.

A budgie is happiest if she has a choice of three or four perches in her cage. Situated at various levels to provide the resident bird with various perspectives on the world beyond the cage bars, these perches should also vary in diameter to help exercise the bird's feet and prevent cramping.

Pet's Peeve

Just say no to sandpaper-covered perches. They are marketed as do-it-yourself avian nail files, but they only serve to give a poor bird sore feet.

When You Get a Budgie, You'll Also Have to Get These

Cage	Toys
Food dishes	Playgym
Water dishes	Nail trimmer
Perches	Sharp barber's scissors (for wing trimming)
Cage cover	Care and training book
Bird bath or spray bottle for misting	

The Best Spot

The cage should be located in a corner of the house that is safe from the heaviest household traffic, drafts, and direct sunlight, but not so remote as to undermine the natural budgie sense of family.

The kitchen is definitely not a good idea for your pet. Elements that we can't smell at all can kill a bird, which is dangerously susceptible to fumes and poisons. This is no comment on your cooking abilities. It's just that birds can be poisoned by the fumes released when nonstick cookware overheats. If the kitchen is the heart of your home, and it's where your budgie would be happiest, get rid of the nonstick pots and pans.

Honoring the Budgie's Love of a Clean House

Your job is to remove any uneaten food from the cage several times a day, change the paper daily, and scrub the entire cage, including all the toys, perches, and dishes, each week. The daily cleaning chores will permit you to examine your pet's droppings.

What fun! Budgies are quite prolific with the droppings. As time passes, you will become very familiar with those droppings, which should be white with a green border. This familiarity will help you notice changes that could indicate health problems.

Pet's Peeve

Never clean cages and cage furnishings with strong, toxic chemicals. Always keep your bird at the other side of the house when you are doing your own housecleaning.

As for the weekly scrubfests, check for sharp edges or broken hardware in the cage that may have emerged either spontaneously or thanks to the diligent beak work of the resident budgie. You should also evaluate the condition of the various perches that you have so kindly supplied to your pet—only to find that she prefers to use them as chew toys. Your inspection may indicate that some replacements are in order.

The Balanced Budgie Diet

Once upon a time, budgie keepers assumed that budgies required seed, and only seed. They learned the hard way, at the expense of many budgie lives, that this is not the case at all. The budgie's diet is actually very much like our own. The bird requires grains and seed, fruits and vegetables, proteins, and a never-ending supply of fresh, clean water. Simple.

What Does a Budgie Eat?

Commercial budgie pellets

Seeds

Fresh fruit

Fresh green and orange vegetables

Cooked pasta

Cooked rice

Whole-wheat bread

Cooked beans

Cooked meat or tuna (sparingly!)

Millet (sparingly!)

Each day the budgie should receive a serving of fresh seeds or pellets, most easily and dependably offered in a commercial mixture available at pet supply stores. Supplement this with a daily ration of fresh vegetables and fruits, preferably those that are either dark green or orange—and chopped up small enough so your budgie can hold each piece easily in her claw.

Budgies can also enjoy cooked pasta or rice, whole-wheat bread, and cooked beans. Some may occasionally enjoy small bites of cooked tuna or other well-cooked meats, but the key word here is "small." Just use your common sense. Forbid junk foods or processed food of any kind, and you'll soon discover that your bird is setting quite a good example for you concerning what you should and shouldn't eat.

Because of the variety inherent in this diet, serve the food in two clean food dishes. If possible, feed your pet fresh rations twice a day. Your bird will appreciate the freshness, and you will appreciate the health benefits to your pet and perhaps an easier cleanup. Keep the water fresh and clean, too, as it is probably the most important component of the overall diet.

The budgie (whose name rhymes with pudgy) is highly susceptible to obesity. Too many seeds and not enough exercise will make your pet budgie a pudgy bird. This, in turn, can lead to illness and overall discomfort, something no pet deserves. So feed your bird with common sense, and treat her regularly to activity both in and out of the cage.

Pampered Pet

A *millet spray* is a cluster of round millet grains that you can hang from the top of your budgie's cage. It is a beloved chewy toy, but it can be quite rich, so offer it only on special occasions.

The Least You Need to Know

➤ Budgies are beautiful, social, easy-care birds that enjoy the company of other budgies and are considered ideal choices for first-time bird owners.

➤ To prevent accidents and escapes, have the budgie's wings clipped regularly— and remember that even a budgie with clipped wings can fly.

➤ When seeking a pet budgie from a breeder or pet shop, look for a bird with uniform feathering, clear eyes and cere (nose area), clean droppings, and a pleasant disposition.

➤ The budgie requires a clean, roomy cage; a variety of perches in a variety of sizes and widths; a stimulating selection of toys; and a diet that combines traditional seed and grain with fresh fruits, vegetables and, proteins.

Chapter 15

Cocky Cockatiels

> ## In This Chapter
>
> ➤ A day in the life of a cockatiel
>
> ➤ Understanding the cockatiel and his world
>
> ➤ A guide to choosing a healthy cockatiel pet
>
> ➤ Cockatiel care made easy

When the cockatiel first came to the pet world's attention, it was a simple gray bird with a yellow head and crest, and orange cheeks. Pretty, but not much variety. It was the cockatiel's personality that brought him early admirers. These are smart, active, affectionate pets. They offer all the charm of their larger cockatoo cousins without the noise, biting, and other problems that often accompany the larger birds.

And then bird breeders discovered something remarkable about the little cockatiel. Its genes are easily manipulated through selective breeding to produce an array of color mutations reminiscent of something you might find in the French Impressionist wing of an art museum. The cockatiel today claims second place behind its fellow Australian, the budgie, in popularity.

Cockatiels As Pets

	light	1	2	3	4	5	heavy
Time commitment					✔		
Grooming				✔			
Feeding				✔			
General cleanup					✔		
Suitable for kids age infant to 5		✔					
Suitable for kids age 5 to 10			✔				
Suitable for kids over 10				✔			
Sociability					✔		
Expense of keeping				✔			

A Day in the Life

Every day the cockatiel wins new fans from two different camps: those who love birds and are driven to invite them into their homes, and those who never imagined living with a bird but find themselves blindsided and forever enchanted by the cockatiel's charm. Don't think you want a bird? The cockatiel can change all that. That's how it happened with Sydney. Let's step into his world for a moment and see just how he and his kind manage to pull this off.

Morning Pleasantries

Your household needs no alarm clock. You have Sydney. Every morning Sydney awakens and greets the day like a refugee from a Disney cartoon—think of all Seven Dwarfs whistling off to work. Sydney's cage is covered by a sheet when he goes off to sleep, but he still emerges with the light. He then begins his lilting homage to the sun: a series of whistles, foot drums, and feather fluffs. Even on weekends. Even when you want to sleep in. Sydney doesn't know the difference. Why would anyone wish to sleep the morning away?

Sometimes you feel like you're living with Shirley Temple. You were out until two the night before. Now it's 6 a.m. and there's Sidney. Stumble out to the family room, his concert hall, pull off the sheet, and there he is, whistling away. You could swear he's smiling at you. Look at those little apple cheeks. He throws you his most endearing oh-aren't-I-so-adorable-and-isn't-this-the-most-wonderful-morning look. Next thing you know, you're smiling. Then laughing. Then feeding him breakfast. Then watching

Saturday morning cartoons with him on your shoulder. Resistance is futile. It has been since the moment you spotted him at the pet shop.

Afternoon Delight

Like all self-respecting cockatiels, Sydney spends the day nibbling on his food: fresh seeds and veggies, perhaps a bit of cooked pasta. When not lounging in his cage munching and whistling, you have him out in a cockatiel-proofed room (no open doors, no open windows, no open water, no mirrors to fly into). Whenever you bend over to clean up some run-away seed hulls from the floor beneath his cage, you again can't quite believe you have a bird as a pet. But you also can't quite imagine life without Sydney.

You both look forward to the daily playgym session, typically reserved for the afternoon. Sydney never ceases to amaze you with his acrobatic skills on the ladder and the swing. Before you put him back into his cage, you take a few moments to change the newspaper at the bottom (in addition to being athletically talented, Sydney is quite a prolific little fellow with the droppings). You take a quick gander at the droppings to make sure there are no dramatic changes in consistency or color. Then you clean the food and water dishes and refill them with fresh rations.

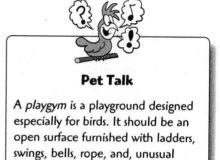

Pet Talk

A *playgym* is a playground designed especially for birds. It should be an open surface furnished with ladders, swings, bells, rope, and, unusual perches.

A Quiet Evening at Home

You eat dinner. Sydney eats dinner. Always eating—that's a cockatiel for you. When not eating or playing, he's chewing. You're careful that he has safe toys to chew on. Otherwise it could be your new, very expensive, reportedly quite rare Bruno Magli shoes or a live electrical cord upon which he chooses to exercise his beak.

At about 9:30 Sydney finally slows down. He sits quietly perched on your lap for about half an hour while you channel surf with the remote, the fleeting images on the television mesmerizing him after a long, busy day. By 10-ish, Sydney's internal time clock tells him it is time to retire. Like almost all cockatiels, he is devoted to his daily routine. He rearranges his wings. He reaches back to scratch an itch on his wing with his beak. You carry him to the cage and tuck him in. Then you turn in your-self—6 a.m. comes around quickly.

Pampered Pet

Do your bird a favor and take him only to a veterinarian who specializes in avian care. You wouldn't go to a dermatologist for brain surgery, would you?

Living with a Cockatiel

When first you bring a new pet into your home, you are filled with hope and excitement. This can fade after awhile, but usually your infatuation is replaced by genuine devotion and respect. To ensure that is what happens, make sure your expectations are realistic.

Expecting your cockatiel to make you rich and famous with his talking abilities is not realistic. Some cockatiels are avid talkers, but some learn just a word or two. And many never talk at all. Expecting your cockatiel to do your organic chemistry homework or program your computer is also not realistic. (Cockatiels are smart, but come on!)

What you can expect is the delightful company of a lovely, affectionate, beautiful bird that with proper care can be family to you for anywhere from 15 to 20 years. You can expect him to reach a maximum length of about 12 inches, more or less. You can expect your pet to thrive best with a daily routine, and to enjoy the meal portions of that routine immensely (even too immensely, if you allow him). You can expect him to be very affectionate toward you and very demanding of your attentions. That last part is the most realistic of all.

Secrets from the Pet Files

No one knows why, but for some reason cockatiels are prone to a condition called night thrashing—an avian version of a bad dream. Perhaps it's those memories of being chased by dingoes or crocodiles across the Outback. The bird awakens and begins thrashing about his cage. To help prevent accident or injury, just do what you would do for a child suffering from a similar condition: Install a night-light near your pet's cage.

Out of Australia

Come and journey back with us to Australia. You hear a deafening chatter from the trees. Cockatiels? Nope, budgies. Cockatiels don't hang out in the trees in large flocks like that. As you're looking up at the small, colorful birds, watch your step. That's where the cockatiels might be, exploring the grasslands for food.

Before he made the fateful journey to the Hawaiian Islands that would mark the end of his travels, not to mention his life, Captain James Cook must have stumbled upon that vision of wild cockatiels when he visited Australia in the late 1800s. His journey is considered the beginning of the cockatiel public-relations tour. England soon knew about the exotic gray birds with the sweet, earthy dispositions. America soon knew, too.

The cockatiel was initially considered less than spectacular when standing alongside some of the more brilliantly feathered members of the bird family. This bird, however, could not be ignored. The cockatiel won, as does each and every person, including the first-time bird owner, who chooses a cockatiel for a companion.

Cockatiel Family Values

We hear a lot these days about family values, but it appears that many who talk about the subject could learn a thing or two from the cockatiel. With this bird, you will find yourself committed to a level of gender equality unmatched by most species, with the exception of the seahorse (the male seahorse gestates the eggs of his young). Unlike many birds, the male cockatiel as well as the female incubates the eggs, and both help care for the young after they have hatched. What a modern outlook!

Pampered Pet

Make sure that when the bird is outside of his cage, doors and windows in the room remain closed at all times. Check, double-check, and check again.

Secrets from the Pet Files

Reminiscent of scenes from *The Exorcist*, cockatiels are rather flexible in the neck. As a protective measure developed to help them keep on the lookout for predators, they can swivel their heads around 180 degrees and look straight behind them. So don't ever assume you'll be able to sneak up on this bird.

But the family values of the cockatiel run even deeper. In addition to the devotion he shows his feathered family, he regards humans as family, too. It's really quite amazing, when you think about it. There are few animals on the planet more different from us than the birds. Yet, by some miracle, we are able to bond. Think about it too much, and you might start thinking there's something supernatural going on here. Maybe there is. Only the cockatiel knows for sure.

The Cockatiel As Companion Animal

Treated with respect, the cockatiel will delight in the company of all family members, young and old, broadcasting his contentment with hums, whistles, and if you are truly worthy, preening of your hair or ear. A cockatiel who preens you is telling you that you are almost a cockatiel. And there is no higher honor.

It should be pretty obvious by now that the cockatiel makes a wonderful pet. He is an easy-keeper and an appropriate choice for both newcomers to and veterans of the bird world. But those from either realm of experience need apply only if they will commit to satisfying this bird's insatiable quest for fun and companionship.

That companionship can include children who have been instructed how to handle a bird, and who are supervised when the cockatiel is out of his cage. Even children who may be frightened by the massive beaks and talons of larger birds can learn to feel comfortable around a cockatiel.

That companionship cannot include other pets. Do not purchase a cockatiel in some misguided attempt to provide a companion to your dog and cat. Yes, these species can coexist, but allowing them to do so up close and personal is to invite disaster. Separate lodgings, separate time out and about in the house: That's the safest way to go. You're talking predator and prey here. Respect the age-old differences that have governed the earth—and the food chain—for millions of years.

Cockatiel Training for Fun and Manners

You are a predator, too, of course, but you are able to transform the predator-prey relationship into one of trust and respect. As your bond, and the trust that holds it together, builds, you will discover that your cockatiel will look to you for guidance, and even for some training.

The methods used to train a cockatiel don't differ all that much from those used to train a dog. You need not teach your bird tricks (although he certainly can learn them), but you will need to teach him a few simple commands so that you can easily get him in and out of his cage. You'll also need to teach him what is acceptable (climbing from your shoulder to your head) and what is not (biting your ear, even in play). Your method? Positive reinforcement. Your tools? Treats, head and neck scratches, and words of praise. Be patient, calm, and consistent, and show your beloved pet that he has every reason to go along with the game.

Secrets from the Pet Files

Cockatiels know they are beautiful, and enjoy posing in front of mirrors and windows. You can hang a small, shatterproof mirror inside his cage, but he may end up falling in love with himself and never quite loving you.

Choosing the Healthiest Cockatiel Pet

Before you run out and start looking for a cockatiel to share and maybe even rule your roost, stop for a moment and think. Yes, cockatiels are beautiful with their crest, long tail, and apple cheeks. But don't choose a cockatiel, or any pet, because you're into some 1970s retro thing and the stripes on the bird's wings remind you of a pair of old bellbottoms you had back in college. A bird is not—definitely not—an ornamental pet.

But you already know that, right? You are enchanted because of the cockatiel's personality. Even that, though, can prove a novelty that eventually wears thin. Be worthy of this oh-so-trusting bird. Commit for the long haul. There is no halfway. Now you may go forth and find your pet.

Pet Talk

Know your bird's body parts. That lovely growth of feathers on the top of his head is the *crest*. The region above his beak that resembles a button is the *cere,* and the two holes it covers and protects are the cockatiel's nostrils, or *nares*. And those long, lovely tail feathers? Sure you can call those the tail feathers, but you will be far more impressive if you refer to them as the *retices*.

Where to Shop?

Cockatiels, being the world's second most popular pet birds, are easy to find. The pet shop, of course, is the most accessible source for most people, but avoid shops that don't seem clean, that overcrowd the birds, or where staff members don't seem to know the first thing about birds and couldn't care less what type of home their birds fly off to.

Pampered Pet

Clipping your bird's wings regularly (don't worry; it doesn't hurt the bird) will keep him from flying into walls and windows. This procedure is best taught by your bird's avian veterinarian.

If more personalized attention is what you seek, there are alternatives to the pet shop. How about a specialized pet shop that sell birds and only birds? Call this paradise for bird lovers. Typically staffed by knowledgeable bird people, such a shop can be an excellent source of well-bred pets, as well as vital information. This is also a good place to get referrals to local avian veterinarians and experienced pet-sitters.

Personalized attention is also available from breeders, especially breeders who offer hand-fed, hand-raised birds. You'll find lots of breeders at bird shows. At these fascinating events, you will see every color and every pattern of the cockatiel rainbow, and no doubt find yourself eternally inspired. But don't allow the dazzling spectacle of it all to cloud that common-sense judgment that simply must accompany your choice of a pet.

Smart Choices, Healthy Birds

Choosing a place to buy your new pet is one thing. Choosing the actual bird is quite another. With the cockatiel, a typically healthy branch of the bird family, this shouldn't be too difficult. A bird that is tame and adjusted to the presence of humans is your best bet (and not too much of a stretch for most cockatiels). Then call upon that common sense we keep harping about, and look for these all-important signs of health:

➤ Bright eyes

➤ A clean cere

➤ Easy, trouble-free breathing

➤ Healthy feet

➤ Efficient beak action in both eating and preening

➤ Smooth feathering

The Secret Language of the Cockatiel Crest

When evaluating a potential pet cockatiel, look to the crest. That lovely tuft on the top of his head is not only decorative but also a barometer of the bird's mood. The crest position, and the bird's mood, will change throughout the day, but it can also offer you some valuable messages about the bird's overall disposition.

Consider the bird's first response to your approach. Is his crest straight up at attention like a soldier's salute? This bird wants to play. Drooped casually behind the bird's head? He is contented, relaxed, and pleased to meet you. If, however, you approach the bird and he turns into a snarling lion, the crest flattened against his back and neck and an otherworldly type of hiss coming from his throat, this is not a happy cockatiel. Don't take him home, thinking he'll feel better later. With this type of behavior, first impressions do count.

Pet's Peeve

Never allow a bird to roam freely through the house—even a bird with clipped wings. Dangers can lurk anywhere, and a curious creature like the cockatiel will inevitably find them.

Words of Warning

While your heart may be soft where animals are concerned, you must harden it up a bit when choosing a new cockatiel pet. A sick, frightened, or timid cockatiel may pull on your heartstrings, but that is simply a tragedy waiting to happen. Beware the classic signs of bird illness: a chronically fluffed-up appearance, raspy breathing, a crusty cere, a lack of interest in food, lethargy, and listlessness. Be wary, too, of a healthy bird amid a flock of others who don't share his robust appearance. Avian diseases can be quite contagious. Your healthy bird today could be ill tomorrow.

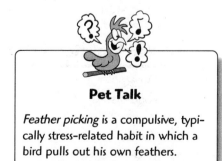

Pet Talk

Feather picking is a compulsive, typically stress-related habit in which a bird pulls out his own feathers.

A bald cockatiel, too, can mean trouble. If the bird is molting (shedding old feathers to make room for new plumage), that is one thing, but if you notice bald patches caused by feather picking, perhaps you had better look elsewhere. Many a bird, being a sensitive creature, may do this temporarily in response to a momentary stress or change in the household, but the condition can become chronic and terribly frustrating.

At Home with a Cockatiel

While cockatiels do enjoy their time at liberty out of the cage, they still need a home of their own within the larger domicile. This is the classic bird cage. While it may seem cruel to confine a creature meant to fly, with proper care and attention that cage can be a place of security and serenity for your bird. It's in your power to make it so.

The cockatiel's cage must be:

➤ Spacious

➤ Properly furnished

➤ Positioned out of direct sunlight, drafts, and heavy household traffic

➤ Clean

➤ Safe

➤ Secure

Start by buying the largest cage possible for your pet—wide enough to allow some rudimentary flight (even a bird with clipped wings can flap those wings and get moving a bit) and full wing stretching. It should also be tall enough to accommodate that high crest at full erect position and that long, lovely tail. So popular are cockatiels, you will even find cages designed especially for them.

In fact, the manufacture of birdcages has become big business. Today there are cages available in all sizes, shapes, and colors for birds of all sizes, shapes, and colors. From traditional wire to white acrylic, from floor-to-ceiling aviaries for an entire flock to spacious cages designed especially to preserve the crest and tail of a cockatiel. If you are truly ambitious—and have some disposable income to play with—you might even look into the cage setups that double as fine furniture. No bird-lover's living room is complete without a finely sculpted armoire that houses not your wardrobe, but your beloved avian pet.

When You Get a Cockatiel, You'll Also Have to Get These

Cage	Toys
Food dishes	Playgym
Water dishes	Nail trimmer
Perches	Sharp barber's scissors (for wing trimming)
Cage cover	Care and training book
Bird bath or spray bottle for misting	

Making the Cage Safe, Secure, and Fun

Mechanically, the cage door of the cockatiel's cage should not be of a dangerous guillotine style (just consider the name and you'll figure out why). It should offer a slide-out tray on the floor to allow for frequent changing of the flooring newspaper, which will quickly be littered with droppings, seed hulls, and food scraps. The cage bars—which should be close enough together to prevent trapping tiny cockatiel heads, but not so close that they trap even tinier cockatiel toes—are typically of acrylic or wire. Many find acrylic the easiest to clean. Regardless of the medium, those bars should remain free of sharp edges. Run your hand over all cage surfaces periodically to make sure nothing has come loose.

You should outfit the cage with a variety of perches at various levels, each of a different diameter to exercise the bird's feet and keep life interesting. Imagine having to stand barefoot on the same hard substance all day, every day, and you'll understand why good perches are important. Most cages come with a perch or two, but they aren't always the right diameter for your cockatiel. The tips of your bird's toenails should go about two thirds of the way around a perch. If the front and back toenails touch or almost meet, the perch is too thin, and your bird will have trouble standing up straight.

Toys, too, are vital components to achieving this goal. Keep them safe, keep them colorful, and keep them rotating. Just as you might do with your own child, periodically rotating the toys will thrill the resident bird to no end. Each time you reintroduce a favorite, the bird believes he is discovering the toy for the first time.

Pampered Pet

Newspaper is considered the safest medium for the cage bottom. Don't even think about sandpaper or anything else with a rough texture!

You should also consider a bird bath, although it need not fit in the cage. Cockatiels do love a bath—or a shower—and it stimulates preening, which helps keep their feathers healthy. A bathtub can simply be a shallow dish of lukewarm water in which the bird can splash around. For the bird that prefers a shower, fill a misting bottle with lukewarm water, and spray it lightly down on the bird, like a gentle rain. The shower is also valuable during the warmer months when a bird appears to be overheating: holding his wings out from his body and panting. A slightly cool mist will help him cool down.

What Does a Cockatiel Cost?

The purchase price of a cockatiel can vary widely, but the average is $105.50.

The average pet bird owner also spends per year:

$68	Bird food
$36	Other supplies
$26	Toys

Keep It Clean

Designing the optimum cage setup for a cockatiel is only the beginning. Now you must keep it as clean and pristine as it looked the day you set everything up. So add a new set of daily and weekly chores to your calendar.

Each day (several times a day, if possible), you will need to change the newspaper lining in the slide-out tray at the bottom of the cage. Water and food dishes, too, require a daily scrubbing. Your weekly chore will be the wholesale cleaning of the cage.

Place the bird in a holding cage, and scrub every inch of the main cage: the bars, the floor, the perches. A clean cage is more pleasant for bird and owners alike, and it fosters good avian health.

Pet's Peeve

Never clean cages and cage furnishings with strong, toxic chemicals. Always keep your bird at the other side of the house when you are doing your own housecleaning.

The Premium Cockatiel Diet

Cockatiels enjoy a good meal, and it is your job to ensure that your bird receives all the important nutrients he requires every day. Just look to your own diet—well, at least to the diet you know you are supposed to have—for clues on what to feed your bird.

What Does a Cockatiel Eat?

Commercial cockatiel pellets

Seeds

Grains

Fresh green and orange vegetables

Fresh fruits

Cooked pasta

Whole-wheat bread

Cooked meat or tuna (sparingly!)

Millet (sparingly!)

The essential ingredients are simple: grains, seeds, and breads (typically in the form of a commercial seed or pellet mixture, as well as some whole wheat bread or cooked pasta), complemented with a serving of chopped fresh fruits and veggies (preferably of the dark-green or orange variety). Your bird's veterinarian may also recommend occasional servings of protein, such as tuna or well-cooked meat, but serve these sparingly.

The same must be said for treats. You'll find out quickly what foods are your pet's favorites. Use this to your advantage: as training aids and as enticements to get back into the cage after playtime. And don't be bullied. If your cockatiel loves grapes and screams and screams and screams for them, don't give in.

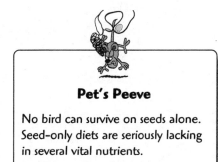

Pet's Peeve

No bird can survive on seeds alone. Seed-only diets are seriously lacking in several vital nutrients.

Cockatiels can also eat themselves into serious obesity. While they may not devour stairway banisters and television remote-control units, as some dogs have been known to do, most just don't know when to stop. Your job, then, is to play watchdog and protect your bird from suffering the gastrointestinal consequences of his own bad habits. Stick to the daily rations, and perhaps a treat now and then, and keep all excess, especially sugary and processed foods, away from the family pet.

And don't forget the water, either. Your pet must have access to fresh, clean water at all times. It's best served up, like the food, in one or two clean dishes within the cage. Monitor the food and water rations throughout the day, and whenever you notice a soiled dish, out with the old and in with the new.

The Least You Need to Know

➤ Once considered the ugly duckling of the pet-bird world, the cockatiel has blossomed into one of the world's most popular, most sociable, and most beautiful pet birds.

➤ Guard your pet cockatiel's health by placing her cage in an area free of fumes, closing all windows and doors when she is out of the cage, keeping her wings clipped to hinder flight, and supervising her activities whenever she is at liberty.

➤ A pet cockatiel requires a clean, roomy cage, and also time spent outside the cage playing with her owner.

➤ The ideal cockatiel cage is tall enough to accommodate the bird's long tail and the expressive crest at the top of her head, and is furnished with a variety of multi-width perches, a door that is not of the life-threatening guillotine style, and a slide-out tray at the bottom that permits easy cleaning.

Part 5
Scales and Slime

And now for the moment you've all been waiting for: your entree into the world of reptiles and amphibians. There's a good chance that much you'll be learning in the chapters ahead that are devoted to lizards, snakes, turtles and tortoises, salamanders, frogs, and toads will be new to you. At the same time, this is a group of animals that is currently experiencing a veritable explosion of popularity, so the more information that starts circulating about their care, and the more novice owners are willing to collect that information, the better.

The challenge is that the care of these animals is probably the most scientific of all the pets. Your first clue to this should be the fact that these are, for the most part, anything but the touchy-feely animals that you think of when you think of pets. Your second clue will come when you discover that reptiles require certain types of lighting and heat, or else they won't survive, while amphibians must be kept cool and moist to preserve the oft-criticized slime on their skin. If you haven't guessed by now, each of these animals is unique and fascinating, and all of them deserve the best care—and the most devoted and knowledgeable owners—possible.

Chapter 16

Leaping Lizards

In This Chapter

➤ A day in the life of an iguana

➤ Getting to know the lizard family

➤ Evaluating and choosing a healthy lizard

➤ The scientific and responsible care of lizards

Children pass through various stages of development as they grow. First solid food. First steps. First words. And, of course, their first dinosaur.

Sometime around the third or fourth year of life, most kids meet a tyrannosaurus rex, or maybe a stegosaurus, at a museum, a toy store, or within the pages of a book. The results are universal: magic. How do we explain the hold these massive lizards, now extinct, have on young minds? After spending several of their formative years with fuzzy stuffed bears, bunnies, and farm animals, little kids meet a dinosaur and they know instinctively that there is something different and wonderful about this creature.

Many kids pass through the dinosaur stage and move on, but some never shake the sense of wonder. These individuals go on to become paleontologists, perhaps, or museum curators, spending their days with the massive skeletons of animals now long gone. Some become lizard owners, and for them, the dinosaurs still live. Just to set the record straight, today's lizards are not direct descendants of those ancient giants—birds are. But lizards seem to evoke the same sense of fascination, probably because of the way they look. A budgie in a cage just doesn't seem like a dinosaur, while an iguana bears a distinct outward resemblance.

Secrets from the Pet Files

Lizards are far more highly regarded by the general public than their cousins, the snakes. In certain parts of Africa, for example, lizards were traditionally considered messengers from God. Lizards were also the inspiration for the Chinese dragon, a symbol of fertility and imperial majesty.

Lizards As Pets

	light	1	2	3	4	5	*heavy*
Time commitment					✔		
Grooming			✔				
Feeding				✔			
General cleanup				✔			
Suitable for kids age infant to 5		✔					
Suitable for kids age 5 to 10			✔				
Suitable for kids over 10					✔		
Sociability			✔				
Expense of keeping					✔		

A Day in the Life

The lizard family covers the gamut in terms of size, lifestyle, color, diet, and temperament. So in exploring the day in the life of a typical lizard, we simply cannot focus on one species and claim that it represents the family at large. We will thus concentrate on one of the most, if not the most, popular pet of the family: the green iguana. We will spend the day with Tiny, who certainly isn't.

Morning, Tiny: Rise and Shine

Tiny was purchased when he was quite young and could fit into the palm of his owner's hand. But those days are long gone. Though he was named for his small size, his owner was well aware that this would change. This small, vibrant chartreuse lizard grew up to be five feet long.

Tiny is rather pleased to meet us—which would not necessarily be true of all iguanas. Some enjoy human company, some don't. They make their individual opinions on the subject known when they reach sexual maturity, somewhere around 18 months of age. Tiny, then, is an excellent, though perhaps somewhat misleading, ambassador of his species.

This morning his sociability is on hold, however, for Tiny is hungry. He jumps down from his tree branch perch within his spacious iguana abode and wiggles around joyfully when his breakfast of fresh chopped veggies is served. For now, that is of greatest interest.

Post-breakfast Activities

With his hunger pangs satisfied, Tiny can get on with the business of being a lizard. Time to bask. He climbs gracefully up the tree within his six-foot-high enclosure (which from the outside resembles a fine piece of furniture), and settles in beneath the special reptile light. He knows instinctively that heat is what he needs to stimulate his appetite and maintain his body temperature and metabolic activity. The light supplies heat, as well as the ultraviolet rays from the sun that Tiny needs to live. He, of course, does not know this in such scientific terms. Tiny is smart, but not *that* smart.

Pampered Pet

A mature green iguana can be four to six feet long. Make sure you can house an animal that size for 10 years or more before you think about getting an iguana.

After a morning of moving back and forth, in and out of the warm light, Tiny is thrilled to realize that the afternoon offers one of his favorite activities, a visit into the great outdoors. He watches from his enclosure as his owner prepares his outdoor accommodations: a sun cage, which will confine him in the backyard while still allowing him to enjoy the fresh air, the natural sunlight, and the soft tickle of grass between his toes. The experience is made even more delightful when he is spritzed with water from a spray bottle while in the warm sun, taking him instinctively home to his native rain forest. Captive-bred though he was, he still has a species memory of what home is like.

Evening for Tiny

Tiny is content. He has spent yet another delightful day, both on his own and in the company of the man he considers to be almost family. He spends the first part of the evening munching on a fresh serving of veggies, which his owner has sprinkled with a vitamin-mineral powder to protect him from the notorious calcium deficiency that plagues so many pet iguanas.

After dinner Tiny meanders around the family room, ultimately resting peacefully along the back of the couch watching his human companion pay the monthly bills. Included in the stack is a rather hefty veterinary bill for a cut Tiny got on his leg two weeks ago. Oh, well. Tiny's worth it, and he knows it. He closes his eyes as his owner tickles his head—part of the bedtime ritual they share each night before Tiny returns to his comfortable abode.

Pet Talk

Although most lizards are *insectivores* (insect eaters), some are *herbivores* (plant eaters), a few are *carnivores* (meat eaters), and many are *omnivores* (they eat plants and animals). Before you decide to add a lizard to your family, make sure you know what that particular species eats.

All Lizards Great and Small

Lizard is the word we use to describe a very large, very popular multifaceted branch of the reptile family tree. This branch boasts more than 4,000 species. The vast differences in character among lizards is testament to the evolutionary success of the family, which has adapted to virtually every type of environment and living situation, from the deserts to the mountains to the rain forests and everywhere in between.

Some lizards climb trees, some burrow into the ground, some even move about through the heavens in a parachute-like action we might best describe as flying. While all have scales, some have smooth-textured skin, some are plated, and still others wear fierce, and often spiked, suits of armor. Some are short and squat, some long and slender, and some don't even have legs. By accepting this diversity as a miracle of nature, and respecting the differences among those lizards in captivity, we can be better lizard owners.

Regarding Reptiles

What is a reptile? Lizards and snakes are reptiles. Turtles and tortoises are, too. Reptiles are an amazing, not to mention ancient, class of animals that have evolved to withstand the effects of some of the most treacherous conditions on the planet. Unlike amphibians, with which they are often mistakenly compared, most reptiles have scaly skin, most are hatched from eggs on dry land, and most require ample exposure to sunlight. Their bodies are also uniquely engineered to retain moisture, which explains why so many reptiles can thrive in some of the earth's hottest, driest deserts. Subject an amphibian to such conditions, or even most mammals we know, and witness the dire results.

Lizards in the Wild

It is impossible to characterize all lizard pets with a single example. The same is true of lizards in the wild. The lifestyle of, say a gregarious green iguana in Central America will vary dramatically from that of a reclusive gila monster in the southwestern United States. Yet despite their vast differences, they remain members of a single reptilian family with many shared characteristics.

In the wild, most lizards spend their days searching for food, regulating their body temperatures, and steering clear of predators. To the untrained eye, their basking behavior might suggest that they live a life of leisure. Those more knowledgeable about life in the wild, however, know that no life is leisurely in nature. Everything the lizard does is an exercise in survival, including lying around in the sun.

What Does a Lizard Cost?

The purchase price of a lizard can vary widely, but the average is $50.

The average lizard owner also spends per year:

$66	Food
$33	Other supplies
$11	Toys

The average iguana owner also spends per year:

$88	Food
$51	Other supplies
$49	Veterinary services
$30	Toys

Members of the Family

As reptiles, all lizards have scales, and all are *ectothermic,* which means they rely on their external environment to warm their internal body temperatures and thus fuel their appetites and overall health. On the reproduction front, most lizards would be unlikely candidates for parent-of-the-year once their young hatch from their eggs, yet they are fairly diligent in protecting those eggs until that time.

While degrees of sight, smell, and hearing vary among species, lizards do share one important characteristic with snakes that significantly enhances their ability to survive. That is the *Jacobson's organ* at the roof of the mouth, which operates in conjunction with the lizard's tongue and brain. The process begins when the lizard flicks his tongue out into his environment, as he constantly does, and picks up scent particles from the air and other surfaces. The tongue carries these particles back into the mouth and deposits them on the Jacobson's organ. The brain then processes the taste and smell information it receives and alerts the lizard that potential food or predators are about.

Secrets from the Pet Files

The *Jacobson's organ* is actually a pair of structures, located in the roof of the mouth below the nose, that are connected to the brain through the olfactory nerve. They are used to identify minute scent particles. Cats, snakes, and other animals also have them.

Lizards in the House

That lizards are immensely popular pets for kids of all ages is not difficult to understand. In an age where wild lands and wild animals are constantly disappearing, reptiles can satisfy our desire to continue to commune with nature. The lizard branch of the animal kingdom does so in a quiet, easy-care manner, making even dedicated, properly prepared newcomers to reptile keeping feel confident. In addition, lizards are not as aloof as some basically wild pets can be. While they are not domestic animals, many can be tamed, actually learning to recognize their keepers and enjoying the time they spend together.

In addition to their very ancient, almost otherworldly appearance, their vast diversity and extraordinary adaptability have contributed to the lizard's popularity as a pet. Of course, not every species is cut out for life as a pet (and some cannot by law be kept as pets), so it is best to heed the recommendations of lizard experts and choose only those species with a positive track record as pets.

Various factors contribute to that positive pet reputation. Diet is one. Because many lizards subsist on a vegetarian diet, they tend to be more readily embraced by people with a passion for reptiles who would rather not keep a pet that, like the snake, requires meat that's still moving. Temperament, too, is a consideration. Even some legally kept lizard species can have foul dispositions both in captivity and in the wild. Such a moody creature is not what most of us have in mind when we crave a wild creature in our homes. This is, after all, supposed to be fun for everyone, human and reptile alike.

Lizards Out and About

Sure you'll see lizards paraded out in public, typically an iguana that rests contentedly on his owner's shoulder or crawls along the grass on a leash. These pets invariably draw a crowd. But this, you must keep in mind, is the exception, not the rule. You are not likely ever to see the shy, aggressive-with-strangers iguana showcased in public, but there are plenty of those about—many of them living private, satisfying lives as adored pets.

Sometimes a lizard's aggression and fearfulness are inborn traits; sometimes they are created—even within the most well-meaning, reptile-adoring households. As is the fate of many a reptile, the lizard is too often bought as a child's pet, the kids and all their friends are allowed to play with the animal at will. They may carry him to school with them every day in a lunch box, send him down the slide at the playground, and take him swimming at the public pool. In case it has not already been made abundantly clear, *the lizard does not like this.*

Pet's Peeve

Lizards are very sensitive to their environment, and an animal that is overhandled will literally die from the stress.

The point is this: Where sociability is concerned, every lizard species and every individual lizard is just that—an individual. When you commit to lizard ownership, you commit to appreciating that individual spirit. Some lizards enjoy human handling. Some don't. Some revel in attention from strangers. Some don't. Respect your own pet's personal take on the subject, and don't try to change his mind if he doesn't quite meet your expectations.

If you happen to have an affinity for a variety of animals, just how do you handle a menagerie of reptiles, mammals, and other members of the animal kingdom? With great care and respect for all, that's how. Only in our wildest imaginations will the lion lie down with the lamb, and the same holds true of, say, a cat and a small, shy desert lizard. Don't cause your reptiles unnecessary stress by forcing them to "play nice" with their sworn enemies, and don't force your resident predators to battle their natural impulses.

Lizards and Salmonella

Most pet lizards, like most reptile species in general, tend to be carriers of salmonella. Owners are wise to become rather obsessive about hand washing and general household cleanliness. If yours is a lizard who enjoys time outside of his enclosure, wash your hands with antibacterial soap before and after handling the animal, and thoroughly clean any surfaces the lizard had contact with once he returns to his enclosure.

This is true, for example, of an iguana who may enjoy swimming in the bathtub, after which the tub should be cleaned thoroughly with an antibacterial cleaning product. Be especially diligent, too, with children who handle reptiles. Assume that all reptiles are salmonella carriers and act accordingly.

Here are some hints that will help prevent the spread of salmonella.

➤ Keep the reptile's habitat clean.

➤ Never use household cleaning articles or the kitchen sink for washing the reptile's things.

➤ Teach the kids (and other family members) to look at the reptile, not touch.

➤ Teach the children how to handle the reptile, keeping it away from their face.

➤ Always wash up well, using an antibacterial soap, after caring for the reptile.

Finding That Healthy Pet Lizard

Given the many lizard species available today as pets, deciding in a responsible manner which might be right for you in terms of size, diet, and care requirements demands some intensive research on your part. Books, breeders, veterinarians who specialize in reptiles and their care, herpetological associations, and even the various pet and reptile Web sites on the Internet are all excellent sources for valuable information—all of which can help make you a better and, we hope, permanent lizard owner.

Secrets from the Pet Files

One of the larger, extended branches of the family tree is the gecko clan. It is a group that is becoming increasingly popular as pets. Ease of care is one reason; vocal talents are another. You see, many geckos are quite talkative, their vocabularies comprised of clicks and squeals that owners find irresistible. In fact, the name gecko actually comes from the propensity of the noisiest of the bunch, the Tokay, to emit a sound that sounds very much like the word "geck-oh."

You will do yourself and your pet a favor by being as prepared and knowledgeable as can be, and by choosing wisely. Your ultimate decision about species and individual lizard should be grounded in both common sense and ethics. Both, as you will see, play important roles in the well-being of individual pet reptiles, and in the well-being of the entire reptile family, as well.

Internet Resources

There is a wealth of information about reptiles on the Internet—far too many sites to list here. What I've done instead is list some of the information clearing houses: Web sites that offer a wide variety of information, or that supply lots of links to other Web sites.

➤ http://www.acmepet.com/reptile

Acme Pet has its own chat rooms and bulletin boards. The Reptile page also offers a Marketplace, and a listing of national and local clubs and events. The Pet Library contains reference materials, articles, and links to other Web sites, sorted by type of animal.

➤ http://home.ptd.net/~herplink/index/html

Hundreds of links to just about everything you can imagine, arranged into the categories Care and FAQs, Organizations, Publications, Herp Pages, Resources and Dealers, plus a search function and a feature that e-mails you every time your favorite herp Web pages are updated.

➤ http://www.herp.com

Links to animal dealers, books, information, exporters, supply dealers, food dealers, herp societies, upcoming events, and other herp pages.

➤ http://www.xmission.com/~gastown.herpmed

A super site with links to everything reptile, from the latest laws to medical information to book catalogs to conservation news, plus every type of herp you can imagine, including crocodiles.

➤ http://netvet.wustl.edu/reptiles.htm

A super list of links and information on every type of herp you can think of. The list of links is particularly well organized.

➤ http://www.petstation.com

PetStation has information on a wide variety of animals. The Herp Hacienda, their herp site, is affiliated with *Reptile & Amphibian* magazine. It also contains a book list, photo gallery, list of publications, clubs and associations, and a bulletin board to communicate with other herpetologists.

➤ http://www.tamebeast.com

The Reptiles page offers a lot of links to other sites, sorted into General Information, Breeders and Dealers, Events, Herpetology, Really Old Reptiles, and Supplies. There's also a Hip Herp Site of the Week.

Responsible Choices

Human negligence is today taking a terrible toll on the various reptile families. Whether it's the illegal wildlife trade that leads to unbridled poaching of these animals for their body parts, illegal collecting of live wild specimens for the burgeoning reptile pet trade, or the wanton destruction of their worldwide habitats, the results are always the same: a decrease in wild populations of these fascinating animals.

And just why should you, the reptile pet owner, be concerned? Because which lizard you choose can have far-reaching effects. When you choose to take a wild-caught lizard into your home, you are directly contributing to the success of the wildlife trade, both legal and illegal, that is diminishing the wild populations of these animals. On the other hand, choose a lizard that has been bred in captivity, and you make a profound statement that you care about the lizards in the wild and support the idea of leaving them there.

In the captive-bred lizard, you are also likely to end up with a vastly superior pet—one that is better suited to life as a pet and is less likely to carry disease and parasites. You set a good example for other would-be lizard owners, who will be so impressed by the quality of your pet that they will follow in your footsteps and obtain a similar captive-bred lizard for themselves. So you see, one person can make a difference.

Secrets from the Pet Files

Someday, if we're not careful, we may find in the more temperate regions of the country bands of feral iguanas roaming the landscape. The reason? All these irresponsible iguana owners who purchase their pets on impulse and then release them into the wild when they become too large and too difficult to handle. In warmer climes, the animals may survive and thus wreak havoc with native wildlife. Whether native or not, no pet lizard—or any reptile—should ever be released into the wild. This is cruel both to the animal and to the ecosystem. Don't do it!

Where to Go When It's Time to Choose

Given the popularity of lizard pets, you will be faced with a variety of sources for these animals when you are finally prepared to take the plunge. Investigate as many as possible, and you will not only increase your education significantly, but also probably end up with a healthier pet.

Pet Shops and Reptile Specialty Stores

The traditional pet shop used to be the only source for lizard pets. The local store carried puppies, a few kittens, turtles, and rabbits, and perhaps some nondescript type of lizard. Today you can still find lizards in traditional pet shops—particularly herds of iguana hatchlings. But if you are seeking a more exotic species, perhaps a skink or a leopard gecko, you may need to enlist the services of a specialty pet shop that deals only in reptiles and amphibians.

Several years ago, such shops were unheard of, but today the good ones have quickly become paradise for those bitten by the reptile-keeping bug. Regardless of the type of establishment you choose, the enclosures must be clean and provide light and heat sources, as well as fresh water to the resident animals. Those animals should not be overcrowded, and they must appear spry and healthy. Add to this a knowledgeable, preferably reptile-crazy staff, and you're in business.

Reptile Shows

Let's say you have decided you want a leopard gecko. You look in the phone book and voilà!, there is a breeder of geckos right up the road. Actually, it's not likely to happen that way. But this does not mean that purchasing a lizard from a breeder is an impossible dream. Do some research in your local newspaper, and you may well discover that a reptile show is being held nearby in the near future. Breeders come from far and wide to participate in these shows, offering would-be owners not only a chance to learn more about their species of choice, but also to meet some of the animals up close and personal.

At the reptile show, you are likely to find a congregation of some very dedicated folks. A great many of these people, as you will quickly discover, are devoted not only to the promotion of captive-bred pets, but also to the conservation of reptiles in the wild. Such sentiments and commitment are all part of the fabric of this fascinating hobby. And they can be highly contagious to visitors.

Animal Shelters and Rescue Groups

As happens whenever a pet becomes popular, more and more of their kind become disposable once the novelty wears off. This is as true of reptiles as it is of various dog breeds that find themselves the fad of the moment after being featured in movies and television shows. Whether *Jurassic Park* has had any bearing on the widespread popularity of iguanas and other lizards is open to debate, but we do know that animal shelters have recently had to add lizards to their lists of unwanted pets.

Pampered Pet

Solo housing is usually best for lizards. Most are solitary, territorial animals and don't enjoy company.

Already-beleaguered shelters do what they can to place these animals in new, this time permanent, homes, so it might be worth your while to call around and see if your perfect reptile might at this very minute be waiting at a local shelter. You might even find rescue groups that specialize in lizards. Perhaps your friendly neighborhood reptile veterinarian will know of such a group in your area, or know of a particular patient who needs a new home. Network a little, and it will be to your advantage.

Choosing a Healthy Lizard

Your research will also prove invaluable when it's time to select your individual pet. Only by understanding the nuances of a particular species will you be prepared to evaluate the animals that cross your path. If the lizard of your dreams is, say, a bearded dragon, look for an exemplary specimen that exudes the ultimate in spiky skin, prominent neck flap "beard," and the sweet temperament for which this species is known. You get the picture.

To generalize, then, look for a lizard that is the picture of health—whatever constitutes the picture of health for the particular species you are looking for (try to say that three times fast!). For most species, this means bright eyes, clear breathing, uniform skin texture, graceful movement, and a good appetite—plus whatever other characteristics the lizard in question is known for. Easy.

Secrets from the Pet Files

One lizard species that is gaining popularity is the chameleon. This tree-dweller is extraordinary not only for his vibrant colors and his ability to change those colors to blend with his surroundings, but also for his prehistoric, rather hump-like body structure, his agile climbing ability, his prehensile tail, and his long, sticky tongue—so adept at picking up insects that seem beyond his grasp. He requires a lot of special care and is best reserved for only the most experienced lizard keeper.

Reptilian Rooming

Here we go again. Just like all lizards, all lizard abodes are not created equal. They should be equal as far as quality, but given the vast differences between species, the character of the accommodations will vary dramatically. Size, for example, is one such element. What is large enough for a small gecko will hardly accommodate a six-foot iguana, which will need a tall, vertical-style enclosure that will accommodate some trees and elevated shelves. Still, some elements are standard for all, if not in kind, then certainly in concept.

The cage style you choose for your pet depends on your lizard and your budget. You may choose a traditional aquarium converted for a resident lizard (meaning it must include a securely locking screen top for safety and ventilation), or a custom-made beauty that looks like it was designed to match your own interior decor. So get to know your lizard, and give him what he needs. And keep it clean. Remove all waste products and leftover food each and every day. Make sure there is a clean water dish filled with clean water within the enclosure, and you'll both live happily ever after.

Pampered Pet

Your lizard will probably need either a vivarium with some land and some water, a desert environment, or a simulated tree house. Make sure you know which!

Furnishings Fit for a Lizard

What you place in your lizard's abode—aside from the lizard, of course—depends on the lizard. Flooring is dictated by species, as a burrower will need a deep substrate layer that will accommodate his habits, while alfalfa pellets or newspaper may suffice for a lizard that spends most of his time in a tree or on a basking shelf.

All lizards deserve a place within their homes where they can hide from the prying eyes of the world—or at least of the kids next door—and retreat when they've had their fill of heat and light. But some lizards, desert species in particular, may prefer several hiding places from which to choose. Appropriate accessories, too, will vary among species. The iguana with his tree is one example. So go wild. Spruce the place up to mimic your lizard's natural habitat. Hunks of driftwood, small stone caves, plants, trees, and logs can all enhance the natural beauty that can be a lizard's abode.

Pampered Pet

Lizards that need a semi-aquatic environment will need all the equipment you need for an aquarium, including a water filter and air pump.

When You Get a Lizard, You'll Also Have to Get These

Appropriate cage or enclosure	Rocks/plants for habitat
Secure cage cover	Heat light and/or ceramic heater
Food dishes	Reptile light supplying UVA and UVB rays
Water dishes	Two thermometers
Substrate material	Basking spot
Hiding places	Care book

Heat and Light: A Legendary Combination

Even those who haven't shared their homes with rep-tiles know that lizards enjoy basking in the sun. What those people may not know is that when the lizard does this, he is keeping the doctor away. Lizards must have heat to stimulate their appetites and digest their food, and they must have ultraviolet light (UVA and UVB) to synthesize vitamin D_3—the lack of which can lead to a serious condition called metabolic bone disease.

The heat side of the equation is classically provided by either an incandescent light or a ceramic heating element perched above the enclosure and out of reach of the resident lizard. Heat only one side of the enclosure so the lizard has a range of temperatures from which to choose. That range will vary from species to species, some preferring higher heats, some lower. An iguana's daytime domicile temperatures, for example, should range from about 85°F at one end of his enclosure to as high as 95°F to 100°F at the opposite end (install thermometers at each end to make sure all is as it should be).

Pet's Peeve

Heat should not be supplied by the so-called hot rock, an electric heat source that sits in the cage. Often touted as an ideal heat source, the hot rock has also been responsible for burning the skin of more reptiles than we would care to think about.

Lighting is equally critical. Lizards are most secure with a sunrise-sunset kind of day: light for 12 hours, dark for 12 hours. Just like people. Artificial lighting can mimic this, and it is best that the lighting be from a special fluorescent bulb designed just for reptiles. With fluorescent lights—again, positioned above and away—the light will provide the vital full-spectrum ultraviolet rays your lizard needs to keep his internal system operating correctly.

While heat and light are of utmost importance to a lizard, it is possible to fry them. Just because some is good, more is not necessarily better. Wild lizards regulate their body temperature by moving in and out of the sun. They must be offered flexibility in their heat sources so they can follow their own instincts in soaking up the optimum amount of heat and light they require at a given moment. Offer them a spacious multidimensional domicile that offers areas of ample heat and light, and other areas where they may retreat for cool and shelter when they've had enough of the warm stuff. Trust your pet. He knows best what he needs.

A pleasant, very natural way to provide a larger lizard with heat and light is to allow him to spend time in a sun cage. This is an escape-proof enclosure placed outdoors on a soft, pesticide-free lawn, where the lizard can revel in some of the more natural joys of life. Within the sun cage, the lizard remains safe, yet at the same time he can wriggle across the grass and rest in the sun. Just make sure the cage provides a solid shelter, as well, in which the lizard can hide once he is sufficiently sunbathed. Otherwise he could overheat.

Keep It Clean

Your lizard needs a clean home. That means picking up any uneaten food and scooping feces every day. It also means cleaning the food and water dishes every day. And the entire enclosure, whether aquatic, arboreal, or terrestrial, will need to be regularly cleaned and disinfected. Get yourself on a schedule, and stick to it.

Pet's Peeve

No animal's enclosure should ever look unkempt or smell bad. If it looks or smells dirty, clean it!

Lizard Cuisine Made Easy

Finally, there is the lizard's diet. As with everything else, the menu is determined by species. But this is an issue you must think about before you even consider which lizard is right for you—a very important issue, as a matter of fact. Lizard diets run the gamut from the vegetarian diet of the iguana to the insect-and-worm diet of the captive leopard gecko to the decidedly carnivorous palates of most of the monitors, and everything in between. Some lizards are exclusively vegetarian, some meat eaters, and some, like the bearded dragon, enjoy a little of each.

What Does a Lizard Eat?

Herbivores		Insectivores	
	Grasses		Crickets
	Leaves		Mealworms
	Vegetables		Flies
	Fruits		Fruitflies
	Flowers		Waxworms
	Grains		Earthworms
	Commercial reptile foods		Commercial fish and reptile foods
	Vitamin-mineral supplements		Vitamin-mineral supplements
Carnivores	Mice		
	Rats	Omnivores	Fruits
	Chicks		Vegetables
	Canned dog food		Insects
	Insects		Meat
	Commercial reptile foods		Vitamin-mineral supplements
	Vitamin-mineral supplements		

The vegetarians can actually be a bit more difficult to feed properly. Balancing this diet requires you to master the intricacies of dietary nutrients in various food items. Even those lizards that prefer vegetarian fare require proteins and all the vital vitamins and minerals. In many cases, though, you can provide those vitamins and minerals with a vitamin-mineral supplement formulated especially for reptiles and amphibians.

Your job is to ensure that the food is fresh and of optimum nutritional quality. Feed according to a schedule, make sure the lizard is properly warmed for appetite stimulation and digestion, feed what you are supposed to feed (don't try to turn a carnivore into a vegetarian), and make sure the lizard has access at all times to fresh, clean water. From a dietary standpoint, this is what healthy captive lizards are made of.

The Least You Need to Know

➤ Pet lizard species come in every imaginable size, color, living situation, and dietary preference.

➤ All reptiles rely on their environmental temperatures to warm their bodies and stimulate appetite and metabolism.

➤ A captive-bred lizard is a superior, more responsible choice than one captured from the wild.

➤ Choose a pet lizard with bright eyes, clear breathing, even skin texture and scales, graceful movement, and a healthy appetite.

➤ The pet lizard requires a roomy enclosure, basking spots, fresh water, a species-appropriate diet, safe flooring, a secluded hiding place, both UVA and UVB ultraviolet lighting, and air temperatures ranging from 85° F at one end of the enclosure to 95° F to 100° F at the other.

Slithering Snakes

In This Chapter

➤ A day in the life of a ball python

➤ Understanding the world of snakes

➤ Choosing a snake that is both healthy and beautiful

➤ Snake care made easy

Snakes aren't for everyone. Nor do they tend to win many converts among confirmed snake haters; very few suddenly discover the error of their ways and decide the snake is the perfect pet for them. No, most snake enthusiasts are born, not made.

That persuasive snake in the Garden of Eden can take most of the blame for this. Ever since that fateful forbidden-fruit-related incident, the snake has been vilified by cultures all over the world. We fear them. We distrust them. We wish them dead. But some among us, those with a special brand of DNA, do not share these sentiments. For us, there is nothing more wonderful, more breathtakingly beautiful, more awe-inspiring, than a snake—not in the grass, but in the house.

We are not talking here about egotistical folks whose only aim is to attract public attention with a so-called scary pet. No, we are talking about, and to, those pure-of-heart snake lovers—and you know who you are. You need not hide your affinities here. You are among friends.

Snakes As Pets

	light	1	2	3	4	5	heavy
Time commitment				✔			
Grooming		✔					
Feeding					✔		
General cleanup				✔			
Suitable for kids age infant to 5		✔					
Suitable for kids age 5 to 10			✔				
Suitable for kids over 10					✔		
Sociability				✔			
Expense of keeping				✔			

A Day in the Life

Meet Betty, a ball python. Scary? Not really. Ball pythons grow to only a few feet long. Betty is probably the quietest pet you could ever dream of. And the cleanest. Feeding time is not for the squeamish, but no pet is perfect, right? So let's take a look at a day in the life of this predator and see just what makes her so terrifying.

Pet's Peeve

Never release a pet snake into the wild. With a snake that is native to the area, you threaten the existing population with disease and parasites. With a snake that is not native, you sentence the snake to an early demise or let loose a monster that will decimate the existing wildlife.

The Early Part of Betty's Day

Betty awakens. She is snuggled into her favorite shelter in her enclosure: half of a hollow log that now acts as a log cabin for a snake. She sees the rays of the sun filtering through the window at the other side of the room. My, what a beautiful morning. Betty stays where she is. How delightful to be alive, to be a snake, on a day like this.

The Middle of Betty's Day

Betty rests comfortably in her log cabin. But she's thinking that perhaps it's time for a stretch. She feels the need to bask. Slowly she unfurls her muscular form from her shelter. She wriggles over to her basking spot, a smooth flat stone situated under the light. Ahh! She may or may not understand that, in basking, she is not only indulg-ing in one of a reptile's ultimate pleasures, but also stimulating her appetite, recharging her metabolism, and keeping herself alive.

Betty is interrupted by a noise at the door. One of the kids is home, and he's got a friend with him. Show-and-tell time. Betty is fortunate that everyone in her family understands her and respects her. The kids wash their hands. They approach. Betty's young owner opens the enclosure and gently strokes the snake inside.

Although ball pythons are named for their habit of curling into a pretzel-like ball when frightened, Betty hasn't had cause to do that in months. Let's hope there won't be reason to break that record now. "Wow!" exclaims the young stranger. "Let's wrap her around your neck and take her outside and scare everyone!" An argument ensues. "We can't do that," says the snake's young caretaker. "But it's so cool," argues his pal. "It's so cruel," says the young snake handler. "And it can be dangerous for the snake. The answer is no." And that's that. Yes, Betty can always depend on the humans in this household, no matter how old—or young— they happen to be.

Pampered Pet

Although some species are more sociable than others, individual snakes vary in how much handling they will tolerate. Know and respect your snake's wishes.

Later in Betty's Day

Betty spends the rest of the day resting and loung-ing. She won't be eating today. She doesn't need to. Betty is a reptile, and reptiles are quiet efficient at retaining moisture and using up all the nutrients in their diets.

This doesn't mean Betty's day is over, though. This particular python enjoys a bit of company at the end of the day. The mom of that responsible little caretaker walks over, gently reaches into the enclosure and lifts Betty up and out. She sits down on the couch and places Betty on her lap as she watches television. Betty enjoys the warmth. Then it's off to bed. The two lights at the top of her roomy enclosure are clicked off. Good night, Betty.

Serpent Social Studies

Indiana Jones, what a courageous guy—or a masochist. Take your pick. On a daily basis he grapples with ancient temples crumbling over his head, booby-trapped daggers seeking out his major arteries, seas of skeletons and rats crawling up his legs, pilotless planes and runaway trains ejecting him to unknown fates, and the flesh-eating powers of the lost ark and the Holy Grail. There is only one thing that frightens this man. Snakes.

Mr. Jones is not alone. You would think that by now we would be accustomed to shar-ing the planet with the more than 2,500 species of snakes that are found throughout the world. But no; the snake is probably the most reviled, feared, utterly despised creature on the face of the earth. Does the snake realize this? Perhaps. But when you

travel through life as a single strand of muscle without benefit of arms, legs, or eyelids, and only a mouth full of teeth and perhaps a dram of poison to protect you, there's not much you can do to change human perceptions, is there? There is, however, much we humans can do to understand snakes and their unique view of the world. In the process, we can learn to accept this animal for what she is, and thus ensure that those snakes who live in captivity receive top-notch care.

Secrets from the Pet Files

We might think that the medical symbol of a snake wrapped around a rod, or caduceus, is a rather odd choice to denote healing. But this symbol dates back to ancient times, surely to Greece, and perhaps even to Egypt, both of them cultures that believed the snake harbored mystical healing powers.

For an animal perceived as the ultimate villain, the snake's life is really not all that exciting. Whether wild or domestic, she just takes one day at a time, knowing that her survival will depend on ample food, moisture, sunlight, and shelter. What's so bad about that?

Snakes may not be the best-loved pet species on earth, but we can safely state that many rank as some of the most beautiful. The colors and patterns on their backs can be nothing short of dazzling. In most cases, this is Mother Nature's way of camouflaging one of her least popular children, but it can also help temper the fiery opinions of people who may be meeting them for the first time.

Snake Biology

Serpents in the wild are rather democratic in their choice of homes. Nimble in their adaptations to every type of living situation, some live in the rain forest, some in the desert, some in the mountains, and some on the prairie. There are snakes who make their homes in trees, in burrowed holes in the ground, and yes, just like that legendary biblical creature, in the garden.

Most lay eggs to procreate, but some give birth to living, breathing miniatures of themselves—a spectacle worthy of admission to the cardiac care unit for those who harbor that universal human fear of snakes.

In terms of diet, snakes are meat eaters all, so don't expect to maintain a snake by offering her a vegetarian diet. Snakes are also what we refer to as *ectothermic,* a characteristic of all reptiles. This means they must rely on the temperature of their environment to warm their bodies—and thus stimulate their appetites and digest their meals. So when you notice a snake, or any reptile, basking in the sun, you'll understand. She knows instinctively that she must use solar power to keep herself alive.

People who have obviously never touched one often describe snakes as slimy. Wrong. Their scaly skin is actually quite dry and cool. It maintains its health by shedding. How you manage the snake during shedding can affect her health, as this is a very vulnerable time for her.

Facing an impending shed, the snake will lose her appetite. She may become obsessed with soaking in her water dish (which you make sure is always filled with fresh, clean water). When not soaking, she may rub up against rough surfaces. Her eyes may take on a cloudy cast, a signal to you that her vision is impaired. As soon as you notice the first of these signs, do not feed or handle the snake. Soon, if your snake is healthy, she will shed her whole skin intact.

Pet's Peeve

Shedding in patches could indicate an illness or a parasitic infestation. Contact the snake's veterinarian immediately.

As if lacking arms and legs isn't enough, snakes are also endowed with less-than-sharp eyesight. This is why they are forever flicking their tongues in and out. When the snake flicks her tongue out, she picks up microscopic chemical particles from her environment. The tongue then transports these particles into the snake's mouth where the *Jacobson's organ* on the roof of the animal's mouth, with help from the brain, interprets the identity of the particles. The snake may thus efficiently locate both food and mates through the scent particles she draws in on her tongue.

Snake Behavior and Temperament

Most snakes are quite jealous of their privacy, a propensity directed at both other snakes and people. They prefer to hide. If you wish to keep more than one snake, of either the same or different species, do your pets a favor and provide them with their own private territories.

Keep your own interactions with them to a minimum, as well. In time, if you prove yourself worthy, your snake may come to trust you and agree to spend time with you. She may even come to look forward to the time you spend together. But keep such interactions private. Most snakes don't appreciate the role of conversation piece.

Snakes and the Family

In the past few years, more and more people are discovering the fascination and convenience of snake ownership, viewing this as an ideal pet for no-pets-allowed living situations. A snake can be a quiet, easy-care pet for those who would like to install a bit of nature into the contemporary household, or for a person with mammal allergies.

But not everyone is right for snake ownership—and not every snake is right for life as a pet. The best pet species include such snakes as the ball python, the garter snake, the corn snake, the various rosy boas, and the king snake. While cobras, anacondas, and the family of massive constrictors may be ideal ego enhancers, they are not appropriate pets.

Proper Respect

As for those snakes that fall into the "appropriate" column, they can be fascinating additions to the household. All they ask for is proper care and a little respect, which means honoring their privacy and keeping the other pets in the household away.

Secrets from the Pet Files

Captive-bred pet species such as corn snakes and rosy boas are now being bred in a wide variety of colors and patterns. A reptile show is the best place to see this rainbow of snakes and decide which one you like best.

We've all seen the novelty photos of, say, a large python wrapped around the neck of a Doberman Pinscher. But you, as a more responsible type, are wise to just say no to such potentially dangerous, certainly stressful foolishness—stressful for both the dog and the snake. The same is true of a snake's interactions with children. Sure, kids can learn to be responsible, respectable snake owners, but they require constant adult supervision in doing so, for the sakes of both the child and the snake.

A Ticklish Issue: Snakes in Public

We've also all seen the macho-type guys in the park with big pythons wrapped around them. Sometimes they're charging money to have your picture taken with the snake draped on you. Sometimes they're just looking to meet women. Whatever their motivation, they are exposing their snakes to unnecessary physical danger and stress. So let's make this perfectly clear: Snakes *do not* like to be taken out into public areas. Those who truly adore snakes and have dedicated their lives to them cringe every time they go out in public and see some show-off strutting around with a python around his neck.

The health of your pet is paramount, but there's another issue here as well. Once you begin to delve into the world of reptiles and those who make a religion of living with them, you will ultimately encounter the great fear inherent in doing so. This is not a fear of the animals, of course. It is a fear of public persecution.

For centuries snakes have been reviled, and while they are becoming increasingly popular as pets, public sentiment has not changed much. With so many reptiles listed as endangered species—and thus off-limits as pets—reptile enthusiasts are forever being investigated and regulated by wildlife authorities. Strutting about in public with a snake, even a legal snake, is of no benefit whatsoever to the snake or to the art of snake keeping. As seasoned snake keepers well know, mass hysteria among those who witness such a public spectacle can feed the momentum that results in legislation prohibiting snake ownership. So go ahead and enjoy the companionship of your pet in the privacy of your own home, but do your fellow snake keepers and their pets a favor, and stay home.

Pet's Peeve

Stress can be just as dangerous to snakes as a fungus or a virus because it weakens the animal and makes her a prime candidate for illness. We don't tend to view snakes as so vulnerable, but they are.

Choosing Your Snake

Suppose you have decided that yes, you are one of those fortunate few who was born to live with snakes. You are prepared to offer a snake care that is complimentary with her wild roots, and yes, you will love, honor, and respect the animal for as long as she lives (which can be a decade or more). Now what?

It's time to explore the details. First, what species of snake should you invite into your home? If you're a beginner, the ball python, the king snake, and the corn snake are excellent choices. Any venomous snake is a no-no. As for a large tropical constrictor—say, the Burmese python—well, at an adult length of 15 feet or more, she can require an enclosure as large as a bedroom and send you to the poorhouse with her voracious appetite, so she is really not practical for most folks.

What Does a Snake Cost?

The purchase price of a snake can vary widely, but the average is $155.79.

The average snake owner also spends per year:

$127	Food
$43	Toys
$42	Other supplies
$13	Veterinary care

Obviously, you must consider the size of the various pet snakes when you are reviewing your options. And diet, too. Most snake owners find pinkie (newborn) mice or rats far less traumatic to feed their pets than the endless supply of rabbits, chickens, and even small pigs that a large snake like a Burmese python will demand.

Remember, too, that some species are not only illegal pet species, but also just not cut out for life as a pet. This latter point applies to individual snakes, as well, even when those individuals are legal. Some snakes, usually snakes taken from the wild, simply don't want to be pets. They will protest by refusing to eat, moping around, ignoring their instincts—in short, by committing suicide.

Pet's Peeve

If you're a rookie, you just might discover that you have been rooked into purchasing a wild-caught snake that is illegal—something you discover when the authorities show up at your door to confiscate the animal.

The Superiority of Home-Grown Snakes

Of probably the greatest importance to those who have dedicated themselves to snake keeping is the issue of wild-caught versus captive-bred pet snakes. Many species may seem ideal for eternally docile lives in captivity, but snakes are not domestic creatures—not even the captive-bred ones. To tear a wild animal from the natural habitat in which she was born is downright cruel, especially when there are so many beautiful, healthy captive-bred snakes available these days.

To choose a wild-caught snake as a pet also supports the insidious trade in illegal wildlife that is plaguing animals throughout the world. Snakes have the misfortune of being not only quite prominent on the various endangered species lists, but also of sporting beautiful skins that many people covet for boots, belts, handbags, and other fashion accessories. If you wouldn't buy a snake belt, but you would buy a wild-caught snake, you're kidding yourself. Both trades are supplied by the same people, who think nothing of trapping a terrified wild animal and transporting it under the harshest conditions.

The Sad State of the Captive Wild Snake

Aside from the moral and ethical issues involved, a wild-caught snake is by far the inferior choice for a pet. She will invariably be unhappy, and she will probably refuse to cooperate with attempts to feed or care for her properly. She is also far more likely to carry disease and parasites.

The moral of the story? The wild-caught snake is a poor choice all around. A captive-bred snake from a reputable source is far more likely to be healthy, content with life in captivity, and less prone to stress. In short, the captive-bred animal is a far better choice for the responsible snake owner who is looking for a long-term relationship.

Where to Find Your Pet Snake

If this is your first foray into the world of snakes, you may be surprised to discover just how many options there are for finding a healthy captive-bred pet snake. Snakes are not just for pet shops anymore. Still, the clean, properly run pet shop can be a good source, especially if it is one of the new-and-improved pet shops that specializes in reptiles and amphibians.

The captive-bred stock in these shops is typically supplied by breeders who specialize in various species. Some of these breeders, believe it or not, also make their stock available through mail order. Don't immediately discount this as cruel or somehow inferior. Some fine breeders operate this way, and they guarantee the animals they sell. Steer clear, though, of the breeder who is a jack-of-all-species, master of none. Opt instead for one who specializes in specific species.

A reptile show is an excellent place to meet a variety of breeders. These fascinating events

Pampered Pet

When looking for a new pet snake, you may be surprised to discover the pet you're looking for at the local animal shelter. Not all shelters take in snakes, and many that do will adopt them out only to proven experts, but it may just be worth your time to call around and investigate.

showcase not only the animals, but the dedicated individuals who care for and breed them. Their enthusiasm and their complete devotion to these animals can be contagious, so keep your guard up. You don't want to go to a reptile show intending just to research different species, and come home with one of each. Sure your heart would be in the right place, but that is not a responsible way to choose a new pet snake.

Pet's Peeve

Small black dots near the scales can mean a mite infestation. Steer clear of any snake that has them, and all snakes that establishment is offering.

Evaluating Pet Serpents

Evaluating prospective pet snakes is fairly black and white. A healthy snake's eyes will be clear, as will her breathing, and her mouth will be free of any redness or white "cheesy" fuzz that can indicate the fungal reptile illness known as mouth rot. She should be amenable to being handled, and when you do handle her, whether she is a youngster or an adult, she should leave the clear impression that you are holding solid muscle in your hands, not a strand of cooked spaghetti.

The healthy snake will have an equally healthy appetite, which you may or may not have the honor of witnessing. Given the infrequency of most snakes' meals, you may have trouble being in the right place at the right time to watch a particular snake eat. This can be even trickier with a ball python, which has a reputation for being finicky about eating, so don't hold it against the snake if she is shy about taking a meal in front of an audience.

Pampered Pet

If you already have other snakes, consider the first two weeks a quarantine period for the newcomer, separating her from the general population until you are sure she is not carrying disease or parasites.

Avoid any snake with skin that exhibits lumps, pits, wounds, or small black dots near the scales. Avoid, too, a snake that seems overly nervous and agitated, or that is housed in a dirty enclosure or a crowded one. Lack of clean water, light, and heat sources in the enclosures are pretty obvious signs that this is not a responsible seller of snakes, and that the resident snakes are probably not all that well cared for.

A Snake in the House

As with any pet you purchase, preparing for a snake's arrival ahead of time is the only way to go. Get the enclosure ready, and then, once you bring your new pet home, be prepared to leave her alone for a while—as long as two weeks actually—so she can get accustomed to her new surroundings and all the unfamiliar scents and sounds. Your respectful distance during those first few weeks will be a welcome sign to your new pet that she has landed with people who are willing to give her the care she deserves.

A House Fit for a Snake

Preparing for your new snake involves first finding an appropriate enclosure. This is typically a glass aquarium-style tank with a sturdy screen top that can be securely locked in place. Size depends on the size of the snake. Smaller snakes, such as slender garters, can fare well in a 10-gallon tank, while larger snakes will require more spacious housing. Bigger is usually better with snake housing.

When You Get a Snake, You'll Also Have to Get These

Appropriate cage or enclosure	Rocks/plants for habitat
Secure cage cover	Heater
Food dishes	Reptile light
Water dishes	Two thermometers
Substrate material	Care book
Hiding places	

If you intend to buy a snake that likes to climb—say, a corn snake—you may want to buy a tank with a more horizontal design so you can install tree branches that will satisfy your pet's urge to cruise the treetops. Even if your snake isn't a climber, the tree branches can come in handy at shedding time as a nice rough surface against which the snake can rub. The tank should be roomy enough to accommodate all the necessary snake accouterments—water dish, hiding place, and so on—and preferably accommodate its resident at adulthood as well as it does during the snake's early months.

Proper Interior Decor

Most snakes hail from regions of the world known for thick foliage and distinctive landscapes. A bare enclosure, then, is not this reptile's idea of a dream home. You should furnish your snake's enclosure with several items that not only play key roles in maintaining the snake's health, but also enhance the hominess of the enclosure.

First, and probably most important to the snake during those first few days, is the hiding box. This can be a regular old cardboard box or the half-log design that our ball python friend Betty used. Whatever you choose, it must be large enough to fully contain the resident snake and, like everything in the enclosure, be kept clean, clean, clean. To round out the furnishings, you will need a heavy ceramic water dish (ever filled with fresh, clean water), two thermometers to keep track of the internal temperature at either end of the enclosure, and some type of basking spot (perhaps a smooth, flat stone).

Pet's Peeve

When designing your snake's abode, give a great deal of thought to where you will be placing it in your house. Avoid drafts and high-traffic areas.

What's Underfoot?

Flooring, too, is an important concern when contemplating snake decor. The simplest, least expensive flooring is newspaper. Stacked in layers on the bottom of the tank, the surface layers can be whisked away quickly and easily on those rare occasions when they become soiled by feces, food or water. Second in popularity is usually a wood-chip product, but this must *not* be made from aromatic—and therefore snake unfriendly—pine or cedar.

The Importance of Heat and Light

As we have learned, snakes, like all reptiles, rely on the temperatures in their environment to keep their bodies properly warmed. This leads us to our next concern: heat and light. Snakes need to live where it is light during the day and dark at night. As for heat, a chilled snake will lose her appetite and possibly develop respiratory problems. Heat for a snake means life.

The ideal temperature for one snake may not be so ideal for the next one, which is why it's important to do some research on your particular species. However, most snakes fall into the same basic range. During the day they may be most comfortable in temperatures ranging from the low 80s (°F) to the mid-90s. In fact, a range of temperatures is best because reptiles regulate their temperature by moving into and out of warm spots. So your snake's basking spot can be in the mid-90s, while the rest of the enclosure is a bit cooler. The mid-70s is usually appropriate for the night.

Snakes must also have pure, unfiltered sunlight, meaning light that has not passed through a window. That's because they need the sun's ultraviolet rays (UVA and UVB) to synthesize vitamin D_3—the lack of which can lead to a serious condition called metabolic bone disease. Since indoor snakes are not likely to get unfiltered sunlight, you must provide them with special reptile fluorescent lights—positioned above and away from the enclosure—that will radiate the vital full-spectrum ultraviolet rays your snake needs.

Providing Heat and Light

Heat and light are usually provided by what is considered a classic combination: an external, top-mounted incandescent light at one end of the tank to provide the heat, and a fluorescent bulb mounted externally at the opposite end to provide full-spectrum lighting without extra heat. The temperature should be monitored by two thermometers, one on each end of the tank.

With the heat source at one end, mounted over the basking area, the snake can move back and forth from warmer to cooler as her instincts dictate. If, however, your pet begins to lose interest in her food and your thermometers tell you that more heat is in order, do not resort to the hot rock, an artificial heating element that sits in the enclosure. This can be dangerous because sometimes these rocks grow too hot and burn a snake's skin as she rests against the rock for warmth. There are better alternatives, such as ceramic heating elements that sit underneath the tank and safely provide heat without light.

Keep It Clean

Your snake needs a clean home. That means picking up any uneaten food and scooping feces right away. It also means cleaning the water dishes every day. No snake's enclosure should ever look or smell bad. If yours does, clean it! And the entire enclosure will need to be regularly cleaned and disinfected. Get yourself on a schedule, and stick to it.

How to Feed a Snake (Very Carefully)

True or false: Snakes must have live food. The answer is false. Those of you who are captivated by snakes but also enjoy watching mice snuggle up together for a nap are in luck. This is not to say that your pet will be a vegetarian. Snakes need meat, and nothing but meat. And they must have that meat whole, if you catch my meaning. It just doesn't need to be alive.

The better acquainted you become with people in the reptile world, the more you will hear this as a prevalent theme: Don't feed live food. An unruly dinner item can injure a snake and certainly put her off eating for a while. Pre-killed and frozen food is far safer for the snake (assuming that frozen food is completely thawed ahead of time), and typically easier for many an owner to offer.

If this dashes any prurient desires you may harbor to witness a life and death duel between a snake and its unsuspecting prey, perhaps you lack the respect for both the predator and the prey that is required for a pet like a snake.

Secrets from the Pet Files

The snake's jaw is amazingly engineered to enable her to eat what can often be rather large prey. The lower jaw can almost disengage, expanding the size of the mouth substantially and allowing the animal to gobble down a large meal.

While it's true that many snakes need to see their food moving before they strike, you can easily accomplish this by wiggling a thawed out mouse. But please use long tweezers or tongs for this operation. You do not want your snake to accidentally strike your hand. You also don't want your snake to associate hands in her enclosure with food because then she may strike when you're reaching in for a routine chore like removing the water dish.

Once you jump on the frozen food bandwagon, your greatest challenge may be where to store the food. You don't want guests finding a container of frozen mice in your kitchen freezer when they're just innocently looking for ice cubes, do you? Store them in colored or opaque airtight containers, and save everyone a shock fit for a horror film.

What to Feed a Snake

Just what food items should be stored in that opaque freezer container depends on the snake species you choose. We've already discussed the voracious and potentially expensive diet of the giant Burmese python (and that animal's larder would require an entire freezer of its own), but what about the more practical snake pets?

What Does a Snake Eat?

Mice	Rabbits
Rats	Insects
Chicks	Goldfish
Frogs	Vitamin-mineral supplements

What a snake eats often depends on how big it is. Garter snakes can actually do pretty well with fish and earthworms, which shouldn't require freezing unless you want to stock up. Ball pythons, the finicky guys of the bunch, and many of the other more common pet species, are happier with mice and rats—ideally pinkie, or newborn, mice and rats, available at pet shops.

As for frequency, the amazingly efficient snake metabolism requires only sporadic feeding. As a guideline and guideline only, midsized snakes require feeding only about once every week or two. But gauge your own pet's needs, with help perhaps from her breeder and/or veterinarian, and feed accordingly.

The Basics of Good Care

The following list of care guidelines will offer preventive medicine for snakes. Follow them in spirit and in deed, and your pet should live a long healthy life.

➤ Keep the housing structure clean, both inside and out; remove soiled flooring regularly.

➤ Feed sparingly, and preferably stick with the same food species throughout the snake's life.

➤ Do not handle your snake when she does not wish to be handled (for example, a ball python rolled into a ball wants to be left alone). Don't allow others to overhandle or bother your pet, either.

➤ Treat the snake with tender loving care during shedding time: no handling, no feeding, peace and quiet.

➤ Provide your snake with hiding places, as well as proper heat and lighting.

➤ Watch the skin for signs of illness, injury, parasites, or infection.

The Least You Need to Know

➤ Despite their legendary negative reputation, snakes are quiet, easy-care pets for people who don't have a lot of time for personal interaction with an animal.

➤ It's best not to parade a pet snake around out in public. This can be dangerous for the snake and result in negative PR for pet snakes at large.

➤ When choosing a new pet snake, think about your would-be pet's dietary preferences and ultimate size—and choose only a captive-bred animal from a reputable source.

➤ A snake is best housed solo in a roomy, private enclosure with a secluded hiding place, a dish of fresh water, safe flooring, a basking spot, a gradient of air temperatures (to stimulate appetite and metabolism), and UVA and UVB ultraviolet lighting.

➤ Snakes are die-hard meat eaters, but despite the most common images to the contrary, it's safest to feed them pre-killed rather than live prey.

Chapter 18

Totally Turtles and Tortoises

> ### In This Chapter
>
> ➤ A day in the life of a tortoise
>
> ➤ Living with turtles and tortoises
>
> ➤ Choosing a healthy pet that could very well outlive you
>
> ➤ Responsible care of turtles and tortoises

There are few creatures as ancient and dignified as turtles and tortoises. Having made their homes in a wide variety of environments, ranging from tropical rain forests to arid deserts, these reptiles have witnessed through the ages just about all of human progress.

And when we say ancient, we mean not only the roots of the chelonian family tree, but also the individual members of that tree, for these are some of the longest-lived animals on the planet. Those who welcome tortoises into their families soon revise their wills to name a legal guardian for the family pet, because it is not at all unusual for a properly cared for tortoise to outlive her owners.

Our goal, then, is to offer these animals such exquisite care that they become family heirlooms, and ensure that they meet each new generation with the robust health and abiding trust that they, as witnesses to history, so richly deserve.

Turtles and Tortoises As Pets

	light	1	2	3	4	5	*heavy*
Time commitment				✔			
Grooming			✔				
Feeding					✔		
General cleanup					✔		
Suitable for kids age infant to 5		✔					
Suitable for kids age 5 to 10			✔				
Suitable for kids over 10					✔		
Sociability				✔			
Expense of keeping				✔			

A Day in the Life

With so many different species of turtles and tortoises from so many different regions of the world, how can we possibly explore a day in the life of a single turtle or tortoise and suggest that it is representative of the care of the entire chelonian family? We can't. That is why we will be spending the day with a single member of that family, a tortoise named Toni. We will allow her to introduce us to what charmed and charming lives these animals can live, regardless of species and care requirements, when they are housed with someone who understands what they need.

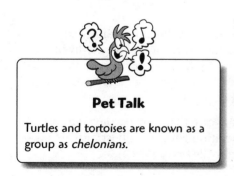

Pet Talk

Turtles and tortoises are known as a group as *chelonians.*

A Morning Introduction

Welcome to Toni's house. Toni is a California desert tortoise. Her species, an endangered one, is an illegal pet species. But before you go calling the Fish and Game Department, let us explain. While the California desert tortoise is not an allowable pet species, certain individuals, specifically those who have been injured, rescued, or bred in captivity, can be kept by people who obtain special permits to do so. Toni lives with a family that did just that.

Toni awakens at dawn and crawls out from her corner by the refrigerator where the air is warm. She awaits her sumptuous breakfast of apples, plums, tomatoes, and dandelion greens that will be served shortly. She may be a slow mover, but when her feeding dish is filled with that delectable cuisine, she can be surprisingly enthusiastic. Her family never tires of watching her feast. And they never stop thinking about what her fate might have been had they not come along to save her.

Life, you see, has not always been so luxurious for this tortoise. Two years ago she was crawling along the floor of California's Mojave Desert, minding her own business, when an all-terrain vehicle sped by, nicked the edge of her shell, and sent her flying into the highway. She was stunned, injured, and immobilized. A car stopped. Two hands reached down and gently picked up the terrified creature. The people in that car brought her to a doctor, who nursed her back to health. Soon life as she knew it was forever changed. She now lives happily with her knights in shining armor, enjoying a lifestyle that takes her both indoors and out, and provides her with all the fresh and luscious food she can eat. Funny where fate takes you sometimes, isn't it?

Secrets from the Pet Files

Given the antiquity of the turtles and tortoises on this planet (they shared the earth with the dinosaurs), it's not surprising that these animals have played a role in folklore throughout the world. One of the most universal images is that of the turtle as creator. Several Native American tales, for example, tell of the world resting on the strong and resilient shell of the turtle.

Sunbathing at Noon

In all her 25-odd years of life, Toni has been a sun worshipper. There's just something instinctive in her that sends her seeking the soft rays that bathe her in warmth. Of course, she probably doesn't understand that she needs that sun to survive. Just the irresistible pleasure of basking in it is good enough for her.

Fortunately, Toni's caretakers do understand the significance of the sun to this reptile. They have thus provided her with accommodations that allow her to take full advantage of it within their California backyard. Before giving her free rein, they surveyed the surrounding fence to ensure that even the most skilled burrower couldn't escape. Then they reviewed the vegetation for pesticides that could prove deadly to a tortoise who loves to graze. They cordoned off an area of the yard that they christened Toni's Area, and set her free in it.

How she loves Toni's Area! There she can bask in the sun, as she is this fine afternoon. And when she's had enough, she can take cover under the large leaves of the dwarf palms along the perimeter or step into her shallow pool for a soak. The desert seems miles away now.

Secrets from the Pet Files

Reptiles are considered a cold-blooded family of animals, but this can be deceiving. In truth, they are animals whose blood is warmed or chilled by whatever external temperature they happen to be exposed to at the moment. This is why we so often see reptiles basking in the sun—do-it-yourself body temperature control. Once their blood has been warmed sufficiently by the sun, they may move into a cooler spot, or use the resulting energy to go out and look for some dinner.

Evening Respite

As the sun begins to descend, Toni begins to slow down—even slower than she already is. She is brought into the house and allowed to meander around the kitchen while dinner is prepared. The family knows to watch their every step during this customary time of family togetherness. The two cats get in on the scene, walking over to nose around their unusual housemate. They mean her no harm. They could do her no harm even if they did. Toni simply retreats into her shell, just as she used to do with the coyotes.

For dinner, Toni munches on her fresh greens. After dinner, she joins the family for some television. At the commercials, her owners gaze at her and smile. They comment on how they would really like to get another Toni someday. They've already proven themselves worthy to take on that responsibility. "She may outlive us," they say. They always say that. The kids know that someday, it will be their refrigerators that Toni retreats behind at bedtime—and perhaps their kids' refrigerators after that. And that is just peachy with them.

Chelonian Social Studies

At the most tender of ages, we begin to hear those words: Slow and steady wins the race. This is the moral, of course, of Aesop's legendary tale about the tortoise and the hare, in which a quick but cocky hare loses a race to a tortoise who plugs along and never loses sight of his goal. That would be the tortoise, all right, say those who know her best. Living as they do with creatures so single-minded in their determination and dignified in their presence, many keepers through the years have found these animals, tortoises and turtles both, to be irresistible companions.

Natural Chelonian History

Reptiles have been making major strides in the popularity department in recent years, thanks to the release of such films as *Jurassic Park,* and restrictive and increasingly urban living situations. But they still tend to get a bad rap. Except the turtles and tortoises, that is. Many people either don't know that these very popular animals are reptiles, or simply would rather not think about their zoological roots. But reptiles they are, and proud of it.

The reptiles are a fascinating family. They have evolved to withstand the challenges of all climates and all environments. There are turtles and tortoises that live on land, in the water, and even buried in the mud. Some live in salt water, some in fresh. Some in the woods, some in the ocean, some in the desert. Despite the lifestyle that ultimately

Secrets from the Pet Files

Approximately 300 species of turtles and tortoises today call the earth home, but those numbers could soon decline dramatically. Thanks to habitat destruction, pollution, predation, and human poaching of turtles and tortoises for their body parts for clothing, carved artifacts, and even soup, many, if not most of these animals now face the finality of extinction.

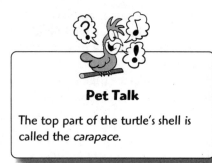

Pet Talk

The top part of the turtle's shell is called the *carapace*.

awaits them, they lay their eggs on land. When they hatch, the young are adults in miniature (and absolutely adorable)—their features identical to what they will be as adults. Their instincts will then lead them to their fate, whether that be swimming the oceans, burrowing into the muddy bank of a pond, or basking in the sun of a suburban backyard.

That Magnificent Shell

The shells worn by most turtles and tortoises are truly Mother Nature's works of art. But nothing in nature is frivolous, and the shell's role as a survival adaptation is un-matched. It protects the soft body of the reptile that would otherwise be defenseless. Without that shell, these animals never would have survived on this planet for 200 million years, nor would individual animals enjoy the long lives many do today. Yet that shell can also be a curse. Wherever you see displays illustrating the horror of the illegal international wildlife trade, you will always see turtles and tortoises featured prominently as victims.

Contrary to the beliefs of poachers and those who purchase their wares, the purpose of the shell is not for jewelry, combs, belts, or decorative carvings. Its purpose is to protect its wearer from predators, rough weather, and even her own clumsiness.

The shape of each individual species' shell actually tells us much about the job for which it was designed in the wild. Avid swimmers, for example, tend to have smooth, flat shells, while those that must contend with dangerous, powerfully jawed predators are protected by shells featuring a series of pointed bumps not unlike the peaks of a jagged mountain range. Biting down on that just once would certainly convince a predator to look elsewhere for dinner.

Turtles and Tortoises: What's the Difference?

As often happens in the animal kingdom, everything is not all black and white. That is certainly true when you are attempting to understand the differences between turtles and tortoises. We will thus generalize, but remember, there are always exceptions.

In a nutshell, or shall we say, turtle shell, turtles and tortoises both require constant access to water, yet turtles (not all, but some) are more inclined to be aquatic in nature. An example is the ever-popular red-eared slider, who inhabits not just human households but also all manner of ponds and lakes—assuming, of course, that there are handy perches on which they can bask in the sun.

The tortoise, on the other hand, tends to be more terrestrial in nature, content to live with her four feet

Pet Talk

A *herpetologist*, derived from the word *herpetology*, is someone who is involved in the study and husbandry of reptiles.

planted firmly on the ground. Tortoises also tend to be the longer-lived of the two, some reaching the century mark with ease. Some even continue to grow throughout their long lives; hence the giant tortoises that so fascinate us whenever we see them in photographs or meandering around the zoo.

A Worthy Role Model

It's tough to withstand the power of the chelonian gaze. Deep within those eyes lurks the wisdom of the ages. Install one of these animals in your home, pay her the respect that is her due, and you may soon feel that you are cohabiting with a Zen master. Soon you can't imagine what it would be like without her quiet presence in your house. Soon the house is not a home without this animal.

Poll a group of turtle and tortoise enthusiasts, and you will come away viewing these animals as gentle role models for the human species—animals that embody grace, dignity, determination, and resolve. You will also discover firsthand the addictive nature of turtle and tortoise keeping, for the majority of people you ask will probably be living with a variety of the animals. Most chelonian species can coexist with others of their own and other species, as long as they have plenty of room to move around—and as long as there is ample grub at mealtimes. Food, you see, can be a sensitive subject among turtles and tortoises.

Kids and Other Pets

Turtles and tortoises can make excellent pets for children, as long as the kids and any friends they might have over are supervised and taught proper respect for this old soul. Go ahead and introduce them, but keep an eye on the situation. You certainly don't want your pet, an animal you may have inherited from your grandmother, to fall victim to unruly kids or teenagers who find it funny to find out just what it takes to make a tortoise retreat into her shell.

Make sure you teach your kids the proper way to handle a turtle or tortoise. Place one hand on each side of the shell and grasp it firmly and securely. Lift the animal up with a smooth motion, your charge's weight distributed equally on each side. Don't be surprised if she begins to paddle her legs as if swimming when airborne. Consider this exercise and maintain your secure grip.

If the animal you're holding is unaccustomed to such handling, be ready for a bite to your hand or even a sudden bowel movement. Contrary to external appearances, life with a turtle or tortoise is never boring.

As for other pets, turtles and tortoises, equipped as they are with their own protection, usually fare well when surrounded by dogs, cats, and other animals. When the family dog or cat becomes overly enthusiastic in socializing, that shell comes in quite handy. But again, keep intentional harassment in check. Undue stress is not good for any creature.

What Does a Turtle or Tortoise Cost?

The purchase price of a chelonian pet can vary widely, but the average is $20.33.

The average turtle or tortoise owner also spends per year:

$44	Food
$30	Other supplies
$10	Veterinary care
$5	Toys

Finding a Pet to Outlive You

Any pet of any species deserves an owner who takes the time to find out just what care the animal requires. Turtles and tortoises are no exception. They aren't ones to complain, but they won't live even a fraction of the long, full life they're genetically entitled to if you don't plan ahead. Much thought should go into the decision to live with a turtle or tortoise, and which one to live with.

Pampered Pet

Whenever you add a new turtle or tortoise to your family, quarantine the newcomer for up to three months to ensure that it will not infect your existing population with an undetected illness or parasites.

What Is Legal, What Is Available?

Given the protected status of the vast majority of the world's turtles and tortoises, only a fraction of the existing 300 species may legally be kept as pets. But there's a related issue to consider: the wild-caught versus captive-bred controversy. Accept a wild-caught animal, and you may be taking in a pet that is miserable in captivity, and is not quite as healthy as its captive-bred counterpart.

Toni, in our story at the beginning of this chapter, is an exception. She was taken in when she would not have survived in the wild. And she is cared for by experienced chelonian keepers who have proven their expertise with other species.

Purchase a wild-caught animal and you may also be inadvertently supporting participants in the illegal wildlife underground—people who trade in animals for both the pet and body-part markets. How fortunate that today so many captive-bred animals are readily available from a variety of sources, improving the possibility of your success as a chelonian keeper and exonerating your conscience.

What Is Right for You?

Care requirements, too, are a critical factor in your choice of a turtle or tortoise. Grounded in individual biological needs and native habitat, they vary as dramatically as the many species who comprise the chelonian family. It's wise for beginners to start out with an easier keeper—say, a red-eared slider or a North American box turtle.

And while you're researching the backgrounds of the various pet chelonians, consider your own native habitat. If you live in Phoenix, Arizona, and you long for a tropical species that requires a humid environment—perhaps the yellow-footed tortoise—call the moving company and get ready to hightail it to Florida because this tortoise will have a tough time of it in the desert, no matter how hard you try to accommodate her. Legal issues, care requirements, environment—you have quite a job ahead of you, don't you? But how rewarding the results can be when you do it right.

Pampered Pet

Be fair to your new pet. Choose a species that you are prepared to care for.

Where to Go for a Healthy Shelled Pet

As the popularity of turtles and tortoises has increased, would-be owners can now find a rich selection of these animals in a variety of venues. Traditional pet shops are the most obvious option. Just be sure to deal only with shops that are clean and house their stock properly. But you may not find some of the more exotic species within their displays. For that you are probably better off seeking out one of the reptile-amphibian specialty shops that are cropping up around the country (again, they must be clean and properly managed). These should not only carry a wider selection of animals, but also employ a knowledgeable staff of reptile-crazy people.

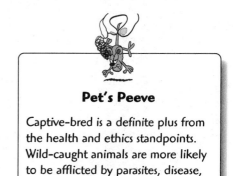

Pet's Peeve

Captive-bred is a definite plus from the health and ethics standpoints. Wild-caught animals are more likely to be afflicted by parasites, disease, and/or debilitating stress.

Don't discount the possibility of the animal shelter or rescue groups, either. Today there are rescue groups devoted solely to the rescue and placement of turtles and tortoises. Some animal shelters are also willing to take in the animals when they are rescued from situations of abuse or neglect, or merely found meandering unclaimed down a quiet street, nibbling on the grass and an occasional flower.

And finally, there are breeders, who are plentiful these days. Attend reptile shows, which are also plentiful these days, and you'll meet a whole herd of turtle and tortoise breeders all gathered together in one fascinating locale. But be careful. Their enthusiasm can be contagious, especially when you meet the animals they have bred. As soon as you witness a family of newly hatched leopard tortoises, tottering about in their seemingly oversized shells, two or three invariably arguing over the plumpest, juiciest mealworm, the most adorable little creatures you've ever seen, you'll understand why these shows invariably gain new converts to the reptile cause.

How to Choose a Healthy Chelonian

You've done your homework, prepared your home for your pet's arrival, and now comes the moment of truth. First you must evaluate the living conditions of your potential companion for cleanliness, spaciousness, and appropriateness. Then do some investigating into the animals' backgrounds. Are they captive-bred or wild-caught? How old are they? What have they been fed? If you like the answers, it's time to meet the candidates.

The ideal candidate, one that, depending on the species, could be with you and your family for the next century, has:

➤ A spring in her step

➤ Strong, muscular legs that are capable of moving her forward with power and efficiency

➤ A healthy appetite

➤ An interest in her surroundings

➤ Clear, bright eyes

➤ Evenly textured skin

➤ Easy, clear breathing

➤ Nose and mouth free of fluid

➤ No shell or skin injuries

➤ Firm, hard shell

➤ A solid feel, as if she's full of water

Beware of an animal with a runny nose or open-mouth breathing, which can indicate respiratory problems. Also steer clear of turtles and tortoises with swollen eyes, and a soft shell in a species meant to be hard shelled—nutritional and sunlight inadequacies could be to blame. Beware, too, of a whitish, fuzzy growth around the mouth and tongue, accompanied by a foul odor. These are the classic signs of mouth rot, or necrotic stomatitis, an extremely contagious disease of the reptile family.

Pampered Pet

The shell of a turtle or tortoise is actually part of the chelonian skeleton, which is why its condition is always a clue to the animal's nutritional health.

The Ideal Chelonian Lifestyle

All in all, turtles and tortoises rank as rather easy-care pets, but this does not let you off the hook in the responsibility and commitment department. While their demands are few and their demeanors quiet, proper housing and respect is just as important to turtles and tortoises as diet, heat, and light. Strive toward providing these in the correct balance for your particular pet, and you will experience firsthand just how rewarding the keeping of turtles and tortoises can be.

The Right Environment for the Right Species

Housing design for turtles and tortoises depends on the species. Some, for example, will require a swimming pool, while the priority for others will be a shallow water pan or heavy ceramic dish for soaking and drinking, and solid footing to maintain their sense of security on the ground. Nevertheless, certain elements remain standard for all.

First, whether you choose to provide outdoor accommodations (ideal for sun baskers during the warmer months of the year), indoor digs, or a combination of the two, the animal's enclosure must be sufficiently chelonian-proofed. Turtles and tortoises can be surprisingly skilled escape artists. Don't learn this the hard way. Indoor-outdoor accommodations may include an indoor wood-framed glass terrarium or aquarium, or a wire exercise pen made for dogs. This is then

Pampered Pet

Turtles that need a semi-aquatic environment will need all the equipment you need for an aquarium, including a water filter and an air pump.

complemented by an outdoor pen—a canine exercise pen, a child's wading pool, or a securely fenced backyard—that keeps the animal confined yet allows her an area for free movement.

The Proper Interior Decor

The turtle or tortoise enclosure designed for a particular species' needs, should be furnished with equally appropriate accessories: a basking spot (perhaps a large flat stone); a spacious, accessible shelter that doubles as a hiding place; and an appropriately sized water source filled with clean water.

Safe flooring, too, is critical, especially for terrestrial turtles and tortoises. Gravel is fine for an aquatic species that will rarely touch the ground, but this can threaten the health of a terrestrial turtle or tortoise. For this animal, whether you choose shredded paper, peat moss, alfalfa pellets, indoor/outdoor carpeting, or the natural grass of

Pet's Peeve

Never, ever, *ever* assume that a logical way to confine a turtle or tortoise to her yard is to drill a hole in her shell, run a chain or rope through it, and tie the other end to a stake. Believe it or not, people do this. It is cruel and unusual punishment to these animals.

an outdoor corral, keep it clean. Remove flooring immediately when it becomes soiled with food, feces, and urine, and change the flooring material completely every week.

If your pet is, say, a box turtle or tortoise who enjoys burrowing, make sure the flooring is deep enough to accommodate that impulse. A hill of moss will be a most-welcomed burrowing element, and you can help maintain environmental moisture by spritzing the hill every few days with water.

The Trinity: Heat, Light, and Moisture

We'd probably rather not even think about all the turtles and tortoises who have died needlessly through the years in the hands of people who were too ignorant or too young to care for them properly. This won't be happening to your pet, though, will it? Oh, no. You know the secret. Turtles and tortoises need heat, they need light, and they need moisture—and you're going to provide them.

When You Get a Turtle or Tortoise, You'll Also Have to Get

Appropriate cage or enclosure	Swimming or soaking pool
Secure cage cover	Heat light and/or ceramic heater
Food dishes	Reptile light
Water dishes	Two thermometers
Substrate material	Basking spot
Hiding places	Care book
Rocks/plants for habitat	

As with all elements of turtle and tortoise keeping, the proper balance of heat, light and moisture for a given animal depends on species. Most species will be fine in daytime temperatures that range somewhere between 75° F and the high 80s. But moisture requirements will vary dramatically depending on whether an animal is aquatic or terrestrial, with tropical or desert origins. Do your homework and get acquainted ahead of time with what your particular pet will require.

Power from the Sun

And now about the lighting. Reptiles must have light. Without it they cannot metabolize their food correctly, and without a combination of heat and light, they won't even eat. This must, however, be the appropriate type of light: full-spectrum, including ultraviolet rays, types A and B. Full-spectrum lighting is most easily, most effectively supplied by the natural light of the sun, in which your pet can bask during her forays into the great outdoors.

In the absence of outdoor accommodations, or during the wan days of winter, you will need to provide an acceptable substitute. That means a full-spectrum reptile light. Install the overhead fluorescent kind at one end of the enclosure to provide the rays without the heat. If you need to raise the heat a bit, too, this can be done with an incandescent light bulb, installed in an overhead position at the end of the enclosure opposite the fluorescent fixture. Your pet may then move about, basking under the light and moving out of the light as needed. Turtle or tortoise knows best.

Safe and Clean

Pet's Peeve

Sunlight filtered through a window or a glass enclosure will not have the UVB rays your pet needs. Without unfiltered sun, only a special reptile light will do.

Turtles are not clean animals. They poop a lot, sometimes even in their swimming pool. That means scooping feces right away, cleaning out the pool as often as is necessary, and picking up any uneaten food. No chelonian's enclosure should ever look or smell bad. If yours does, clean it! And the entire enclosure will need to be regularly cleaned and disinfected. Get yourself on a schedule, and stick to it.

A Word About Salmonella

Several decades back, a law was passed to protect children. The law said no chelonian could be offered for sale that is smaller than four inches across. That meant those tiny, ever-popular red-eared sliders, staple items at the local drug store, would no longer be available for purchase. The idea behind banning the young turtles was that children would not contract salmonella by placing their pets in their mouths or placing their fingers in their mouths after handling the turtles.

While the idea was a bit skewed, this law unexpectedly ended up protecting the turtles, too. No longer relegated to the care of young children and a short life span due to less than stellar care, these tiny turtles were offered the chance to grow up and shed their disposable pet image.

But the danger from salmonella is real. Most reptile species tend to be carriers of salmonella. Owners are wise to become rather obsessive about hand washing and general household cleanliness. You'll find some hints that will help prevent the spread of salmonella in Chapter 16, Leaping Lizards.

Satisfying a Voracious Appetite

At first glance, given the genteel countenance of the turtle and tortoise, we would naturally assume that these animals must be vegetarians. But that assumption would be only half correct. In the wild turtles and tortoises dine on a combination of vegetation and animal protein, the latter typically obtained in the form of insects and worms. Your job is to mimic this natural diet as closely as you can within a captive environment.

What Does a Chelonian Eat?

Terrestrial chelonians	Fresh vegetables (except lettuce)
	Fresh fruits
	Earthworms
	Insects
	Mealworms
	Lean dog food
	Vitamin/mineral supplement
Aquatic chelonians	Live goldfish
	Earthworms
	Snails
	Commercial trout pellets
	Leafy greens (very sparingly!)

The bulk of the diet for most species should be vegetarian-based: fresh fruits and veggies, such as squash, tomatoes, apples, plums, cantaloupe, strawberries, and okra. Go easy with the greens, and try to limit them to collard greens, romaine lettuce, dandelion greens, and escarole. For protein, you can offer your pet meat on the hoof, including snails, crickets, night crawlers, or, if the live food makes you squeamish, a high-quality commercial dog food.

The recipe for a nutritionally healthy turtle and tortoise includes the following practices:

➤ Feed your pet once each day.

➤ Remove old food when it's time for the next day's meal.

➤ If at all possible, allow your pet to graze in a pesticide-free yard from time to time, where she can nibble on her own preferred greens and maybe even hunt her own bugs.

Pampered Pet

A healthy, varied diet is top priority for a turtle. Captive turtles are very susceptible to dietary deficiencies, and nutritional problems are probably the leading cause of death.

A Long Winter's Nap

As autumn approaches and the mercury begins to fall, along with the changing leaves you may notice some changes in your turtle or tortoise. The appetite diminishes, and the animal becomes sluggish and restless, roaming aimlessly in search of shelter. The hibernation impulse has been triggered.

Not all turtles and tortoises hibernate, and among those who do, not all of them should. Sick, malnourished, or otherwise weakened animals absolutely must be prevented from taking a winter's snooze, as should most of the tropical species. Only the healthiest, most robust turtles and tortoises of species for whom hibernation is common should be allowed to indulge: California desert tortoises and box turtles, to name two.

Hibernation Tips

You must assist your pet in her hibernation endeavors. Success is directly related to an owner's participation. Start by figuring out where hibernation will occur and in what type of shelter. Some owners opt for outdoor hibernation, but this is safe only in regions where winter temperatures do not dip below about 38°F. Otherwise, indoors it is.

Pet's Peeve

A hibernating turtle or tortoise housed for the winter in a garage must be safely ensconced in a corner or closet free of exhaust fumes, rats, and drafts. These can all be deadly to the sleeping chelonian.

Hibernation accommodations can range from an igloo-type doghouse in the backyard that you elevate above the ground and insulate with newspaper, hay, or leaves, to a high-sided cardboard box in the garage. Mainstream household locations are typically too warm to foster hibernation, but if you've got an unheated basement, that may do the trick. Check the hibernation site periodically throughout the winter to make sure it remains insulated and sheltered, and be ready come spring to welcome your well-rested and soon-to-realize-she-is-very-hungry pet back into the real world.

The Least You Need to Know

➤ The typical day in the life of a chelonian (turtle or tortoise) depends on whether the animal is aquatic or terrestrial; a vegetarian or a carnivore; a tropic, lake, pond, or desert dweller.

➤ Choose a captive-bred turtle or tortoise rather than one that is captured from the wild. Many species are endangered and are key targets of the international illegal wildlife trade.

➤ Depending on the species, turtles and tortoises can be housed either indoors or out—or a combination of both. Just make sure to design your pet's home (and diet) according to the needs of her particular species.

➤ Like all reptiles, turtles and tortoises require heat and UVA and UVB ultraviolet light—and the flexibility to move around to seek shelter or soak up whatever rays they require at a given moment.

➤ Choose a chelonian pet from a reputable breeder, pet shop, or rescue facility, and look for an animal with a healthy, uniform shell; bright eyes; clear breathing; a clean mouth; springy movement; even skin texture; and a healthy appetite.

Chapter 19

Secretive Salamanders

In This Chapter

➤ A day in the life of a salamander

➤ Learning to respect the salamander and his survival instincts

➤ Choosing a salamander of your own

➤ A primer on salamander care

We all began as salamanders. Well, sort of. You've heard of the primordial ooze, haven't you? Humans like to speak of that fateful moment in history when a small, simple ocean-dwelling creature emerged from its aquatic home and made a revolutionary step onto dry ground. You can almost hear the orchestra swelling. That moment, according to the most romantic renditions of evolutionary theory, would spawn every creature, every scientific discovery, every architectural marvel, every work of art that collectively would become the planet Earth.

It's a romantic vision, but the basic facts are true. When an unobtrusive sea creature mustered the necessary courage and momentum, ventured up and out of the primordial ooze, and realized that yes, he (or she) could breath oxygen and navigate on dry land, life on this planet would be forever changed. Capable of beginning life under the sea and then adapting almost miraculously to life on dry ground, this animal was what

we call an amphibian. All of evolution, then, may have been set into motion by a quiet, unassuming creature that probably looked very much like the salamanders that live among us today.

These creatures deserve some respect, then, wouldn't you think? But, like a well-known comedian always says, they just can't seem to get any. Perhaps that's because the salamander—a slimy creature with an enormous mouth—just isn't as cute and cuddly as a puppy or a bunny. No, we are more inclined to view the salamander with disgust. And the salamander's reaction? He simply prefers to be left alone.

Salamanders As Pets

	light	1	2	3	4	5	*heavy*
Time commitment			✔				
Grooming		✔					
Feeding					✔		
General cleanup				✔			
Suitable for kids age infant to 5		✔					
Suitable for kids age 5 to 10			✔				
Suitable for kids over 10					✔		
Sociability		✔					
Expense of keeping			✔				

A Day in the Life

Sammy is a salamander, and a lucky one. The people who own him know amphibians and they know salamanders. They thus know to leave Sammy alone, and to admire him from afar. They know that he doesn't like to be touched. It's nothing personal. It's just that for millions of years his kind have shied away from physical contact. They've had to. It's the slime. They must preserve the slime and thus their skin, their most vital organ. What a lucky salamander Sammy is. He lives with people who respect him and his slimy skin, who accept him for who and what he is.

Secrets from the Pet Files

While many of us think of a newt as simply an important ingredient in witches' brews, it is actually a close cousin to the salamander, and is almost exclusively aquatic. The newt's habitat is thus more of a challenge to maintain, more akin to an aquarium than to the terrestrial digs of most salamanders.

Sammy's Morning

It's morning, and Sammy's hungry. Sammy is often hungry. Those know-it-all owners of his know this, too, and first thing in the morning they're ready with the chow. They open the door to Sammy's well-appointed vivarium that so beautifully mimics a dark, damp woodland area. He's a bit irritated by what ensues. A string dangles into the terrarium. On the end is tied a small piece of raw meat. It flits around in a lame attempt to imitate the real thing. Those owners of his aren't real crazy about feeding their pet live food. They're always trying to convince him that perhaps raw meat dangled on a string is just as good. They've heard of some salamanders that have been convinced. Not Sammy. He's a purist, through and through. Nice try, though.

Admitting their defeat, they surrender the string. The door opens again. They let loose a fat, healthy nightcrawler. Sammy sits like a statue, a skilled hunter ready to pounce. Any minute now. Ready . . . gotcha! In an instant, he has captured his quarry within his large mouth.

Breakfast ended up being quite satisfying, and Sammy wriggles across to the other side of the vivarium for a rest. There he finds his favorite spot: a nest of sphagnum moss behind a thick branch that doubles as a fallen log. He settles in, protected from full view by some large leaves. This is the life. A full tummy and a secluded resting area. Those people out there think of everything.

Sammy's Afternoon and Evening

Not much new to report. Sammy's still hiding behind the fallen log. He's quite content there. Oh, wait a minute, there he is. He moves out very smoothly, very slowly, and looks around. He thought he detected some familiar movement out here. He did. A hand slowly enters the enclosure with a spray bottle that directs its contents at the moss hill. And the moss hill only. Sammy enjoys the brief spectacle, probably even understanding the significance of what is taking place.

As the afternoon wears on, Sammy just does more of the same. He rests among the moss and protects his skin. That's just what salamanders do. It's what they've done for

millions of years. Sammy is carrying on a lifestyle that probably goes back further than any other lifestyle on earth.

After awhile, he emerges from his sheltered spot and surveys his domain. How satisfying it all is. No, it's not a genuine woodland, but his instincts tell him that it's certainly the next best thing. He has ample space in which to move and ample and appropriate hiding places in which to protect himself and his skin.

The fluorescent light atop his terrarium has been shut off. Time for some shut-eye. Good-night, Sammy. See you in the morning for more of the same.

Salamander Social Studies

Some animals love company. Some love being touched and cuddled and hugged. The salamander is not such an animal. He has no choice in the matter. It's an issue of life or death for this fascinating amphibian. Touching and handling risks the health of the salamander's skin, the most important organ of the animal's body. That means the survival instinct for the salamander translates into an instinct to protect his skin.

Never underestimate this instinctive drive. It is the core to the salamander's existence and will affect your relationship with your pet from the moment he enters your home. Indeed, the more we learn about salamanders and their very logical priorities, the better we respect them and the more content our slimy pets will be.

What Is an Amphibian, Anyway?

What amazing creatures comprise the amphibian family of the animal kingdom! All amphibians share similar physical characteristics:

➤ Large heads and mouths—assets to these quintessential carnivores that are ever-hungry for live food

➤ Moist skin that plays a pivotal role in respiration and hydration

➤ Protective coloring and patterns that can range from spots to stripes, to help hide the animal from predators in whatever region of the world he happens to call home

➤ Delicate, almost human-like hands that offer both balance and propulsion when the animals move

Even more dramatic is the amazing biological programming of amphibians—the internal blueprints that govern their development. While as adults a particular species of amphibians may live primarily in water or on land, or a mix of the two, many begin life under water. Young amphibians must therefore be excellent swimmers and be able to breathe exclusively under water.

As time passes, they experience a miraculous transformation. They sprout legs and a new respiratory system designed for breathing on land. Isn't nature grand?

Biologically speaking, amphibians are considered somewhere between fish and reptiles, a definition in keeping with the amphibian's adaptations to both water and land. Do not assume, however, that because of his lizard-like appearance, that a salamander should be treated like a reptile. Reptiles require regular exposure to ultraviolet light, either artificially in a captive habitat, or by basking in the sun. Subject an amphibian to such treatment, however, and you will dry out the critter's skin, dehydrate his entire system, and ultimately kill him.

The Salamander's Place in the Family Tree

The salamander is a somewhat unsung member of the amphibian family, playing second fiddle to the more adorable, more beloved frog. He tends to move slowly and methodically, except when predators are about. He typically moves with a zig-zag, almost snakelike twisting of his thick, muscular body; and his long, thick tail whips back and forth as part of that zig-zag motion. In an effort to protect his precious skin from dehydration and himself from predators, he will spend a good deal of his time undercover, typically in sheltered woodland areas. He must. Careless exposure means death.

Pet's Peeve

Every day humankind gobbles up the secluded and sheltered woodland areas that amphibians of all kinds call home, in the name of development and progress. The result is a decline in wild lands and in amphibian populations.

Your Role as Slime Protector

We humans talk endlessly about maintaining the youthful moisture of our skin, but for the salamander, it's not a vanity issue. It's life or death. Salamanders, you see, breathe through their skin, survive because of the camouflage it provides, and remain plump and hydrated because of its moisture. Faced with such massive responsibilities, that skin must remain moist and protected.

Your mission the moment you decide to bring a salamander into your family is to commit to the preservation of your pet's slime. Now this doesn't mean you have to slather petroleum jelly on him every night before bed (in fact, please don't do anything like that!). It does mean that you must honor this animal's quiet, protective nature; provide him with ample moisture and hiding places within his home; watch for signs of illness and injury to the delicate salamander skin; and keep handling to a minimum. Through these simple actions, you will maintain the slime. The salamander's body, protected from direct sun and dry air, will do the rest.

Taking Clues from Salamanders in the Wild

So now you may consider yourself properly prepared. You understand the salamander's priorities, and you understand that a salamander, like a fish, is a pet that is best seen and not touched. Salamanders are obviously survivors, yet they can be felled quickly by improper care and stress, so you can be a better owner by learning about salamanders in the wild. Honor the salamander's penchant for dark and damp, provide him with a diet akin to what he would seek in the wild, and you may count yourself as one who respects the salamander for what he is and what he has been for hundreds of millions of years.

Pet's Peeve

Salamanders are most prone to bacterial and fungal illnesses. The classic sign of trouble is fuzzy white patches on the skin. Veterinary attention is required.

The joy of salamander ownership comes not from daily companionship, mutual communication, and tactile bonding, but from installing in your home a habitat that mimics what you would find in the most secluded, untouched recesses of the wild. The satisfaction of caring for such a pet comes from respecting what is in every sense both a wild and a legendary animal. In this way you may thank the salamander for making your existence possible.

Adding a Salamander to the Family

Since that first salamander-like creature left the water world behind, the salamander family has grown dramatically. Today hundreds of salamander species in every imaginable color and pattern populate planet Earth. Some are extremely slimy, while others feel almost dry to the touch. Some are rough-skinned, some are smooth. Some sport neon colors, tiger stripes, and leopard spots, while others, thanks to their home territories, prefer the more conservative earth tones.

Regardless of the particular type of salamander that strikes your fancy, this is not the simplest pet species to locate. It's less popular than frogs and most of the reptiles, so the salamander is best purchased from an individual or shop that values amphibians, understands them, houses them properly, and makes available only animals that have been bred in captivity. Doing so helps to ensure that you will wind up with a pet that is both well-adjusted and healthy. Not a bad place to start.

Pet Shops

While there are pet shops out there—and people who work in them—that fill this bill, you must use common sense when evaluating them. Imagine that you have combed your area exhaustively for shops that carry salamanders, all to no avail. At last you find a shop with available salamanders. But you look closer and discover that the display tank is inadequate (no hiding places, too dry). The employees are apathetic and not all that knowledgeable about where the animals came from or how they have been cared for. You notice a white fuzzy patch at the base of one of the animal's tails. What should you do? Continue your search, no matter how long it takes.

If you're lucky and diligent in your search, you'll find one of the up-and-coming pet shops that specializes in amphibians and reptiles and hires dedicated hobbyists to staff them. Even aquarium shops may carry salamanders, in honor of the animals' roots as fish. But regardless of the establishment you find, even one with an expertise in salamanders and a healthy stock of them to match, don't let down your guard. Evaluate them carefully, and don't settle for anything less than what your common sense tells you is right.

The Wild-Caught Salamander: A Ticklish Issue

There is one more source of salamander pets of which many an owner has taken advantage through the years. That would be venturing out into the animal's native woodland and simply taking a salamander home. Hey, why not? Because it's not really ethical, and it's not very wise, either.

In recent years, enthusiasts have voted almost unanimously that a captive-bred specimen is far superior as a pet to one captured from the wild. The wild animal will never really adjust to a captive environment, and it will spend its remaining days stressed and possibly ill. If you have other salamander pets, the wild-caught newcomer could transmit diseases from the wild to the existing population. No matter how you slice it, taking a salamander from the wild to be your new pet is simply not a good idea.

Setting a Pet Free

Taking a salamander from the wild can also lead to another rather serious side effect. Too often people adopt a wild amphibian and decide after a few days, weeks, or months of improper care that no, this isn't the pet they wanted after all. They tromp back out to the woods and set the animal free.

Pampered Pet

Out of respect for its solitary nature, each salamander pet should be housed separately.

Releasing a salamander back into the wild can be disastrous. It exposes the wild population to any illnesses or parasites to which the now-former pet may have been exposed during his unfortunate incarceration. The result? An epidemic in the wild population. It's a sad situation all around, and one that can be avoided by obtaining a captive-bred pet and making the proper preparations and commitments.

Believe it or not, the consequences can be even more disastrous if you release a captive-bred salamander into the wild. First is the same danger of disease. Next, your captive-bred pet does not know how to survive in the wild, and will most likely die.

However, if he's lucky enough to survive, things could be even worse. If he's not native to the area, he could begin breeding, creating a hybrid species that upsets the delicate ecosystem in the area. Non-native species have been known to take over areas, driving out all the native ones.

A Picture of Salamander Health

Once you have found the ideal source for salamanders, you should choose the healthiest salamander possible to come home with you. As you probably have guessed, temperament won't play much of a role here. Appearances, however, will.

Proper diet, air temperature, and humidity levels will all make themselves known in a salamander's external appearance. When evaluating potential salamander pets, then, look for a bright-eyed animal that is plump, moist, and muscular from head to tail. Steer clear of salamanders with skin lesions or those telltale signs of white fuzz that indicate infection—and steer clear of those that share a tank with infected salamanders, as well.

Bringing Your Slimy Pet Home

The steps are simple when you finally pick the right salamander for you. The first and most obvious step is to set up the salamander's vivarium before you bring your new pet home. A pet that thrives best in aquarium-like solitude can't really be expected to wait around in the living room twiddling his slimy, very human-like thumbs while you set up his house, now can he? No, that should all be taken care of in advance. Your confused, uprooted little amphibian will appreciate your foresight.

What Does a Salamander Cost?

The purchase price of a salamander can vary widely, but the average is $25.

The average salamander owner also spends per year:

$55	Regular veterinary care
$50	Food
$45	Other supplies
$10	Toys

When it's time to bring the slimy little dear home, remember that even during a short trip from the pet shop, you must preserve the moisture of the salamander's skin. This is best done by transporting him home in a small, secure, properly ventilated plastic box, complete with a clump of moistened sphagnum moss for his traveling and hiding comfort. Gently usher the little guy into his personal traveling compartment, and take him home. When you discover how stress-free this method is for all involved, you may just opt, like so many salamander owners have, to use it in lieu of direct handling whenever you need to remove your pet from his domicile.

Once home, release the salamander into his new abode and leave him alone for a few days. Depending on his personal adjustment to his new home, this may even mean waiting a few days before offering him his first meal. Just peek in on him every now and then to make sure all is well, and once he ventures out of seclusion to check out his new environment, offer him a cricket, or maybe a nightcrawler. He'll soon understand that this place can be trusted, that no predators lurk beyond the water dish, and that someone somewhere is providing the meals.

When You Get a Salamander, You'll Also Have to Get These

Vivarium with secure cover	Shelters and hiding spots
Water dishes	Mister
Sphagnum moss flooring	Holding box
Potted plants	Care book
Fluorescent light	

Admiration from Afar

Designing your salamander's new home is a serious responsibility, but it also adds an exciting new dimension to your home. It invites a little corner of nature into the modern household, much to the pleasure of the humans in that household and the salamander for whom it is all being done.

Playing Mother Nature

Dark, quiet, and damp: That is a salamander dream home. This does not mean he should be kept in complete darkness, cut off from all sensory stimulation. It simply means he should be offered the option. Your goal is to create a natural environment, much like the one he would choose to occupy in the wild.

First you must consider the structure. While elaborate pond-like ecosystem setups are available that can house a variety of animals together in the most natural setting possible, the traditional fish tank setup converted to a terrarium is the most commonly seen salamander habitat. When choosing your pet's tank, make sure the seams are secure and free of sharp edges that could cut that delicate skin. A well-ventilated top is equally critical, ideally in the form of a wood-framed, small-mesh, screen-style top that fits securely and is free of holes and tears.

In the wild, salamanders seek out environs that are cool and damp. Most species will thrive best in temperatures ranging from 65° to 75°F, so you are wise to re-create this for the salamander pet. And make sure the salamander's habitat is located in a corner of the house that is somewhat secluded and out of direct sunlight. Neither sun nor crowds make for a contented salamander.

Home Sweet Salamander Home

As for furnishings, every salamander needs a water dish, both for drinking and to assist in maintaining the proper humidity levels. For most species, the kind of dish that goes under a flower pot, filled each day with fresh water, will suffice quite nicely. Because of the nature of the salamander's diet, a feeding dish will be unnecessary, but other accessories will enhance the comfort of your pet's home. Soft flooring, for one, is a must. An ideal medium for this is fresh, soft sphagnum moss, which will protect the salamander's sensitive skin and give a very natural feel to the terrarium.

An ample supply of hiding places will also enhance your design of an imitation, almost bog-like, woodland floor. Furnish the abode with stone caves, driftwood, smooth rocks, pesticide-free leaves, and even live plants. For easiest maintenance, plants are best planted in individual pots that you can then embed

Pet's Peeve

Make sure the rocks, plants, and other hiding places have no sharp edges that could tear a salamander's delicate skin.

in the mossy flooring. And speaking of that moss again, a hill or two of moist moss is a salamander's delight. That would be so in the wild, and it is so in your home, as well.

While they will typically seek out the darker, more secluded recesses of their environment, most salamander species live in regions where sunlight does penetrate. You may create your own *photoperiods*—intervals of light and dark that simulate day and night— by installing a light at the top of your pet's terrarium that remains on during the day and is clicked off at night. Just like the sun. The safest, most effective light source is a fluorescent light that will provide the necessary full-spectrum lighting without heating or drying the cool, damp air so critical to salamander health.

Critical Humidity

In your zeal to keep your pet and his home moist and cool, you might inadvertently over-dampen the terrarium. The formula for maintaining proper humidity is really quite simple. Again, that sphagnum moss can be your most handy tool. Make a hill of the moss a staple in the terrarium, mist that hill and only that hill every other day or so, and you will achieve humidity nirvana. This practice, coupled with the presence of the shallow water dish and the cool 65° to 75°F air temperature, should be all your pet requires.

Housekeeping Chores

Your salamander cannot be healthy if his home isn't clean. Follow these guidelines and you'll find that cleanliness is next to happiness:

➤ Remove soiled bedding and uneaten food daily.

➤ Change the water in the water dish every day.

➤ Do not over-mist the habitat; a sloppy, wet environment invites a buildup of bacteria and fungi.

➤ Clean the entire habitat whenever it looks or smells dirty.

➤ Make sure to rinse all soap and chemical residue from every nook and cranny of the tank and all its furnishings.

Although handling of a salamander should be kept to a minimum, when it's time for a whole-sale cleaning of your pet's home, you'll have to remove your pet. Clean, moist hands are a must. Wash your hands thoroughly before touching your pet, and keep them moist and free of soaps or chemicals so as not to irritate the salamander's delicate skin. Many a concerned handler has even opted to nix the bare hands altogether, and handle their pets with latex gloves moistened

Pet's Peeve

Never grab a salamander by his tail. Not only does this endanger the animal's skin, but as a defense mechanism the tail will break off when handled that way.

with water. Such precautions only serve to protect the skin and prevent the dreaded stress that can leave your salamander open to illness.

Live Food Only

If feeding live food to a pet makes you squeamish, perhaps the salamander, or any amphibian, isn't right for you. While some owners have been known to convince their pets to take a morsel of raw meat that they bounce around on the end of a string in a weak imitation of life, this will not provide the animal with the balanced nutrition he requires, and it's not fair to expect him to settle for less-than-perfect nutrition.

What Does a Salamander Eat?

Earthworms	Mealworms
Crickets	Flying insects
Nightcrawlers	Vitamin-mineral supplements

Once you have decided you can deal with this particular component of salamander stewardship—a decision best made before you take a salamander as a pet—you will probably find that feeding time is not as gruesome as some believe. Salamander dietary staples include earthworms (preferably nightcrawlers), crickets, mealworms, and virtually any type of flying insect, many of which are available commercially. Feed him once each day, and only as much as he can ingest in a single sitting. You can further enhance his diet by dusting your pet's dinner first with a sprinkling of vitamin-mineral powder designed especially for amphibians and reptiles before sending it off to its fate.

At least its fate will come quickly. What may surprise you most about feeding your salamander is the gusto with which this quintessential carnivore approaches his meals. He starts off slow and graceful, watching his prey from afar. At this point it's hard to believe that this seemingly cumbersome creature will ever be able to catch so quick a mover as an insect or even a wiggly worm. You need not worry. When the time is right, he will strike, and his prey will never know what hit it. He has perfected this skill for millions upon millions of years. The fact that he is still with us is testament to his ability as a hunter. *Bon appetite!*

The Least You Need to Know

➤ Salamanders are solitary creatures that are best seen and not touched or played with. Their moist protective skin can be damaged or infected through mishandling or exposure to the elements.

➤ On those rare occasions when you must handle a salamander, make sure your hands are clean and moist.

➤ The ideal salamander habitat is dark and damp with a wealth of hiding places and a cool atmospheric temperature of 65° to 75°F.

➤ Maintain the proper moisture within a salamander habitat by building a small hill out of sphagnum moss, which you spritz every other day or so with water from a spray bottle.

➤ Devout carnivores, salamanders eat only live food, such as earthworms, crickets, mealworms, and flying insects.

Chapter 20

Fantastic Frogs and Terrific Toads

In This Chapter

➤ A day in the life of a frog

➤ Learning to respect and live with frogs and toads

➤ Choosing healthy frog and toad pets

➤ Natural care of frogs and toads

What is it about frogs and toads that makes us just want to drop whatever we're doing, dress them up in tuxedos, and listen to their funny witticisms about life? There is something otherworldly about these animals that together compose the largest and most notable branch of the amphibian family tree. We consider them ugly, yet at the same time we consider them cute. We cut them up in school, yet we fancy them to be princes in disguise. Their images are powerful fixtures, good luck charms, even totems, in societies around the world, evoking a combination of affection, respect, and revulsion.

From the very irresistible Kermit, to the melodically gifted Budweiser frogs, to that open-minded princess who sought a prince by kissing a frog, to the many fables featuring frog and toad protagonists, these animals are, and have always been, cultural icons. Perhaps it's the large, luminous eyes and permanent smile that hint at an inner wisdom and wit, or the lilting song that mesmerizes us on a warm summer evening when we hear frogs serenading one another as they laze about a pond waiting for flies to pass by. It's just one of those attractions that cannot be explained—or denied.

Many of us have sought the good karma frogs and toads promise by inviting the real animals to come into our homes and live with us. Good-natured as always, they comply, although they would rather not spend their days stuffed into the pocket of a child's jeans or locked away in a screw-top jar with holes punched in the top. In fact, they won't survive that way, as so many young children have found out. Contrary to these "charming" images of yesteryear, the care of amphibians in general, and frogs and toads in particular, is far more complex than any child, or his parents, ever suspected. Read on.

Frogs and Toads As Pets

	light	1	2	3	4	5	*heavy*
Time commitment				✔			
Grooming		✔					
Feeding					✔		
General cleanup				✔			
Suitable for kids age infant to 5		✔					
Suitable for kids age 5 to 10			✔				
Suitable for kids over 10					✔		
Sociability			✔				
Expense of keeping			✔				

A Day in the Life

With the many hundreds of frogs and toads found throughout the world in every imaginable type of environment, it would be impossible to paint a portrait of a day in the life of one of these animals that would speak for them all. We will thus spend our day with Buster, a bullfrog. Don't expect to meet any other frogs or toads in his abode. Buster lives alone. Were he to share his digs with another bullfrog, or any other amphibians, he would probably eat them for dinner—or be eaten himself. That's just how it is in the often brutal, not to mention carnivorous, frog-eat-frog world.

Morning with Buster

The sun peeks through the window. Only a diffused light enters Buster's densely landscaped terrarium, but Buster begins to stir. He's hungry. Nothing new about that. He moves out from the stone cave in which he had been snoozing.

Soon, a hand comes down through the top of the tank. Buster remains still. Though excited by the concept of prey being released into his abode, he knows not to move a muscle. An earthworm wriggles around on the soft mossy flooring of the enclosure. No contest here. Buster waits until the worm's wriggling brings it into striking distance and then snap! Got him.

Pet Talk

A *terrarium* is a glass (or plastic) aquarium for a reptile or amphibian that includes live plants and has a relatively high humidity.

The Middle of the Day with Buster

His hunger pangs relieved, Buster can get on with the other projects at hand. He hops around a bit, explores this corner, then that one. Most of the time, though, he's just content to hide away in one of the many sheltering structures within his domicile: the stone cave, the live plants with large protective leaves, the moss hill.

And speaking of that moss hill, it looks like it's time for a misting. The hand descends once more from the top of the tank, this time holding a spray bottle. The moss hill gets a light misting. Buster has no idea that this act is helping to keep his skin nice and slimy. He just appreciates the results: a cool, moist place in which to hide from any light and heat that might try to infiltrate his sanctuary and dry his all-important skin.

Secrets from the Pet Files

Although they are not typically as highly regarded as their cuter frog cousins, toads, too, lay a substantial claim to cultural fame. On the more negative end, they have long been falsely accused of causing warts. A more positive view is held by people in rural areas of the United States, who believe that when newlyweds spot a toad in the road, their marriage is destined to be filled with happiness and good fortune.

The Rest of the Day with Buster

Nothing much new to report from Buster. He has enjoyed the coolness of the day, just as he does every day. And he has enjoyed the ample opportunities to go undercover, just as he does every day. He begins to feel a bit more energetic as those dangerous, skin-drying rays of the sun retreat. Only then can a frog's skin be safe out in the open. A frog may be safer from predators in the evening, too, although Buster doesn't need to worry about that. In celebration of the promise of dusk, he exercises his voice a bit, much to the delight of the humans who maintain his private world—a world not at all unlike what he would occupy if he were a wild frog.

The Secret Lives of Frogs and Toads

Our fascination with frogs and toads is nothing new. We have long regarded their body parts as powerful aphrodisiacs and contraceptives, and we have viewed the frogs and toads themselves as symbols of good luck. This last role is obviously alive and well to this day, apparent in the number of people who fill their homes with frog figurines and other frog and toad collectibles, and the vast number of cartoons, greeting cards, and children's stories in which they appear.

Real flesh-and-slime frogs and toads of every imaginable shape, size, and color are found throughout the world in every imaginable environment. Although their voices are universally recognized, their lives remain quite secret. Whether they live on land, in trees, burrowed under the ground, or in water, they enjoy their privacy. As you will see, for a frog or a toad, privacy equals survival. In getting to know these fascinating amphibians, your goal should be to understand them so well that you can reliably duplicate their home environments—and thus their privacy—so that all may live happily ever after.

Frogs and Toads: Celebrate the Similarities

One look at a frog or toad of any species, and it is obvious that they are members of the same clan. They share the same basic, typically ribless body structure; the large head; the enormous, ever-smiling mouth; and those large, bulging eyes that are the stuff cartoon caricatures are made of.

Both are *amphibians,* animals that exhibit a fascinating set of characteristics. Content to be neither exclusively water nor land dwellers, these animals seek the best of both worlds, and have for hundreds of millions of years. Most amphibians rely on water for breeding and development purposes, then make a giant leap, literally, onto land, where they adapt to breathing oxygen from the open air. The skin is an amphibian's most vital organ, playing a multiple role as breathing instrument, camouflage and—programmed to alert its wearer to predators and his own prey—sensory organ.

Pampered Pet

All amphibians, including frogs and toads, are consummate carnivores.

Most come into the world as fish-like tadpoles, soon to experience an extraordinary metamorphosis that, dictated by an unseen genetic code, will see the slender tadpole sprout arms, legs, fingers and toes that look almost human in design. The head will thicken, the mouth will broaden, and the lungs designed for breathing underwater will miraculously leave their watery ways behind and adapt to life above the ground. If this transformation weren't a documented scientific fact that we witness with our own two eyes, we would never believe it possible.

Frogs and Toads: Vive la Différence

As for the difference between frogs and toads, well, that's not quite so easily defined. All we really have are some generalizations. There is a handful of characteristics that applies to frogs and another that applies to toads, but there are also exceptions to almost every rule.

In the name of broad generalizations, we can safely say that most toads are ground dwellers, preferring to spend their days camouflaged within a secluded corner of the world, imitating stones, mushrooms, or leaves with their earthy skin tones and patterns. And they are quite skilled at this. In fact, there could be a toad at your feet right this minute, and you might never even notice until he opened his mouth.

Frogs, on the other hand, which tend to be more agile and gregarious than their toad cousins, are more inclined to wear bright colors, made all the brighter by the greater moisture on their slimy skin. Frogs are more inclined to hop and/or swim while their toad cousins walk, and they are as a whole more attracted to water.

But it doesn't really matter which is which, does it? When you're looking for a frog or a toad as a pet, listen not to scientific delineations, but to that inner voice that says, "Wow, I like this one." "This one" could be a tiny, delicate, vivid chartreuse mantella frog, or a good old muddy-hued American bullfrog that exhibits many of the classic toad characteristics. No matter. Whichever one you like is the right one for you.

What Does a Frog or Toad Cost?

The purchase price of a frog or toad can vary widely, but the average is $25.

The average frog or toad owner also spends per year:

$55	Regular veterinary care
$50	Food
$45	Other supplies
$5	Toys

A Biology Lesson (No Dissections, Please)

Okay, now don't drift off. This is stuff you have to know if you intend to live successfully with frogs and toads and benefit from all that ancient wisdom that we seem to assume they possess. While we may enjoy conjuring up tales about frogs that behave and move and even dress very much like humans, we cannot for a moment forget that they are what they are: unique biological entities with specific needs. Commit to your long-term memory the three most important needs of frogs and toads, and you will be better prepared to meet those needs for them in a captive environment.

Number One: Skin Care

When many of us think of frogs, we think of that slimy skin. While it can be a tad repulsive to some Mother Nature never designs anything without a purpose. The frog was not endowed with that particular skin texture to disgust you. In fact, the frog or toad could not survive without his slime.

Millions of years in the making, that slimy skin is the ultimate survival tool. A frog or toad literally breathes through his skin, and it must be moist to facilitate this. Like a thirsty kitchen sponge, the skin sops up molecules of moisture from the animal's environment, fueling mucus production and keeping the animal plump and healthy inside and out.

Pet's Peeve

The greatest threats to a frog or toad are direct sunlight and excess heat, and their ability to zap a moist amphibian of his moisture and hence, his life.

Number Two: Live Food

While many a neophyte owner might like to believe that frogs and toads are gentle, dignified vegetarians, that image could not be further from the truth. Bloodthirsty, voracious carnivores is more like it. While not particularly vicious hunters, they are skilled. And sneaky, too.

In a typical hunt, a toad rests beneath a mushroom that could pass as his brother. No one would give him a second look. With those big eyes he watches his prospective quarry, say an earthworm or a fly. It wanders closer . . . closer . . . closer . . . *Snap!* Now you know just why these animals have such large eyes and even larger mouths. The better to eat you with, my dear.

Number Three: Hiding Places

If frogs and toads were to choose an anthem, it would no doubt be *Gimme Shelter*. These animals spend their lives seeking protection not only from predators, but from the elements, too. They arrive on this planet knowing innately, like all the frogs and toads who came before them, that their mission is to protect their most precious treasure: their skin. Only under cover of leaves, vegetation, logs, and other natural hiding places can they steer clear of those deadly rays from the sun. They usually wait until the evening hours to emerge from their sanctuaries, knowing that moonlight, shade, and cool air are a frog's and a toad's best friends.

Secrets from the Pet Files

The fabled image of the frog or toad who has only his wits on which to rely for survival is grounded in truth. Aside from those few species graced with toxins in their skin to ward off predators, these animals are armed with only the camouflage and sensitivity of their skin as protective weaponry in a large, very dangerous, predator-laden world.

This Is Not a Toy

The idea of a frog or a toad as a pet invokes images of Tom Sawyer sauntering down a dirt trail, the stick in his hand clattering against the wood of the fence he'll soon be whitewashing, a faint croak emanating from this pocket. This is not appropriate care for an amphibian pet. Yes, these animals can be a delightful, smiling presence in our lives, but they must be seen and not touched if they are to survive in a human household.

The frog and the toad, then, are pets more akin to fish in an aquarium than to dogs that are out and about playing with their owners. Frogs and toads need shelter and protection. They don't need constant handling or companionship from their

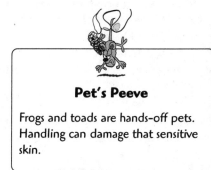

Pet's Peeve

Frogs and toads are hands-off pets. Handling can damage that sensitive skin.

owners (although some species do enjoy cohabiting with others of their own kind). Your role in their lives is not as playmate, but as caretaker, housekeeper, and food preparer. Your pet's role is as a fascinating household presence, an ambassador from the wild, offering over-civilized humans a glimpse into a natural and very ancient world.

A Very Healthy Addiction

Assuming everyone holds up his or her end of the bargain, a really very lovely symbiotic relationship can emerge between you and your amphibian. Though this is not what we classically consider a bond, you may quickly discover just why keeping frogs and toads can become so addictive. The more you observe your pets, and the more you learn about their larger family, the more inspired you may be to expand your own extended family of frogs and toads.

Soon your home may be filled with frog and toad terrariums (or *vivariums,* as they are called), and maybe even some frog aquariums should you venture into the aquatic species. You'll strive with each to provide a home that resembles as closely as possible the natural habitat from which he hails: a desert environment for a desert toad and a tropical rainforest for a family of tree frogs, for example.

Each is a beautiful addition to your home, as are the lilting songs of these animals that have for so many centuries regaled us with their music. And in the midst of all this, you discover that, wonder of wonders, your luck has improved dramatically. With a house full of happy singing frogs and toads to guide you, perhaps now would be a good time to start playing the lottery.

Pet's Peeve

Never, ever release a former pet back into the wild. It can place an inexperienced amphibian at a disadvantage; introduce a wild population to new diseases; and wreak havoc with the carefully balanced ecosystem upon which so many animals rely.

Choosing a Hopping Good Pet

A frog or a toad can be one of the most inexpensive pets you might obtain. Just go out to a local amphibian habitat—say, a pond or even the neighbor's swimming pool—and there you are, a new frog owner. But that really isn't the most responsible or the most compassionate route to take. In doing so, you are actually kidnapping the animal from his home, then thrusting him into a situation that is completely foreign to him.

A kinder, more responsible way is to find a frog or a toad that has been bred and raised in captivity. The good news is that amphibians and reptiles have been skyrocketing in popularity, so there are more of them available all the time. Once you start looking, you'll be amazed.

Where to Find Your Frog or Toad

Okay, so your backyard or any other "wild" environs are off limits for pet collecting. Then where are you to go? There are several options open to you. The first of these, of course, is the traditional pet shop. Frogs and toads, popular pets that they are, are readily available at such shops.

If you're lucky, you'll find a specialty shop that carries only reptiles and amphibians. These shops typically carry a wide range of species and supplies, and are usually staffed by knowledgeable folks who are devout hobbyists themselves. Just be sure that any shop you patronize is clean and avoids over-crowding its available animals.

Another option is the frog breeder. This isn't as odd as it sounds. They're out there, and they can be valuable sources not only of pets, but also of information. Breeding amphibians, and managing that legendary journey from water to land, requires knowledge and experience. Breeders may also specialize in a particular species that you are unable to find anywhere else.

> **Pampered Pet**
>
> Even if you decide to go with a frog from a pet shop in the beginning, keep breeders in mind as your ad-diction to these animals grows.

Where do you find breeders? Reptile shows that are held periodically throughout the country are the best places to start. Nowhere will you find such a vast array of frogs and toads—and of experienced amphibian keepers. You will also find directories in the back of reptile and amphibian magazines. Pet shops may also be able to put you in touch with the breeders they buy from—especially if you promise to buy your equip-ment from the shop.

How to Choose Your Pet

Given that frogs and toads are jealous of their privacy and ask only to be left alone, you won't be choosing your new pet based on how affectionate he is toward you. Your concerns when choosing are grounded instead in health, pure and simple.

A portrait of quintessential amphibian health is what you should look for:

➤ Bright, open eyes

➤ Muscular legs

➤ Plumpness

➤ Good appetite

➤ Natural color (not too dark or too light)

➤ Skin that is clean and uniformly moist

➤ The absence of abrasions or fuzzy white patches that could indicate infection

➤ Hops when gently prodded

➤ Fluid, easy hopping motion

Pet's Peeve

Beware of amphibians whose room-mates exhibit white patches, because these infections are contagious.

When you get your pet home, these same signs will tell you if he's well. Any pet you deem worthy of sharing your home with is also worthy of veterinary care. Fortunately, it's not as difficult these days to find a veterinarian who cares for amphibians and reptiles. Should you notice tell-tale signs of frog or toad illness—such as a loss of appetite, uncharacteristic listlessness or a white fuzzy growth on the skin—veterinary attention is in order. You can usually locate frog and toad special-ists through reptile shops, other veterinarians or referrals from other frog and toad owners.

Handle with Care

The key to successful frog and toad keeping is education. With so many species to choose from—and with so many variables at play in their care—the better educated you are, the better amphibian keeper you will be. A green tree frog, for instance, will require a housing situation quite different from that of a burrowing toad. Do your homework before you succumb to the charms of a particular frog peering out at you from a pet shop display case, and you take the first important step toward a long and mutually happy association.

To start with, most species prefer to live alone. Frogs and toads live in a frog-eat-bug world. It's also a frog-eat-frog world, where they, too, are often the prey of other larger animals, including other amphibians. They go through life knowing there's always someone bigger ready to gobble them up. Life is tough when you're a frog or a toad. You'll understand, then, why your pet frog won't be all that interested in meeting the larger frog in the vivarium next door.

A Castle Fit for This Prince

There is no one perfect housing situation for all frogs and toads. What is right for a burrowing desert toad, which will be more concerned with conserving energy and protecting his skin from light and heat, would be inappropriate for a tropical tree-dwelling frog, which will thrive best in a tall, vertical terrarium complete with live plants with branches for climbing. But certain tenets hold true regardless of which frog or toad you invite in to share your home.

Although specialty housing is available (like that vertical setup for climbers that seem to have suction cups for feet), the traditional glass aquarium is the most popular amphibian domicile. This is especially true if you will be housing a frog that spends the majority of his time swimming, so you will need a tank setup much like a fish tank.

But the majority of frogs and toads will fare well in that traditional tank setup with no sharp edges and a securely fitting, small-mesh screen top (the screen is for ventilation), an ample collection of hiding places (smooth surfaces only), a shallow water dish, and a floor of soft sphagnum moss.

Pampered Pet

Frogs and toads that need a swimming hole will also need all the equipment needed for an aquarium, including a water filter and an air pump.

When You Get a Frog or Toad, You'll Also Have to Get These

Vivarium with secure cover	Shelters and hiding spots
Water dishes	Mister
Sphagnum moss flooring	Holding box
Potted plants	Care book
Full-spectrum fluorescent light	

Making That Castle a Home

That sphagnum moss can be an amphibian's best friend because it is an ideal toad and frog flooring, easy on delicate amphibian feet and instrumental in maintaining the proper humidity levels in the vivarium. Just make sure that soiled moss is removed daily and that the layer of moss is thick enough to accommodate your pets' particular species. A tree frog, for instance, won't be spending much time on terra firma, but he still requires proper flooring. Our burrowing toad friend, on the other hand, will need nice deep layers where he might effectively use his digging skills.

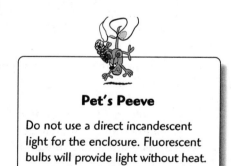

Pet's Peeve

Do not use a direct incandescent light for the enclosure. Fluorescent bulbs will provide light without heat.

Live plants are another nice addition to the frog and toad house, best installed in individual pots that are embedded in the flooring. The plants will need light, as will the resident frog or toad. This is best supplied by a fluorescent light above the enclosure that will provide full-spectrum lighting to both the plants and the frogs or toads.

Respecting Slime

Protecting your frog's or toad's skin is just as critical as protecting his heart or his brain. In addition to supplying these animals with proper shelter, you should also refrain from handling them more than is necessary. Aside from the stress this can cause the animal, invisible chemical residues and even the natural salts of human skin can cause them great irritation.

If you must handle your pets, wash your hands thoroughly and then moisten them with water to make them more compatible with the slimy animal you will be holding. Indeed, as someone who lives with frogs and toads, you will have to become quite obsessive about hand washing. Wash your hands before and after handling the frog and anything in his enclosure. And always wash your hands between frogs and toads when handling more than one.

You are wise to become just as obsessive about keeping your pet's home clean as he is about protecting his skin. Clean the water dish and remove uneaten or leftover food every day. And when it's time to clean the entire tank (which will vary from tank to tank, animal to animal), make sure every last molecule of soap and cleaner is rinsed away from every surface. That delicate amphibian skin doesn't need exposure, to toxic and painful chemical substances.

To prevent the stress and irritation when your pet must be moved for tank cleaning, set up a holding box. Place a clump of moistened sphagnum moss in a small, clean plastic or cardboard box with holes punched in it for ventilation. Place the box within your pet's terrarium and usher him in gently with a clean, bare hand (you can protect your pet even more by wearing a moistened latex glove) and then cover it. Your pet is now safely confined without risk of skin irritation, escape or injury.

Moist, but Not Too Moist

While moisture is critical to amphibian health and the maintenance of that slimy skin, too much moisture will lead to illness and fungal infection. Be careful not to over-moisten your pet's home.

Frogs require moisture, but you need not mist the frog, his tank walls, and everything in his home to provide the proper humidity. A simpler, more practical, more effective method is to simply install a hill of sphagnum moss in a secluded corner of the vivarium and spray it every other day or so with a misting bottle. This will not only maintain humidity (along with the open water dish), but also provide the resident amphibian with a much-favored shelter.

Today's Menu: Hopping, Slithering, Flying Food

Living with a frog or a toad offers you a front-row view of the brutal entity we call the food chain. In the wild, your pet would be ever looking over his shoulder at mealtimes, wondering if he was next. But in the captive environment you create, he can cast away such worries and concentrate instead on simply satisfying that voracious appetite of his.

What Does a Frog or Toad Eat?

Live insects	Smaller frogs and toads
Fish	Mealworms
Small lizards	Earthworms
New born mice	

Only live food will do. Balanced nutrition for a frog or toad means the stuff is still kicking. Crickets, earthworms, mealworms, fruit flies, and beetles are some of the most palatable delicacies. Variety is another component of a balanced diet. In other words, frogs do not live by crickets alone.

Most of these menu items are available commercially, and many can also be captured by a wily keeper who is handy with a fine-weave butterfly net. You can further foster that coveted balance by sprinkling crickets or worms once or twice a week with a vitamin-mineral powder formulated especially for amphibians and reptiles.

A Voracious Appetite

Remember, too, that like the young boys that have always been so attracted to them, frogs and toads are almost always hungry. You can't feed them (the boys or the amphibians) constantly, of course, but you can help stave off those hunger pangs by feeding them moderate amounts each day. You may want to extend this to every other day for some of the large toads, but the daily ration is a pretty safe rule of thumb for the majority of pet frogs and toads.

Pet's Peeve

Be careful not to feed garden bugs that have come in contact with pesticides.

You, then, can rest easy knowing that feeding frogs and toads is pretty darn inexpensive, and your pets can rest easy knowing that there's not a chance they'll ever be asked to share their breakfast with you.

The Least You Need to Know

➤ Frogs and toads have moist skin that helps them to breathe and protects them from the elements. Owners must help protect the skin and keep handling to a minimum (and then only with clean, moist hands).

➤ Regardless of species, whether aquatic or terrestrial, frogs and toads require a dark, moist environment. Provide them with ample shelter and, ideally, a hill of sphagnum moss that is moistened every few days with water from a spray bottle.

➤ Choose a frog with bright eyes; a healthy appetite; muscular legs; moist, evenly textured skin (free of wounds or fuzzy growths); and graceful movement.

➤ Frogs and toads require skin care (minimal handling, hiding places, moisture), live food offered daily (such as earthworms, crickets, and flying insects), and housing situations appropriate to their particular species.

Part 6
In a Class by Themselves

And now here we are in our last section, which is devoted to animals that truly are in a class by themselves. From a particular type of fish that doesn't seem unusual until you learn that the way 98 percent of us house them is incorrect, to a big hairy spider that has for years scared the daylights out of us silly humans, to a smallish pig with a large tummy, to an adorable garden-dwelling carnivore with spines all over his back, to a wiry little member of the weasel family whose mission seems to be finding out how effectively she can commit suicide—see? A class by themselves.

Would-be owners thus have to take this fact very much to heart. For instance, do you want a ferret as a cute, fun conversation piece, or do you genuinely look forward to spending your time with one of the pet world's most demanding creatures? Do you covet a hedgehog because he's the up-and-coming "hip" pet, or a tarantula to show off to—and terrify—the less knowledgeable neighbors? Choosing a pet from this group, and choosing responsibly—is going to take a lot of soul-searching. So buckle your seatbelts. Your journey starts here.

EXCEPTIONAL PETS CLASS

Feisty Ferrets

You know those cartoon tornadoes that spin around like a top, bouncing off this object, gobbling up that one. That's what it's like to have a ferret around the house. At first glance you are entranced by the bright, mischievous eyes; the long, tubular body; and the ever-twitching nose. But do you really want a tornado in your house 24 hours a day, 365 days a year?

If you're like most people, probably not. If, on the other hand, you can dream of nothing but ferret-induced pandemonium in your home, go for it. Just be prepared. There is literally never a dull moment when a ferret is about. If there is, well, then you're doing something wrong as an owner or your ferret is ill.

Needless to say, this pet is not at all for the faint of heart, the lazy, or those who dislike spontaneity. You must be up to the challenge, or you will soon find that you are taking orders from a lithe, agile little critter that is no bigger than a cat and that more closely resembles a sock puppet than a third-world dictator.

Ferrets as Pets

	light	1	2	3	4	5	heavy
Time commitment						✔	
Grooming						✔	
Feeding				✔			
General cleanup					✔		
Suitable for kids age infant to 5		✔					
Suitable for kids age 5 to 10		✔					
Suitable for kids over 10				✔			
Sociability						✔	
Expense of keeping					✔		

A Day in the Life

The grand challenge to ferret owners is to balance their leadership position with the ferret's insatiable quest for activity, and to blend it all gracefully within the day-to-day rhythms of the household. That's how it is in the household of the ferret we are about to meet. Her name is Bonnie, and although her owners like to say that she owns them, Bonnie would confess that they do have the upper hand.

Attention Everybody: Bonnie Is Ready to Get Up!

Well then, we will just have to answer her majesty's call, won't we? She wiggles excitedly at the door of her custom-made floor-to-ceiling ferret house, ready to get on with things. But before she is set free, it's time for breakfast. A dish of fresh kitten food is placed before her. She eats her fill. A quick visit to the litter box. A quick drink from her hanging water bottle. "Okay! Here I am! I want out now!"

Again, her calls are answered. Bonnie is freed, but business before play. She sits patiently on her mistress's lap as the woman runs her fingers down Bonnie's lithe form from head to tail. She leans down and smells Bonnie's ears, examines her feet and nails, and then looks into her eyes. Just checking. She doesn't expect to find signs of a budding problem—Bonnie was spayed as a youngster, and she is well-fed, properly groomed, and taken regularly to a veterinarian who keeps ferrets herself—but it's always smart to look. The woman runs a soft brush through the ferret's coat. Tummy too. Then, we're off.

High Noon

If she could, Bonnie would be in the laundry room right now, slipping into the dryer to slide around on the rounded walls of the drying compartment. But no, that room is forbidden territory to her. If she could, Bonnie would be under the range in the kitchen right now. But no, that was blocked off from her access as soon as Bonnie came to live here and started nosing around the inviting dark crevice that promised such fun. If she could, Bonnie would be burrowing into the reclining rocker in the living room hiding from . . . no, strike that. That recliner—the number-one danger to ferrets everywhere—was sold before Bonnie entered her new home. If she could, Bonnie would be tunneling under sheets of her owners' bed right now. In fact, that's where she is. What bliss!

But not for long. She hears her name being called from the other room. She hears the footsteps. Uh-oh, she's been discovered. She struggles and wiggles when she is removed from her haven. Gosh, they just don't let her do anything! "Poor baby," says her mistress as she carries Bonnie into the family room. Bonnie continues to protest with her squiggles, until, ooh, what's that over there? Is that a new toy? And she's off.

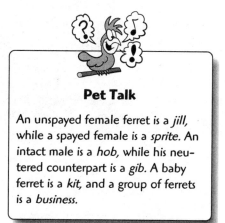

Pet Talk

An unspayed female ferret is a *jill*, while a spayed female is a *sprite*. An intact male is a *hob*, while his neutered counterpart is a *gib*. A baby ferret is a *kit*, and a group of ferrets is a *business*.

Evening Fun and Games

After Bonnie's afternoon nap (yes, ferrets can and do take naps), she joins her family out on the deck in the backyard. It's late afternoon, before dinner. Bonnie jumps around. So what else is new? Bonnie rolls around in the grass. Yes, she likes that, too. The family dog lounges nearby. He's an old dog. He likes the resident wiggle-worm all right, but just watching her makes him tired. When Bonnie runs up to him to invite him to play, he declines politely by turning his head the other way. Sometimes she snuggles in between the dog's front paws and drifts off to sleep. He'll lay his head down beside her and join her siesta.

But napping is the last thing on Bonnie's mind right now. She's over there scaling the stack of wood next to the back door. Now she's chasing a Ping-Pong ball on the deck. Now she's climbing up on the seat of the lawn mower. Now she's up on the patio table. Now she's scampering out to the garden. Now she's . . . oh, never mind. How can we possibly keep up?

By nine o'clock in the evening, Bonnie is finally slowing down, and her family is downright exhausted. Bonnie is pleased to return to her home, which has been carpeted with freshly laundered blankets while she was out. She snuggles into her cozy bed at the far corner and closes her eyes, sure to dream the happy dreams reserved only for a much-loved ferret.

Secrets from the Pet Files

The pet ferret's closest living relative is the black-footed ferret. We use the phrase "living relative" here because only a few short years ago our domestic pet's wild cousin was thought to be extinct. But then, on an autumn morning in 1981, a Wyoming rancher discovered that his dog had killed an odd little masked creature that turned out to be a black-footed ferret. The colony from which this animal had come was located, and ever since then valiant efforts have been made to save this American original. Hope now springs eternal for the black-footed ferret, an animal that lives or dies based on the well-being of its primary prey, the prairie dog, and that may just have a chance at making a successful comeback. And no, don't even think about making her a pet. She is a wild animal. Period.

Life Will Never Be the Same

The concept of living with ferrets is nothing new. Ferrets were domesticated thousands of years ago, yet they remain somewhat misunderstood in their roles as pets and companions. Read on, and I'll try to clarify some of those misunderstandings.

Ferret Pets, Technically Speaking

Ferret domestication occurred, as it did for all domestic animals, as a direct offshoot of humans once again looking to the animal kingdom for help. The ferret, a fearless hunter within the proper context, was quite successfully enlisted in ancient Egypt and

Europe to hunt rabbits and exterminate a variety of rodents—a calling it answered in the United States, too, beginning some 300-odd years ago. Throughout this long process, ferrets and humans decided that they really enjoyed each other's company, and the pet aspect of the relationship grew from there. So no, this is no newcomer to domestication. The love affair between people and ferrets has been going on for a very, very long time.

Pet's Peeve

Let us set the record straight here and now: Ferrets are *not* wild animals. They are domesticated pet animals—not tame, not captive, not held against their will—and have been for thousands of years.

On the pet spectrum, the ferret falls somewhere be-tween the cat and the dog in terms of care responsi-bilities and activity levels. The properly socialized, well-kept ferret is an irrepressible busy-body who is a companion in every sense of the word. She thrusts her twitching little nose into every activity of the household and demands that her high-powered energy levels be accommodated with fun and play, both in and out of her cage. She may also be litter-box trained.

The ferret is a true carnivore and a member of the weasel family, and her sharp teeth are those of a meat eater. Physically, the ferret is long and tubular, with a wiry, muscu-lar physique and a small head but no small brain. She is ready and able to outsmart her owner at a moment's notice, and if you're not careful, she'll do just that.

A Bad Rap for Ferrets

Unfortunately, ferrets have been on the losing end of some misguided public relations during the past few years. The buzz is that ferrets are mean, they're vicious, they smell bad. Who would want such an animal for a pet? Thousands, if not millions, of people do. They know that the ferret's bad reputation, while based in fact for certain animals, is caused by owner negligence and not by the genuine character of this gregarious critter. Even the American Medical Association and the American Veterinary Medical Association, both of whom have investigated ferret-attack cases, have come to this conclusion.

That the ferret is not a pet for everyone should come as no surprise. That it is not an ideal children's pet, and certainly not a babysitter (the way a large dog can be), must be understood from the outset. But mean, vicious, and stinky? Well, you would be too if you were cared for by people who kept you locked up all the time and who failed to pay attention to the cleanliness of your home and your person.

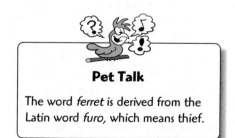

Pet Talk

The word *ferret* is derived from the Latin word *furo*, which means thief.

Instead, we are regaled with horror stories about how a ferret mauled a child (that's what happens when you trap a ferret in a crib with a toddler to promote bonding), or how a ferret viciously killed a pet rabbit during a play session (ferrets were originally domesticated to hunt rabbits and other small animals—hint, hint). When all ferrets are owned by responsible people who understand them, the ferret's reputation will improve dramatically. Until then, the good owners out there are doing all they can to dispel the myths and earn their pets a more honored—and in some cases, legal—niche in society.

Thief in a Fur Coat

As new ferret owners quickly learn, their homes must be ferret-proofed completely from the very beginning. Everything and anything is a source of eternal fascination to a healthy ferret, and she is quite adept at worming her lithe frame into any nook or cranny that strikes her fancy. This little bandit is also most willing to steal anything that strikes her fancy—and almost everything does. Go ahead and seal off entry to such ferret-threatening rooms as the laundry room and the kitchen, but remember that everything within the rooms that are ferret-legal are fair game.

And just what does the ferret do with her treasures? She hides them, of course. She just never knows when she might need a set of keys, a sock, a spoon, or a pair of jeans for tunneling purposes. And when the knowing owner discovers the stash? Well, reserve punishment for a genuine felony. This is just natural ferret behavior, the kind that makes you giggle. If you're the right owner for a ferret, you'll probably find that it's best to decide all these little infractions make you giggle.

Ferrets, Pets, and Kids

Ferrets are sociable critters. When properly socialized, they adore people, and they can learn to live quite happily with other ferrets, either in the same very spacious abode or, better yet, in separate cages placed side by side.

Pet's Peeve

Two unneutered males cannot be housed together. They could end up fighting out their differences, literally to the death.

Despite this friendly nature, it is unwise to invite a ferret in to play social director for a menagerie of rabbits, lizards, or hamsters—unless, of course, you don't mind your social director attacking and probably killing some of her charges. Rabbits, for example, are the species for which the ferret was originally enlisted to hunt, and those little rodents—gerbils, mice, hamsters, and the like—won't stand a chance. Even hedgehogs aren't safe from ferrets, so if you do wish to keep these animals, keep them safe from the family ferret.

This is not to say that a ferret should be kept isolated from all other animals. Her fellow predators, cats, and dogs, can learn to coexist quite nicely with her, and vice versa. Rover and Fluffy are better equipped to keep that wiggly little sock puppet in line.

Ferrets and kids can be either a disaster or a delight. It all depends on the parents. If parents allow the kids to handle the ferret without supervision, fail to teach them how to handle her correctly, or allow ferrets around infants at all, they are inviting disaster. If, however, there is a formal separation between kid and ferret, all interactions are carefully monitored, and kid and ferret are both trained in the proper protocols of interaction, an idyllic relationship grounded in mutual respect and affection could be budding.

Choosing the Right Ferret for Your Family

You know the ferret will require specialized care, special toys and equipment, and veterinary attention. You know you will have to spend a great deal of time each and every day playing with your ferret and keeping her and her home clean, clean, clean. You know you will have to ferret-proof your house—your entire house—and your pet will require constant supervision when she is out of her cage, even when you are not sharing a formal play session.

Now you must find out if the ferret is legal. Ferrets are not legal in every state or in every area. Many people in *ferret non grata* areas still keep them, but they take a great risk in doing so. This has happened because some states and localities mistakenly classify ferrets as wild animals. Ferret clubs are working hard to correct this misconception and get the laws changed.

Pampered Pet

Contact a local ferret club, animal shelter, veterinarian, or animal control office to find out if ferrets are legal in your area.

Breeders and Pet Shops

When you begin your quest for your perfect ferret pet, you will no doubt discover that the two most logical sources for ferrets are pet shops and breeders. There is always an element of risk with a pet shop because you may not know where the animals came from and what efforts have been made to socialize them, and you may not even get the straight scoop on where ferrets can be kept legally and where they can't. But don't discount pet shops altogether. You may just stumble across a shop that is clean and pristine; that houses its ferrets in spacious, mind-stimulating display cages; and that offers sound advice on care from a knowledgeable staff.

The breeder is probably your best bet, though, and the increasing popularity of ferrets has made breeders far more accessible than they once were. An ethical breeder with only the well-being of their animals at heart will put much thought and effort into the breeding of ferrets and will guaran-

Pampered Pet

Ferret Central has lots of information and links to other ferret Web sites. Find it at http://www.ferretcentral.org.

tee the fruits of their labors. To locate such individuals, turn to the ferret network. It's a very active, very enthusiastic, very opinionated bunch. You can locate the network through local veterinarians, animal shelters, ferret associations and even on the Internet. And you'll no doubt learn a great deal more about ferrets and ferret people along the way.

What Does a Ferret Cost?

The purchase price of a ferret can vary widely, but the average is $116.18.

The average ferret owner also spends per year:

$99	Regular veterinary care
$54	Food
$30	Other supplies
$20	Toys
$3	Grooming

The Adoption Option

Another option when you are looking for a new pet ferret is an animal shelter or ferret rescue group. It's a sad fact that the more popular a pet species becomes, the more it is likely to start showing up as homeless, abandoned, and neglected. Unfortunately, the ferret falls into this category.

Some lovely pets can show up in shelters or fall into the waiting arms of rescue groups, both of whom will work to get the orphans placed in new homes. In many cases, there is nothing wrong with the ferrets; the problem was owners who were not sufficiently prepared for the responsibilities of ferret ownership.

Ready for Pet Life

A ferret kit does not pop out into the world ready and able to be the ideal pet. No, some preparation is in order. The best ferret pet is the spayed or neutered one. The altered, or neutered, male will be calmer in disposition and perhaps emit less of an odor. And for a female ferret, spaying is literally a life-or-death issue. For some reason, she was engineered with a system whose button may be shut off only by the act of breeding. Without this, she will eventually die. Spaying, however, eliminates this need entirely.

Pampered Pet

While much is still to be learned about ferret health, two vaccines are typically recommended: rabies and canine distemper.

We certainly don't want every female ferret to be bred because that would result in far too many ferrets without homes, and because we want only those truly devoted to the animals to carry out their breeding. That means every pet ferret should be spayed or neutered.

Leave the breeding to the breeders. Play it safe and spay or neuter your ferret *before* it reaches six months of age.

While the spaying and neutering of ferret pets invite little debate, the descenting procedure does. Many breeders and owners believe a ferret should be spayed or neutered and descented before the young animal ever enters its new home. There are others who claim descenting is unnecessary and even cruel, that the same results can be obtained from a weekly bath.

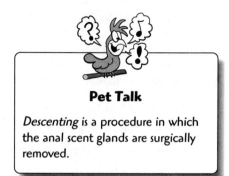

Pet Talk

Descenting is a procedure in which the anal scent glands are surgically removed.

In truth, the descenting procedure is quite simple and can be done quickly and cleanly during a young ferret's spaying or neutering surgery. But it's also true that the sex hormones level out as a result of neutering, which greatly reduces the productivity of the scent glands. So this is something you're going to have to talk over with your veterinarian and decide for yourself.

Absolutely no debate surrounds the issue of early socialization. The earlier a young ferret is introduced to people and schooled in proper behavior for a human household, the better. The conscientious breeder will pay as much attention to the socialization of their animals as the color, size, or markings. This breeder knows that nothing is more important than proper socialization, and that this, combined with spaying, neutering, and descenting, offers a ferret her best chance of finding a permanent and loving home.

Evaluating Ferret Health and Temperament

Thanks to breeding programs that strive to produce healthy as well as physically attractive animals, ferrets today are found in a variety of colors. Aside from the traditional dark brown (known as sable) and light brown (chocolate) that we all know and love, there now champagne ferrets, albino ferrets, and so on. But color is definitely secondary when you are choosing a pet ferret that you hope will remain with you for the next six to 10 years. Health and temperament are far more important to a long and fruitful partnership.

The healthy ferret:

➤ Has a shiny, lustrous coat

➤ Has a clean nose

➤ Has bright, shiny eyes

➤ Has clean ears

➤ Breathes clearly

➤ Shows a natural curiosity and enthusiasm

The ferret you choose should also exhibit a natural affection for you. Some ferrets just naturally like some people better than others, and vice versa. It helps to seek a ferret that has been hand raised and socialized by loving keepers and has only positive experiences with humans stored in her long-term memory. But in the end, it's personal. Love at first sight, animal magnetism—call it what you will.

What should you avoid? The classic signs of ferret illness include:

➤ A sudden loss of appetite

➤ Listless, lethargic behavior

➤ Diarrhea

➤ A dull coat

➤ Discharge from the nose or mouth

➤ Breathing difficulties

➤ Coughing

➤ Hair loss

➤ Skin problems

➤ Unclean ears

➤ Watery eyes

A Ferret in the House

If we were looking for some sort of experience that could compare to ferret ownership, that would have to be life with a human toddler. I know this will send some of you screaming into the hills, and perhaps it should; such a demanding critter is not the right pet for everyone. But for those of you who are still interested, read on for the details on just how you can adequately meet the needs of this sprightly character.

Pet's Peeve

Ferrets are highly susceptible to respiratory illness, so watch for the signs. The quicker a health problem is diagnosed, the better the chance it can be treated successfully.

Secure and Comfortable Housing

While ferrets enjoy immensely time spent outside of their cages or enclosures, and need it each day, their cage is not simply a holding pen and must offer the height of ferret comfort. When designing your pet's private accommodations, keep in mind at all times the ferret character—this is, for example, a consummate escape artist—and proceed accordingly.

The cage can vary from a large, traditional cage with a solid floor, to a wooden hutch-type enclosure, or to one of any number of homemade designs. What you want is the largest, roomiest ferret house you can both afford and fit into your home.

When You Get a Ferret, You'll Also Have to Get These

Secure enclosure	Bedding material
Food dish	Litter boxes
Water bottle	Litter scooper
Brush	Litter
Nail trimmer	Harness
Play toys	Carrier
Cage furniture (ramps, tunnels, hammocks, etc.)	Feline or ferret shampoo
Box or bed	Care and training book

When designing your ferret's home, don't be restricted by the horizontal. Ferrets are wiry little creatures that love to move, climb and jump, and to see the world from every perspective. If at all possible, provide your pet with height as well as width in which to do this. A floor-to-ceiling homemade enclosure can be outfitted with shelves, ladders, lots and lots of tunnels, and all kinds of delightful furnishings to make life within the ferret house just as adventurous and exciting as it is outside. Just make sure that regardless of which housing style you choose, the enclosure is escape-proof. That includes the door. Never underestimate the power of the ferret to figure out just how a locking door mechanism can be unlocked.

Interior Decorating for a Finicky Ferret

Ferrets like order and organization, and you should arrange the interior of the enclosure so that each area is designated for separate purposes. One corner can be the ferret's bedroom, one can be the dining area, and one, preferably the end opposite the sleeping and dining areas, can be the litter box area. As for the rest of the space, that can be reserved for toys and the various architectural wonders you're erecting to make the cage interesting.

Furnish each of these separate areas with the proper accouterments: food dishes and hanging water bottle in the dining area; the litter box (with clean litter only, please) in the litter box area; and a bed/hiding box in the sleeping quarters. The bed should be cozy, yet spacious enough to conceal the ferret entirely from the world. The ferret should know that if she ever feels in need of sanctuary, she can find it right there in her own home.

Clean towels or blankets will provide both the proper bedding and the proper flooring for the

Pampered Pet

Keep a litter box in every room the ferret will be allowed loose in. And scoop every box as soon as you see something in it.

base of the enclosure. Steer clear of wood shavings or other such flooring materials that are used for rodents and rabbits and the like. This isn't a rodent.

Ferret Feeding Made Easy

Ferrets are often compared to cats, and for good reason. Both are skilled and agile hunters, both shared similar paths to domestication, both are quiet yet demanding animals that continue to embody many of their wild sensibilities, and both are die-hard carnivores. Both need plenty of meat and extra taurine.

Pampered Pet

Ferrets have a high energy level and a short digestive tract, so they need to eat every three or four hours.

Because of the similarities, ferrets have for years been sustained on high-quality, animal protein–based commercial diets formulated for kittens. Recently, however, the pet food industry has responded to their popularity and formulated foods specifically for ferrets. There is some controversy, however, over which is more nutritious for ferrets.

What Does a Ferret Eat?

Commercial dry ferret food

Commercial dry kitten food

Fruit or cooked meats as treats (sparingly!)

The kitten-food camp points to all the ferrets who have thrived on kitten foods, which are the products of years and years of nutritional research. Meanwhile, ferret-food proponents hold that a ferret's nutritional needs differ from those of a cat—a contention countered by the opposition with claims that ferret foods still have not proven themselves superior, let alone worthy. Time will tell, no doubt, but as long as a pet ferret receives daily rations of a high-quality version of one or the other, and has constant access to it to fuel her phenomenal energy needs, she will probably do just fine.

Ferret Grooming Made Easy

A ferret's grooming habits also resemble those of a cat, all the way down to the practice of licking her front paws and then using them to wash her face. Both share similar physical aversions to strong shampoos or dips, so it should come as no surprise that ferrets have for years been bathed, dipped, and groomed with milder products made for kittens. But here, too, ferrets now also have grooming products formulated especially for them. And here, too, many veteran owners still swear by the original kitten products. No matter, as long as they are being groomed and bathed.

Ferrets are fastidious on their own about their grooming, although they also have a reputation for being stinkier than your average pet. Many an owner has found that weekly baths with ultra-mild products will help.

Pampered Pet

You'll also need to regularly clip your pet's nails and clean her ears. Ask your veterinarian to show you how.

Daily grooming also offers you the ideal opportunity to examine for lumps and bumps, skin irritations and reactions, hair loss and dullness, and anything else that seems not quite right. Short but regular brushing sessions in which you brush your pet with a soft brush should help you stay ahead of any physical problems she may be having, many of which will make themselves known through the coat and skin.

Ferret-Proofing Your Home

They say that curiosity killed the cat. Well it can do a pretty nasty job on the ferret, too, so it is your job to protect your pet from herself. Reclining chairs, open windows and doors, live electrical cords, a hot stove, a clothes dryer: All can be deadly to a ferret, yet all invariably seem to attract her devoted attention.

Just as you would with a toddler, get down to your pet's level (and then the next level up, and the next, since ferrets can wind up anywhere at any time), and look for the unexpected dangers lurking there. You certainly want to be the one to find it first. And when you do, get it taken care of—removed, sealed off, sold at the garage sale—whatever you must do to keep your ferret safe and to make your own life a little easier, too.

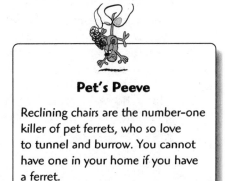

Pet's Peeve

Reclining chairs are the number-one killer of pet ferrets, who so love to tunnel and burrow. You cannot have one in your home if you have a ferret.

Ferrets have an insatiable appetite for fun, and watching them play is well worth the effort of ferret-proofing your home. They view every event, every object, as a new and oh-so-profound adventure. The family room rug is a tunnel, the fine linen tablecloth in the dining room is a tent in the desert, the stuffed tiger on your bed is a foe to be vanquished. And that large tube sock that somehow fell to the floor after your morning workout, well, that is gone in a flash and transformed into a ferret tunnel and a comforting reminder—via scent—of the person your ferret loves best.

Ferret Training Made Easy

Needless to say, this incessant sense of fun can get a wee carnivore in trouble. You simply cannot allow her to run amok. Thank goodness ferrets can—and should—be trained. Treats and positive reinforcement will be your most valuable tools.

303

Teach your pet where she is allowed to be and what she is allowed to do. When litter-box training, for example, look for the telltale restless pacing behavior and quickly whisk your pet away and into the litter box. Then issue a command. If she obliges, praise, praise, praise. If she doesn't, well, forget the punishment. That will not accomplish anything. Just remember that tomorrow is another day, and ferrets are smart enough to learn this behavior—eventually. Patience and a sense of humor should come in handy, too, when dealing with ferrets; actually, they are a must.

Pampered Pet

No rich, nutrition-free treats when training, please. Try slivers of raisin and specially formulated ferret treats instead.

Ferrets love the great outdoors, and one way you can allow them to enjoy fresh air, sunshine, and companionship safely is by teaching them to walk on a leash. Most will learn quickly to tolerate the harness that securely hugs their bodies and the tug of the leash that gently reminds them that the person on the other end of the leash is in control. Introduce the activity gradually—ideally indoors—and gradually increase the time of your training sessions.

Soon your ferret will be doing back flips the minute she sees you take out the leash. You may even find that suddenly you've gotten to know more of your neighbors, because most people just can't resist visiting with a ferret out and about on a leash—oh yeah, and the person who is walking her, too.

Even if your ferret excels at training, you must never assume that her knack for learning liberates you from your duties as sentry. Your mission: to supervise and monitor the ferret and her interactions with the family at every turn. Your ferret's skills and her understanding of human language may change dramatically as you instruct her in the code of manners that long-term ferret-owner relationships are made of. Your responsibilities, however, remain the same. That's simply part of the contract to which you agreed the moment you decided to bring a ferret into your home. So enjoy it. And make your pet proud.

The Least You Need to Know

➤ Hardly a pet for the faint of heart, the ferret requires daily activity, attention, companionship, training, leadership, and supervision—and a ferret-proofed household.

➤ Consummate hunters, ferrets will view smaller pets in the household, especially rabbits and rodents, as prey. They should also never be left unsupervised with small children.

➤ Look for a ferret that exudes all-around health, is lively, has a friendly temperament that comes from early socialization, and, ideally, has been descented and spayed or neutered.

➤ The care of ferrets is similar to that of cats. Many owners feed their ferrets high-quality feline diets and keep them beautiful with grooming products made for kittens.

➤ A ferret requires a clean, spacious, secure enclosure with separate areas for eating, sleeping, playing, and bathroom duties.

Chapter 22

Tickly Tarantulas

> **In This Chapter**
>
> ➤ A day in the life of a big hairy spider
>
> ➤ Understanding and respecting tarantulas
>
> ➤ Selecting a big hairy spider of your very own
>
> ➤ Tarantula care and feeding

It's no secret that exotic pets are growing in popularity these days, the legendary tarantula is just about as exotic as you can get without entering the illegal-pet zone. The tarantula is casting her spell on more and more people all the time. Entranced by the spider's mystique, these individuals are taking to the streets—and to the wide open fields—in search of big hairy spiders of their own. But once they get them home, they had better be prepared to offer the care they require, or the whole experience could become just like a horror movie, leaving a grim memory for all.

Before we take a look at tarantulas, a word of advice: Beware of bad information. The world is riddled with poor information regarding the care of tarantulas, and as a result, far too many of these quiet, dignified pets meet sad and premature ends. Such advice as "house a tarantula in a dry, desert-like environment," and "when it's time for the spider to shed its exoskeleton, keep the atmosphere as dry as possible," makes the heads of dedicated enthusiasts explode (it will also kill your tarantula). To protect the heads of these individuals, follow the guidelines issued by the American Tarantula Society, which is the root of the advice you will find in this chapter. (The Society's address is in Appendix B.)

Tarantulas As Pets

	light	1	2	3	4	5	*heavy*
Time commitment			✔				
Grooming		✔					
Feeding				✔			
General cleanup			✔				
Suitable for kids age infant to 5		✔					
Suitable for kids age 5 to 10			✔				
Suitable for kids over 10				✔			
Sociability		✔					
Expense of keeping			✔				

A Day in the Life

Meet Pamela. What a lovely creature she is. That lustrous ebony hair. That agile way of moving. Those long legs that never seem to end. You can't take your eyes off of her. And if you love one leg, there are seven more to admire. And that ebony hair is actually a collective of spiky, very sensitive hair-like structures that cover most of Pamela's body. All very normal, all very lovely, for a Mexican redknee tarantula. Let's spend a day with Pamela, shall we?

Morning with Pamela

Pamela's owner awakens and looks in on his little pet. There she is. She sits outside of the overturned log shelter and stretches her legs. Time for breakfast. Her owner drops a plump, healthy cricket into Pamela's cozy home. This is usually the one time she is guaranteed to show some rather undignified enthusiasm. But today she's not interested. Important sign. It looks like she is preparing to molt—to shed her exoskeleton. Her attentive caretaker removes the cricket, which could be dangerous to a soon-to-be-molting tarantula.

Noon with Pamela

Pamela is lounging at home, not doing much of anything. This is just what tarantulas do, and Pamela is no exception. Her owner watches attentively. Knowing that soon Pamela will molt, he spritzes the vermiculite flooring of her enclosure with water from a spray bottle to increase the all-important humidity that is the key to successful molting.

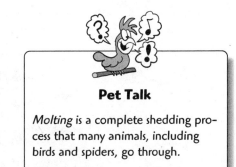

Pet Talk

Molting is a complete shedding process that many animals, including birds and spiders, go through.

Evening with Pamela

More lounging. More relaxing. This is why the tarantula can indeed be the ideal pet. Lovely to look at (yes, that *is* in the eye of the beholder). Quiet. Unusual. Her caretaker has developed a genuine affection for Pamela. He hopes she will be around for the next decade or more. With the care and attention he gives her, she very well could be.

Secrets from the Pet Files

Much is yet to be learned about tarantulas, and the quiet spiders are not all that forthcoming with information. But we do know female tarantulas tend to outlive their male counterparts, and burrowing tarantulas tend to outlive tree-dwelling spiders. We also know that properly-cared-for females of certain species can celebrate their 30th birthday in captivity. Males can live about 10 years in captivity, which is still substantially longer than the life span of wild males.

Lifestyles of the Big, Hairy, and Eight-Legged

Tarantulas, along with, oh, black widows and daddy longlegs, are probably the most well-known members of the vast arachnid family. But only one of these falls into the pet category. Although the tarantula, star of film, television, and every local haunted mansion, has for generations succeeded in frightening us merely by showing up, she has also enjoyed a closeted, rather unspoken respect from the human species.

Consider the young mother living in the hills of southern California who gently fishes a drowning tarantula out of the swimming pool with a net and sends her on her way. A line of traffic waits on a rural road in Texas as a tarantula, so large she is easily visible to the drivers, makes her way carefully across the asphalt to the other side. Rather amazing responses, actually.

An Uneasy Alliance

The root of the esteem in which we hold spiders is no great mystery. It rests with an uneasy alliance that our species long ago forged with the spiders of the world. While we fear the poisonous ones (which only a handful of the tarantulas are—more on that in a moment), we need spiders. Without them, humans would not have evolved into the so-called dominant species that we are today. No, without the spiders on our side, the insects probably would have taken over the earth long ago.

A Marriage of Tolerance and Luck

In cultures throughout the world, spiders have long been considered good-luck charms. Folklore suggests that to kill a spider is to invite a rash of terrible luck. It would seem that even people in centuries past knew that without the spiders as gatekeepers, we would all now be paying our taxes to the vast and all-powerful insect regime.

And just how do we repay them? Well, many of us try to leave them alone, feigning a disgust for extermination that ultimately lets the spider be. We find them in our homes and are more diligent about clearing out the cobwebs than the eight-legged artists that spin them. And the tarantula? Well, sure we'd like to let bygones be bygones, and let the spiders be spiders, but you simply can't allow these massive creatures to take up residence in the corner of your kitchen. But you can invite them to take up residence in your home as pets.

Secrets from the Pet Files

Perhaps our most contemporary spider hero is Charlotte, from E. B. White's classic children's novel, *Charlotte's Web*. If ever there was a good-luck charm, both for pigs and for people, it was Charlotte.

Or at least some of them. More than 800 species of tarantula today call the earth home (and perhaps hundreds more that we don't yet know about), and only a handful of these are acceptable as pets. Behavioral, breeding, and housing complexities can all render a species an unfit pet. So can the fact that a species is endangered. Like so many other animals today, tarantulas, too, must face the uncertainty of survival in the new millennium. Another way we may thank tarantulas, then, for all the good the spider members of the arachnid family have done for us, is to preserve their natural habitats so they may continue to thrive both in the wild and as pets.

What Does a Tarantula Cost?

The purchase price of a tarantula can vary widely, but the average is $10 to $20.

The average tarantula owner also spends per year:

$50	Food
$30	Other supplies

The Truth About Tarantulas

The first step toward being a worthy tarantula owner is to get to know the wild tarantula. Some tarantulas live in trees, while others spend their days burrowed underground. But whether tarantulas are natives of the American Southwest or the jungles of South America, all are guided by the same list of priorities: find food (live meat), preserve body moisture, protect that all-important abdomen, and make new baby spiders.

So now you have some clues as to what you must do as an owner of one of these shy, stunning spiders. First, you can forget about the making baby spiders part; that is best reserved for the experts. But the rest you are honor-bound to provide. Offer the spider an environment commensurate with what she would choose in the wild (climbing opportunities for the tree-dweller, thick flooring for the burrower, hiding places for all to preserve moisture). Understand that there is no turning this consummate carnivore

Pet's Peeve

How delicate is that abdomen? A fall of just six inches can kill a tarantula.

into a vegetarian, and do all you can to ensure that she is never dropped or handled in any way that might lead to a rupture of her delicate abdomen. One fall and the abdomen, encased in a firm-bodied exoskeleton, can split. And that is the end of the spider.

The Venom Thing

The tarantula gets a mighty bad rap as far as media images go. That fierce, hairy form, coupled with her size, is just an our-hero-is-almost-killed-by-a-big-scary-spider scene waiting to happen. Of course, it's all hogwash. Rarely will you find so quiet an addition to your household, so gentle a creature (of course, a cricket confronting a hungry tarantula at mealtime might beg to differ). And never has a case been documented where a secret agent has been fatally poisoned in his sleep by a tarantula under his pillow. Never. Not once.

Like nearly all spiders, tarantulas do have venom. They also have fangs, which they use as a delivery system. The venom is primarily used to procure prey, by paralyzing the creature the tarantula wishes to eat. It may also be used for defense, but that is not its primary purpose.

For nearly all tarantulas (except a few varieties that nobody should be keeping as pets), the bite is no more serious than a hornet sting. In other words, it hurts, but it's not dangerous. There are no confirmed instances of a human death caused directly by tarantula venom, and they are not considered a significant medical problem anywhere.

If you do get bitten, don't panic. Clean the site thoroughly with soap and water, and apply an antibiotic cream. Then watch the site for a few days, not for signs of poisoning, but of infection. And remember, that bite is actually more dangerous to the tarantula than it is to you because the shock of it, especially if you happen to be holding the spider at the time, could result in your dropping and fatally injuring your pet.

TLC and the Tarantula

In fact, we humans pose a far greater threat to the tarantula than the tarantula does to us. Consider, for example, the adult woman who, in the name of Halloween fun, perches a member of the burrowing species of tarantulas on her shoulder as an attention-getter at a party. Perhaps she doesn't understand that in committing this grievous act, she could kill what is at the moment a very terrified spider who knows instinctively that she should keep all eight legs on the ground at all times. One slip and bye-bye spider.

A good rule of thumb is to nix the attention-getting business. This is a pet—and a pet who might be described most accurately as the quintessential homebody. Allow burrowing species to remain in their homes on the ground, and allow tree-dwellers to climb only in the safety of their own spacious aviary-style digs. This way, you will not subject the spider to potential injury, infection, stress or even a fatal squeeze or fall in the hands of a jittery, inexperienced handler.

Veteran tarantula keepers handle their spiders very little, and novices should handle them even less. Tarantulas are not interactive pets. However, there will be times when you have to take your spider out of her enclosure to clean it. Veterans usually master the fine art of firmly, though gently, lifting the spider into the air without risk of dropping or injuring her (be warned, though, that the hairs of some species can irritate human skin).

Pet Talk

Arachnid is the name of the class of eight-legged animals that includes spiders, scorpions, and mites. Needless to say, most of the members of this group would never be discussed seriously in a book about pets.

Beginners are wise, however, to try a simpler, safer (for the spider) method, and they may be most comfortable wearing gloves to start. First, tap the spider on the leg to warn her of your intentions. Place your flattened palm down in front of the spider and gently tap her from behind, urging her to walk forward onto your hand. Most relaxed spiders will comply. As a variation, you can use the same method but urge the spider into a small, secure box—anything that makes you most comfortable, and thus guards your pet's safety.

Where to Get a Tarantula Pet

You wake up one morning and realize that you simply must bring a tarantula into your life. Quiet, clean, beautiful in her own inimitable way: the perfect pet. An impulse buy is, of course, out of the question, so you prepare for your new pet, educate yourself on her care, and then begin your quest for a most unique companion, ideal for virtually any living situation.

Why a Tarantula, for Heaven's Sake?

Only the purest of heart need apply when the prize is tarantula ownership. Unfortunately for the spiders, there are a great many would-be and actual tarantula owners out there who do not satisfy this qualification. Before you consider taking a tarantula as a pet, evaluate your motives honestly. Perhaps making a list will help. If you find that your list includes such statements as "will enhance my macho image" or "will look great with my new Halloween costume," well, perhaps a tarantula is not right for you.

If, however, you have written, "It would be rewarding to care for one of these fascinating animals in the style to which she is accustomed and deserves" and even "I really want a pet, but my apartment complex doesn't allow pets," you're on the right track. A variety of honest, legitimate motives sends people looking for tarantulas. Even viewing the large, legendary spider as an ambassador of Mother Nature within your home speaks of respect and good intentions. And that is really all this spider asks for.

While a tarantula is certainly not a children's pet, she can be a valuable educational tool within the household. The responsibility for the care of the spider must rest with the adults, and the spider is not to be viewed as a novelty toy that the kids can show off to their friends. On that there is no debate. However, in witnessing adults tend to this delicate creature with a considerate and nurturing hand—misting the spider's home at molting time, honoring the spider's privacy, feeding the spider with respect for both predator and prey—children learn a profound respect for nature. That is something they will carry with them into their own adult lives, and it is an attitude we certainly could use more of these days.

Pet Shops?

As soon as you decide your motives for wanting a tarantula pet are the right ones, you need to start scouring the landscape to find out just where that spider of your dreams might be waiting. The most obvious first stop is the pet shop, but you're likely to be disappointed.

In general, pet shops tend to be a bit behind the times when it comes to tarantulas. They don't all carry them, for one thing. This is a rather *exotic* exotic—and hardly a cute, cuddly exotic, at that—and the pool of potential buyers is limited. Plus, it can be a challenge to ensure that the staff cares for them properly—and will agree to do so. Even when shops do carry tarantulas, the spiders aren't always housed properly, and their species is not always properly identified. But as long as the spider is healthy, improper housing for a very short period and an incorrect name may not matter.

Now, this is not meant to suggest that all pet shops that offer tarantulas are substandard in their care and marketing of the creatures. That wouldn't be fair, now would it? There are always exceptions, and what a pleasure it is to discover an unexpected treasure waiting where you least expect it—perhaps the mom-and-pop pet shop right down the street from you. Spend some time to look around, and if you're lucky, you may find a pet shop with a knowledgeable staff, proper display cases, and healthy spiders.

Pet's Peeve

If you do take a wild tarantula as a pet, don't consider this license to offer it anything less than the best care possible. The value of an animal's life is in no way related to what you paid for it.

From the Wild?

While reptiles, birds, amphibians, and rodents should *not* be taken from the wild to be pets, the tarantula is one species for which this might be okay. The world as we know it won't come to an end if you happen to spot a tarantula roaming along a road in California, Texas, or Arizona and decide to invite him in for a life of leisure as a pet. It will indeed probably be a him, because females are most comfortable tending the home fires while the males meander about in the great outdoors.

Breeders (Yes, Breeders)

Imagine you are walking down the street of a typical suburban neighborhood. You approach one particular two-story tract home that closely resembles the others in the neighborhood. You knock. You are welcomed into the living room. Nothing unusual there. Comfortable couch, a piano. The family room? Lovely. Big-screen TV. The kitchen? Spacious and clean. Then you are ushered upstairs.

You take a breath and follow your guide up the stairs. This is the room. As you enter, you catch your breath. Shelves line the walls of this room from floor to ceiling. And on those shelves are stacks and stacks of plastic shoe-box-size boxes. And in those boxes? Spiders—big hairy spiders with huge, bulbous abdomens. Ten thousand of them! Welcome to the home of your regular, everyday tarantula breeder.

Not everyone has easy access to the home of a regular, everyday tarantula breeder and the 10,000-odd spiders in his or her care. Not everyone would *want* easy access. So what's a would-be tarantula owner seeking a lovely captive-bred spider to do? Well, mail-order is an option—perhaps the only option for someone who wants a certain species that is available only from a particular breeder across the country.

Another option is the reptile show. Arachnids are definitely not reptiles, but they are just as exotic in character as the scaly creatures one finds featured at such shows. Tarantula breeders thus consider this a natural venue to show off the lovely products of their breeding efforts—and spectators seem to agree.

Secrets from the Pet Files

While there are differences in male and female tarantulas in regard to life span and size, and to some extent even behavior (females tend to be plumper and more relaxed), it is usually impossible to tell male from female in juvenile spiders. Even in adults, you need to look right after a molt. At that time, a male will exhibit a structure called the *palpal bulb* on the underside of the front leg-like structure called the *pedipalp*.

Choosing for Health and Beauty

When selecting a pet tarantula, you don't always have many specimens from which to choose. Still, you are wise to approach this decision with the same long-term goals that you would have in choosing any pet. In other words, look for the healthiest, most robust spider you can find.

After consulting the experts and doing your own research on the subject, you may have some preferences regarding species: say, a more docile spider such as a Mexican redknee or a Chilean rose. Or perhaps you believe that bigger is better and have found yourself captivated by a big red Goliath birdeater.

Beyond species considerations, you should look for an alert spider that responds to motions and actions in her environment. The spider's legs should be strong, without any hint of inner curling. The abdomen, too, is a valuable indicator of health. It should be plump, round, and free of wounds or other damage. Avoid the spider with a pinched abdomen, which is a warning signal that the spider might be suffering from malnutrition or dehydration—the latter being the leading cause of death in tarantulas.

When evaluating a potential pet tarantula, don't necessarily discount a particular spider because her abdomen has a bald spot or she happens to be missing a leg. The bald spot is usually a side effect of some species' habit of flicking barbed hairs called *urticating hairs* from their abdomens at predators or handlers who fail to practice proper handling protocol. As for that missing leg, broken appendages are commonplace when you're a spider. As long as the spider is healthy in all other respects, the leg should be regenerated after the next exoskeleton molt.

Do, however, make sure that the cage is clean and well-misted. Spiders in dirty surroundings can develop mites later on. Make sure the cage has clean water, clean substrate, and a proper heat source. These are all signs of good tarantula care.

Making a Sweet Tarantula Home

When all is said and done, the tarantula is really one of the easiest pets to care for—and an excellent choice for frequent travelers. A pet of few demands and even fewer complaints, she can thrive with minimum attention and cost. This easy lifestyle all hinges, however, on the foundation of proper care that you build for your pet. Do this, and the rest is cake.

Pampered Pet

With proper care and regular removal of flooring soiled with food leftovers and feces, a tarantula's enclosure may require wholesale cleaning and disinfecting only twice a year. I told you the tarantula might be the perfect roommate!

Living Solo

Before we move on to the brass tacks of providing your pet with her tarantula dream home, be advised that it is not wise to house more than one tarantula together. Single is best. In most cases, the two, three, or four tarantulas sharing the same enclosure will ultimately become one—the biggest one, no doubt. Need I say more?

Simple Architecture

When designing your tarantula's humble abode, the spider's safety must be your primary concern. A burrowing spider's home will probably differ dramatically from that of a tree-dweller, and that high-sided tree-dweller's home could injure the adventurous burrower who attempts to scale her own personal version of Mount Everest.

But there is nothing more simple than preparing a comfy home for our burrowing friend—and, frankly, the tree-dweller, too, who needs not climb to be content. Just take a trip to your local discount department store. You'll find an incredible selection of tarantula homes in the housewares section. A plastic sweater or shoe box with a secure snap-on lid is ideal. The low walls and secure top (with small holes punched into it for ventilation) promote safety, and the plastic structure is easy to clean.

Two other safe options for these spiders are a plastic jar-like container with a secure, hole-punched, screw-on top, or a commercially available terrarium that many an owner may find more complimentary to their own home's decor. Regardless of the style you choose, make the security of the top a priority. You must never underestimate the spider's ability to remove a loose enclosure lid. Ignoring this advice could result in a big hairy spider running loose in your house, so that should be motivation enough to pay attention.

Special Abodes for Tree-Dwellers

Tree-dwelling tarantulas may actually be happily housed in the more terrestrial digs that are the burrower's ideal, but offering them a more natural habitat can be fascinating for you, as well as fun and interesting for your pet.

A traditional glass aquarium is perfect for a tree-dwelling tarantula, whose legs are specially engineered to stick to the surfaces she climbs and thus prevent those nasty falls that can result in abdomen breakage. Outfit this enclosure with small tree branches for your pet's climbing pleasure, and a tight-fitting ventilated lid, and you'll have a lovely miniature jungle in your home with an unexpected little creature in residence.

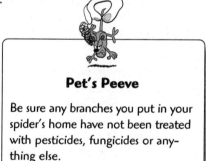

Pet's Peeve

Be sure any branches you put in your spider's home have not been treated with pesticides, fungicides or anything else.

Safe Accessorizing

Although a tarantula will hardly complain, she would appreciate some furnishings in her happy home. Flooring, for one, is of great concern, especially to the burrower. You may see photos of captive tarantulas posing on sand, but resist the temptation to follow that lead. Sand can irritate your poor pet. Also avoid wood shavings, bark chips, and anything made from paper.

One excellent—make that ideal—flooring material is pea- or corn-sized vermiculite, a multi-purpose material for both burrowers and tree-dwellers that facilitates burrowing, is easily cleaned, and helps maintain the proper humidity levels in the enclosure.

When You Get a Tarantula, You'll Also Have to Get These

Secure enclosure	Heat source
Low, shallow water dish	Misting bottle
Substrate material	Forceps or tongs (for feeding)
Hiding place	Care book
Tree branch (for arboreal spiders)	

Furniture need not be expensive or lavish, but it should be functional. A hiding place, for example, is of utmost importance for those times when your spider just doesn't feel like being the center of attention. This can be half of a log that has been hollowed out, a commercially available stone cave or a flower pot turned over on its side. Just make sure that whatever you place within the enclosure is firmly planted within the flooring material. Safety first, remember. You don't want that cave toppling over onto your pet and learning the hard way about the severity of tarantula abdominal injuries.

Heat and Moisture

Take a look at the native homelands of most tarantula species: the deserts of the southwestern United States and the hot, humid rainforests of South America. These animals must like it hot. In fact, warm temperatures are an important ingredient in maintaining a healthy tarantula—ideally, temperatures that range from about 75° to 90°F. A cold tarantula won't eat, and a tarantula that won't eat isn't going to live very long.

If the room you keep your tarantula in is constantly within this range, you won't need an extra heat source. But if it tends to dip below 75°F in the winter months, you'll need an extra heat source. There are under-tank heaters designed for reptile homes that will work well in an aquarium setup. For plastic houses, an incandescent spotlight overhead can provide heat. Just remember that the more heat you provide, the more you'll have to mist the substrate.

A discussion of tarantulas and heat is not meant to suggest that the tarantula is a sun worshipper. Nothing could be further from the truth. Tarantulas spend a great deal of time hiding from the sun in an attempt to retain the moisture within their bodies—and thus stave off the deadly scourge of dehydration and ease the molting process. You, too, must concern yourself with the humidity within your pet's abode. This is most easily done by anchoring a shallow water dish in the enclosure's flooring. A tree-dwelling spider may require a bit more moisture, which can be provided by giving the vermiculite flooring a few spare spritzes from a mister bottle now and then, but be careful not to over-moisturize. That can lead to fungus, which can be dangerous to the resident spider.

The Molt

A tarantula is protected by a firm shell-like coating called the *exoskeleton*. As she grows, she must shed this skeletal structure periodically to make way for her new, larger physique. This can be a dangerous time for the spider, who will let you know of her impending molt by growing lethargic and refusing to eat.

Pampered Pet

Keep all prey away from your spider both before and for a few days after the molt, as the prey can injure the predator during this vulnerable time.

Humidity is a key player in ensuring a smooth molt. The normal steps you take to maintain humidity should accommodate the spider's need for moisture during molting, but you may want to increase it a bit now—especially for tree-dwelling spiders—by misting the vermiculite a bit more frequently. Then just sit back and welcome your newly minted, now a bit larger, pet.

The Tarantula Gourmet

We have already discussed the fact that tarantulas require a diet of live food. That we must accept. In fact, it is the movement of the prey that often sparks the interest of the spider to capture it, liquefy it, and ingest the delectable meal she has created in so gruesome a manner. Now we will delve in to just how this demanding palate may be satisfied.

What Does a Tarantula Eat?

Crickets	Beetles
Mealworms	Other small insects
Moths	Vitamin-mineral supplements

The tarantula menu is simple enough. For most species, it consists of the staple item of live, well-hydrated crickets—a diet that can be supplemented from time to time with live mealworms, small insects, moths, and beetles. The typical tarantula will usually fare best on two or three crickets a week—preferably crickets that have been sprinkled with a vitamin-mineral powder. These can be offered in two feedings over the course of the week. If the spider seems particularly voracious, feel free to increase the number of crickets, one at a time, until she slows down.

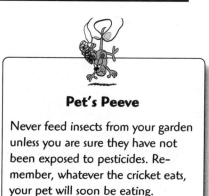

Pet's Peeve

Never feed insects from your garden unless you are sure they have not been exposed to pesticides. Remember, whatever the cricket eats, your pet will soon be eating.

Always supervise your spider's mealtimes to detect signs of an impending molt and to evaluate whether your pet needs seconds or thirds. With the help of the tarantula keeper's best friend—a pair of long forceps—you can place the food in the enclosure (only one cricket or worm at a time, please), and remove either the empty shells or a lucky cricket that, because of a spider's lack of appetite, has won a brief reprieve.

The Least You Need to Know

➤ Handle a tarantula only when necessary. A fall can mortally wound the delicate exoskeleton that protects the spider from a world that is more threatening to the spider than she is to the world.

➤ While a burrowing, land-loving tarantula will live contentedly in a clean plastic sweater or shoe box furnished with a small shallow water dish and a hiding place, a tree-dwelling species will appreciate a taller enclosure furnished with a shallow water dish and trees for climbing. Vermiculite is an excellent flooring material for both setups.

➤ Choose a robust tarantula with a round, plump abdomen; strong legs; an alert disposition; and a healthy appetite.

➤ Tarantulas eat only live food (crickets, mealworms, small insects), several of which can be offered one at a time every few days or so.

➤ When the tarantula molts, keep her enclosure moist by spritzing a corner of the vermiculite flooring with water from a spray bottle and withhold food until the process is complete.

Chapter 23

Hip Hedgehogs

In This Chapter

➤ A day in the life of a hedgehog

➤ A journey into the unique world of the hedgehog

➤ Choosing a spiky pet of your own

➤ A short course on hedgehog care

Wouldn't it be lovely? You saunter out into the cool evening air of an English country garden: the ivy-covered stone walls, the quilt of flowers and plants, the humming insects. Then, you spot movement at the foot of the high stone walls. You step closer. And closer. There, snuffling along the foot of the wall, you see spikes. And then an adorable face. A pointy snout capped at the end by a moist black nose. Twinkling round ebony eyes. And, believe it or not, the little creature almost seems to be smiling at you.

Is it an elf? No, it's a hedgehog—a most unusual, rather unsung, decidedly adaptable little critter with an illustrious past and enough charm to warm the most skeptical heart. That includes the hearts of the English, who love their gardens to distraction but can't help but smile at the sight of a prickly hedgehog rummaging through the garden on a cool spring evening. And, now, contemporary pet owners are beginning to fall under that same spell.

Secrets from the Pet Files

Hedgehogs have several rather adorable vocalizations. Their repertoire includes the purr of the contented adult hedgehog, the chirp of the young hedgehog, the huff and chuff of the hedgehog that has been abruptly awakened or otherwise irritated, and the scream of the frightened or hurt hedgehog.

But before we go any further, a word of warning: The hedgehog is currently considered a trend pet, a title that never benefits any animal species. Popularity does attract people whose affection is genuine and who commit themselves fully to an exotic pet. But it also attracts people whose intentions are anything but honorable—people who jump on the breeding bandwagon to make a buck, and people who must always festoon themselves with the latest trend—even when that latest trend is a living, breathing creature in need of a complex code of care. So, do the hedgehog a favor and evaluate honestly your own intentions before jumping in and inviting one of these undeniably charming little animals into your home.

Hedgehogs As Pets

	light	1	2	3	4	5	heavy
Time commitment				✔			
Grooming			✔				
Feeding					✔		
General cleanup					✔		
Suitable for kids age infant to 5		✔					
Suitable for kids age 5 to 10			✔				
Suitable for kids over 10					✔		
Sociability					✔		
Expense of keeping				✔			

A Day in the Life

This section should actually be called "A Night in the Life" because hedgehogs are nocturnal. Day for them is night for us. But most of our interactions with hedgehogs take place during our day, so that is the time we will spend with this friendly hedgehog who has so kindly invited us in to see what being a hedgehog is all about. His name is Nigel. His species hails from Africa, but Nigel is from Minneapolis. Isn't that just like a hedgehog? So adaptable.

Morning

As the sun rises, Nigel is grooming himself. Bedtime bath. He likes to feel clean when it's time to hit the hay—or in this case, the wood shavings. First he wanders over to the water bottle for one more sip before bed. Then he nudges a small multi-colored ball that sits in the middle of his spacious cage. But he can't play now. The sun is in full swing and he's exhausted. Quite an exciting night last night. He waddles over to the cozy box that is his bed, disappears through the door on his delicate feet, and it's good night . . . er, good morning, Nigel. Sleep tight.

Noon

Please do not disturb. Nigel is sleeping.

Evening

As the afternoon wanes, Nigel begins to stir. The long shadows call to him, signaling to the nocturnal rhythms that have through the ages guided the hedgehog's daily routine. He emerges from his cozy den. His owner is waiting. Nigel knows this. He recognizes the scent.

It's still warm outside, so Nigel's attentive owner decides that today's out-of-cage activities will include a visit to the great outdoors. Gently he carries his pet out into the backyard and puts him down within the secure outdoor enclosure—a large wire canine exercise pen. Here Nigel can trundle about on the grass, snuffling through the delicate blades for bugs, and enjoy the fresh air, yet still remain safe and confined.

When they return to the house, Nigel is offered free run of the kitchen, chasing after a small plastic train while dinner is prepared. Time for Nigel's dinner, too. Back within the confines of his spacious abode he munches on a luscious ration of dry cat food with a bit of canned cat food on the side—chicken flavor. He attacks the meal with gusto. After his meal has settled, he is once again invited out for a visit. This time in the family room. He waddles about, landing eventually in the lap of his owner, who sits with Nigel on the floor. Nigel never flinches as his owner gently moves a finger between his pet's quills in search of flakes or other signs that could indicate emerging health or skin problems. All clear. After a quiet evening, Nigel returns to his cage. It is well prepared to accommodate his nightly activities, including a selection of toys placed in his midst. He'll play until dawn. Then it begins all over again.

The Social Life of Hedgehogs

The hedgehog can't help but immediately charm that lucky individual who comes face to face with him for the first time. Can this animal possibly be real? Look at the quills. Can I touch them? And his eyes like shiny ebony buttons. And that smile. He's actually smiling at me! He has to be something out of a children's book. He is, of course. Mrs. Tiggywinkle, remember? From Beatrix Potter?

But there is so much more to the hedgehog than just that storybook smile. Or even those quills. So many quirks. So many unexpected surprises. Read on and you'll find out just why this animal is so captivating—and so impossible to pin down.

Pet Talk

The African pygmy hedgehog is just that—a pygmy. He weighs about one pound and is just six to nine inches long.

Out of Africa

I will be referring to the pet hedgehog as simply a hedgehog, but in more formal circles he is known by his given name: African pygmy hedgehog. He hails from Africa. Much of Africa, actually. From the hot arid grasslands where life is difficult—survival even more so—and where one would never expect to find a smiling critter who has served as a sweet and gentle inspiration and model for more children's stories than we can count. But the hedgehog, as you can see, is full of surprises.

You're thinking again about that critter in the English country garden, right? The European hedgehog is about 12 inches long and weighs about three pounds. It is also a protected species, because so much of its habitat has been destroyed. You won't find these bigger hedgehogs in the pet trade, although you should be delighted to find one in your garden—they eat up to one-third of their body weight in slugs, snails, and insects each and every day.

The Hedgehog's Wild Side

As with any animal that is relatively new to the pet world, the more you know about the animal's natural existence in the wild—his likes, dislikes, diet, housing, habits, and fears—the better caretaker you will be of the animal in a captive environment. This advice holds true, of course, for the hedgehog, who has long seemed amenable to both the wild life and one that is, shall we say, a bit more civilized. Whatever fate throws his way seems to be fine with him—as long as those who join him mind their manners.

So to help us mind our manners, let's explore the hedgehog's character a bit, and his experiences as a wild animal. First, and this is a biggie, he is nocturnal. That does not mean he will fall into an unconscious stupor all day and emerge at sunset for all-night parties. But you must consider this a warning, all the same. He will be most alert for your quality time together in the morning and late afternoon and evening, and yes, he may be inclined to make some noise at night. That's just the way it is. Don't try to change what can't be changed.

But you need not worry much about those nighttime escapades because the hedgehog is most content when his home is located in a secluded corner of the house—an arrangement that benefits both his daytime sleeping habits and your nighttime ones. He needs warmth and privacy, but he also needs regular companionship, attention, and exercise, including daily interaction and activity outside of his cage. He can be a little spitfire when it comes time to play, and you must commit to being his playmate.

But do control yourself, please. Those quills on the hedgehog's back are a neon clue that while he is curious and affectionate, he has also evolved with a natural suspicion of predators. Handle him gently, with respect, and not too often—and make sure others follow your lead.

Pampered Pet

The hedgehog is blessed with a keen sense of smell. He will learn to identify those he knows and loves best by scent, and will react with enthusiasm when they approach.

The hedgehog is docile, friendly, and clean, but he will bite if frightened or provoked—and scream, too. And despite that genteel demeanor that almost makes you believe he sits down daily for afternoon tea, the hedgehog is a consummate hunter. He subsists in the wild on live insects, snails, and such, and he relishes the hunt. He is also a loner when it comes to those of his own kind, preferring to live in his own private abode both in the wild and in captivity. So take the hint and honor his wishes. Cohabitation, especially between males, can lead to some pretty nasty rows—despite, and because of, those quills.

About Those Quills

The most obvious characteristic of the hedgehog is those stiff, sharp, prickly quills he wears from the top of his head to his back and down the sides of his rather top-heavy physique. Although breeding efforts have resulted in several hedgehog color variations, the classic is a salt-and-pepper mix of quills, where each quill is brown and black, tipped with white. As you have probably surmised, those quills were designed to protect the hedgehog from predators.

Indeed, that coat of spikes has served the hedgehog handsomely through the ages, repelling the predatory advances of some animals with the largest teeth and most powerful jaws on the African plains. And now that the hedgehog is finding an increasingly popular niche with sometimes ill-mannered human predators in more so-called civilized environs, those quills continue to guard his soft-furred underbelly.

Secrets from the Pet Files

While those who know no better may confuse the hedgehog with the porcupine, the hedgehog is actually the original groundhog. In other words, America's Groundhog Day is actually Hedgehog Day. The Romans, you see, believed that if the hedgehog emerged from his den on February 2 and saw his shadow, six more weeks of winter would follow. They never did explain why this nocturnal creature never happened to be sleeping during the middle of the day on February 2, but such questions are not what folklore is made of.

The Quills at Work

When frightened or stressed by, say, an unsupervised four-year-old human, the hedgehog will roll up in a ball that is virtually impenetrable. Attempts to unroll him can prove quite painful to the unsuspecting intruder. One look at this ball, and it is no wonder Lewis Carroll chose hedgehogs to be the croquet balls in his classic *Alice in Wonderland*.

The moral of the story is that you must try your darnedest to guard your pet from stress or fear so that he doesn't spend his time impersonating a pin cushion. Regard this protective reflex as a barometer, a periodic report card on your success as an owner. If your hedgehog rarely sees fit to engage the amazing engineering system that facilitates that roll-into-a-spiky-ball reflex, consider yourself a successful hedgehog keeper. If, however, you and your hedgehog are quite familiar with the reflex, it's time for some caretaking adjustments on your part.

How to Find a Healthy Hedgehog

Be careful. You might get yourself in a hedgehog frenzy, ready to run right out to get one of these delightful critters of your own, only to discover at the first pet shop you visit that hedgehogs are illegal in your state, or perhaps just your city. Hmm. Guess it's time to put the house on the market.

While you're waiting to move, there are several important issues to consider when obtaining a hedgehog pet. The animal should be captive-bred, well socialized to people (that means he should be bred by people who care about the long-term well-being of their animals), healthy, and, of course, legal in your area.

Pampered Pet

There may be times when you must interrupt your pet's daytime slumber. Lift him gently, sit down, and place him on your lap. This will allow him to wake up gradually and free from stress. Just don't make a habit of it.

What Does a Hedgehog Cost?

The purchase price of a hedgehog can vary widely, but the average is $92.50.

The average hedgehog owner also spends per year:

$65	Food
$30	Other supplies
$10	Regular veterinary care

You may be wondering just why this wonderful little critter is considered contraband in certain areas. Well, the reasons are complex, a little silly and perhaps somewhat legitimate. A fear of rabies is one reason, probably because of the hedgehog's odd self-anointing behavior that gives them a rabies-like appearance as they froth at the mouth. The other reason is local and state authorities fear that if pet hedgehogs escaped, they might roam the countryside disrupting the balance of native wildlife. They've got a point. But it's sad to think that we must automatically assume that people will either negligently lose their pets or release them into the wild when they tire of them. We humans have a poor track record in this area.

So Just Where Do You Find a Hedgehog?

Good question! Sitting as they are on the precipice of popularity, hedgehogs are not yet household names. Because breeders are not yet a dime a dozen (and we hope they never will be), they're not easy to find. Pet shops may be your only option to begin your search. There are good ones out there that are clean, knowledgeably staffed, and well versed in the care of hedgehogs. Just don't settle for second best. If, for example,

Pampered Pet

Call around to the local animal shelters. More and more exotic pets are coming their way, and you may just be at the right place at the right time to take in a hedgehog whose previous owners just didn't understand him.

you find only one shop that sells hedgehogs and it's just not up to snuff, keep looking. Even if you have to drive a bit. Start out on the right foot for both of your sakes.

In the meantime, don't give up on the breeders, either. Some do offer to ship hedgehogs long distance, and you may even find some devoted souls who travel from out of state to introduce their animals at local pet shows, fairs, and even reptile shows where exotic pets are featured (assuming, of course, we are talking about shows held where hedgehogs are legal).

Evaluating the Hedgehog Seller

Whenever a pet species is either at the height of trendiness or standing on the threshold, evaluating whoever is selling the pets becomes even more critical. That would certainly be the case with the hedgehog. If you step into a breeder's establishment and suddenly feel like you've entered a used-car lot, accosted by people who are more concerned with what you want (and how much you are willing to pay for it) than with the well-being of their animals, turn right around and go back where you came from.

If, on the other hand, you find you are barraged with questions regarding your intentions toward this animal—Why do you want a hedgehog? Do you know anything about housing hedgehogs? Do you understand that hedgehogs are nocturnal? Are you aware that they are meat eaters?—then you may have found a good breeder.

This suspicion will be further validated when you begin to quiz the quizzer. If you discover that the hedgehogs have been well cared for in proper, private, clean housing situations and that much effort has been spent on socialization—and you witness a gentle confidence in the way the breeder handles the animals—regard these as positive signs. Also positive is the breeder or pet-shop representative who will not allow a young hedgehog to be sold until it reaches at least six weeks of age (six to 12 weeks is considered the optimum age for a hedgehog to leave the nest and bond with people), who knows the animals so well that he or she can tell you what this one likes and this one doesn't, and who exhibits a genuine affection for the animals while explaining these delightful differences.

Selecting a Healthy Hedgehog

When it's time to make that fateful decision about just which hedgehog will be coming home with you, do not let that adorable mug undermine your common sense. Arm yourself with the ability to evaluate for a battery of signs that bespeak of health and longevity. In a very black-and-white nutshell, look for these signs of health in a hedgehog:

➤ Dark eyes that shine clearly and brightly

➤ Clean, soft and smooth-edged ears

➤ Skin that is free of abrasions, dandruff, or other flakes

➤ Quills that are free of any matter

➤ Clean and clear nose

➤ Hearty appetite

➤ An obvious enthusiasm for the world around him

Gauging enthusiasm may be a tough one because, as you know, hedgehogs are nocturnal. To visit them for evaluations in the middle of the day and expect them to be up, active and excited about your arrival is hardly fair. That would be like your boss calling a meeting at 3 a.m. and expecting you to be at your best. So give the little guy a break. Try, try, try to meet potential hedgehog pets in the morning or late afternoon, when they will be more awake and more themselves.

Secrets from the Pet Files

Hedgehogs exhibit an unusual behavior called *self-anointing*, usually ignited when the hedgehog encounters a strange or unusual object. He begins to salivate and grow increasingly excited, ultimately resulting in a buildup of a thick foam around his mouth. Then, almost uncontrollably, he begins to swing his head back and forth, flinging the foam onto the spines of his back. Shocking? Well, sure, the first time you see it. Dangerous? Not a bit.

The Temperament Quandary

Take some of the behavior you witness with a grain of salt, too. Remember, these are docile but secretive little animals who are not all that crazy about being the center of a large alien-scented audience's attention. If one rolls into a ball upon your first meeting, well, that's no indication of some deep and irreversible psychosis. It's just a natural case of stage fright. If he unrolls soon thereafter, unable to squelch his natural hedgehog curiosity, then he's probably a fairly stable, well-socialized little guy. If, however, that initial glimpse was the one and only look you got of his ebony eyes before he disappeared behind his quills, perhaps he has not received the positive socialization that he should have.

Pampered Pet

When creating your hedgehog home, remember that your hedgehog was originally from Africa, not England.

Lifestyles of the Cute and Spiny

Just because the hedgehog has traditionally been considered a welcome addition to the garden, you cannot bring your new pet home and just set him free to fend for himself in the backyard. Sure he might enjoy supervised forays outdoors from time to time, but his well-being commands a far more traditional indoor accommodation.

Three Hedgehog Housing Options

Your challenge when designing your hedgehog's new home is to find a perfect balance between ventilation and warmth. This gives you three basic housing choices. All have their advantages and disadvantages. The rules that apply equally to all, however, are:

➤ Bigger is better.

➤ The hedgehog's home must be placed in a quiet corner of the house, out of high-traffic areas.

➤ The hedgehog's home must be away from direct sunlight or drafts.

➤ The enclosure must include a thick layer of bedding on the floor.

➤ The bedding must be commercially available wood shavings (no irritating pine or cedar, please) or shredded paper manufactured specifically for small-animal housing.

The first of these options is the traditional wire cage with a solid floor (to protect those delicate hedgehog toes) and a securely locking door. This obviously satisfies the ventilation requirement, but what of the temperature? Just make sure the corner of your home in which the cage is situated remains somewhere between 75° and 80°F. Temperatures much cooler than this invite respiratory infection.

The second option is the glass aquarium—at least a 20-gallon tank. Here ventilation is at a disadvantage. You can improve the situation by outfitting the tank with a securely fitting wood-framed screen top. The answer is *not* to place the tank under an air-conditioning vent. Remember, no drafts!

The third option, also lacking in the ventilation department, is the dog crate made for airline travel. The advantage of this choice, other than the warmth it provides (not warmer than that 75° to 80°F, though), is that it keeps the hedgehog quiet and secluded during his daytime sleep. Such housing does, however, demand that the resident hedgehog be afforded ample time outside his home each day—but of course, that holds true for a hedgehog housed in any of these abodes.

When You Get a Hedgehog, You'll Also Have to Get These

Cage	Bedding material
Exercise pen	Litter box
Food dishes	Litter
Water bottle	Nail clippers
Exercise toys	Toothbrush (for grooming)
Play toys	Tweezers (for grooming)
Nest box	Care book

The Properly Appointed Hedgehog Home

A hedgehog cannot live by aquarium, cage, or kennel alone. Granted, he comes from the savannas of Africa where vegetation is sparse, but he is a curious critter and should be afforded some semblance of variety in his happy home. First, every hedgehog simply must have a hiding/nest box complete with clean, dry bedding. Whether cardboard or wood, it must be large enough for the resident hedgehog to conceal himself completely and to turn around in. A chunk of PVC piping can also be fun both for play and hiding, as can a variety of toys, such as an exercise wheel, a squeaky hedgehog toy, and a ball. Rotate the toys periodically to keep life exciting.

Hedgehog Fun and Games

Which brings us to the subject of hedgehog leisure time. Hedgehogs, while hardly the rocket scientists of the animal kingdom, do like to have fun. And sharing fun and games with this gregarious pet is something that should have drawn you to the hedgehog in the first place. Such communal activities, which for obvious nocturnal reasons are best reserved for mornings and evenings, can be carried out both indoors and out, and they should be part of you and your pet's daily routine.

Indoor Fun

Indoor fun can consist simply of allowing the hedgehog to meander around the family room in the evening while the family looks on, to explore your bed while you read, or letting him run around with some toys in the bathtub in a bathroom lit only by a night light.

Use your imagination and you'll find exciting new toys everywhere in your household: a child's toy truck or an empty toilet-paper roll perhaps. Just be sure that other household pets, particularly dogs and cats, don't view the hedgehog as their personal

Pet's Peeve

Any time you have your hedgehog on a raised surface, such as your bed or a table, keep your eyes on him. You don't want him falling off the edge.

plaything. The hedgehog should be fine, but the unsuspecting, even well-meaning dog or cat will learn pretty quickly and painfully that the hedgehog is not a toy.

Outdoor Fun

While supervision is required whenever a hedgehog is out and about, this is even more true when he is out and about in the great outdoors. When it's warm and dry out, go ahead and allow your pet to enjoy the nice weather, but do take the necessary precautions. The animal should remain confined, either in a roomy cage (a dog crate or aquarium could overheat), or in a larger pen, such as a spacious wire crate or exercise pen made for dogs. Whatever you choose should be secure and free from gaps through which a hedgehog might escape. The hedgehog will be delighted if the play yard's floor is natural grass—especially if he happens to find an earthworm or a snail meandering across the blades.

Pet's Peeve

Never put a hedgehog down on grass that has been treated with chemical fertilizers, herbicides, pesticides or anything else.

Make sure your outdoor play yard also includes shelter for the animal, should he decide to retreat from the sun, and fresh, cool water to drink. A combination of quiet companionship time and rowdy exercise each and every day will keep a hedgehog happy, satisfied, and affectionate toward the family that cares enough to spend time with their unusual pet.

Hedgehog Grooming

Virtually every pet species you can name craves cleanliness both in themselves and in their homes. The hedgehog is no exception. Remove soiled bedding and leftover food daily, and change the bedding entirely at least once a month. If you're very patient, your hedgehog can be litter box trained. Check the bedding every day anyway, and, of course, scoop the litter box daily.

As for the hedgehog himself, he'll take care of much of his own grooming. But he will need help with his nails, which you should clip with a simple nail clipper. You can also help out from time to time with a soft toothbrush and a pair of tweezers. Use the tweezers to remove pieces of bedding and such stuck between the quills, and use the toothbrush to brush gently the areas between the quills and the quills themselves.

A Voracious Carnivore

Despite his association with the garden, the hedgehog is no vegetarian. Quite the opposite. In fact, hedgehogs are welcomed in gardens because they are a natural, chemical-free, oh-so-charming form of pest control. You see, in the wild hedgehogs dine on whatever live delicacy is available: snails, spiders, slugs, beetles, earthworms.

But don't worry. This is not what you will have to feed your pet hedgehog. However, he will require meat.

What Does a Hedgehog Eat?

Dry hedgehog or cat food (meat flavors only)	Mealworms
Canned cat food (meat flavors only)	Waxworms
Cottage cheese	Crickets
Cooked eggs	
Cooked chicken or ground beef	

The meat you offer your pet need not be alive. A moderate helping of a high-quality commercial dry cat food each day should suffice. Supplement this with some sort of moist food, such as a teaspoon or so of canned cat or dog food, low-fat cottage cheese, boiled or scrambled egg, or cooked hamburger.

As for treats, they can be items that harken back to the hedgehog's wild roots. How about offering a mealworm once or twice a week? Do so, and you may be absolutely shocked when the worm's wiggling inflames the wild hunter within your friendly, docile pet and he becomes the voracious predator of the garden. Whether cat food or mealworm, serve all food in a shallow, heavy-bottomed dish that sits securely in the flooring of the hedgehog's home.

Beware of hedgehog obesity. The hedgehog is and should be charged with energy—anything but a couch potato. Time spent rolling up to fend off predators, surveying a massive territory, and foraging for food keeps a body slim and trim. In captivity, however, the pampered pet hedgehog's needs are all met without much effort on the animal's part, and his life is far more sedentary. You must then take great care not to overfeed your hedgehog and to provide him with ample exercise time outside of his enclosure, which will be good for his mind as well as his body.

Pampered Pet

How do you pick up a hedgehog? Very carefully! Put one hand on each side of the animal and gently scoop your hands beneath his body. Remain still for a moment as the animal settles in and makes himself comfortable, then lift.

Of course, no hedgehog diet is complete without a constant supply of fresh, clean water. This is best served in a traditional water bottle that hangs on the side of the hedgehog's cage, kennel, or glass tank. Not convinced? You'd rather use a water dish that matches the feeding dish? You'll change your mind about that as soon as your pet goes running in circles around his cage and makes a royal and very wet mess of everything. Clean the water bottle and the feeding dish daily, and your pet should be a happy, healthy hedgehog indeed.

The Least You Need to Know

➤ Hedgehogs are available from breeders and pet shops, but they are illegal in some areas, so do your research.

➤ Look for a healthy hedgehog with dark, shining eyes; smooth-edged ears, flake-free quills and skin; and a healthy appetite.

➤ Because hedgehogs are nocturnal creatures, evaluate prospective pets in the morning or late afternoon when you can catch a glimpse of the animals' true personalities.

➤ A hedgehog values his privacy and is best housed separately in a clean, well-ventilated enclosure with a secluded sleeping/hiding place, a collection of toys, fresh bedding, and an air temperature of 75° to 80°F.

➤ Devout carnivores, hedgehogs thrive on a diet of high-quality dry cat food supplemented with a bit of canned cat or dog food, low-fat cottage cheese, boiled or scrambled egg, or cooked hamburger—and perhaps a live mealworm once or twice a week.

Chapter 24

Gorgeous Goldfish

In This Chapter

➤ A day in the life of a goldfish

➤ Unraveling all the misunderstandings about goldfish

➤ Choosing a school of your own

➤ An aquarium-eye view of goldfish care

Name a pet that almost every single person you know—and even most of the people you don't know—have owned at one time or another. Give up? It's the goldfish, of course. You may not have lived with a goldfish since you were about five years old, and that fish probably didn't last long. That's par for the course with goldfish, and do you know why? Because most people don't know the first thing about caring for them.

How can that be? We all know how to take care of goldfish: Just fill up a bowl with water. Pour the goldfish in from a plastic sandwich bag. Sprinkle a lot of food into the water. And that's it. End of story. Sure, the fish will be dead in a few months, maybe even in a few weeks, but that's just the life span of a goldfish, right? Wrong! Anyone going through life thinking this is all there is to goldfish keeping is in need of some education on the subject, and this is just the place to start.

Goldfish As Pets

	light	1	2	3	4	5	*heavy*
Time commitment			✔				
Grooming		✔					
Feeding			✔				
General cleanup				✔			
Suitable for kids age infant to 5			✔				
Suitable for kids age 5 to 10			✔				
Suitable for kids over 10					✔		
Sociability		✔					
Expense of keeping				✔			

A Day in the Life

Meet Goldie the goldfish. His keepers don't know that Goldie is really a male, but they do know that he is the typical run-of-the-mill goldfish. Nevertheless, they treat him like a very special fish. In fact, they treat him as all fish should be treated: with respect and with the proper equipment. Goldie's keepers, you see, know how it is for most goldfish—the fish bowl and some food now and then—but they vowed it would be different for their fish.

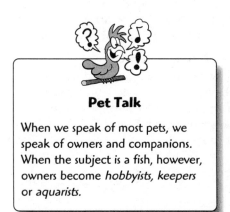

Pet Talk

When we speak of most pets, we speak of owners and companions. When the subject is a fish, however, owners become *hobbyists, keepers* or *aquarists.*

The First Half of Goldie's Day

Morning. The sun peeks in the window. The light is clicked on over Goldie's aquarium. Yes, Goldie lives in an aquarium. Lucky little goldfish. He awakens from his slumber on the floor of the tank and swims. And he swims and he swims. Breakfast is served. He glides up to the surface to greet the few flakes of food that have been sprinkled onto the top of the water. A nibble here, a nibble there. Once he's had his fill, it's back to the business at hand. He dives down to the floor, then back up to the surface again. He hides among the plants that flutter in the current. The greenery tickles his tail. Then he swims and he swims some more.

The Last Half of Goldie's Day

It's afternoon now. Time for a partial water change. But that, of course, is of more concern to Goldie's keepers than it is to him. They take some water out of the tank and then replace it with fresh water. As for Goldie, he swims and he swims. He dives down to check out the little Mickey Mouse in scuba gear standing in the gravel on the tank floor. Then he swims and he swims some more.

It's evening now. The light is clicked off in the aquarium. That's the signal that it's time for sleep. Goldie glides down to the floor, his fins fluttering gently to keep him balanced, and he drifts off to sleep. Happy fish dreams, little Goldie.

Goldfish Societies

Goldfish have been coexisting with humans for a very long time. In fact, it is believed the Chinese first domesticated the goldfish sometime around the 10th century. The raising of goldfish began as a communal project during the second part of the Chin Dynasty and blossomed during the subsequent Ming Dynasty when individuals began taking goldfish into their homes as pets. Thus a tradition was born that is today shared in almost every nation of the world.

That this tradition began with the Chinese, and that it spread quickly to Japan, is no surprise. The Asian cultures have a long history of elevating fishkeeping to an art form, and they have developed many of the fancy goldfish species.

It was not until relatively recently that the Western cultures decided to follow their lead. Today, the aquarium hobby is big business; you can even find pet shops dedicated solely to aquarium fish. The masses just need to be convinced that goldfish, too, are part of the aquarium hobby—a hobby that can be extremely satisfying intellectually, and extremely relaxing emotionally.

Secrets from the Pet Files

How relaxing it is to peer into an aquarium, watch the fish glide with the current (countless doctors and dentists who have installed fish tanks in their offices to soothe their patients can't be wrong!). But what about the flip side? Do the fish watch us? The answer is probably. Although severely nearsighted, fish can probably see colors. Attentive hobbyists insist that their pets do know their keepers and enjoy their presence. They report that the fish will respond to the sight of people outside the tank wall, swim joyfully when they notice the hand raised above the surface for the sprinkling of food, and hide when someone approaches the tank in a threatening manner.

What Exactly Is a Goldfish?

Here we go again. Asking silly, obvious questions. What is a goldfish? Goldfish are those little orange-colored fish that you win at school fairs and keep in a bowl on your kitchen counter for a while. Next question?

Wait just a minute. Before we move on, let's spend a little more time on this question. First, contrary to popular ignorance, there is no one type of goldfish. There are more than 100 varieties in an astounding array of sizes, shapes, fin lengths, colors, and even facial structures. Some are gold, some are black, some are orange, some are white, and some are combinations of any or all of the above. Some are plain and simple; some look like they're wearing long, flowing orange wedding dresses, fully equipped with veils and trains. Some are small, some are large, some have small eyes, and some have enormous bubble eyes that look like they might pop like balloons if the fish aren't careful.

Secrets from the Pet Files

All goldfish today are presumed to be cousins of the koi, the prized carp of Asia. Both are, by nature, pond fish that are typically found in the same mix of colors. Both are hardy and should be long-lived, and, while they typically enjoy the company of others of their own kind, they are usually not all that accepting of other types of fish. The most dramatic difference would probably be in their price tags. Koi can command tens of thousands of dollars, while goldfish can be purchased for pocket change. This does not mean, however, that you should not value and care for them.

Goldfish are arguably the most popular pet on the planet—or at least the most widely kept. They are also the most inexpensive pet on the planet, a phenomenon that has made them highly disposable and lends credence to the notion that people don't value what they don't pay much for. In fact, the phrase "free to a good home" is a way of life for the goldfish. Almost all of us have lived with goldfish, yet very few of us have paid much, if anything, for them. Many of us have also had our first lessons in dealing with the death of a pet through the demise of a goldfish that probably met its end prematurely thanks to a lack of proper care.

Goldfish and Mice: Separated at Birth?

Although one swims and one lives on land, there are actually several similarities between mice and goldfish. On the sadder side, both are regarded as rather disposable pets. They are frequently sacrificed at the altar of hey-let's-teach-the-kids-how-to-take-care-of-a-pet-by-themselves. Both are also purchased periodically as food for other animals. Goldfish destined for this sad end are referred to as "feeder fish" for other fish and amphibians, while many mice are purchased as dinner for reptiles.

Both mice and goldfish are often treated as inanimate interior decorations, but this can be a blessing in disguise if the animals are cared for properly. They are most content if left alone and admired from afar. Neither mice nor goldfish enjoy handling (downright impossible with a goldfish, anyway), and neither appreciate being held aloft by their tails. Both are most content in social groups of their own kind and enjoy feeding time immensely. So similar are they that mice are often referred to as aquarium-style pets, best seen and not bothered. Perhaps we can similarly refer to goldfish as mouse-like pets—yet another hint that goldfish belong in a spacious aquarium environment.

Secrets from the Pet Files

Ancient peoples, from the Egyptians to the Phoenicians to the Chinese, viewed the fish, with its ability to lay and fertilize great quantities of eggs, as the ultimate symbol of fertility.

Goldfish Etiquette

Goldfish can be scrappy little denizens of the deep. Yet at the same time, they do find comfort in the company of other goldfish and tend to get along well together. They do not, however, tend to get along with other types of fish. They can't help but flaunt their superior stamina and health in front of other fish—boasting that can lead to aggression, injury, and death to the other fish who don't have the distinction of being born goldfish.

And just what lesson can we learn from this? Goldfish should only be kept with other goldfish, and even more specifically, only with goldfish of the same type. After so many centuries of living according to the rules of survival of the fittest, the goldfish has emerged as the fittest of the tropical fish that people enjoy installing in their homes. You don't typically see goldfish swimming around with the angelfish and other such exotic beauties in those lovely mixed-fish aquarium setups. It's not because the goldfish aren't lovely enough. It's because they just can't get along.

A Whole New Underwater World

A warning: Fishkeeping can be highly addictive, and the goldfish tends to be the springboard, the fish with which it all begins. The goldfish, you see, is a hardy fish that is probably the one and only pet we might say is appropriate for virtually every owner. It is also the ideal starter fish for anyone with an interest in aquariums.

Before you know it, you're hooked. You start with a goldfish or two, set up the aquarium, and find that you enjoy the challenge. Balancing the water components, installing the filters, maintaining the substrate and plants—it's a kick being lord of this tiny underwater world. So inspired, you try your hand at some other types of fresh-water fish. More success. Then the greatest challenge: saltwater fish. You find yourself doing all you can to re-create the ocean in your living room.

The tanks in your home begin to multiply like mice. They expand in size, decor and accessories. Soon the fish you choose become more and more exotic and expensive. And all thanks to that one little goldfish that ushered you into this beautiful world those many years ago.

Realistic Expectations

When you bring a goldfish into the house, this pet will prove to be quite different from a dog, a cat, or even a gerbil. This is without a doubt the quietest pet you can get, and the one that will be welcomed with open arms into condominiums and apartments that otherwise enforce strict "no pets" policies.

What Does a Goldfish Cost?

The purchase price of a goldfish can vary widely, but the average is 25 cents to a dollar. Fancy varieties can be much more.

The average freshwater fish owner also spends per year:

$30	Equipment
$19	Fish food
$17	Aquarium lighting
$13	Chemicals
$10	Health items

But while the goldfish has documented soothing effects on the human psyche, it will not satisfy each and every longing you might have when you think about pets. You must approach this pet with realistic expectations. Look at the following list to see just what you can and cannot expect from this pet. If the goldfish falls short of what you are looking for, then go ahead and keep the fish, but feel free to get another pet, too. It need not be a question of one or the other: The goldfish doesn't mind sharing you—as long as you keep the cat's paws out of the fish tank.

To make it easy, here's a list of what you cannot expect of your pet goldfish:

➤ Don't expect obedience and affection.

➤ Don't expect to get exercise walking your pet goldfish on a leash; they haven't yet made a collar small enough to fit a goldfish.

➤ Don't expect to housetrain or litter-box train your goldfish.

➤ Don't expect the goldfish to view you as anything more than a dispenser of food.

➤ Don't overestimate the kids' ability to care for the fish without adult supervision.

➤ Don't underestimate the kids' affection for the fish.

➤ Don't overestimate the kids' affection for the fish.

Choosing a Pet Goldfish

Sometimes you have no say in choosing the goldfish that comes home to live with you. The most common scenario is the young child who comes home from the school fair, all smiles on his face, a goldfish swimming in a bag in his hand. He won the fish at the fair. Or perhaps you attended the fair and won it for him.

Or maybe you chose to have a goldfish pet but never thought about choosing your particular fish. The idea of it never even occurred to you. You just went to the pet shop and asked for one. The fish is brought out to you and that's that.

Well, with the exception perhaps of the prize goldfish at the school fair, you can and should have a say in which fish you end up with. This choice, combined with the proper care that you will provide, all work together to elevate fish keeping to a more fulfilling and fascinating experience—for the fish as well as its keeper.

Pampered Pet

All goldfish are brown when young. Any that have brown or black markings on them may change to orange later. In fact, it is common for goldfish to change color or markings as they age.

Where to Go

As we have already seen, sometimes a goldfish comes into our lives when we least expect it. Nevertheless, there are those who purposely set out to find a goldfish or two, and they inevitably discover that the options are rich.

The pet shop, of course, is the most logical place to find a pet goldfish, but it isn't the only place. Today, thanks to the burgeoning popularity of the aquarium hobby, pet shops devoted solely to fish have cropped up around the country. Do not be ashamed to walk into one of these stores and tell them you would like to see the goldfish, thank you very much. Yes, you will be surrounded by much more exotic creatures swimming about, but stick to your choice. You can learn a lot from the people who work at such stores, and should you find yourself hooked on the hobby, this will be an excellent resource when you decide to keep other species.

What to Look For

When you discover just how plentiful a store's collection of available goldfish is, you may find yourself getting dizzy. How do you choose? Well, first examine the environment. Are the tank and the water it holds clean? Is the tank wall-to-wall fish? Be wary of overcrowded display tanks, which can be breeding grounds for contagious disease. Beware, too, of a tank that is housing several fish that are listless or not very skilled in their swimming abilities. And make a quick about face if you notice strange growths on any of the fishes' scales or fins. Disease within a tank can be contagious almost instantly.

The healthy goldfish should swim with power and enthusiasm. A fish that swims almost exclusively on the top of the tank or on the bottom should be avoided, as should the fish that is floating on the top of the water. Not a good choice.

One, Two, or Your Own Personal School?

Go ahead and get several fish, but don't overcrowd the tank. A 10-gallon tank can hold about eight goldfish. It's best, too, to house like fish together. While goldfish are, as a whole, hardy fish, there are some delicate members of the family (those bubble-eyed varieties, for example) that will require some special care and perhaps some special experience on the part of their keepers. Fish can also be bullies. They just can't seem to get away from that "survival of the fittest" stuff, even though they've been domesticated for more than 1,000 years. They will hone in instantly on a fish among them that is ill or injured or in any way weaker than the pack.

When choosing members for your school, try to choose fish that are similar physically. They should be of similar sizes and types. All should swim powerfully and enthusiastically, exuding health and vitality with every swish of the tail. You should note no sign of illness. The gills and scales should be free of infection, as should those of the other fish in the display tank.

Pampered Pet

Goldfish eat more, and excrete more, than many other types of fish. That means you can put fewer of them in your aquarium.

The Real Story on Goldfish Care

We can't really go into all the minute detail of fishkeeping because, probably unlike any other pet you could choose, the successful keeping of this pet is a science. No kidding. It involves chemistry and biology and wastewater management: subjects people attend college for years and years to earn Ph.D.s in. But don't worry, you can qualify for goldfish ownership without a doctorate. You will need to do your homework, though, and, if possible, find a mentor, perhaps a helpful staff member at your friendly local aquarium store.

The Classic Fish Bowl—A Poor Choice

If you don't feel you've had the message appropriately drummed into your head yet, here we go again: The classic fish bowl, or giant brandy snifter, or oversized bud vase, or novelty table lamp, or whatever it is people have at one time or another deemed a goldfish would look cute swimming around in, is *not* an appropriate home for a goldfish.

All fish are fish. Remember that. Why would one type of fish require the natural environment provided by an aquarium, with filtering, oxygen, light and heat, while another deserves only some tap water poured into a tiny bowl? Where did this idea come from?

The traditional fishbowl makes a great planter, but it is an inappropriate goldfish home—not simply because it is restrictive and boring for its resident free-swimmer, but also because it exposes an extremely limited surface area of water to the open air for the exchange of oxygen (see, we told you science would be involved). While fish can breathe underwater, they do require oxygen, and as much as we can possibly supply them.

When You Get a Goldfish, You'll Also Have to Get These

Aquarium tank	Aquarium lights
Tank cover	Aeration system
Filter	Aquarium gravel
Water test kit	Plants and decorations
Heater	Fish net
Thermometer	Care book

A Real Aquarium

Now that we have learned our lesson about the goldfish bowl, just what should we house our goldfish in? Well, if given their choice, goldfish, like their koi cousins, would choose a pond as their ideal home. But since most of us get goldfish as pets because we don't have backyards, it's doubtful that many of us have goldfish ponds, either.

So what's a goldfish to do? He needs water surface area for oxygen exchange, he needs ample space in which to swim around, and he needs a home compact enough to fit into a somewhat size-restricted living space. We have just the answer: the aquarium. The goldfish may be a little bit less expensive than most other fish you can buy, but his needs are no different from those of hizzzs fishy brethren.

The Science of Goldfish Tank Maintenance

This is not meant to be the final dissertation on aquarium maintenance. The aquarium hobby is practically a religion, comprising a rich body of knowledge firmly grounded in the hard sciences. We can, however, go over the basics of the freshwater aquarium, which will dictate what your concerns will be day to day as you work to maintain the ideal home for your fish, and what pieces of equipment and materials you will need for that mission.

Filtration

Healthy fish require a clean tank. Scavengers that they are, goldfish will probably make valiant efforts to ingest everything they see floating around the water, but you will need to pick up what they don't. This is best done with a filtration system, of which there are three types available. These are the undergravel filter (possibly too complicated for the beginner), the internal box filter (considered by most experts to be inadequate when used alone), and the external box system (the preferred system for its power and efficiency).

Pet's Peeve

Never simply dump a fish into tap water. Water must be tested, treated, and brought to the right temperature before a fish can live in it.

Acidity

Water acidity is measured as pH. Your goldfish tank should have a pH somewhere from 6.5 to 7.5, measured weekly with a simple test kit designed specifically for this purpose. If your pH is not right, there are chemicals you can add to the water to adjust it.

Temperature

Different varieties of goldfish thrive in different temperatures, but all in all the goldfish family is tolerant of temperatures lower than those appropriate for other popular aquarium fish. Your fish may fare just fine without a heater, but it's still smart to install a thermometer to monitor the tank temperature.

Oxygen

Fish breathe oxygen, not water, so the water in which they swim must receive a steady infusion of fresh oxygen all the time. In addition to the water circulation and aeration provided by the power filter, it's wise to install an aeration system of some kind. This includes an air pump and airstones that will keep the water fish-friendly.

Light

Fish take their signals about when it's time to sleep and time to wake from light. Because direct sunlight can heat the water, it's best to use an artificial light source. Try a fluorescent light that is simple to turn on and off, and that will not shed excess heat.

You'll need to establish a regular schedule for turning the light on and off. When it comes on, the goldfish wake up hungry. When it goes off, they'll have the darkness they require for a restful night's sleep. Your fish will then probably float down to the bottom of the tank and drift off with his eyes wide open. He has no eyelids, you see.

Pet Talk

Goldfish are *diurnal*. They work and play during the day and sleep at night. And, like us, they simply must have their beauty sleep if they are to thrive.

Accessories

Rounding out this environment is vegetation and decoration. Beginners may want to wait a while before delving into the challenging world of live plants, but you should provide your fish with some type of decor that not only makes the aquarium more fun to look at, but also provides hiding places for the fish. Artificial plants, castles, sunken ships—all can make the aquarium a cheerier, even more natural, place for a fish to be.

At the very least, you need some aquarium gravel. This gives your tank a nice look, gives the fish a little something to dig around in, and gives you a medium to stick your plants and decorations into.

Laying the Groundwork

When you decide that you will be adopting a goldfish or two, you must begin ahead of time. To rush the process is to risk your pet's health.

First you must purchase the appropriate equipment: a spacious glass tank with a leakproof frame, a cover for the tank to prevent escapees who might accidentally leap for joy right out of the water, the gravel, the filtering system, the aeration system, the lighting system, a fish net for capturing fish when necessary, the pH test kit, the heater (optional), an aquarium thermometer, and the fish food.

Pampered Pet

How critical is a regular cleaning regimen? Fish swim in their toilet. You need to flush it for them.

Now is the perfect time, too, to commit to the cleanliness regimen that will be so critical to your role as fishkeeper. Wash everything with a gentle soap and water, and rinse every surface thoroughly. Rinse off the gravel for the aquarium floor (no soap!). Plan where you will be keeping the aquarium, too. It must rest on a solid, secure surface that is out of the high-traffic areas of the house that can lead to an overturned aquarium, and out of direct sunlight, which will only invite overheating and algae growth.

Believe it or not, once you have all the supplies assembled, you're still not ready to throw in the fish. Nope. First you have to age the water. This means filling the aquarium with water, getting all the equipment up and running, and allowing the toxic materials in the water to evaporate, thus creating a more fish-friendly environment. Now, granted, the goldfish is one of the hardier members of the pet fish family, and given all those goldfish that have been thrown into un-aged water through the years and lived to glub-glub about it, it's apparent that the aging process isn't absolutely critical to its survival. But we want to do this right, don't we? We want to give our pets every chance we can.

Once the fish are in, maintenance is an ongoing affair. If there is one phrase that should be considered the mantra of fishkeepers everywhere, that would be "partial

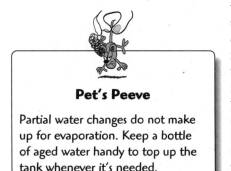

Pet's Peeve

Partial water changes do not make up for evaporation. Keep a bottle of aged water handy to top up the tank whenever it's needed.

water changes." There is no greater tool for keeping the tank clean and the fish healthy than to change a portion of the water in the tank every week to 10 days. This involves removing approximately 10 to 20 percent of the tank water, followed by replacing that water with a fresh supply. If you were to make a wholesale change, you would have to wait a few days for the new water to age before you could return the fish to their new, freshly filled aquarium. Partial water changes: Say it in your sleep, on your way to work, while you exercise, while you feed the fish, and while you change the water partially.

Chow Time in the Fish Tank

Goldfish are easy keepers that will eat almost anything. You must not feed them according to this biological inclination, however. Goldfish are phenomenally simple to feed, and even easier to overfeed.

What Does a Goldfish Eat?

Flaked goldfish food
Dry goldfish food

While some experienced keepers like to get fancy with their fish at mealtimes, for the keeper who would like to keep it simple, flaked and dry foods are the simplest choice for a well-balanced diet. Not just any flaked or dried food, however. Not all foods, or even all fish, are created equal, so you must choose food that is specifically formulated for goldfish. Nothing else will do.

Meals are best served twice a day, preferably morning and evening. That's easy enough to remember. And because a goldfish will eat himself to death if offered the chance, you must monitor the amounts. One accepted formula calls for feeding the fish as much as it will eat in five minutes. This way, your fish will not outgrow his tank.

The Least You Need to Know

➤ Despite the image of the traditional fish bowl, goldfish are best—and most humanely—housed in full aquarium setups where the water is properly filtered, chemically balanced (pH should be somewhere between 6.5 and 7.5), and aerated.

➤ Maintain the health of your goldfish and his home with regular partial water changes.

➤ Goldfish tend to get along well with their own kind but not with fish of other species.

➤ When choosing a goldfish, look first for a clean display tank environment; then look for a fish that swims powerfully and displays healthy skin, scales, and fins.

➤ Avoid the pitfall of overfeeding your goldfish. A sprinkle twice daily in which the fish is allowed to eat as much fresh goldfish food as he can in five minutes will suffice.

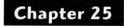

Chapter 25

This Little Miniature Potbellied Pig

> ### In This Chapter
>
> ➤ A day in the life of a potbellied pig
>
> ➤ A look at pigs and their place in the world
>
> ➤ Choosing a healthy, sweet-tempered pig pet
>
> ➤ Tender-loving care of the potbellied pig

The 1980s: a decade of excess; a decade of self-indulgence; a decade of potbellied pigs. Back in the 1980s, a great many people found themselves with more money and more status symbols than they had ever dreamed possible. Some of those people saw a photo of a tiny black pig, held securely in a woman's fine-boned palms. "Miniature potbellied pig," the caption read. "I don't have that," they thought, "and none of my friends do either." That, of course, was about to change.

Soon pet stores were featuring tiny potbellied pigs. At the same time, breeders jumped on the potbellied bandwagon, touting the small pig as a dream come true—the perfect pet for everyone, and my, what an attention-grabber. What they neglected to tell these status-seeking would-be owners was that the pig portrayed in the photo and featured in the pet shop window was just a baby, a pig*let*. They neglected to inform buyers that the healthy miniature potbellied pig, aside from growing sour, nasty, and spoiled in inexperienced or lackadaisical hands, would one day grow to 60, 70, 80, even 90 pounds. Sure, that's miniature by pig standards, but such an animal would hardly fit comfortably in the palms of her owner's hands.

Pet Talk

A pig is a smaller hog, and both are members of the *porcine* family of animals—animals that actually, as we are now discovering, aren't really all that far removed physically and intellectually from humans.

There are some special people who genuinely love this animal for what and who she is. This does not include everyone who made killings in real estate and junk bonds in the 1980s, only to lose those fortunes when the 1990s rolled around. The "me generation" came to an end, and so did the heyday of the potbellied pig. Soon those misleading ads were replaced by announcements of potbellied pig sanctuaries, but this painful transition would actually prove healthier for the pig. Left standing were those special souls who today continue to consider a life without a potbellied pig a life not worth living. Perhaps you are one of these people. Perhaps you aren't. Perhaps the following will help you figure it out.

Miniature Potbellied Pigs As Pets

	light	1	2	3	4	5	heavy
Time commitment						✔	
Grooming					✔		
Feeding					✔		
General cleanup						✔	
Suitable for kids age infant to 5		✔					
Suitable for kids age 5 to 10			✔				
Suitable for kids over 10			✔				
Sociability						✔	
Expense of keeping						✔	

A Day in the Life

Here we are at Pearl's house. Pearl is a miniature potbellied pig. She weighs in at about 82 pounds, and she is beautiful by potbellied standards. Her dark hair is coarse and thick, her skin wrinkled in all the right places, and a tuft of white hair sprouts up on her forehead between her eyes. Her plump belly is of just the right size and curve relative to her overall size—we can't have that belly dragging on the ground, now can we? She is championship material from head to toe.

The prognosis for a day spent with a potbellied pig depends on the nature of the pig. Hang out with a spoiled animal, and that will probably be the last day you will ever care to spend with that or any pig. But spend it with a well-adjusted pig who has been raised by a firm yet understanding pig-savvy owner—a pig like Pearl—and you may leave wishing for a pig of your very own.

Breakfast with Pearl

Pearl's devoted mistress—we'll call her Jeanie—walks out into the backyard to greet her porcine pet. Pearl emerges regally from her clean igloo-shaped doghouse, her countenance mimicking that of the Queen of England. She surveys her secure and spacious realm for a moment and then looks at Jeanie with that meaningful expression: "Time for breakfast, isn't it?" Jeanie is ready, as always, to give Pearl what she wants—up to a point.

Needless to say, breakfast at Pearl's house does not include bacon or ham for anyone in the family. As for Pearl, she munches on a generous helping of fresh pig chow, followed by a generous helping of fresh, clean water. Her tail spins through it all. This ultimate gesture of approval never stops. If Jeanie keeps doing everything right, it never will.

Doing Lunch with Pearl

It's been a rather warm morning, so Pearl has rested quietly in the shade. A longtime friend visits Jeanie, and they sit out on the back patio sharing a light lunch, watching Pearl as they dine. They reminisce about the day they met Pearl for the first time. Together they visited the breeder, and there she was: a tiny piglet snuggled in with her two sisters and two brothers in a precious pig line, their heads resting comfortably on their tiny hoofed feet, their tails spinning in happy unison behind them.

After lunch, they decide that perhaps Pearl would like to take a dip. Jeanie fills Pearl's wading pool with fresh water. Pearl approaches, enters, and begins to soak. Ah, she adores this so. This is what she would do if she were a wild pig on a hot day. When Pearl's body has been sufficiently cooled, she steps out of her pool and retreats once more to the shade under the tree in her enclosure. She settles in for a nap. Her third one today. "This is not a day for much activity," she seems to say.

Pampered Pet

We usually think of pigs wallowing in mud, and they do if there is no other way to cool down. But a dip in cool water is just as good, and a lot cleaner.

The Evening Meal with Pearl

As the afternoon cools, Pearl becomes a bit more sociable. She munches on some chopped fruits and veggies, throwing the food about exuberantly when the inspiration moves her, spilling her water

when it's time for a drink. Then, because Pearl is such a well-behaved creature, she is invited indoors for a while.

Pearl steps delicately with her cloven hooves on the slick kitchen tile. She walks gingerly into the family room and seeks out her favorite corner: a comfy pillow upon which are stored several squeaky toys that she enjoys throwing about. She waddles over to Jeanie on the couch, nuzzles her knee and asks for a scratch behind the ear. Pearl is very insistent. They enjoy the camaraderie they have come to know in the past two years.

Then bedtime rolls around. Pearl willingly walks to the sliding door to the backyard, and just as willingly returns to her spacious enclosure. She knows the routine. She understands what Jeanie expects of her—and Jeanie understands what Pearl expects of her, too. Such mutual respect is what happy, and permanent, person-pig relationships are made of.

Getting to Know Pigs

Miniature potbellied pigs live in the jungles of China and Vietnam, where they use their long snouts and excellent sense of smell to dig up their food. They are not descendants of the domestic pigs we've been raising on farms for centuries. But they are cousins. And all are pigs, sharing certain piggy characteristics.

Research—respected research, mind you—tells us that we're not all that different from pigs. Some of us eat until we almost pop, some of us have pot bellies, some of us . . . wait, not *those* similarities. These are far more scientific: our brain structures, our skin, our parenting techniques, even our intelligence.

Get to know a pig, and you'll understand. These are extremely sensitive, intelligent animals that just don't get the respect they deserve. Indeed, if they did, if more people understood just what special creatures these animals are, bacon burgers probably would not be nearly as popular as they are today.

The Pig as Cultural Icon

Our understanding of pigs, and our undeniable attraction to them, isn't some new phenomenon launched by the popularity of such beloved contemporary pigs as Babe in the film of the same name, and Wilbur from *Charlotte's Web*. Farmers, writers, artists, and the like who have, through the centuries, known pigs well have documented their porcine charms. They have struggled, often in vain, to convince the general public that pigs are clean, intelligent, sensitive, and friendly—and not all that different from humans in character.

We may have tried to ignore the message, perhaps to justify our ham steaks, but it has hit a chord on a subconscious level. That would explain the mass popularity of pigs as cartoon characters, film stars, greeting-card subjects, and collector figurines. And it would help to explain why the public was so eager to embrace the misguided promise of a tiny pet pig who could live happily as a pet in the palms of her owner's hands.

Being a Proper Owner of a Potbellied Pig

Those who have studied pig character are also those most likely to bond with a potbellied pig in a unique pet owner relationship that is unlike the relationship between any other person and pet. These individuals must not, however, be merely suckers for a pretty piggy face. Oh, no. They must have backbone. They must know the meaning of the word "no" and possess the constitution to use it consistently, even when confronted with the demands, wants, and desires of a four-trottered critter that might be their equal in stubbornness, determination, and even smarts.

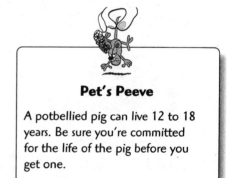

Pet's Peeve

A potbellied pig can live 12 to 18 years. Be sure you're committed for the life of the pig before you get one.

Allow the pig to claim dominance, and you will find yourself sharing your home with a spoiled, domineering animal who will gladly take over your household and refuse to relinquish control. This would explain why so many of these pigs have ended up in shelters and sanctuaries over the years, wouldn't it? And why only a certain type of individual is up to the job of living with them.

Potbellied pigs do not reach maturity until 18 months to two years of age. When they do, watch out. Feeling confident in who and what they are, newly maturing pigs typically begin to assert themselves to their owners. A successful outcome hinges upon the relationship you have forged with your pet up to this point. If you have allowed yourself to be lulled into a dangerous sense of permissiveness by the sweet snuffling and chortling of your adorable pet, you will have much difficulty convincing her now that your word is the gospel. If, on the other hand, you have all along established a foundation built on firm handling, consistency, and affection, you should be able to pass through this pivotal stage in your relationship successfully. It's your choice.

Beware the Realities of Living with Potbellied Pigs

Living with a potbellied pig isn't easy. We've already seen that the pigs' size can be prohibitive for many living situations. But their natural character, too, can be a challenge for most people. These animals can be rather headstrong, and their natural habits, while not inherently nasty, can be too much for some to handle. Their table manners, for one, can leave a bit to be desired. If you plan to feed your pet in your house, be prepared to mop down the dining area afterwards.

What Does a Potbellied Pig Cost?

The purchase price of a potbellied pig can vary widely, but the average is $75

The average potbellied pig owner also spends per year:

$340	Food
$75	Toys
$50	Veterinary care
$12	Other supplies

And if you're a gardener, well, you'll have to make arrangements to keep the pig out of the garden. Spurred on by an instinctive compulsion to do so, pigs will root for food buried underground and nestle into the earth to cool their bodies on a hot afternoon. Even refined, well-fed potbellied pigs in a contemporary, often suburban, environment, can transform a garden, and even an entire backyard, into a veritable minefield. It's just natural for the pig. Not something you can change or punish out of her. Just something you must accept.

Pampered Pet

You can share your garden with your pig. Give her a spacious enclosure where she can root, and keep your flower beds on the other side of the yard.

Their intelligence can also lead these animals down the road to ruin, resulting in serious battles of wills between pig and person that a weak-willed owner is destined to lose. Too many such battles, too many pig victories, and the pet/owner relationship is doomed. Even with proper handling and training, potbellied pigs can be demanding, domineering, and not at all amenable to the presence of children or other pets. In fact, some breeders will not sell potbellied pigs into households with children. Demanding as they are, pigs can fancy themselves equal in position to the kids and become jealous. Breeders who are not so obstinate on the subject tend to prefer that the pig in question be raised by an owner who is experienced and skillful enough to convince the animal in a positive manner just who is who and what is what within the family.

One point on which all agree is that the pig should be afforded a peaceful and private environment, and that any and all interactions between children and pigs must be supervised carefully by adults. Honor your pig's opinions on such matters, respect her unique character, and you'll increase the odds significantly that all will live happier ever after.

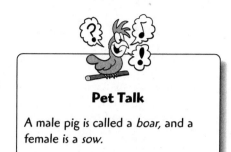

Pet Talk

A male pig is called a *boar,* and a female is a *sow.*

Revel in the Delights of Living with Pigs

On the more positive front, potbellied pigs who are given proper and compassionate care are known to forge deep bonds with their owners—the two living in harmony for many years. They are inherently clean animals, most of whom can even be housetrained like a dog to eliminate in a designated spot outdoors. Although hardly qualifying as easy-care pets, the dietary needs of potbellied pigs are easily met, and most will repay their owners with companionship and fun.

New owners quickly understand what all the ruckus is about when the subject is pigs. While traditionally we have demeaned the animals by labeling them filthy and gluttonous, those who spend time with pigs find them friendly, communicative, and almost human in their interactions with the people they know best. When living with potbellied pigs is approached in the right way, with full knowledge of what to expect from the experience, first-time owners are often downright shocked to realize how quickly a new pet can worm her way into the family, making herself both at home and downright irreplaceable. That is the magic of pigs. We cannot deny their charm.

Secrets from the Pet Files

Water is very important to potbellied pigs. They must have a constant supply of fresh, clean water to drink. Given their ability to cause tidal waves in the water bowl, keeping that bowl filled can be a challenge. The pig should also have access to a water source in which she can soak—a child's wading pool will fill this bill handsomely—both to keep her clean and to cool her down.

Choosing a Healthy Pig Pet

Now, consider yourself properly warned, properly prepared. The potbellied pig is a pet challenge, pure and simple. But those willing to tackle that challenge, to establish realistic expectations and live in harmony with this animal, find the experience satisfying and rewarding—and often quite exasperating, but in a good way. A positive experience hinges, of course, on your initial choice of a healthy, well-adjusted potbellied pig. And this, as any responsible pet owner knows, involves some homework.

Avoiding Impulse Pig-Buying

It would be inaccurate to suggest that forging a healthy, promising relationship with a pet potbellied pig begins when you walk into the local mall to purchase some underwear and leave instead with an adorable potbellied pig that you happened to see in the front window of the mall's pet shop. Danger, danger! Do you have any idea where that pig came from? Do you know anything about her care? Do you know what sort of socialization she has received up to this point?

While it's unfair to generalize, it's a fairly safe bet that whoever was willing to sell you a potbellied pig on your spontaneous whim was also one who would not hesitate to tell you that the tiny pig wouldn't get much bigger, and sure, she could live happily in your 500-square-foot apartment. Shame on that individual, and shame on you.

But that isn't you, of course. That was just an imaginary you. You would never dream of purchasing a pig so impulsively. The real you would observe the following guidelines when making the momentous step into the complex world of potbellied pig ownership.

Breeder? Shelter? Pig Rescue?

Notice that something is missing from the list of potential sources of pet potbellied pigs above? That would be the pet shop. For the most part, it really is not all that safe to purchase what is essentially a farm animal from a shop that does not deal in such animals. Safer choices would be the breeder, the shelter, or the pig-rescue group. Here you will find staff members who are more likely to be better educated about the care of potbellied pigs, and more highly motivated to ensure that their pigs land in the right homes.

Evaluating the Pig Seller

In the case of breeders, you should feel comfortable with their intentions, their ethics, and their actions. If you meet them at a potbellied pig show—held independently or in conjunction with county and state fairs—you can usually get a good idea of how involved they are with the potbellied pig community at large and how committed they are to the cause.

When you visit a breeder's operation, look over the grounds and the pigs carefully. Then ask yourself the following questions. If you answer no to any of them, perhaps it's best to look elsewhere.

➤ Are the enclosures clean and spacious and properly appointed with sleeping areas, shelter, clean feeding dishes, and toys?

➤ Are the pigs healthy, clean, friendly, and content?

➤ Does the breeder know each of the pigs personally?

➤ Can he or she tell you all about each pig's likes, dislikes, and special quirks?

➤ Does the breeder question you about your intentions and living situation?

➤ Will the breeder take the pig back if things don't work out?

Beware of unscrupulous breeders. This applies not only to those who would try to convince you that the tiny pig you are holding in your hands is a full-grown potbellied pig that will willingly obey your every command, but also to those who would sell you an agricultural breed of pig, claiming it is a minia-ture potbellied pig. What's so bad about that? Miniature potbellied pigs are big enough, but regular-size pigs weigh in at several hundred pounds as adults. While such deceptions occur less frequently now than they once did, there are still breeders out there who know how to appeal to that very human desire to have what is new, different, and unlike anything the neighbors might have. So buyer beware.

Pampered Pet

Use your common sense. Whether you're talking to breeders, shelters, or rescuers, in most cases you'll know the good ones when you meet them.

The same questions should be asked when meeting pigs available from animal shelters and pig-rescue groups. In those cases, the challenge is even greater to ensure the successful placement of pigs that may be a bit scared and in need of some therapy after a previous negative experience. Beware of the adoption representative whose sole intention is to place pigs without regard to whether they are placed in proper and permanent homes.

Which Pig Is Right for You?

Questions will also arise when it comes time to decide just which type of pig you would like. Should you purchase or adopt a pig or a piglet? While raising a potbellied pig from infancy to adulthood is an awesome responsibility, it could actually be better than a beginner taking on an adult pig who is need of some rehabilitation. By the same token, you might find a well-adjusted adult who is well-versed in pig manners and would fit in famously in your household. It all depends on the individual pig.

The same can be said when discussing males and females. Which is superior? You'll never get a unanimous answer on that one.

Signs of Potbellied Pig Health and Vitality

In an ideal world, the ideal pet pig candidate is one that is lively and friendly, vaccinated, housetrained, properly socialized, spayed or neutered, trained to wear a harness and walk on a leash, and has a level-headed disposition. This animal, aside from harboring a natural affinity for humans and being properly prepared to live with them, is, on top of everything else, also a picture of health. Look for a pig:

➤ With bright, clear eyes

➤ With skin that's free of rashes

➤ That does not scratch incessantly

➤ That's pleasingly plump

This last point is critical. It is wise to steer clear of very small, delicate pigs and piglets, whose size could mean a pig's bone structure will not adequately support her weight someday. Beware, too, of pigs with tremendous bellies that drag on the ground. Look instead for a pig whose weight and overall size are in proper proportion to her bone structure, and who can move smoothly and comfortably. Mismatched or poor conformation can result someday in poor health, leg problems, and excessive veterinary bills.

Check the Law

Before you bring a potbellied pig home, make sure the zoning restrictions in your area will allow you to do so. In many areas, if not most, potbellied pigs are classified as farm animals and are forbidden. By the same token, your particular area may make a special dispensation for pigs of the miniature potbellied variety.

A special livestock permit may also be required to document both your pet's health and your right to keep her as a pet. Call your state and local agricultural and health departments, and research the requirements ahead of time—before you find yourself head over heels in love with a pig that is doomed to be evicted and/or confiscated from her happy home.

A Question of Ethics

While people may disagree about the best way to train a pig, or whether they like boars or sows better, the one issue on which you will find a practically unanimous vote is spaying and neutering. Hear that resounding, almost deafening, "Yes, do it!" Those would be the voices of all those responsible, ethical breeders out there. If you have no intention of breeding a potbellied pig, the animal should be spayed or neutered. Certainly, in this era of restricted demand, pet owners—beginners and veterans alike—should not be breeding their pigs. If your pet has not already been spayed or neutered, find a veterinarian who is experienced in caring for potbellied pigs, have the procedure done, and you will end up with a healthier, more relaxed, and just an all-around better pet. Case closed.

The Potbellied Pig at Home

Somewhere along the line, we decided that pigs love mud, dirt, and filth. Wrong, wrong, wrong. Just ask your pig. She'd tell you, if she could. Let us set the record straight here and now: Pigs are most comfortable when both they and their homes are clean and pristine. Read on for more tips on just how you can, as an owner, provide a pig pet with all she needs to thrive mentally, physically, and even emotionally.

Accommodations Everyone Can Live With

I have discussed in almost every chapter of this book the fact that just about all pets should live indoors with their families. Potbellied pigs are the exception. They are actually more comfortable, and more easily and logically, kept outdoors.

This does not mean your pet should be exiled completely from your home. Many potbellied pigs enjoy spending time with their families indoors. The pig's primary residence, however, should be outside. If you believe otherwise and have never lived with one of these animals, you'll probably change your mind on the subject once you have shared your bedroom, your kitchen, and your family room with a demanding critter who has claimed your house as her very own.

The ideal is an indoor-outdoor arrangement. The pig's primary home is outdoors, yet she is so well-trained and so intimately bonded to her family that she can spend quality time indoors, as well. This way, everyone's needs—those of pigs and people alike—can be met with ease and flexibility.

Pampered Pet

Remember, this little piggy comes from the jungle. Provide heated shelter for your pet when the weather gets cool.

Living Like a Dog

The ideal potbellied pig home is very much what one would expect of ideal outdoor accommodations for a dog. The pig requires plenty of room in which to move around—and to sleep, eat, play, lie in the sun, lie in the shade, swim, and relieve herself whenever she feels the urge.

The enclosure—a small yard, really—should be large enough so that each of these functions may be assigned designated corners of the pig's home. Pigs, potbellied and otherwise, tend to be organization fanatics, most comfortable when everything is in its place. So, too, can the pig use her extraordinary wiles and strength to escape if she sees an opening, so you should surround that spacious enclosure with a sound, deeply planted fence with a gate that can be locked, and always is—securely.

The enclosure should have a large patch of ground where your pig can dig and root to her heart's content. It should also have a swimming pool—a plastic wading pool will do—that you fill daily with fresh, clean water for cooling down and taking a bath. And finally, the enclosure should have toys your intelligent pig can play with to keep her busy.

The most important furnishing within that enclosure will be the pig's house. In its simplest, easiest form, this is a dog house, either a heavy, igloo-style plastic model that is easy to clean, or a traditional wooden house. The house must be large enough for the adult pig to enter and turn around in, and it should be carpeted with an ample supply of clean blankets and/or towels, or a thick, fragrant layer of clean hay.

Pampered Pet

Hay may be better bedding for male pigs, who have been known to get rather aggressive with blankets.

The house should be positioned out of drafts and direct sunlight, but the resident pig should have access to both sunlight and shade outside of her house. The house should also be elevated above the ground—most igloo houses are already designed this way—which will further protect the pig from the elements.

And finally, remember that while some pigs can cohabitate with other pigs, for others, sharing space is a fate worse than death. Respect your territorial pig's wishes in this matter, and err toward the conservative: solo housing.

When You Get a Potbellied Pig, You'll Also Have to Get These

Secure fencing for the pig enclosure	Wading pool
Pig shelter/bed	Soft-bristle brush
Bedding material	Harness and leash
Large, sturdy food dishes	Toys
Large, sturdy water dishes	Care and behavior book

Out and About with Your Pig

Sensitive creatures that they are, potbellied pigs are extremely prone to the stress of separation anxiety when their owners leave them alone. You can help prevent this by getting out and about with your pig. Get active and exercise. Play with your pet, take her out on a leash, participate in potbellied pig showing—activities that in the long run will be good for you both.

Most potbellied pigs can be trained to walk on a leash. All you will need is a harness and leash that are specially made for walking a pig. Then just remember that pigs love treats, and gather an ample supply of your pet's favorites. Bribe the pig into understanding just how rewarding wearing the harness and obeying the gentle tug on the leash can be. Work with your pet gradually, consistently, and without anger or frustration, and eventually you should be able to convince her that walking on a leash is as fun as it is gastronomically fruitful—so much so that soon you'll discover the treat bribes are no longer necessary.

Eating Like a Pig

That folklore about slovenly pigs has also followed these animals into the nutrition department. Give a pig a bunch of garbage, the leftovers, the refuse; she'll love it.

Wrong, wrong, wrong again. Let us once again set the record straight. The pig is a mammal. While her sturdy constitution may prevent her from keeling over dead after eating from a trough of rotten food, that is not what the optimum pig diet is made of. And that is not what you should feed your beloved potbellied pig.

Pampered Pet

Always serve both food and water in freshly washed dishes. Make sure they're big and heavy enough so your pig can't spill everything instantly.

The potbellied pig's food should be fresh and appropriate for her particular dietary needs. Look to your own dietary needs for clues. What is best for a pig is a diet that is high in fiber, low in fat. Sound familiar? The foundation of this diet should be a fresh, carefully stored, high-quality pelleted commercial pig chow, the kind formulated specifically for miniature pigs. Because variety is the spice of the potbellied pig's nutritional life, rounding out the animal's optimum diet are fresh fruits, vegetables, hay and alfalfa, and pesticide-free grasses. In fact, your pig may be able to get some grass herself while grazing within her well-appointed enclosure.

To keep that "It's afternoon and I'm starving" feeling at bay, it's best to feed a potbellied pig twice a day, morning and late afternoon. Divide the daily pig chow ration in two, and supplement this with the fresh goodies, which can also serve as treats (healthy yet effective). Steer clear of processed and sugary foods that will offer the pig nothing but excess pounds (again, sound familiar?).

What Does a Potbellied Pig Eat?

Commercial pig chow	Hay
Fresh fruits	Alfalfa
Fresh vegetables	Grass

Eat, Drink, but Don't Be Piggy

Potbellied pigs love food—of that there can be no denial. Use this fact to your advantage at training time because the pig will pay attention to anything you are attempting to teach her if treat rewards are involved. But don't overdo it. If you learn nothing else about potbellied pigs, please take this one important point to heart: Do not overfeed your pig.

But these are *potbellied* pigs, you might say. Yes, and that body structure is genetic. You don't need to help it along. Remember, you're not fattening your pig up for the market. Health, longevity, and quality of life are the pet owner's concerns. The pig's food should be fresh, it should be appropriate for a pig's consumption, and it should be offered in moderation.

Pigs Need Doctors, Too

If your pet potbellied's tail stops its spinning—or you notice a loss of appetite, energy, and zest for life; or perhaps diarrhea, breathing troubles, or skin problems—get your pet to her veterinarian as soon as possible. In the meantime, you can help keep your potbellied pig healthy by having her dewormed and vaccinated regularly (the types of vaccines will depend on the agriculturally recommended norm for pigs in your particular area), and by feeding her in moderation to prevent obesity.

Protect your pet further by having her spayed (and having males neutered), preventing her from becoming chilled or overheated, keeping her environment clean, and taking her to the veterinarian twice a year for checkups.

All in all, a pig thrives on the same type of basic care that humans do—and they exhibit similar symptoms when they fall ill. So observe the Golden Rule with your pet: Treat your potbellied pig as you would have her treat you. Amen.

The Least You Need to Know

➤ A spoiled potbellied pig is not pretty. Prevent this with consistent and constant training and socialization of this unique, and extremely intelligent and manipulative, animal.

➤ Potbellied pigs can be sloppy eaters and drinkers; they enjoy rooting in gardens; they can be jealous of an owner's attentions; and, despite what some unethical advertising propaganda may suggest, the healthy adult pig typically weighs in at about 90 pounds.

➤ The ideal potbellied pig pet comes from a reliable breeder and is well-socialized, vaccinated, leash-trained, housetrained, and spayed or neutered.

➤ While potbellied pigs can spend time indoors with their families, the pig should have a spacious, secure outdoor yard or pen with a shelter (a dog house works well), a wading pool, shade, and toys.

➤ Feed a potbellied pig a high-quality miniature pig chow, supplemented with fresh fruits, vegetables, hay, and pesticide-free grasses. Feed twice a day and don't overfeed.

A Glossary of Pet Terms

agouti   A color combination in which each individual hair alternates with light and dark bands of color.

amphibians   Animals able to live and breathe both in the water and on land (not simultaneously, but at various stages of their development).

arachnid   The class of eight-legged animals that includes spiders, scorpions, and mites.

avian   Pertaining to birds.

aviary   A large home for birds.

aviculture   The care and raising of birds.

boar   A male pig.

budgie   Short for budgerigar, the technically correct name for a bird sometimes known as a parakeet.

business   A group of ferrets.

carapace   The top part of the turtle's shell.

carnivores   Meat eaters.

cecotropes   Soft pellets that are produced within a rabbit's large intestine.

cere   The area just above the budgie's beak that covers the nostrils.

chelonians   A group of reptiles that comprises turtles and tortoises.

crepuscular   Animals that are active at dawn and dusk.

crest   The lovely growth of feathers on the top of a bird's head.

cute response   The ability of baby animals to elicit nurturing and protection from their elders.

descenting   A procedure where the anal scent glands of a ferret are surgically removed.

diurnal   Animals that are active during the day.

domestication   The process of selective breeding whereby animals truly loose their wildness and are, in fact, unable to survive on their own in the wild.

ectothermic   Animals whose bodies are warmed and cooled (and their appetites stimulated) by their exterior temperature.

exoskeleton   A firm shell-like coating on animals such as the tarantula.

fancy   The aficionados of a certain type of animal—the people who breed and show them; often used with dogs and cats, but can be applied to other pets as well.

fancy mice and rats   Specially bred mice and rats with particular coat, color, or pattern characteristics.

feather picking   A compulsive, typically stress-related habit in which a bird pulls out its own feathers.

gib   A neutered male ferret.

herbivores   Plant eaters.

herpetoculture   The practice of breeding and raising reptiles and amphibians.

herpetologists   People who study and keep reptiles and amphibians.

herpetology   The study of reptiles and amphibians.

herps   A fond term herpetologists use for their pets.

hob   An intact male ferret.

insectivores   Insect eaters.

jill   An intact, or unspayed, female ferret.

kit   A baby ferret.

lagomorph   A plant-eating mammal with fully furred feet and two pairs of upper incisors; a rabbit is a lagomorph.

molt   A complete shedding process that many animals, including birds and spiders, go through.

nares   A bird's nostrils.

natural dog   The animal that would result if dogs were allowed to breed freely.

nocturnal   Animals that are active during the night.

omnivores   Animals that eat both plants and meat.

pedigree   The family tree of an animal; with purebred pets, the pedigree will be an official document that traces the pet's parents back several generations.

photoperiods   Intervals of light and dark that simulate day and night.

playgym   A miniature playground for birds, furnished with toys and games for special out-of-the-cage fun.

porcine   Of or relating to pigs.

puppy raisers   Dedicated individuals who volunteer to raise service dog puppies for the animals' first two years or so of life.

ranchers   The traditional term for chinchilla breeders.

retices   A bird's tail feathers.

rodent   A family of animals with extended front teeth that continue to grow throughout their lives.

rosettes   The cowlick pattern on the fur of some types of guinea pigs.

sow   A female pig.

sprite   A spayed female ferret.

tame   A wild animal that has been conditioned to live among humans, but is always wild in its essential nature.

terrarium   Usually a glass (or part glass) aquarium or cage for a terrestrial amphibian or reptile; it may contain live plants and have a relatively high humidity.

urticating hairs   Barbed hairs on the abdomens of tarantulas that they fling at predators.

vivarium   A terrarium-style housing unit for reptiles and amphibians.

warren   An underground series of tunnels where a colony of rabbits will live in the wild.

whorls   The swirled cowlick pattern on the fur of some types of guinea pigs.

zoonosis   An illness that people can catch from animals.

Where to Go for More Information

In your quest for information about the various pet species discussed in this book, the following organizations and Internet Web sites should prove helpful.

A great new place to find information on the care of small pets (a previously rather neglected area of the pet world) is the Internet. Many excellent Web sites now exist—and more are cropping up every day—where dedicated and experienced owners gather to discuss everything from mice to gerbils to potbellied pigs. Owners should be warned, however, that all advice is not to be taken as gospel. Discuss any new ideas with your pet's veterinarian before making drastic changes.

By no means a complete list, this will nevertheless get you started, and you will find that one organization or Web site leads you to another, and so on, and so on, and so on…

All Pets

Acme Pet
http://www.acempet.com/

The American Humane Association
63 Inverness Drive, E
Englewood, CO 80112
(303) 792-9900
http://www.sni.net/aha/

American Veterinary Medical Association
1931 north Meacham Rd., St. 100
Schaumburg, IL 60173
(847) 925-8070
http://www.avma.org

The Humane Society of the United States
2100 L Street, NW
Washington, DC 20037
(202) 452-1100
http://www.hsus.org

Project Breed
P.O. Box 15888
Chevy Chase, MD 20825-5888
(An excellent source for locating rescue groups throughout the country for cats, dogs, and other animals.)

Budgies

The American Budgerigar Society
1704 Kangaroo
Killeen, TX 76543

The Society of Parrot Breeders and Exhibitors
P.O. Box 369
Groton, MA 01450

Cats

The American Cat Fanciers Association
P.O. Box 203
Point Lookout, MO 65726

The Cat Fanciers' Association
P.O. Box 1005
Manasquan, NJ 08736-0805
http://www.cfainc.org/

Project Breed
P.O. Box 15888
Chevy Chase, MD 20825-5888
(An excellent source for locating rescue groups throughout the country for cats, dogs, and other animals.)

Chinchillas

Chinchilla World
http://members.tripod.com/~Chinchilla_World/index.htm

ChinNet
http://www.chin.buffnet.net/

Cockatiels

The National Cockatiel Society
286 Broad Street, #140
Manchester, CT 06040

The National Parrot Association
8 N. Hoffman Lane
Hauppauge, NY 11788

Dogs

The American Kennel Club
51 Madison Avenue
New York, NY 10010
(212) 696-8200
http://www.akc.org

Project Breed
P.O. Box 15888
Chevy Chase, MD 20825-5888
(An excellent source for locating rescue groups throughout the country for dogs, cats, and other animals.)

The United Kennel Club
100 E. Kilgore Road
Kalamazoo, MI 49001-5598
(616) 343-9020

Ferrets

The American Ferret Association
P.O. Box 3986
Frederick, MD 21705

The Ferret Fanciers Club
713 Chautauga Ct.
Pittsburgh, PA 15214

Ferrets Anonymous
P.O. Box 3395
San Diego, CA 92163

The North American Ferret Association
P.O. Box 1963
Dale City, VA 22193

Goldfish

The American Society of Icthyologists and Herpetologists
P.O. Box 1897
Lawrence, KS 66044-8897
http://www.utexas.edu/depts/asih/

RedKat's Goldfish Place
http://www.geocities.com/Heartland/Prairie/3503/REDSPLACE_CONT.HTML

Guinea Pigs

The American Cavy Breeders Association
c/o ARBA
1925 S. Main Street
Box 426
Bloomington, IL 61704

The Home for Unwanted and Abandoned Guinea Pigs
3772 Pin Oak Circle
Doraville, GA 30340

The House Rabbit Society
P.O. Box 3242
Redmond, WA 98073-3242
or
1524 Benton Street
Alameda, CA 94501

The National Cavy Club
Olney Park Cottage, Yardley Road
Olney, Bucks HP13 5NN
England

Hamsters

The American Rat, Mouse and Hamster Society
9370 Adlai Road
Lakeside, CA 92040-4834

Hedgehogs

The International Hedgehog Fanciers Society
P.O. Box 1417
Oroville, WA 98844-1217

The North American Hedgehog Association
601 Tijeras NW, #201
Albuquerque, NM 87102

Potbellied Pigs

National Committees on Potbellied Pigs
P.O. Box 2282
Oakhurst, CA 93644

Southern California Association of Miniature Potbellied Pigs
P.O. Box 8638
Riverside, CA 92515

Rabbits

The American Rabbit Breeders Association
1925 S. Main Street
Box 426
Bloomington, IL 61704

The House Rabbit Society
P.O. Box 3242
Redmond, WA 98073-3242
or
1524 Benton Street
Alameda, CA 94501

Rats and Mice

The American Fancy Rat and Mouse Association
9230 64th Street
Riverside, CA 92509

The American Rat, Mouse and Hamster Society
9370 Adlai Road
Lakeside, CA 92040-4834

The Rat Fan Club
857 Lindo Lane
Chico, CA 95973

Reptiles and Amphibians

The American Federation of Herpetoculturists
P.O. Box 300067
Escondido, CA 92030-0067

The American Society of Icthyologists and Herpetologists
P.O. Box 1897
Lawrence, KS 66044-8897
http://www.utexas.edu/depts/asih/

The Basking Spot
http://www.baskingspot.com/societies.shtml

The National Herpetological Alliance
P.O. Box 5143
Chicago, IL 60680-5143

Tarantulas

The American Tarantula Society
P.O. Box 1617
Artesia, NM 88211-1617
http://www.concentric.net/~Dmartin/ats/

Turtles and Tortoises

(See also Reptiles and Amphibians)

The California Turtle and Tortoise Club
P.O. Box 51002
Pasadena, CA 91115-1002
http://www.tortoise.org/

Read All About It

Budgies

Gallerstein, Gary. *The Complete Bird Owner's Handbook,* Howell Book House, 1994.

O'Neil, Jacqueline. *The Complete Idiot's Guide to Bird Care and Training,* Alpha Books, 1998.

Palika, Liz. *The Consumer's Guide to Feeding Birds,* Howell Book House, 1997.

Rach, Julie. *An Owner's Guide to a Happy Healthy Pet: The Budgie,* Howell Book House, 1997.

Cats

Church, Christine. *Housecat: How to Keep Your Indoor Cat Sane and Sound,* Howell Book House, 1998.

Commings, Karen. *Shelter Cats,* Howell Book House, 1998.

Fogle, Bruce, DVM. *The Cat's Mind,* Howell Book House, 1992.

Gebhart, Richard. *The Complete Cat Book,* Howell Book House, 1995.

Giffin, James, MD, and Delbert Carlson, DVM. *Cat Owner's Home Veterinary Handbook,* Howell Book House, 1995.

Palika, Liz. *The Consumer's Guide to Cat Food,* Howell Book House, 1996.

Shojai, Amy. *An Owner's Guide to a Happy Healthy Pet: Kitten Care & Training,* Howell Book House, 1996.

Chinchillas

Barrie, Anmarie. *Guide to Owning a Chinchilla,* TFH Publications, 1997

Röder-Thiede, Maike. *Chinchillas,* Barron's 1993.

Zeihnert, Karen. *All About Chinchillas*. TFH Publications, 1988.

Cockatiels

Doane, Bonnie. *My Parrot, My Friend: An Owner's Guide to Parrot Behavior,* Howell Book House, 1994.

Gallerstein, Gary. *The Complete Bird Owner's Handbook,* Howell Book House, 1994.

Grindol, Diane. *The Complete Book of Cockatiels,* Howell Book House, 1998.

O'Neil, Jacqueline. *The Complete Idiot's Guide to Bird Care and Training,* Alpha Books, 1998.

Palika, Liz. *The Consumer's Guide to Feeding Birds,* Howell Book House, 1997.

Rach, Julie. *An Owner's Guide to a Happy Healthy Pet: The Cockatiel,* Howell Book House, 1997.

Dogs

American Kennel Club. *The Complete Dog Book,* 19th Edition, Revised, Howell Book House, 1998.

Benjamin, Carol Lea. *Dog Training in 10 Minutes,* Howell Book House, 1996.

———. *Mother Knows Best: The Natural Way to Train Your Dog,* Howell Book House, 1985.

Fogle, Bruce, DVM. *The Dog's Mind,* Howell Book House, 1990.

Giffin, James, MD, and Delbert Carlson, DVM. *Dog Owner's Home Veterinary Handbook,* Howell Book House, 1992.

McLennan, Bardi. *An Owner's Guide to a Happy Healthy Pet: Puppy Care & Training,* Howell Book House, 1996.

Morn, September. *An Owner's Guide to a Happy Healthy Pet: Housebreaking,* Howell Book House, 1998.

Palika, Liz. *The Consumer's Guide to Dog Food,* Howell Book House, 1996.

Ferrets

Bell, Judith A., DVM. *The Pet Ferret Owner's Manual,* Christopher Maggio Studio, Inc., and Miracle Workers, 1995.

Jeans, Deborah. *A Practical Guide to Ferret Care,* Ferrets Inc., 1994.

Shefferman, Mary. *An Owner's Guide to a Happy Healthy Pet: The Ferret,* Howell Book House, 1996.

Winsted, Wendy. *Ferrets in Your Home,* TFH Publications, 1995.

Frogs and Toads

Flank, Lenny, Jr. *Herp Help,* Howell Book House, 1998.

Grenard, Steve. *Amphibians: Their Care and Keeping,* Howell Book House, 1998.

———. *An Owner's Guide to a Happy Healthy Pet: Frogs and Toads,* Howell Book House, 1998.

Mattison, Chris. *Frogs and Toads of the World,* Blandford Press, 1998.

Palika, Liz. *The Complete Idiot's Guide to Reptiles and Amphibians,* Alpha Books, 1998.

Gerbils

Engfer, Leeanne. *My Pet Hamster & Gerbils,* Lerner Publications, 1997.

Gudas, Raymond. *Gerbils,* Barron's, 1995.

Hearne, Tina. *Gerbils: Responsible Pet Care,* The Rourke Book Company, 1989.

Putman, Perry. *Guide to Owning a Gerbil,* TFH Publications, 1997.

Goldfish

Andrew, Chris. *A Fishkeeper's Guide to Fancy Goldfishes,* Tetra Press, 1995.

DeVito, Carlo. *An Owner's Guide to a Happy Healthy Pet: The Goldfish,* Howell Book House, 1996.

Ostrow, Marshall E. *Goldfish: Everything About Aquariums, Varieties, Care, Nutrition, Diseases, and Breeding,* Barron's, 1997.

Skomal, Gregory. *An Owner's Guide to a Happy Healthy Pet: Setting Up a Freshwater Aquarium,* Howell Book House, 1997.

Wickham, Mike. *The Complete Idiot's Guide to Freshwater Aquariums,* Alpha Books, 1998.

Guinea Pigs

Barrett, Norman. *Guinea Pigs,* Watts Publications, 1990.

Brehend, Katrin. *Guinea Pigs: A Complete Pet Owner's Manual,* Barron's, 1991.

Hansen, Elvig. *Guinea Pigs,* The Lerner Group, 1995.

Lasell, Vicki. *The Complete Book on Taming and Training Your Guinea Pig,* Silver Sea Press, 1987.

Pavia, Audrey. *An Owner's Guide to a Happy Healthy Pet: The Guinea Pig,* Howell Book House, 1997.

Hamsters

Engfer, Leeanne. *My Pet Hamster & Gerbils,* Lerner Publications, 1997.

Parslow, Percy. *Hamsters,* TFH Publications, 1995.

Siino, Betsy Sikora. *An Owner's Guide to a Happy Healthy Pet: The Hamster,* Howell Book House, 1997.

von Frisch, Otto. *Hamsters: A Complete Pet Owner's Manual,* Barron's, 1989.

Hedgehogs

Kelsey-Wood, Dennis. *African Pygmy Hedgehogs As Your New Pet,* TFH Publications, 1995.

Morris, Pat. *Hedgehogs,* Whittet Books Ltd., 1992.

Stocker, Les. *The Complete Hedgehog,* Chatto & Windus, 1987.

Wrobel, Dawn. *An Owner's Guide to a Happy Healthy Pet: The Hedgehog,* Howell Book House, 1997.

Lizards

Flank, Lenny, Jr. *Herp Help,* Howell Book House, 1998.

Grenard, Steve. *An Owner's Guide to a Happy Healthy Pet: The Lizard,* Howell Book House, 1996.

Palika, Liz. *The Complete Idiot's Guide to Reptiles and Amphibians,* Alpha Books, 1998.

———. *The Consumer's Guide to Feeding Reptiles,* Howell Book House, 1997.

Rosenthal, Karen, DVM. *An Owner's Guide to a Happy Healthy Pet: The Iguana,* Howell Book House, 1996.

Mice

Bailey, Jill. *Discovering Rats and Mice,* Bookwright, 1987.

Bielfeld, Horst. *Mice: A Complete Pet Owner's Manual,* Barron's, 1985.

Henwood, Chris. *Fancy Mice,* TFH Publications, 1992.

Young, Jack. *Mice as a Hobby,* TFH Publications, 1995.

Miniature Potbellied Pigs

Huckaby, Lisa Hall. *Pot-Bellied Pigs and Other Miniature Pet Pigs,* TFH Publications, 1992.

Mull, Kayla and Lorrie Blackburn. *Pot Bellied Pet Pigs: Mini-Pig Care and Training,* All Publishing Company, 1990.

Storer, Pat. *Pot Bellies and Other Miniature Pigs,* Barron's, 1992.

Rabbits

Campbell, Darlene. *Proper Care of Rabbits,* TFH Publications, 1992.

Fraser, Samantha. *Hop to It!: A Guide to Training Your Pet Rabbit,* Barron's, 1991.

Pavia, Audrey. *An Owner's Guide to a Happy Healthy Pet: The Rabbit,* Howell Book House, 1997.

Wegler, Monika. *Rabbits: A Complete Pet Owner's Manual,* Barron's, 1990.

Rats

Bailey, Jill. *Discovering Rats and Mice,* Bookwright, 1987.

Cardinal, Ginger. *An Owner's Guide to a Happy Healthy Pet: The Rat,* Howell Book House, 1998.

Himsel, Carol A. *Rats,* Barron's, 1991.

Mays, Nick. *The Proper Care of Fancy Rats,* TFH Publications, 1993.

Salamanders

Flank, Lenny, Jr. *Herp Help,* Howell Book House, 1998.

Grenard, Steve. *Amphibians: Their Care and Keeping,* Howell Book House, 1998.

Mattison, Chris. *Keeping and Breeding Amphibians,* Blandford Press, 1993.

Palika, Liz. *The Complete Idiot's Guide to Reptiles and Amphibians,* Alpha Books, 1998.

Snakes

Flank, Lenny, Jr. *Herp Help,* Howell Book House, 1998.

———. *Snakes: Their Care and Keeping,* Howell Book House, 1998.

———. *An Owner's Guide to a Happy Healthy Pet: The Snake,* Howell Book House, 1996.

Palika, Liz. *The Complete Idiot's Guide to Reptiles and Amphibians,* Alpha Books, 1998.

———. *The Consumer's Guide to Feeding Reptiles,* Howell Book House, 1997.

Tarantulas

Baerg, W. J. *The Tarantula,* Fitzgerald Publishing, 1997.

Flank, Lenny, Jr. *An Owner's Guide to a Happy Healthy Pet: The Tarantula,* Howell Book House, 1998.

Marshall, Sam. *Tarantulas and Other Arachnids,* Barron's, 1996.

Schultz, Stanley and Marguerite Schultz. *The Tarantula Keeper's Guide,* Barron's, 1998.

Turtles and Tortoises

Flank, Lenny, Jr. *Herp Help,* Howell Book House, 1998.

———. *An Owner's Guide to a Happy Healthy Pet: The Turtle,* Howell Book House, 1997.

Palika, Liz. *The Complete Idiot's Guide to Turtles & Tortoises,* Alpha Books, 1998.

———. *The Consumer's Guide to Feeding Reptiles,* Howell Book House, 1997.

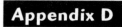

The Pet Comparison Chart

		light	1	2	3	4	5	heavy
Budgies	Time commitment				✓			
	Grooming				✓			
	Feeding				✓			
	General cleanup					✓		
	Suitable for kids age infant to 5		✓					
	Suitable for kids age 5 to 10			✓				
	Suitable for kids over 10				✓			
	Sociability				✓			
	Expense of keeping				✓			
Cats	Time commitment				✓			
	Grooming					✓		
	Feeding			✓				
	General cleanup			✓				
	Suitable for kids age infant to 5		✓					
	Suitable for kids age 5 to 10				✓			
	Suitable for kids over 10					✓		
	Sociability					✓		
	Expense of keeping					✓		

		light	1	2	3	4	5	heavy
Chinchillas	Time commitment				✓			
	Grooming					✓		
	Feeding				✓			
	General cleanup					✓		
	Suitable for kids age infant to 5		✓					
	Suitable for kids age 5 to 10				✓			
	Suitable for kids over 10						✓	
	Sociability					✓		
	Expense of keeping				✓			
Cockatiels	Time commitment					✓		
	Grooming				✓			
	Feeding				✓			
	General cleanup					✓		
	Suitable for kids age infant to 5		✓					
	Suitable for kids age 5 to 10			✓				
	Suitable for kids over 10				✓			
	Sociability					✓		
	Expense of keeping				✓			
Dogs	Time commitment						✓	
	Grooming						✓	
	Feeding			✓				
	General cleanup				✓			
	Suitable for kids age infant to 5			✓				
	Suitable for kids age 5 to 10				✓			
	Suitable for kids over 10					✓		
	Sociability						✓	
	Expense of keeping						✓	

		light	1	2	3	4	5	heavy
Ferrets	Time commitment						✓	
	Grooming						✓	
	Feeding				✓			
	General cleanup					✓		
	Suitable for kids age infant to 5		✓					
	Suitable for kids age 5 to 10		✓					
	Suitable for kids over 10				✓			
	Sociability						✓	
	Expense of keeping					✓		
Frogs & Toads	Time commitment				✓			
	Grooming		✓					
	Feeding					✓		
	General cleanup				✓			
	Suitable for kids age infant to 5		✓					
	Suitable for kids age 5 to 10			✓				
	Suitable for kids over 10					✓		
	Sociability			✓				
	Expense of keeping			✓				
Gerbils	Time commitment				✓			
	Grooming			✓				
	Feeding				✓			
	General cleanup				✓			
	Suitable for kids age infant to 5		✓					
	Suitable for kids age 5 to 10				✓			
	Suitable for kids over 10					✓		
	Sociability				✓			
	Expense of keeping				✓			

381

		light	1	2	3	4	5	heavy
Goldfish	Time commitment			✓				
	Grooming		✓					
	Feeding			✓				
	General cleanup				✓			
	Suitable for kids age infant to 5			✓				
	Suitable for kids age 5 to 10			✓				
	Suitable for kids over 10					✓		
	Sociability		✓					
	Expense of keeping				✓			
Guinea Pigs	Time commitment				✓			
	Grooming				✓			
	Feeding				✓			
	General cleanup				✓			
	Suitable for kids age infant to 5		✓					
	Suitable for kids age 5 to 10				✓			
	Suitable for kids over 10					✓		
	Sociability				✓			
	Expense of keeping				✓			
Hamsters	Time commitment				✓			
	Grooming			✓				
	Feeding				✓			
	General cleanup				✓			
	Suitable for kids age infant to 5		✓					
	Suitable for kids age 5 to 10				✓			
	Suitable for kids over 10					✓		
	Sociability			✓				
	Expense of keeping				✓			

	light	1	2	3	4	5	heavy
Hedgehogs Time commitment				✓			
Grooming			✓				
Feeding					✓		
General cleanup					✓		
Suitable for kids age infant to 5		✓					
Suitable for kids age 5 to 10			✓				
Suitable for kids over 10					✓		
Sociability					✓		
Expense of keeping				✓			
Lizards Time commitment					✓		
Grooming			✓				
Feeding				✓			
General cleanup				✓			
Suitable for kids age infant to 5		✓					
Suitable for kids age 5 to 10			✓				
Suitable for kids over 10					✓		
Sociability			✓				
Expense of keeping					✓		
Mice Time commitment			✓				
Grooming			✓				
Feeding				✓			
General cleanup				✓			
Suitable for kids age infant to 5		✓					
Suitable for kids age 5 to 10			✓				
Suitable for kids over 10					✓		
Sociability		✓					
Expense of keeping			✓				

	light	1	2	3	4	5	heavy
Miniature Potbellied Pigs Time commitment						✓	
Grooming					✓		
Feeding					✓		
General cleanup						✓	
Suitable for kids age infant to 5		✓					
Suitable for kids age 5 to 10			✓				
Suitable for kids over 10			✓				
Sociability						✓	
Expense of keeping						✓	
Rabbits Time commitment				✓			
Grooming				✓			
Feeding				✓			
General cleanup				✓			
Suitable for kids age infant to 5		✓					
Suitable for kids age 5 to 10				✓			
Suitable for kids over 10					✓		
Sociability				✓			
Expense of keeping				✓			
Rats Time commitment				✓			
Grooming			✓				
Feeding				✓			
General cleanup				✓			
Suitable for kids age infant to 5		✓					
Suitable for kids age 5 to 10				✓			
Suitable for kids over 10						✓	
Sociability					✓		
Expense of keeping				✓			

	light	1	2	3	4	5	heavy
Salamanders Time commitment			✓				
Grooming		✓					
Feeding					✓		
General cleanup				✓			
Suitable for kids age infant to 5		✓					
Suitable for kids age 5 to 10			✓				
Suitable for kids over 10					✓		
Sociability		✓					
Expense of keeping			✓				
Snakes Time commitment				✓			
Grooming		✓					
Feeding					✓		
General cleanup				✓			
Suitable for kids age infant to 5		✓					
Suitable for kids age 5 to 10			✓				
Suitable for kids over 10					✓		
Sociability				✓			
Expense of keeping				✓			
Tarantulas Time commitment			✓				
Grooming		✓					
Feeding				✓			
General cleanup			✓				
Suitable for kids age infant to 5		✓					
Suitable for kids age 5 to 10			✓				
Suitable for kids over 10				✓			
Sociability		✓					
Expense of keeping			✓				

	light	1	2	3	4	5	heavy
Turtles & Time commitment				✓			
Tortoises Grooming			✓				
Feeding					✓		
General cleanup					✓		
Suitable for kids age infant to 5		✓					
Suitable for kids age 5 to 10			✓				
Suitable for kids over 10					✓		
Sociability				✓			
Expense of keeping				✓			

Saying Good-bye to a Beloved Pet

Perhaps the most difficult part of living with a pet is knowing that, with the exception of some parrots and tortoises, we'll probably outlive our beloved companion. Living with animals also means that the time inevitably comes when we must say *good-bye*. That is the heartbreaking reality of living with animals.

Sad and Unexpected Ends

It's never easy. Sometimes the end comes abruptly, the result of illness or injury. Sometimes it is expected, as an animal reaches the later years of his projected life span. Sometimes the animal drifts away in his sleep. Sometimes you, the owner, must make the fateful decision to have your beloved pet humanely euthanized. With this act you bring peace and solace from pain and suffering—a very difficult decision indeed, but a courageous one. However it happens, it's never easy.

And it used to be even more difficult. Why? Because when a pet passed on, the grief was real, but most people simply didn't understand. Pet owners would hear things like, "It was only a cat," or, "You'd think that dog was your child!" Fortunately, today most of us have become more respectful of the significance of animals in our lives and are sensitive to the profound effects of their loss.

Seeking Support from Friends and Family

When the loss does occur—and it will—don't be ashamed of your grief. For centuries, humans have expressed their love for their deceased pets, often secretly, sometimes commemorating them in heartfelt epitaphs, poems, and other artistic outlets. Following your own loss, you may be surprised at the natural support group out there waiting to offer a sympathetic ear. Pet-owning friends and family members are logical sources, as are the pet-loss support groups that have sprung up nationwide.

And believe it or not, you may even find the support group you are looking for on the Internet. Along with all the other pet-related Web sites now online, there are many devoted to pet loss. These offer individuals the opportunity to discuss their grief with others, and to pay tribute to the pets that have passed on.

Getting Back on the Horse

When it first happens, you may swear that's it. You'll never own another pet. Deep down, though, you know that's not true. Inviting another pet into your home is a very personal journey. For some, the only remedy is to get another pet immediately. For others, a period of mourning is necessary. Go with your gut and do what's right for you, regardless of the advice you may receive from well-meaning supporters.

However you choose to approach this important decision, remember that you cannot expect to replace the animal that has passed on. Each pet is unique in character and spirit. Each pet brings his own special magic into your home and into your life. Respect the newcomer for who and what he is. In no way will this diminish your love for, and memories of the pet that has passed on.

Index

D

U-V

W-X-Z